Developing Competent Readers and Writers in the Middle Grades

Martha Combs
University of Nevada, Reno

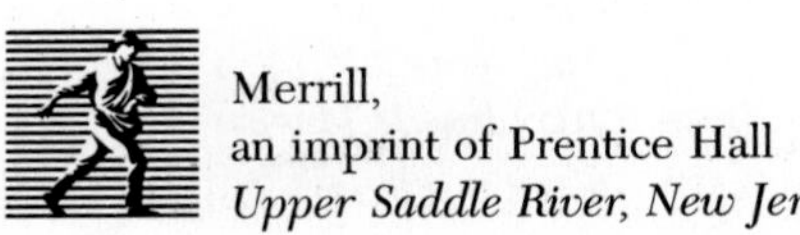

Merrill,
an imprint of Prentice Hall
Upper Saddle River, New Jersey *Columbus, Ohio*

Library of Congress Cataloging-in-Publication Data
Combs, Martha.
Developing competent readers and writers in the middle grades / Martha Combs.
p. cm.
Includes bibliographical references and index.
ISBN 0-13-376435-4
1. Reading (Middle school) 2. English language—Composition and exercises—Study and teaching (Middle school) 3. Young adult literature—Study and teaching (Middle school) I. Title.
LB1632.C576 1997
428.4'071'2—dc21 96-39205
CIP

Cover photo: © Daemmrich, Uniphoto
Editor: Bradley J. Potthoff
Production Editor: Sheryl Glicker Langner
Photo Coordinator: Nancy Harre Ritz
Design Coordinator: Karrie M. Converse
Text Designer: Anne Flanagan
Cover Designer: Frankenberry Design
Production Manager: Pamela D. Bennett
Electronic Text Management: Karen L. Bretz
Director of Marketing: Kevin Flanagan
Advertising/Marketing Coordinator: Julie Shough

This book was set in Caledonia by The Clarinda Company and was printed and bound by Courier/Kendallville, Inc. The cover was printed by Phoenix Color Corp.

Photo credits: pp. 9, 13, 39, 52, 65, 156, 167, 185, 189, 214, 332, 346 by Anne Vega/Merrill; pp. 22, 112 by Linda Peterson/Merrill; pp. 101, 126, 134, 218 by Scott Cunningham/Merrill.

Printed in the United States of America

10 9 8 7 6 5 4 3 2 1

ISBN: 0-13-376435-4

Prentice-Hall International (UK) Limited, *London*
Prentice-Hall of Australia Pty. Limited, *Sydney*
Prentice-Hall of Canada, Inc., *Toronto*
Prentice-Hall Hispanoamericana, S. A., *Mexico*
Prentice-Hall of India Private Limited, *New Delhi*
Prentice-Hall of Japan, Inc., *Tokyo*
Simon & Schuster Asia Pte. Ltd., *Singapore*
Editora Prentice-Hall do Brasil, Ltda., *Rio de Janeiro*

For William R. Powell,
mentor and "more knowledgeable other"

Preface

This text is about engaging students from fourth through eighth grade in literacy experiences. Our focus is on students who are typically ages 10 through 14, often referred to as early adolescents. *Great Transitions* (1996), the concluding report from the Carnegie Council on Adolescent Development, reaffirms for us that

> Adolescence is one of the most fascinating and complex transitions in the life span: a time of accelerated growth and change second only to infancy; a time of expanding horizons, self-discovery, and emerging independence; a time of metamorphosis from childhood to adulthood. (p. 7)

What a challenge we face as teachers of adolescents!

This book is intended to help expand your knowledge of this age group and to explore ways of engaging these students in meaningful literacy learning. To help you focus on your own learning, I present instructional approaches that others have used successfully with middle grade students. We will examine each approach in some depth, to more fully consider the possibilities it may hold for each of you and your students (or prospective students). We will eavesdrop on middle grade teachers as they engage students in whole-class, small-group, and individual reading and writing experiences.

As we follow these teachers, you will experience some of their thinking and decision making. I believe these two areas, teacher thinking and decision making, are among the most difficult areas to learn. Throughout this course, you must work to confront and understand your own thinking and decision making, the knowledge base you draw on for teaching, and how you carry through on your decisions. The teachers in this text can be your teachers, the "more knowledgeable others" (Vygotsky, 1962) who will help you advance your understanding of teaching middle grade students.

Part One (Chapters 1–4) provides selected theoretical foundations for developmental reading and writing, knowledge considered basic to classroom learning for students in grades four through eight. We develop these foundations in depth in Part Two (Chapters 5–12), emphasizing the reasoning processes teachers use to make informed decisions for instruction.

To support and extend your thinking, this text includes the following features:

- *Your Turn. . . My Turn.* This feature encourages you to participate in your reading, and to be a decision maker for classroom practice. Opportunities occur throughout this text to stop and reflect on the reading, to use your background of experience, and to apply knowledge from your reading.
- *In This Chapter. . .* At the beginning of each chapter an overview of chapter highlights helps you anticipate the contents and prepare yourself to read.
- *Before You Get Started. . .* This alerts you to works of literature that receive significant attention in a chapter. Knowledge of these books will enhance your study. It is particularly important to have a copy of *Hatchet* by Gary Paulsen (1987); it is the touchstone book throughout the text.
- *Take a Moment and Reflect.* At the end of each chapter we recap chapter highlights and let you check your understanding of the most important issues in the chapter.
- *Sample scripts, lesson frameworks, and units.* These elements are presented throughout as examples of theory applied to classroom practice.

- *Emphasis on teacher thinking and decision making.* In addition, we will explore instructional approaches in depth, providing opportunities for you to develop your thinking and decision making.
- *Authentic literature.* Authentic literature plays an integral role throughout this text. I emphasize using quality literature because your students must have worthwhile materials that engage their thinking.

Teaching in today's classrooms challenges you to engage students in creative and critical ways, preparing young adolescents for a most uncertain world. This text provides ways for you to examine your own creative and critical thinking about the reading and writing processes of early adolescents and will challenge you to be a better decision maker, to consider issues in literacy that are critical for your students' future, and to gain the confidence that provides literate environments for middle grade students. You must not accept students' failure to become engaged with print and the thinking that it stimulates. Every student must enjoy the power and personal satisfaction that literacy provides. As a teacher of middle grade students, you are a key to that power!

ACKNOWLEDGMENTS

This book is very much a team effort. Without the expertise of my colleagues at Merrill/Prentice Hall, this text would not be a reality. The idea for this text began a number of years ago when I first met Linda Scharp McElhiney, Developmental Editor for Merrill College Division. Linda believed in my vision and I thank her for that. Her efforts in the development of this text were enthusiastically supported by Brad Potthoff and Jeff Johnston. My thanks especially to Brad for his patience and encouragement throughout this process, and his belief in me as a writer. The preparation of this manuscript for production has been under the careful direction of Sheryl Langner, whose expertise has made the entire process a wonderful experience for me. My thanks to freelance copyeditor Robert L. Marcum, who once again refined my thinking and brought consistency to my ideas. Thank you all so very much!

I would like to express my thanks to the reviewers of this book for their thoughtful comments and suggestions: Howard E. Blake, Temple University; Barbara Perry-Sheldon, North Carolina Wesleyan College; Mary Anne Pollock, Morehead State University; and Katherine L. Schlick Noe, Seattle University.

The artwork at the beginning of each chapter was created by one of my daughters, Heather Combs. Thank you, Heather, for breathing life into my idea.

My life as a teacher and learner continues to be touched by so many other teachers and learners, in particular the undergraduate and graduate students at the University of Nevada, Reno and Oklahoma State University, my colleagues at both institutions, and so many teachers in Washoe, Douglas, and Lyon Counties, Nevada. I am especially greatful to Kim Muncy, Kristen Felten, Lou Loftin, Louise Kingsbery, and my good friend Vickie Cannon.

Finally, to my husband, Randy Koetting, for your love, support, and encouragement during this past year. Without you, my world would just be ordinary!

Martha Combs

REFERENCES

Carnegie Council on Adolescent Development. (1996). *Great transitions.* Washington, DC: Author.

Vygotsky, L. S. (1962). *Thought and language* (E. Hanfmann & G. Vakar, Eds. & Trans.). Cambridge, MA: MIT Press.

Brief Contents

Contents

9

Writer's Workshop and Beyond: Learning to Write and Writing to Learn 208

10

Word Study: Patterns for Word Recognition and Spelling 242

11
Using a Basal Reading Series Effectively: Teaching from a Literature-Based Perspective 269

12
Teaching with Integrated Units: Balancing Information and Narrative Texts 331

Part I

Learners, Processes, and Possibilities

We begin our exploration of literacy issues for the middle grades by considering what middle grade students are like and by defining your role as their teacher. In the remainder of Part One we turn our attention to seminal issues in reading and writing development. Together, these chapters form a theoretical foundation for reading and writing programs rooted in knowledge of the development of early adolescents and supported by meaningful, thought-provoking activity.

In Chapter 2, *Growing Toward Maturity as Readers*, we discuss the reading process and the stages of reading development, thinking in narrative and information texts, and how to monitor students' progress as readers. We will apply this fundamental knowledge throughout Part Two as we examine the importance of reading aloud to students and providing opportunities for independent reading, and discuss teaching reading with authentic literature, a basal reading series, and integrated units.

Writing should be an integral part of every reading program. Chapter 3, *Growing Toward Maturity as Writers*, provides an overview of issues in writing development and instruction, including the role of thinking in writing. We discuss both informal and formal writing, and present an overview of a writer's workshop. We then explore these issues in depth in Chapter 9, *Writer's Workshop and Beyond*, and integrate them throughout chapters that focus primarily on reading development.

Chapter 4, *Growing Toward Maturity in Word Knowledge*, links reading and writing through the study of the stages of word knowledge, essential to fluency in both, emphasizing phonics and structural analysis. This background knowledge is essential if you are to make relevant decisions about word recognition and spelling instruction, and not be tied to a commercial text in each area. We apply knowledge in this chapter in-depth in Chapter 10, *Word Study: Patterns for Word Recognition and Spelling*, and integrate it throughout the remaining chapters in Part Two.

1

Developing Competent Readers and Writers

An Introduction

In this chapter . . .

We discuss the background knowledge about middle grade students and their learning you will need to be an effective teacher. You must begin now to understand the powerful role you play as a teacher of early adolescents, by considering:

- intellectual, physical, psychological, social, and moral and ethical development of middle grade students,
- learning environments that encourage and support the development of competence and independence,
- your role as a teacher-mediator, and
- teaching with authentic literature.

We also describe how to use the features of this text to your best learning advantage.

"Middle grades students are in a time of transition physically, socially, emotionally, and intellectually. Their intense interest in themselves, their social interactions, their emotional ups and downs, and their new capacity for analytical thought can be used to help them become literate" (Irvin, 1990, p. 6). "A growing body of knowledge shows that what happens to students between the ages of ten and fourteen determines not only their future success in school, but success in life as well" (Wiles & Bondi, 1993, p. 24). The literacy program that you plan for middle grade students should enable them to "read and write the world" to meet their needs and interests, "taking from and making of the world" what is meaningful to them (Shannon, 1992, p. 1). ■

What types of literacy experiences do students in this stage of development find meaningful and challenging? To address this question, you must have a clear understanding of middle grade students, typically defined as those in grades four through eight. In addition, you must have a strong theoretical and pedagogical knowledge base from which to make appropriate decisions for instruction.

In Part I of this text we discuss the nature of middle grade students and the theory base from which you will make decisions about reading and writing experiences for students. In Part II, we use that base to explore and participate in creating challenging and meaningful instructional experiences for middle grade students.

Early Adolescents in Today's Society

With the exception of the years from birth to age 3, there is no other period in life when we experience the magnitude of change that occurs during early adolescence, approximately 10 to 14 years of age. Eichhorn (1966) refers to this period of development as *transescence*, which he describes as

> the stage of development which begins before the onset of puberty and extends through the early stages of adolescence. Since puberty does not occur for all precisely at the same chronological age in human development, the transescent designation is based on the many physical, social, emotional, and intellectual changes in body chemistry that appear before the time in which the body gains a practical degree of stabilization over these complex pubescent changes. (p. 3)

Transescence suggests a process of "becoming" that can be filled with uncertainly and anxiety. What do you recall of this period in your own life?

The California State Department of Education's report, *Caught in the Middle: Educational Reform for Young Adolescents in California Public Schools* (1987) provides an excellent description of students in the transescent stage. The following lists of intellectual, physical, physiological, social, and moral and ethical development attributes are quoted from the California report (pp. 144–148). Let's take a moment to consider these descriptions of early adolescents.

Middle grade students display the following *intellectual development:*

1. Display a wide range of individual intellectual development as their minds experience transition from the concrete-manipulatory stage to the capacity for abstract thought. This transition ultimately makes possible:
   - Propositional thought
   - Consideration of ideas contrary to fact

- Reasoning with hypotheses involving two or more variables
- Appreciation for the elegance of mathematical logic expressed in symbols
- Insight into the nuances of poetic metaphor and musical notation
- Analysis of the power of political ideology
- Ability to project thought into the future, to anticipate, and to formulate goals
- Insight into the sources of previously unquestioned attitudes, behaviors, and values
- Interpretation of larger concepts and generalizations of traditional wisdom expressed through sayings, axioms, and aphorisms

2. Are intensely curious;
3. Prefer active over passive learning experiences; favor interaction with peers during learning activities;
4. Exhibit a strong willingness to learn things they consider to be useful; enjoy using skills to resolve real life problems;
5. Are egocentric; argue to convince others; exhibit independent, critical thought;
6. Consider academic goals as a secondary level of priority; personal-social concerns dominate thoughts and activities;
7. Experience the phenomenon of metacognition—the ability to know what one knows and does not know;
8. Are intellectually at-risk; face decisions that have the potential to affect major academic values with lifelong consequences.

Middle grade students display the following *physical development*:

1. Experience accelerated physical development marked by increases in weight, height, heart size, lung capacity, and muscular strength;
2. Mature at varying speed. Girls tend to be taller than boys for the first two years of early adolescence and are ordinarily more physically developed than boys;
3. Experience bone growth faster than muscle development; uneven muscle/bone development results in lack of coordination and awkwardness; bones may lack protection of covering muscles and supporting tendons;
4. Reflect a wide range of individual differences which begin to appear in prepubertal and pubertal stages of development. Boys tend to lag behind girls. There are marked individual differences in physical development for boys and girls. The greatest variability in physiological development and size occurs at about age thirteen;
5. Experience biological development five years sooner than adolescents of the last century; the average age of menarche has dropped from seventeen to twelve years of age;
6. Face responsibility for sexual behavior before full emotional and social maturity has occurred;
7. Show changes in body contour including temporarily large noses, protruding ears, long arms; have posture problems;
8. Are often disturbed by body changes:
    - Girls are anxious about physical changes that accompany sexual maturation;
    - Boys are anxious about receding chins, cowlicks, dimples, and change in their voices;

9. Experience fluctuations in basal metabolism which can cause extreme restlessness at times and equally extreme listlessness at other moments;
10. Have ravenous appetites and peculiar tastes; may overtax digestive system with large quantities of improper foods;
11. Lack physical health; have poor levels of endurance, strength, and flexibility; as a group are fatter and unhealthier;
12. Are physically at-risk; causes of death are homicide, suicide, accident, and leukemia.

Middle grade students display the following *psychological development:*

1. Are often erratic and inconsistent in their behavior; anxiety and fear are contrasted with periods of bravado; feelings shift between superiority and inferiority;
2. Have chemical and hormonal imbalances which often trigger emotions that are frightening and poorly understood; may regress to more childish behavior patterns at this point;
3. Are easily offended and are sensitive to criticism of personal shortcomings;
4. Tend to exaggerate simple occurrences and believe that personal problems, experiences, and feelings are unique to themselves;
5. Are moody, restless; often feel self-conscious and alienated; lack self-esteem; are introspective;
6. Are searching for adult identity and acceptance even in the midst of intense peer group relationships;
7. Are vulnerable to naive opinions, one-sided arguments;
8. Are searching to form a conscious sense of individual uniqueness—"Who am I?"
9. Have emerging sense of humor based on increased intellectual ability to see abstract relationship; appreciate the "double entendre";
10. Are basically optimistic, hopeful;
11. Are psychologically at-risk; at no other point in human development is an individual likely to encounter so much diversity in relation to oneself and others.

Middle grade students display the following *social development:*

1. Experience often traumatic conflicts due to conflicting loyalties to peer groups and family;
2. Refer to peers as sources for standards and models of behavior; media heroes and heroines are also singularly important in shaping behavior and fashion;
3. May be rebellious towards parents but still strongly dependent on parental values; want to make own choices, but the authority of the family is a critical factor in ultimate decisions;
4. Are impacted by high level of mobility in society; may become anxious and disoriented when peer group ties are broken because of family relocation to other communities;
5. Are often confused and frightened by new school settings which are large and impersonal;
6. Act out unusual and drastic behavior at times; may be aggressive, daring, boisterous, argumentative;

7. Are fiercely loyal to peer group values; sometimes cruel or insensitive to those outside the peer group;
8. Want to know and feel that significant adults, including parents and teachers, love and accept them; need frequent affirmation;
9. Sense negative impact of adolescent behaviors on parents and teachers; realize thin edge between tolerance and rejection; feelings of adult rejection drive adolescent into the relatively secure social environment of the peer group;
10. Strive to define sexual characteristics; search to establish positive social relationships with members of the same and opposite sex;
11. Experience low risk-trust relationships with adults who show lack of sensitivity to adolescent characteristics and needs;
12. Challenge authority figures; test limits of acceptable behavior;
13. Are socially at-risk; adult values are largely shaped conceptually during adolescence; negative interactions with peers, parents, and teachers may compromise ideals and commitments.

Middle grade students display the following *moral and ethical development:*

1. Are essentially idealistic; have a strong sense of fairness in human relationships;
2. Experience thoughts and feelings of awe and wonder related to their expanding intellectual and emotional awareness;
3. Ask large unanswerable questions about the meaning of life; do not expect absolute answers but are turned off by trivial adult responses;
4. Are reflective, analytical, and introspective about their thoughts and feelings;
5. Confront hard moral and ethical questions for which they are unprepared to cope;
6. Are at-risk in the development of moral and ethical choices and behaviors; primary dependency on the influences of home and church for moral and ethical development seriously compromises adolescents for whom these resources are absent; adolescents want to explore the moral and ethical issues which are confronted in the curriculum, in the media, and in the daily interactions they experience in their families and peer groups.

As a teacher or prospective teacher of students in grades four through eight, what aspects of early adolescent development do you consider important to include when creating classroom learning environments?

With the uncertainty of transescence, early adolescents need to develop views of themselves as valuable, able, and responsible people. School experiences, including literacy experiences, must promote feelings of security, support, and success. The curriculum should engage students in issues that are important to them, to help them resolve conflicting viewpoints, and to reexamine their own views in light of the views of others. Meaningful reading and writing are excellent tools for such exploration.

Middle grade education received special recognition with the publication of *Turning Points: Preparing American Youth for the 21st Century* (Carnegie Council on Adolescent Development, 1989). The council recommended the following:

- Create small communities for learning.
- Teach a core academic program.
- Ensure success for all students.
- Empower teachers and administrators to make decisions about the experiences of middle grade students.
- Staff middle grade schools with teachers who are expert at teaching young adolescents.
- Improve academic performance through fostering the health and fitness of young adolescents.
- Re-engage families in the education of young adolescents.
- Connect schools with communities.

The council's recommendations closely parallel the description of 10- to 14-year-olds given by the California State Department of Education. Keep these recommendations in mind as we explore the development of reading and writing experiences for young adolescents.

Expect wide variation in stages of development among the middle grade students you work with. This variation occurs not only across learners, but also within individuals (Smart & Smart, 1973). For example, it is possible for a student to think abstractly in one subject area but not in another. As we consider the theoretical base for your developing middle grade literacy curriculum, we will frequently reflect on the characteristics of early adolescents identified in this chapter and their implications for your teaching.

Learning Environments in the Middle Grades

Developmental theories provide the base for constructing learning environments that encourage and support competent, independent behavior (Holdaway, 1979; Vygotsky, 1962, 1978). Such environments for middle grade students should include the following:

- "Knowledgeable others" who model clearly purposeful and successful use of the skills/strategies to be learned
- Support and encouragement for approximations toward mature behavior
- A noncompetitive learning atmosphere
- Opportunities for practice that are motivated and paced by the learner
- Opportunities for learners to correct and evaluate their own growth
- Encouragement and support that lead toward independent functioning

In the sections that follow, we describe Hiro's fifth-grade and Kristen's seventh-grade developmental reading classrooms to illustrate how teachers consciously create classroom learning environments that support early adolescent development.

Knowledgeable Others

Each of us, regardless of our stage of development, see "knowledgeable others" model behaviors with obvious purpose and success, and we may try to emulate these behaviors. These knowledgeable others help us form expectations for the behaviors we hope to attain. They also help us set benchmarks for ourselves, so that we may evaluate our development as individuals. As we observe the literacy behaviors of knowledgeable others, we learn about personal, as well as "real-world," reasons to read and write.

Manning (1995) suggests that "many adolescents particularly do not understand who they are or why they behave as they do" (p. 658). He suggests that for adolescents, knowledgeable others live in children's and young adult literature, particularly biography and historical fiction. Early adolescents can find in the lives of others "some purpose, direction, and fulfillment in their own" (p. 658).

In his fifth-grade classroom, Hiro models reading for pleasure during independent free-choice reading periods. His face and body show his pleasure. He even laughs aloud on occasion. During writer's workshop, Hiro writes for the first 10 minutes of each class, while the students are also writing. Periodically he shares his writing to get feedback from the students. To model how competent readers think about their reading, Kristen shares some of her strategies by thinking out loud while reading books that are familiar to her seventh-grade students. Hiro and Kristen each serve as a knowledgeable other for their students.

Supporting Approximations

Developmental processes, such as learning to read and write, mature slowly over many years. There are times in our learning when our performance is less than proficient, and even quite poor in comparison to mature performance. How the knowledgeable others in our lives respond to us as we attempt to learn greatly influences our willingness to persevere. If those around us support us and recognize our attempts, we are more likely to sustain our efforts. If, however, those around us expect more immediate success or perfection, we may question our ability to learn and may expend less effort in the process.

Meaningful learning experiences require a supportive classroom environment and a teacher-mediator.

As teachers, we must recognize that many middle grade students are not yet mature readers and writers and that they need our continued support for their approximations toward new, more mature literacy behaviors. We also must remember that it is through students' interactions with us, their teachers, in the sociocultural environment of the classroom that they learn to read, write, and engage in academic discourse (Goatley, Brock, & Raphael, 1995, p. 355).

Hiro and Kristen support their students' attempts through conferences and compliments. During both reading and writing instruction, they have face-to-face conferences with students. Hiro makes careful notes about student progress during each conference. By referring to his notes and to samples of student work, Hiro is able to identify even the smallest progress that his students make in their reading and writing. He is then able to make specific compliments to support students' approximations toward more complex behavior, such as recognizing an author's use of foreshadowing to develop tension in a plot. In addition to her conferences, Kristen writes specific compliments in students' reading journals as she responds to letters that students write to her.

Noncompetitive Environments

An environment that encourages and supports students' willingness to take risks in their attempts to learn will not emphasize competition between students. Competition that aids learning occurs within ourselves, when we push ourselves to learn something new.

Holdaway (1980) extends our understanding of competition when he states: "The real business of learning is concerned with performing better today than yesterday or last week; it has absolutely nothing to do with performing better than someone else. [Students] want to learn any developmental task in order to be the same as their peers, not better than them" (p. 18).

Early adolescence is already filled with periods of great uncertainty. Competitive environments only cause greater doubt as students question their ability to be successful. There are more losers than winners in competitions; students in middle grade classrooms have more to gain in inclusive, collaborative literacy environments.

The students in Hiro's and Kristen's classes keep individual records about the books they read. There are no class charts that compare the amount of reading that students do. Instead, Hiro has students reflect on their reading each week and make comparisons to previous weeks. Students individually graph the amount of time and number of pages read each week, then write a self-evaluation of their reading progress. Students are easily able to see their own improvement. Kristen asks her seventh-grade students to complete personal self-assessments in their reading logs at the midpoint and end of each grading period.

Self-Motivated, Self-Paced Practice

Learning complex processes such as reading and writing requires a great deal of practice. When our own desire drives our learning, we are more likely to practice. Choice fuels that desire and fosters a sense of control over our learning.

Independent learners typically set their own goals for learning and pace themselves to suit their goals. In Hiro's classroom, students select their own reading materials and determine a reading pace that fits them and the text, and decide when they will write responses to texts and when they wish to pursue an extension project for a text they found meaningful. Both Kristen's and Hiro's students participate in reader's and writer's workshops, forms of individualized reading and writing that allow for student choice.

Self-Correction and Self-Evaluation

Mature readers and writers are responsible for monitoring the accuracy and quality of their own thinking. For middle grade students to achieve similar independence, they must develop the ability to monitor the quality of their own learning.

The reading and writing curriculum in middle grade classrooms must treat students as worthwhile individuals who know something about themselves as learners. We must encourage them to trust their knowledge of themselves, combined with corrective feedback from reliable sources, to move toward independence.

In Hiro's classroom, students keep a learning portfolio that reflects their assessment of themselves as readers, writers, and learners. They add new work samples and self-evaluation reports at least once each grading period. Hiro works with his students to help them develop personal criteria for judging the value of their efforts. Kristen's, students also are learning to evaluate themselves as readers and as learners. In addition, Kristen works with members of her middle school team to help her students follow through with self-evaluation in other subject areas.

Independence Is the Goal

Our goal for students in school, as in life, should be independence! Independent learners are confident in their own abilities and are competent users of skills and strategies. If we are to successfully promote independence, we must set up and sustain developmental learning environments. We should let students' successes in independent learning outside of school teach us about the possibilities for learning in school.

BEING A TEACHER-MEDIATOR

As teachers, we are more knowledgeable others for our students, assisting them in becoming independent and competent individuals. How will you function in this role? In this text, we view the role of teacher as that of a mediator between learners and various types of texts (Dixon-Krauss, 1994), whose goal is to move students toward independence as readers, writers, and thinkers. *Texts* are defined as constructions of meaning, and may be either written or unwritten. For example, writers have a "text in the head" they attempt to recreate as a "text in print." The reader of that text creates still another "text in the head" in an attempt to construct meaning with print.

This view of teacher as mediator is influenced by the research of Russian psychologist Lev Vygotsky (1978), who describes the relationship between learners' development and instruction as a *zone of proximal development.* The zone is the range between where learners function independently (actual development) and where they function with the assistance of a more knowledgeable other (potential development). In Vygotsky's (1962) view, instruction should lead development. He states: "What the child can do in cooperation today he can do alone tomorrow. Therefore the only good kind of instruction is that which marches ahead of development and leads it; it must be aimed not so much at the ripe as at the ripening functions" (p. 104).

What does Vygotsky's theory suggest for us as middle grade teachers? We must think of instruction as paving the way for students to move from their present level of independent functioning to a higher level by providing assistance in tasks that students cannot yet do by themselves. To do this, we must know our students well enough to provide learning experiences that are *just ahead* of what they currently do independently. What a challenge, especially when we may meet several classes of students each day!

As we provide instruction within a student's zone of proximal development, we should: (1) mediate or augment a student's learning through our social interactions with the student, and (2) be flexible and adjust our support/assistance (amount and type) based on the feedback we receive from the student during the learning activity (Dixon-Krauss, 1996).

We cannot completely determine our role before we begin to interact with students. To help students move toward independence, we must determine our role based on what students show us they need from us as the more knowledgeable other. During any learning experience, the type of support we provide can range from vague hints to explicit responses. Student feedback during learning activities should tell us about the role they need us to take.

Teaching with Authentic Literature

Literature as Mirrors and Windows

Cullinan (1989), an expert in children's literature, asks, "Is a story a window through which we see the world, or a mirror in which we see ourselves?" (p. 390). While she uses this question as an introduction into her chapter on realistic fiction, the question is relevant to other forms of text. Cullinan speaks of the power of story and suggests the following:

- Stories "cause us to reflect on life and show us lives" (p. 390) that, because of time and space, we may never attain.
- They "allow us many experiences in the safety and security of our own lives" (p. 390).
- They allow us to mentally "rehearse experiences we might someday have" (p. 390).
- Stories enable us to draw analogies between those we read and those that we tell ourselves about our own lives.

These are powerful ideas! In literature, we are able to live inside the story frame where we are safe. Evil can exist in the story without hurting us. Experimentation, even failure, within a story provides lessons about life without having to experience the actual consequences. The joys of others in a story are also ours to share and revel in. We can use the safety and security of the story frame to work out ideas about life without the trial and error so commonly associated with learning to live in this world. We have the opportunity to try life twice, and more, by living vicariously in good literature and also in reality. We can help students have these experiences if we become knowledgeable about the range of literature available for 10- to 14-year-olds and openly share our knowledge with them.

Literature for Diversity

Seeing ourselves in the lives of book characters validates who we are and models who we might wish to become. If used thoughtfully, literature can play an important role in helping students learn about new ideas, new worlds, or different ways of doing things, which benefits them as human beings (Rasinski & Padak, 1990).

The Commission on Minority Participation in Education and American Life estimates that by the year 2000, 42 percent of schoolage children will be children of color (cited in Gonzalez, 1990). Literature that reflects the achievements, lifestyles, and values of these ethnic groups will help students have a better understanding of who they are and what contributions they can make to this country (Martinez & Nash, 1990). For

Reading authentic literature engages students with people, places, and times they might never experience first-hand.

this reason, it is important that we select literature for the classroom that represents the rapidly changing racial and ethnic makeup of this nation.

In selecting multicultural literature, Reimer (1992) cautions us to take care that the literature selected does not present "cultural conglomerates." For example, to use the term *Hispanic* to refer to all Spanish-speaking children does not acknowledge the specific contributions of Mexican-Americans, Puerto Ricans, and others.

Authentic multicultural literature, literature that is "culturally conscious" (Sims, 1983), helps us become more familiar with the cultural backgrounds of our students. Such books may focus on heritage, everyday experiences, battles against racism and discrimination, urban living, friendship, family relationships, and growing up. We may wish to look particularly for books written by members of a specific culture, to provide more of an insider's view. Appendix B contains lists of suggested books, sorted by cultural focus and primary topic or genre.

Extensive and Intensive Literature Experiences

By the time students reach the middle grades their past experiences with literature will largely explain their differences as readers and writers. Some students have had many and varied literary experiences, others will have had very few. Some students have intensely personal interests in particular literature, others see no reason to read. This range of experience and interest presents a distinct challenge for middle grade teachers.

We must plan extensive experiences with literature, for our reluctant readers and writers in particular. Across all subject areas and topics of study, we must engage students in exploring the range of ideas that others share through print. From CD-ROMs to information trade books, from novels about personal experiences of other early adolescents to biographies of extraordinary people living ordinary lives, our students must become aware of the possibilities of literature.

In addition to extensive experiences, our literacy programs must include opportunities for students to pursue their passions, the things that are intensely interesting to them during early adolescence. We know that our middle grade students are questioning many things, particularly themselves. Literature's varied forms and topics have something for everyone. Our challenge is to help students make the personal links that can lead to lifelong reading. Mature readers use reading for personal and career interests. We must immerse our middle grade students in literacy programs that support their exploration and development of personal interests through reading.

WORKING WITH THIS TEXT

Part I—Learners, Processes, and Possibilities (Theoretical Foundations)

To assist in formulating your understanding of your role as teacher-mediator, Part I (chapters 1 to 4) is concerned with fundamental issues in the teaching of reading, writing, and word knowledge with middle grade students. Your theory base for teaching middle grade students must be drawn from many sources, and you must weigh each idea and make decisions about its theoretical and practical value. Part I supplies important basic information for this task.

Your Turn/My Turn

The Your Turn/My Turn feature is designed to "nudge" your thinking as you read. This feature is my way of encouraging you to momentarily stop your reading and take time to reflect, to make connections with something you already know or with ideas previously presented in this text. Your Turn/My Turn segments occur at strategic locations throughout the text to support your processing of ideas. You may wish to dedicate a notebook to your answers for handy retrieval throughout this course. I hope you will choose to use the feature. Ideally, it will complement your own individual style of helping yourself process text.

Part II—Applying Methods and Strategies (Classroom Applications)

In Part II we explore how the foundations of reading and writing can be put to work in a variety of middle grade classrooms. We will visit Lou's sixth-grade classroom as students engage in whole-class literature study; learn from both Lou and Melodia, a sixth- and seventh-grade teacher, as they try out book clubs and literature circles with their students; observe Kristen, a beginning seventh- and eight-grade teacher, have a go at self-selected reading; and read as both Kristen and fifth-grade teacher Kim describe how they implement reading and writing workshops. We also will study lessons that other middle grade teachers have learned while engaging students in meaningful reading and writing activities. In addition, I will guide and encourage you to seek your own experiences, learn your own lessons, and form your own foundation for growth as a teacher.

Using Authentic Literature

We will use authentic literature as examples throughout this text. Whether you use a basal reading series, authentic literature, or a combination as your main source of reading instruction, children's and young adult literature must still be an integral part of instruction each day to offer students literacy experiences that are motivating and meaningful. Teaching with "real" books in some part of the instructional day helps students find meaningful reasons to read and write (Tunnell & Jacobs, 1989).

The literature used in chapter examples and scenarios will be most helpful to you if you are thoroughly familiar with the texts. At the beginning of each chapter, we identify the essential literature for that chapter. Having personal copies of these essential texts to study will enhance your study of the chapter.

Monitoring Students' Growth

Teaching from a developmental perspective suggests that we are constantly considering each student's progress in light of what we know about that individual, as well as what we know is possible based on developmental learning theory and current knowledge of literacy learning. To build a whole picture of what students know and do as readers and writers, we should be active participants with our students in their assessment and evaluation.

In this text, I use the term *assessment* to refer to the gathering of data through observations, conferences, and samples of student work to inform our curricular and instructional decisions. The term *evaluation* refers to the way in which we place value on the data collected according to our instructional purposes or outcomes. Working from a developmental perspective suggests that we cannot hold the same expectations for all students at any one point in the school year.

Writing from a developmental perspective, Ruddell and Ruddell (1995) state that assessment and evaluation (1) should be based on continuous observation of students engaging in authentic reading and writing tasks over a substantial period of time, and (2) should use a variety of measures, by both teacher and student, that reflect appropriate instructional purposes and account for diversity among learners.

We discuss assessment and evaluation issues throughout the text. Each of the subsequent chapters contains a section entitled, "Monitoring Students' Growth," that addresses assessment and evaluation issues as they pertain to the chapter content.

Respecting Diversity

Diversity has always existed in our society, whether it be of gender, social class, ethnic groups, learning styles, physical or mental abilities, personal interests, religious beliefs, first language, or the like (Harris, 1994). It is the unique contributions of each of these groups that have made the United States the country that it is (Ramirez & Ramirez, 1994).

The diversity of society shows itself in our classrooms. We find students that differ in their backgrounds of knowledge, their ability to make use of their experiences, their preferences for learning, and their motivation to engage in new learning experiences. As a result of the changes experienced by 10- to 14-year-olds, classroom diversity is accentuated at the middle grade level.

When we know such diversity exists, it is our responsibility to use that knowledge constructively in our teaching. As Hilliard (1994) reminds us,

> Diversity is the norm in human society, even when homogeneity appears on the surface. . . . When educators do not notice diversity, when they give negative notice, or

when they lose the opportunity to give positive notice of the natural diversity that is always there, they create a bogus reality for teaching and learning. (p. x)

As we enter today's classrooms we are challenged to move beyond our own recollections of school and be open for today's students to teach us about who they are as individuals and as learners. We each have at least 13,000+ hours as students in grades K–12 (Lortie, 1975) that influence our expectations of what life will be like as a teacher. We must be cautious as we draw on our own school experiences to inform us about classroom life in this rapidly changing world.

Issues of diversity are integrated throughout this text. Each of the subsequent chapters contains a section entitled, "Respecting Diversity," to call attention to issues in diversity as they relate to chapter content.

Our role as teachers of early adolescents can have far-reaching impact. We need literate individuals who are competent to deal with the problems that face us as world citizens. The curriculum and learning environment that we provide for middle grade students is an essential part of their development as literate individuals.

TAKE A MOMENT AND REFLECT

Middle grade students are:

- in transescence, a time of transition between childhood and adolescence
- intellectually diverse and moving toward the capacity for abstract thought
- physically maturing at varying speeds and are physically at risk
- psychologically erratic, inconsistent, and vulnerable
- socially in conflict between parents (society) and their peers and are socially at risk
- challenged by moral and ethical issues and are at risk when support from the home and church are absent

Developmental learning environments are excellent models for literacy learning and are characterized by:

- "knowledgeable others" who model clearly purposeful and successful use of the skills/strategies to be learned
- support and encouragement for approximations toward mature behavior
- a noncompetitive environment for learning
- opportunities for learners to engage in self-motivated, self-paced practice
- opportunities for learners to correct and evaluate their own growth
- encouragement and support that leads toward independent functioning

Teachers:

- are the "more knowledgeable other" for many students
- should be mediators between learners and texts in both reading and writing
- should aim instruction just beyond where students can function independently and should lead students' development
- must use feedback from students to determine where to target instruction

Authentic literature should be an essential instructional component because:

- literature serves as both a mirror for students to view themselves and as a window through which they can view lives and times beyond their own
- literature can reflect the diversity of students in middle grade classrooms

Middle grade students need:

- extensive literature experiences to show the possibilities of what literature has to offer
- intensive literature experiences to pursue passions and areas of deep interest

REFERENCES

California State Department of Education. (1987). *Caught in the middle: Educational reform for young adolescents in California public schools.* Sacramento, CA: Author.

Carnegie Council on Adolescent Development. (1989). *Turning points: Preparing American youth for the 21st century.* Washington, DC: Author.

Cullinan, B. E. (1989). *Literature and the child.* San Diego, CA: Harcourt Brace Jovanovich.

Dixon-Krauss, L. (1994, September). A mediation model for dynamic literacy instruction. Paper presented at the International Conference on L. S. Vygotsky and the Contemporary Human Sciences in Moscow, Russia.

Dixon-Krauss, L. (1996). Vygotsky's sociohistorical perspective on learning and its application to western literacy instruction. In L. Dixon-Krauss (Ed.), *Vygotsky in the classroom: Mediated literacy instruction and assessment.* White Plains, NY: Longman.

Eichhorn, D. (1966). *The middle school.* New York: Center for Applied Research in Education.

Goatley, V. J., Brock, C. H., & Raphael, T. E. (1995). Diverse learners participating in regular education "book clubs." *Reading Research Quarterly, 30,* 352–380.

Gonzalez, R. D. (1990). When minority becomes majority: The changing face of English classrooms. *English Journal, 79,* 16–23.

Harris, V. J. (1994). Multiculturalism and children's literature. In F. Lehr & J. Osborn (Eds.), *Reading, language and literacy* (pp. 201–214). Hillsdale, NJ: Erlbaum.

Hilliard, A. (1994). In E. W. King, M. Chipman & M. Cruz-Janzen (Eds.), *Educating young children in a diverse society* (p. x). Boston: Allyn and Bacon.

Holdaway, D. (1979). *Foundations of literacy.* Sydney, Australia: Ashton.

Holdaway, D. (1980). *Independence in reading.* Portsmouth, NH: Heinemann.

Irvin, J. L. (1990). *Reading and the middle school student: Strategies to enhance literacy.* Boston: Allyn and Bacon.

Lortie, D. (1975). *Schoolteacher.* Chicago: University of Chicago Press.

Manning, J. C. (1995). "Ariston metron." *The Reading Teacher, 48,* 650–659.

Martinez, M., & Nash, M. F. (1990). Bookalogues: Talking about children's literature. *Language Arts, 67,* 599-606.

Ramirez, G., & Ramirez, J. L. (1994). *Multiethnic children's literature.* Albany, NY: Delmar.

Rasinski, T., & Padak, N. D. (1990). Multicultural learning through children's literature. *Language Arts, 67,* 576–580.

Reimer, K. M. (1992). Multiethnic literature: Holding fast to dreams. *Language Arts, 69,* 14–21.

Ruddell, R. B., & Ruddell, M. R. (1995). *Teaching children to read and write: Becoming an influential teacher.* Boston: Allyn and Bacon.

Shannon, P. (Ed.). (1992). *Becoming political: Reading and writing in the politics of literacy education.* Portsmouth, NH: Heinemann.

Sims, R. (1983). What has happened to the "all white" world of children's books? *Phi Delta Kappan, 64,* 650–653.

Smart, M. S., & Smart, R. C. (1973). *Adolescence.* Upper Saddle River, NJ: Merrill/Prentice Hall.

Tunnell, M. O., & Jacobs, J. S. (1989). Using "real" books: Research findings on literature based reading instruction. *The Reading Teacher, 42,* 470–477.

Vygotsky, L. S.(1962). *Thought and language* (E. Hanfmann & G. Vakar, Eds. & Trans.). Cambridge, MA: MIT Press.

Vygotsky, L. S. (1978). *Mind in society* (M.Cole, V. John-Steiner, S. Scribner, & E. Sounerman, Eds. & Trans.). Cambridge, MA: Harvard University Press.

Wiles, J., & Bondi, J. (1993). *The essential middle school.* Upper Saddle River, NJ: Merrill/Prentice Hall.

2

Growing Toward Maturity as Readers

In this chapter . . .

We consider a range of issues that influence how we make meaning with text, including

- our knowledge of the process of reading and making meaning,
- stages we pass through as readers on our way to maturity,
- behaviors we use to monitor our reading as we make meaning,
- explicit, implicit, critical, and creative/personal thinking while we read,
- engagement with literature,
- taking efferent and aesthetic stances as readers,
- ways that we respond to literature,
- the need to know about literary elements as we read narrative writing,
- ways that we think when we read informational writing,
- matching readers with texts of varying difficulty,
- monitoring growth in readers through observation, conferences, and collecting samples of work, and
- respecting diversity in the ways that readers make meaning with texts.

Before you get started . . .

Time for Andrew: A Ghost Story by Mary Downing Hahn (1994) and *Hatchet* by Gary Paulsen (1987) are featured as examples and in Your Turn/My Turn activities in this chapter.

Some Opening Thoughts

Louise Rosenblatt (1978) said that words are mere "inkspots on paper until a reader transforms them into a set of meaningful symbols" (p. 25). Thomson (1987) views this "transformation" as a process of getting better and better at making a text in our heads that has meaning for us, and as a process of becoming more intellectually and emotionally active while we read. Readers transform the symbols on a page to make and share meanings "as ways of exploring and understanding what it means to live" (Thomson, 1987, p. 13).

Making meaning with any one text, however, is not the same for all readers:

- Schon (1983) suggests that each reader is unique, in effect "a universe of one," and as such the meanings we make are in some way unique unto ourselves (p. 333).
- Holdaway (1980) describes the act of reading as "an individual and intensely personal thing. We cannot speak of reading as thinking without emphasizing the individual nature of the process: groups don't think" (p. 51).
- C. S. Lewis (1978), author of the classic *Chronicles of Narnia* fantasy series, suggests that any particular story can be read in different ways by different readers. The same reader also reads a text differently at different times.
- Golden and Guthrie (1986) believe that meaning does not reside in the text; rather, readers actively construct meaning, and their backgrounds and experiences influence the process.
- Bloome and Bailey (1992) suggest that in addition to background knowledge and cultural understanding, meaning making is also influenced by our environment while we are reading and by other texts we have read.

While our individual interpretations presumably differ, commonalities of meaning within any community of readers emerge as we share backgrounds, experiences, attitudes, and strategies as readers (Beach & Hynds, 1991, p. 455). Many adult readers have a sense of community with friends and colleagues with whom they share texts, both printed and visual (television and film). Students come to the middle grades with great variation in their experiences and ability, both in and out of school. It is our task to build a community of readers who share common experiences as they draw on their varied backgrounds.

In this text, particularly in this chapter, we consider issues that surround the reader, the text, and the context in which the reading occurs. In Part II of this text, we will draw on our shared knowledge from this chapter and our individual experiences as we consider instructional approaches for engaging middle grade students in reading processes and literacy experiences. We begin with a discussion of reading processes and the stages through which we all progress as readers.

Reading Process and Making Meaning

We have learned from research that reading is "a high-speed, automatic, simultaneous operation of complex linguistic and cognitive processes. At any moment, a reader of any level of proficiency must keep in mind story meaning, sentence meaning, sentence syntax, and some metacognitive awareness of fit, while simultaneously, perceiving and identifying words, word-parts, and punctuation marks" (Jones, 1995, p. 44).

What might Noel Jones mean by this statement? Let's read it again, this time pulling it apart and analyzing the meaningful words. In the first sentence, Jones's use of the terms in the left column can be restated as in the right column:

linguistic	Using the units and structure of our language,
cognitive	we organize what we know and think,

processes	into a series of actions leading to a particular end (meaning).
simultaneous	Several operations occur at the same time,
high-speed	as information is processed by the brain in milliseconds,
automatic	often without our conscious control.

When we read, our knowledge of language and our ability to think work together very rapidly to make meaning, often without conscious control. When meaning breaks down, we consciously use what we know and have learned from our past experience as readers to repair the breakdown. We will address such monitoring, or use of reading strategies to check meaning, in a later section.

Now, consider the remaining part of Jones's statement. At any moment in the process of making meaning, a reader must keep the following in mind:

- *story meaning and sentence meaning*—We must not only hold in our heads the overall meaning we have constructed thus far, but also must attend to the meaning of each new sentence.
- *sentence syntax*—To construct meaning with each new sentence, we draw on our knowledge of the grammar or structure of our language.
- *and some metacognitive awareness of fit*—We check our thinking to determine if the meanings we are making are possible and appropriate considering the structure of our language and what we know about the topic.
- *while simultaneously, perceiving and identifying words, word-parts, and punctuation marks* —At the same time, we sample just enough of the actual print on the page to confirm whether what we are thinking as we make meanings fits both the sentence and the overall meaning.

For us, as mature readers, this process of drawing on meaning, grammar, and visual cues to make meaning operates so automatically that what we do appears to be effortless. In addition, when we read we focus our attention on meaning cues, drawing on visual cues, language structure, and other sources of information only as they seem necessary to make a meaningful text in our heads. For less experienced readers, however, these processes require much more conscious control and time spent problem solving.

To emphasize the complexity of reading processes, Jones (1995, p. 45) identifies other factors affecting any act of reading:

- Personal choice (emerging from a complex mix of interests, feelings, and ideas)
- Activation of prior knowledge (calling on our organized systems for conceptualizing and understanding something)
- Level of engagement with text (the degree to which we are emotionally and intellectually involved with a text)
- Metacognitive control (awareness of our own knowledge and thought processes that support our meaning making, and our strategic use of that knowledge to monitor meaning)
- Integration of new experiences with our existing knowledge and feelings
- Judgment and evaluation of the meanings we make

How might this discussion affect our sense of purpose in reading instruction? I believe our purpose should be to engage less experienced readers in acts of making meaningful texts using meaning, grammar, and visual cues, so that students learn to rely on meaning with only subsidiary attention to other cues, until making meaning becomes virtually automatic. We must also share our metacognitive knowledge that enables us to monitor our reading processes.

By the middle grades, students should be moving toward mature reading. To break through, students must understand what mature readers know and do. Emphasizing mature reading behaviors, then, is a main purpose of reading instruction in the middle grades.

Before moving on to a new section of text, you may find it helpful to stop for a moment to reflect on our discussion of reading processes. Without looking back in the text, describe your current understanding of reading processes.

Now, look back and see which elements of the process you included as meaningful for you. Perhaps you see those elements in yourself as a reader. The elements that you omitted signify ideas that are not yet meaningful to you.

STAGES OF READING DEVELOPMENT

Reading ability develops in clearly identifiable stages (Holdaway, 1980; Juel, 1991). With the diversity of today's middle grade classrooms, it is likely that several stages of reading development will be represented among the students. In this text we discuss the following stages of reading development:

- emerging
- developing
- transitional
- mature

Emerging Readers

We are actually emergent readers from birth, as we learn to "read" the world. All during the preschool years we see print in use in our environment and, slowly, we begin to realize that the print has meaning. We know where to get hamburgers and french fries, which box holds our favorite cereal, and that the red sign on the street corner says "STOP." Our natural desire to understand leads us to explore and emulate what the significant people in our lives show us about the purposes and functions of print (Teale, 1986).

During the emerging reading stage tremendous growth takes place. We begin to internalize purposes for print, concepts of how print works, ideas about its permanence, and concepts about words and the functions letters serve. The knowledge we develop during this time is very important, but not more important than the attitudes and motivations we, as children, have toward print and its usefulness in our lives.

We are contextual readers during this stage; we need a familiar context to be able to use the print knowledge we are acquiring. We can "read" picture books that have been read to us, but we are most comfortable with patterned repetitive text with illustrations that are highly predictable.

Emerging readers typically read texts that range from beginning reading level to those that average midyear first-grade students can comfortably read and understand.

Middle grade students who engage in sustained silent reading in longer texts are typically in the transitional and mature stages of reading development.

Developing Readers

Over time we begin to sense the patterns of our language as we gain competence with the directional nature of print. We consciously try to match the visual cues of print with what we know as we read aloud. In this stage our reading is "outside of ourselves" because we haven't yet learned to internalize our thoughts through inner speech (Vygotsky, 1978). Our reading is more like word-to-word matching (Holdaway, 1980), when we are literally glued to the print in our efforts to make sense.

In our early reading we find ourselves rerunning text or self-correcting quite a bit as we struggle to make sense of print. If we spend a lot of time in text that is relatively easy we build the confidence that helps us persevere when text is more difficult. Practicing in easy text also gives us time to organize what we know about print.

As our confidence grows, our ability to monitor and correct our own reading becomes more natural. Self-correction demonstrates our ability to make meaning. If the adults around us continue to correct our miscues during oral reading, it takes away our drive to self-correct.

Toward the end of this stage, typically around the early third-grade reading level, we move toward silent reading, and our reading becomes more of a private, rather than public, affair. In this transition, our oral reading becomes subvocalized. When we read to ourselves others may hear murmurs, but not words. It is silent reading that lets us focus on our reactions to a text, rather than on the words. Now, we can truly begin to read for personal satisfaction and understanding. Developing readers typically read text that ranges in difficulty from middle first-grade to early third-grade reading level.

Transitional Readers

Early in the transitional stage we experience some difficulty moving back and forth between oral and silent reading. We have learned how to monitor our oral reading (assuming the surrounding adults allow us to) and are now learning to effectively monitor our silent reading.

The more we move into silent reading, the more likely we are to become truly absorbed in our reading. This also is about the time we move from picture books to chapter books or novels, which provide more extensive description and more development of plot and characters.

Spending our time in the privacy of silent reading helps us begin to sense our own "style" of reading. As a part of our style, we begin to sense the rate at which we can comfortably move through a variety of texts, the amount of attention we must give to different reading tasks, and the range of behaviors we have that help us make meaning with text.

Later in this stage, we become more flexible in our reading. Reading extensively in easy texts lets us feel what fluent reading is like. Extensive, fluent reading helps us add to our understanding of how we make adjustments in our reading depending on the demands of the text. As we move toward the end of this stage we are reading texts that are typically at about sixth-grade reading level and preparing to break into mature reading. Transitional readers typically read texts that range in difficulty from early third-grade to sixth-grade reading level.

Mature Readers

This is the current reading stage for most literate adults. There is no upper limit to this stage, but rather it "constitutes a body of learning strategies which allow the mature reader to extend and develop new skills or refinements of skill to meet changing life purposes" (Holdaway, 1980, p. 30). It is during this stage that our reading becomes "interest-and-vocation-centered" (p. 30). Our comprehension becomes quite rapid, first in areas where we spend the most time reading and have the greatest familiarity and understanding.

Mature readers not only read texts of sixth-grade reading level and above but also use reading strategies in specific ways to make meaning (see the next section). Remember, as we consider stages of development we are thinking broadly about reading behaviors. Behaviors in the early part of a stage may look very different from those at the end of that same stage. As we move from one stage to another, new tasks with increased difficulty may cause us to exhibit "old" behaviors until we are able to gain greater control over new behaviors.

Monitoring Our Reading: Becoming Strategic Readers

As competent readers, we know that reading should make sense and, consequently, we monitor our own meaning making. We recognize when meaning breaks down and deliberately use our knowledge of reading at appropriate times and under a variety of conditions to repair breakdowns when they occur (Paris, Wasik, & Turner, 1991). This ability to self-monitor means that we can function independently with a variety of forms of print (Holdaway, 1980). Middle grade students who are maturing as readers must also become proficient at monitoring their own reading.

When we monitor, we use a variety of strategies to make meaning:

We use our prior knowledge.

- We know that we can use what we already know to acquire further knowledge or information.

We anticipate/make reasonable predictions.

- We draw on prior reading experiences to anticipate what we might need to do to make meaning.
- As we read, we use what seems reasonable to anticipate upcoming text (words or ideas). We sample just enough text to either confirm or change our predictions.

We self-correct miscues.

- We realize when a miscue, or a reading different from the actual text, has occurred. At that point, we activate appropriate fixup strategies that we have learned over time.

- Fixup strategies include reading on to see if key ideas are yet to come, rereading the text in question, and skipping particular sections of text because they may not be important to our purpose.

We adjust our reading strategies to meet the purposes of different types of texts.

- The presentation of ideas in narrative text is typically linear (plot sequence), but ideas in information texts can be structured in a variety of ways within the same piece (description, comparison, ordered, cause/effect, etc.). Such knowledge causes us to look for clues to how ideas are structured.
- We adjust the speed of our reading to the difficulty level of the text, our purpose(s) for reading, and our familiarity with the topic.
- Textual information is organized in particular ways. Reference sources such as indexes, tables of contents, and glossaries can help us locate specific information. Headings, subheadings, charts and graphs, and boldface print are also clues to how information is organized within the text.
- In narrative text, authors use literary elements to engage us in the telling of the story.
- Authors writing in a particular form (such as prose or poetry) or within a particular genre (such as fantasy or mystery), use the rules of the form and/or the characteristics of the genre in their writing.

Which strategies do you notice most in yourself when you read?

When we monitor our reading we become aware of our own reading behaviors. We are also aware of how we use our cognitive abilities to make sense of an author's ideas. In the next section we consider different ways that we think as we consider an author's words.

THINKING AS WE READ

Our thinking is influenced by many factors as we read, including our schema for the topic and the particular type of text, our motivation for making the text meaningful, the level of text difficulty, and our ability to monitor for meaning.

A well-formed schema for written language helps students organize personal experiences into abstract representations that are independent of the original stimuli (Schanklin, 1982). Abstraction allows knowledge to be used in different contexts to make sense of new experiences. Within a schema, knowledge is organized into a hierarchical framework of concepts and procedures (Adams & Collins, 1985; Schank & Abelson, 1975). If a student's schema does not already include an appropriate place to "file" the new information, she must create a new "file" within the existing framework by inferring how the new information might relate to existing concepts or procedures.

Explicit Thinking—Knowing the Author's Words

We think in explicit ways when we are aware of the need to remember and use details. In certain reading situations, we realize that we must retain ideas from the reading for later use and that it is important to listen explicitly to the author's words.

Our ability to explicitly understand the author's words depends, in part, on our ability to recognize the words in a text and on our knowledge of the topic. If the topic is completely unknown we will have difficulty understanding, and most likely will not be able to think along with the author.

Implicit Thinking—Thinking between the Author's Words

Authors do not always explicitly tell us what we may need to know. It would be impossible for an author to anticipate everything that every reader might need to know about the topic at hand. The author assumes that we know some things about the topic and that, depending on our purposes, we will "work" to make sense by filling in or linking the author's ideas. This act of filling in or linking is *implicit thinking* and is the base from which we make inferences while we read.

Anderson and Pearson (1984) identify four types of implicit thinking that we as readers use to fill in the author's ideas:

- We draw on our prior knowledge of a topic to fill in ideas that are missing in the text.
- We mentally link specific ideas that relate to an idea but that do not appear together in the text.
- We combine our prior knowledge with clues from the author (essentially a combination of the first two types of implicit thinking).
- We use logical reasoning to fill in our incomplete understanding of a text, but without enough clues from the author or our prior knowledge to check the accuracy of our thinking.

The first three types of thinking can lead us to appropriate conclusions through varying combinations of our schema and the ideas in a text. The last type, however, can be problematic if our line of reasoning leads to misconceptions about the ideas in the text.

As competent readers, we learn to think our way through a text and operate as if it should make sense. So at times we will fill in missing pieces even if it leads us to what might be an inappropriate conclusion. We will eventually be confronted by situations that contain the accurate information, and because we monitor our reading, we will question our inappropriate prior knowledge and, hopefully, change our thinking.

Critical Thinking—Questioning and Valuing the Author's Ideas

Each of us must make critical judgments about the value or merit of an author's ideas based on a self-determined set of criteria. We develop our criteria through our experiences as readers. Making critical judgments requires us to use our background knowledge accurately and to approach reading as a thinking process.

As readers we must know that, while we consider our own ideas to make judgments, we must make those judgments in light of the author's ideas or arguments. We cannot ignore the author. We must also realize that authors have intentions. They write from a particular perspective. They have their own experiences that influence their view of the world. As we read, we question the author's view and critically consider the support that is provided. Here, as in explicit thinking, we take an efferent stance (see the section, "Literary Stance," later in this chapter) and are concerned with the ideas we will have when we leave the reading.

Creative/Personal Thinking— Unique Ways of Seeing the Author's Ideas

When we think in creative or personal ways, we engage with an author for personal reasons and not because we are required to achieve a specific purpose. We take an aesthetic stance as readers (see the section, "Literary Stance," later in this chapter) and focus on our lived-through experience with the author, rather than on what we will take from the reading. While we may initially be influenced by the author's ideas, we soon realize that our response does not bind us to the author's way of thinking. We go beyond the author and let our own ideas take over.

Results of the most recent National Assessment of Educational Progress (NAEP), "the nation's only ongoing, comparable, and representative assessment of student achievement" (Mullis, Campbell, & Farstrup, 1993, p. 1), suggest that our middle grade students continue to need opportunities to develop their thinking abilities. Students are asked to do the following on the NAEP assessment:

Student reading tasks:	*Type of thinking:*
Demonstrate basic understanding	explicit
Develop an interpretation	implicit
Articulate a personal reflection and response	creative
Demonstrate a critical stance	critical

The majority of fourth- and eighth-grade students who participate in this assessment typically do not demonstrate more than basic proficiency in their thinking about text. They are able to demonstrate explicit thinking, but need additional experiences in implicit, critical, and creative/personal thinking.

The ability to think in different ways with a variety of texts develops slowly, through many reading and literary experiences. Students must become aware of the stance they take as readers to know the purposes for their reading and to develop their own criteria for evaluating ideas in text.

In today's classrooms, we engage students in reading experiences with *authentic* literature, that is, with real books rather than with texts created solely for literacy instruction. The effective use of literature requires that we think about text, not only from a reading perspective, but also from a literary perspective. Our interest in thinking or our intellectual responses to text during reading must expand to include consideration of our emotional responses to text. In addition to instruction in the actual processes of reading, we must provide opportunities for middle grade students to engage in literary experiences, the experiences that we hope will serve to lure them back into literature throughout their lives.

Literary Experiences

Our understanding of literary experience is informed by theories about readers' responses to texts. In reader-response theory, meaning is believed to emerge in the *transaction* between reader and text (Rosenblatt, 1978). In this sense, a transaction is like a negotiation between two parties, a reader and a text, that brings about a change in one or both. A transaction between reader and text, however, cannot occur without *engagement*.

Engagement

Engagement with a literary text is at the heart of reader-response theory. Slatoff (1970) suggests that the very nature of a literary work is to "affect the emotions and to compel various sorts of involvement" (p. 36). Engagement is more than merely emotional response; it is a process of involving "both mind and emotion" (p. 53). Rosenblatt (1978) agrees when she states that literary study should be a "working harmony" between reason and emotion where students "develop the ability to think rationally within an emotionally colored context" (pp. 227–228).

Bruner (1986) adds that in a learning environment emotion and thought are not separate, because emotion is deeply rooted and produced within a cultural reality, where "emotion comes from the knowledge of the situation that arouses it" (p. 117). Think of yourself as a reader. How does your own emotional response to literature draw you into that literature? Do you believe that your emotional engagement calls on your mind to reason in response?

What happens when readers do not engage with a text? For these readers the words on the page are merely symbols, without meaning for them. But for readers with a high level of engagement the very same page of text may be pure delight, entertainment, or enlightenment.

Literary Stance

Readers both transform and are transformed by literary works. Rosenblatt (1985) states that the reading experience is influenced by the literary stance readers take toward texts as well as the cognitive and psychological processes they bring to the reading process. What might Rosenblatt mean by the term *literary stance?*

Readers have certain expectations of a text and of the reading/literary experience, and as a result adopt one of two reading stances (Rosenblatt, 1978): an efferent stance or an aesthetic stance.

An *efferent stance* is a type of reading in which the primary concern of the reader is what she will carry away from the reading or what will remain with her afterwards, such as the information to be acquired, the logical solution to a problem, or the actions to be carried out.

An *aesthetic stance* is a type of reading in which the reader focuses attention on the lived-through experience of the reading, the thoughts and feelings that are being stirred within the reader, the beauty of the writer's ideas and style of expression, and the past experiences that these words call up.

Rosenblatt (1985) views the possibilities for a reader's stance as an efferent–aesthetic continuum. "Since much of our linguistic activity hovers near the middle of the 'efferent–aesthetic' continuum, it becomes essential that in any particular speaking/listening/writing/reading event we adopt the predominant stance appropriate to our purpose" (p. 102). The stance that we take as readers directly affects the quality of our literary experience.

Let's apply the definitions of *efferent* and *aesthetic* reading to the classroom. Imagine that you plan to engage your sixth-grade students in reading *Hatchet* (Paulsen, 1987), in which 13-year-old Brian, on his way to visit his father, who works in the Canadian oil fields, survives a plane crash and lives alone in the wilderness for 54 days. If you emphasize the survival techniques that can be learned from Brian's ordeal, what type of stance are you encouraging students to take? Why?

If, however, you read this text aloud with expression and respond to the way that Paulsen uses words to evoke the feelings of isolation that Brian must have felt, what type of stance would you be encouraging students to take? Why?

If you provide opportunities for students to meet in student-led literature groups and encourage them to find what is meaningful for themselves in the text, what type of stance would you be encouraging students to take? Why?

If I use *Hatchet* to form concepts about survival techniques, I am pushing students toward an *efferent stance*, to focus on what they will take away from the text that will help them understand social studies/science concepts. If I read *Hatchet* aloud to encourage students to appreciate the beauty and emotion of the text, I focus on the experience itself rather than on what students will take from it. This encourages them to take an *aesthetic stance*. If, however, students know that they will meet in student-led groups and set their own directions for discussions, the possibilities for responses can extend across the efferent–aesthetic continuum, depending on their previous literary experiences and their level of engagement with the text.

A major goal of your literature instruction should be to help middle grade students develop a sophisticated repertoire of response options to use in a variety of literary situations. As you plan instructional experiences, you must consider how to engage students and how to help them learn to evaluate the effectiveness of the stances they take as readers.

As readers, our schema for literature and reading influences the processes we use for responding to text. In the next section we consider various ways that readers use intellect and emotion in response to literature.

Responding to Literature

We respond emotionally and intellectually to texts that we read. Our responses to text can be described as engagement, conceiving, connecting, problem solving and question asking, explaining, interpreting, and judging.

Engagement. Engagement rests heavily on the breadth, depth, and quality of our previous literary experiences. The more positively we feel toward the act of reading in general, and toward the reading of a particular text, the more likely we are to have a high degree of engagement with that text. If our experience has taught us that reading is trying to find the "right answer" or that reading is physically hard because we are asked to read texts that are too difficult for us, then we are not likely to have positive feelings toward reading and are less likely to engage in the reading.

Our expectations for a text affect our level of engagement with it. How engaged we become in fiction or fantasy relates to our sense of reality and willingness to accept the fictional world of a literary text as distinct from our own. How engaged we become with information text or biography relates to our interest in the topic, our desire to learn about the topic, and the relevance we see for our own lives. Without engagement, other forms of response are not probable.

Conceiving. Depending on the level at which we engage with a text, we develop conceptions or perceptions of that text. Readers who have difficulty defining their emotional responses to a text also have difficulty describing their conceptions of it (Miall, 1985). Personal conceptions formed in the real world influence our responses in a fictional world. Readers with a more well-organized schema for literature and reading tend to have "more elaborate and complex interpretations of the actions and behaviors of literary characters" (Hynds, 1985, p. 401).

Connecting. As readers, we connect literary texts with related experiences, other texts, and personal attitudes (Beach, 1987; Harste, 1986). Elaborating on our own life experiences, attitudes, and knowledge makes us better able to use that experience as we interpret literary texts. As we make these connections, we often draw on past literary experiences to make new interpretations. It is in our connections to text that we are able to generalize from a broad base of knowledge.

Problem Solving and Question Asking. When we monitor our reading and are able to articulate our difficulties in understanding text, we are better able to use problem-solving strategies to enhance understanding (Newkirk, 1984). Posing our own questions while reading helps us demonstrate better story understanding than if we did not pose such questions. Mature readers interact with the author and with themselves as sense makers.

Explaining. *Explaining* is making a clarifying statement, describing what something means to us. When we read, we may be better able to explain our personal feelings about a text rather than our interpretations. Our explanations may be based more on emotion than thought and, consequently, may lack systematic supporting evidence from the text. Our attitudes toward reading or the information provided in a text can influence our ability to explain (Black & Seifert, 1985). Text that is rich in description provides increased opportunity for engagement and the identification of supporting detail to explain our stance as readers.

Interpreting. Interpretation is considered to be the thinking side of making meaning. When we interpret as readers, we think beyond the literal meaning and "read between the lines." Our interpretations of a text are influenced by our previous literary experiences (Black & Seifert, 1985; Heath, 1985). The more experience we have with literature, at home and at school, the more likely we are to make interpretations (Martinez, 1983; Svensson, 1985). Analyzing or generalizing are more likely to occur when text is familiar.

Less experienced readers are more likely to be oriented to finding information in a text (information driven) or to following a story line (story driven), rather than to making interpretations about the author's intention (point driven) (Hunt & Vipond, 1985, 1986). They are more likely to use retelling, engaging, evaluation, or inferring in response to literature than to generalize about or analyze a text. Such behavior may be a reflection of school experiences with literature.

Judging. Knowledge of literature influences the processes we use as we make judgments about text. With experience, we begin to focus more on the form and complexity of literary text than on story content (Britton, 1984). When less experienced readers make judgments based on story content rather than on form, they are likely to negatively judge a story they do not understand. The relationship between readers' interests and their cognitive maturity also affects their making judgments about the aesthetic quality of literature (Beach & Hynds, 1991).

As readers, we use a variety of processes or strategies in our responses to literature. We seldom use one process in isolation from other response processes. "It is difficult to make generalizations about discrete response types, since responses such as explaining or describing are often embedded in superordinate strategies such as judging or interpreting" (Beach & Hynds, 1991, p. 463).

To engage students effectively in a reading and literature program, you must consider the nature of the texts you will use and how those texts influence the making of meaning. In the next sections of this chapter we turn our attention to issues of narrative and informational texts. What your students know about these texts influences their level of engagement as they make meaning.

Narrative Writing: Becoming Aware of Literary Elements

To think as mature readers, we must have a well-developed sense of how authors use literary elements. Knowing the possibilities helps us develop expectations for narrative writing. The genres of realistic fiction, fantasy, and folk literature draw heavily on narrative writing, which is characterized by the use of such literary elements as setting, characters, plot, point of view, theme, and style. We will examine here literary elements as used in children's literature and consider the importance of each element.

We draw our examples from *Time for Andrew: A Ghost Story,* a mystery by Mary Downing Hahn (1994), in which Andrew, nicknamed Drew, is tricked into trading places in time by the ghost of Andrew, an ancestor who died of diphtheria several generations earlier. Drew must then figure out how to get back to the present. A Your Turn/My Turn activity, using *Hatchet,* by Gary Paulsen (1987), provides opportunity for you to apply your understanding of literary elements.

Setting

Types of Settings. In some stories the author focuses on character development, making the setting seem somewhat unimportant. The setting is merely a *backdrop* and we do not pay much attention to it. We realize where and when the story is taking place, but we also realize that the setting does not influence our attention to the conflict the main character is experiencing. In contrast, the author may choose to use the setting in a more *integral* way, where the setting actually has a specific function in the story.

Functions of Setting.

Integral Settings Can Affect the Mood of a Story. Sometimes an author uses description of the setting to create a particular mood that supports the telling of the story. For example, in *Time for Andrew*, Hahn uses description of dreary, windy, rainy weather and a post–Civil War house, believed to be haunted, to create an eerie mood. We expect that the setting will be important to the upcoming events, so we become engaged.

Setting Can Illuminate a Character. Settings can be used to show us a side of a character that might not be evident in any other way. Being in Aunt Blythe's haunted house puts Drew in a situation he has never experienced and we see a courageous side of him that we might not see in his everyday life.

Setting Can Act as an Antagonist. Lukens (1990) defines *antagonist* as an opposing force to the *protagonist,* or main character. It is the conflict between the protagonist and antagonist that creates plot in many stories. We see the setting as antagonist most prominently in stories in which characters struggle with nature or society, rather than with self or others. Nature and society push characters to show us parts of themselves we might not otherwise see.

Setting Can Symbolize a Figurative Meaning. Authors use concrete objects and color to represent abstract or implied meanings. For example, the darkness that Hahn uses to evoke feeling also symbolizes the death that overshadows Aunt Blythe's house. Figurative meanings are typically present in folk literature, especially myths and legends, but can also be present in other forms of narrative.

Your Turn

What type of setting does Gary Paulsen use in *Hatchet* (1987)? What function(s) does the setting play? What leads you to think that?

My Turn

The setting in *Hatchet* is integral to the development of Paulsen's story. After the plane crash the setting actually becomes the antagonist, the character opposing Brian. The solitude of the setting affects our anticipation of upcoming events, and consequently affects the mood of the story.

Character

Learning about Characters. As we listen to an author describe a character, we learn about the character's physical appearance, actions, possibly the character's thoughts, and, if the author is narrating the story, we know what the author thinks about the character. Through dialogue we listen to the character's words and also what others say about the character. Then it is our job as readers to put these pieces of information together to form our own understanding of that character.

Types of Characters. Characters are described by how much is known about them and the degree to which they change during the development of the plot. Our knowledge of some characters is *round* because we know a lot about them, while our knowledge of other characters is rather *flat*. Main characters are typically round. We need to know them well if we are to engage with them in the story. Other characters are flat because we don't need to know much about them.

Characters can also be described by how much they change during the development of the plot. Some characters are affected by the events of the plot and show us how they grow and change as a result of their experiences. Characters that change are called *dynamic* characters. In contrast, some characters are *static*, showing consistent traits throughout a story. Depending on the duration of the plot, both types of characters may be needed to tell a believable story.

In *Time for Andrew*, Drew (living) and Andrew (ghost) are round characters; we must know them well. Throughout the story we watch Drew change as a result of his experience (dynamic), while Andrew remains predominantly the same (static) as a contrast to Drew. It seems logical for Andrew to remain the same, as he is a ghost. His static qualities enable us to see Drew's change more clearly.

There are two other types of characters that we are likely to meet in various story genres: stereotyped and anthropomorphic. When characters are described as if they represent generalized characteristics of a group rather than as true individuals, we say they are *stereotyped*. In folk literature stereotyped characters, such as evil witches, are common because the genre is intended to teach lessons about life and the characters' traits must be easily identified. In contrast, we would not want to have stereotyped characters in realistic fiction because the author should be developing individuals who are unique and believable. If any round, flat, or stereotyped characters are living or inanimate nonhuman beings (animals, trees, vehicles, books, etc.) that act human, they are considered to be *anthropomorphic*. This type of character is often found in fantasies where the author wants the reader to suspend disbelief and respond to a fully imaginary world.

Functions of Characters. An author uses characters to create an interesting story, and also may consciously use characters to serve specific purposes. The main character, the protagonist, leads or propels the action. To keep the plot moving along, the author may create an antagonist, the opposing force(s) that pushes or challenges the main character. Sometimes the opposing force is the setting, but most often it is another character. In *Time for Andrew,* Drew is our protagonist. His actions keep the plot moving. Andrew is the antagonist.

The author may also create a character who is a *foil*. When the author needs to push the protagonist in a particular direction or cause that character to show a particular side of themselves, but the antagonist cannot serve that purpose, the author creates a character with a limited, and often short-lived, role. A foil character has a specific purpose and will usually disappear after serving it. *Time for Andrew* has several foil characters. The father serves the purpose of getting Drew to the old house so that the story can take place. We understand who Andrew is because Aunt Blythe serves the function of filling in background information for us.

Unity between Characters and Their Actions. Once a character is introduced to the reader, authors should be consistent in the further development of that character in action and speech. Unity of character and action is what makes for a believable story. If an author wants the reader to emotionally invest in a character, unity is vitally important, especially in the genres of realistic and historical fiction, fantasy, and biography. There is unity of character and action in *Time for Andrew*. Drew's actions remain true to his character.

Your Turn

In *Hatchet*, what type of character is Brian? How do you learn about him? Is there unity between Brian's character and his actions? What leads you to think that?

My Turn

Brian is a round, dynamic character. Through the author's omniscient point of view we are able to know all of Brian's actions and thoughts. This is necessary to the development of the story since there are no other characters in the wilderness to help disclose Brian's inner self. There is unity of character and action. What we learn about Brian through his thoughts seems consistent with his actions. Brian's thoughts give us hints about changes occurring within him before we see the changes in his actions.

Plot

Types of Plots. As authors move characters through a series of actions and reactions, two basic types of plots emerge: progressive and episodic. In a *progressive* plot the author builds the tension between characters and events as the plot develops over a period of time. In a chapter book a progressive plot usually keeps us involved from chapter to chapter, anticipating what will happen next.

In contrast, an *episodic* plot typically focuses on one life event in a picture book, or events seem to begin anew with each new chapter in a chapter book. As readers, we do not feel the same type of tension in the development of an episode as we do with a progressive plot. While we follow a main character or two, each chapter is usually a new episode in their life and not necessarily linked directly to the previous chapter.

The plot in *Time for Andrew* is progressive; its series of events link together to make one story. The "Little House" series by Laura Ingalls Wilder is an example of episodic plots in chapter books, with each chapter beginning a new episode that may or may not be connected to the previous episode or chapter.

Order in Plots. Probably one of the most noticeable aspects of plot is order. For most stories, it makes sense for an author to tell the story in a *chronological* order. At other times it is easier for an author to "hook" us by beginning a story as a *flashback*, reconstructing a story that has already occurred. Flashback also can be used within a progressive plot to temporarily go back to fill in missing pieces of information for us.

In *Time for Andrew*, we begin in the present with Drew, travel back in time when Drew and Andrew trade places, follow Drew as he lives Andrew's life, occasionally visit the present to see what is happening with Andrew living Drew's life, then return permanently to the present when Drew wins back his real life. This is a progressive plot that moves between two settings.

Patterns of Action. Good stories keep us engaged, as we wait to find out what happens. The "what happens" is often tied to the solving of a problem or dilemma that faces a significant character. As we follow characters through a plot, a skillful author builds in just enough *suspense* or tension to keep us waiting to see how the situation is resolved. The author may heighten our suspense through *foreshadowing*, giving clues to coming events.

The tension may build to a *climax* or breaking point, then the author must decide what to do with the character's dilemma: end in a cliffhanger, or with an open or closed resolution. Some authors choose to leave us at the climax, creating a *cliffhanger*, and letting us decide for ourselves what else might occur. Adults often enjoy this type of participation in a plot, but children can find the lack of closure unsettling. Realistically, most of the events of our lives do not end as cliffhangers, but instead are resolved in some way. A *closed resolution* leaves little doubt in our mind about what followed the climax. Bringing closure can be reassuring for the reader who sees life as definitive and wants to know "the answer." In contrast, some authors end with an *open resolution*, leaving some doubt in our minds about the final outcome and letting us contribute by making our own "endings." Open resolutions are very effective with older students who are able to use their knowledge of life and story characters to carry on the story.

Time for Andrew is filled with foreshadowings, which heighten the suspense of the mystery. In Chapter 2, as Drew stumbles into his great-grandfather's room, the old man says to him, "You've come back. . . . But it won't do any good. It's my house now, not yours" (p. 11). His great-grandfather had known Andrew as a boy, but we do not yet know that. The pattern of action is a climax with a closed resolution. Andrew was excellent at playing marbles. Drew beats Andrew at Ringer, a marble game, to win his way back into the present. We leave the story with Drew safely back in his own time and we know clearly what happened to Andrew and the other characters from his time. We are assured at the end that the mystery is resolved.

Conflict in Plots. Conflicts in our everyday lives influence many of our actions and reactions. We are aware of things that we do that are motivated by struggles and desires within ourselves, with other people, with our environment, or with the conventions of society. Our lives are influenced by the way we act and react with the conflicts we encounter. Because narratives tell the stories of people's lives, narrative naturally centers around the conflicts in which people find themselves.

There are at least four types of conflict found in narratives: conflict with self, conflicts with other people, conflicts with nature, and conflicts with society. Without these conflicts, how could there be tension in a plot? How could tension build to a point that a climax would be needed to resolve it? Without conflict, what would keep us interested in reading to find out what happens next?

In *Time for Andrew*, Drew's conflict with Andrew (conflict with people) drives the plot. Once in Andrew's time, Drew is torn between returning to his own time and family and staying in Andrew's time with Hannah (conflict with self).

Your Turn

Describe the plot of *Hatchet*, including type, order, action, and conflict. What leads you to your conclusions?

My Turn

The story that Gary Paulsen tells in *Hatchet* is a progressive plot, mostly chronological, with a few flashbacks to fill us in about events concerning his parents. As we anticipate a rescue taking place, tensions build and subside slightly throughout, with the climax coming when the plane lands on the lake. The tensions result from Brian's conflicts with nature and with himself as he learns to live alone in the wilderness. Paulsen adds an epilogue to bring closure to the story, providing additional information about what followed the rescue.

Point of View

Types of Point of View. One of the choices that authors make about the way they want to engage the reader concerns point of view, or who is telling the story. Sometimes the author takes the role of an *objective narrator* who seems to be suspended over the characters and setting, with the ability to see and hear all that goes on. Then it is up to us, the readers, to judge the meaning or significance of events, actions, and speech.

If the author allows us to know the thoughts of one or more of the characters, in addition to knowing and hearing all that was done and said, the point of view becomes *omniscient*. In some plots it is important for us to know what a particular character is thinking to help us become more involved and better understand characters' motivations.

Sometimes the author allows a character to tell the story in their own, or *first person,* point of view. We see all of the events of plot through that character's eyes. When we read a story that is written from a first person point of view, it is important to realize that we are seeing only one view of the events and that view is influenced by the teller's feelings. First person is the point of view of *Time for Andrew*. Drew tells us what happens to him. We have firsthand knowledge of his view of all of the events. It is hard to know about the other characters except through Drew's eyes.

Your Turn

From what point of view is *Hatchet* told? How does the point of view affect the story? What leads you to think that?

Hatchet is told from an omniscient point of view, which draws the reader to Brian and his dilemma. Knowing Brian's thoughts increases the possibilities for engagement between Brian and the reader.

Theme

Types of Themes. The themes of stories help us think about important aspects of life: friendships, loyalty, death, courage, cleverness, and so on. In some genres, particularly folk literature, the theme is *explicit*, or clearly stated, but most often themes are *implicit*, and must be inferred. As readers we make inferences based on what we think is important about a story. Our inferences are influenced by our experiences as readers and in life. Because inference is involved in interpreting implicit themes, it is possible for different readers to "see" themes differently.

In *Time for Andrew*, I feel that two main themes are (1) learning to trust ourselves and (2) meeting challenges that come our way. In the beginning, Drew's Dad is overheard telling Aunt Blythe that Drew is insecure and nervous, and I had the impression that Drew would shy away from things that might be hard to do. When Drew assumes Andrew's identity, he meets Hannah, Andrew's older sister, who teaches Drew how to have more faith in himself and meet challenges.

What themes do you find in Brian's story as told in *Hatchet*? What leads you to your interpretations?

One theme I see is, "We can find inner strength in times of crisis." At the beginning of the book, Brian's thoughts following the pilot's death suggest that he is not very confident of himself. Over the 54 days that he must fend for himself, he shows courage and resourcefulness.

Style

We hear the voice of authors in their writing as they use language to engage us as readers. How well we relate to an author's style influences our engagement with that author.

Sentence Structure and Patterns. One of the first things we notice about writing is the structure of sentences. Sometimes an author will use sentence structures to accentuate certain words or ideas, getting us to notice something the author thinks is important. For example, as we are introduced to Drew in Chapter 1 of *Time for Andrew*, his thoughts of Martin, a boy from school, tell us something about Drew's sense of himself:

> Martin—his scowling face floated between me and the rows of corn stretching away to the horizon. Whenever I dropped a ball, fumbled, or struck out, Martin was there sneering and jeering. He stole my lunch money, copied my homework, beat me up, called me names like Drew Pee-you and Death Breath. (p. 2)

Uses of Language. As we consider the maturity and experience that our students have with language, particularly with book language, we also consider the ways that authors use words. Some authors use words to help readers make mental images or comparisons that are more concrete. Some authors play with language in new and creative ways. Some authors appeal to our senses through the use of language.

Imagery describes an author's use of words to make pictures that appeal to our senses. Imagery is also instrumental when an author tries to make pictures to help us understand something we may lack firsthand experience of. Imagery helps the author reach out to us, encouraging us to respond to the sensations that words can evoke. Images are especially powerful when they remind us of something familiar that we connect to our own experiences, as in the following examples from *Time for Andrew:*

- The driveway leading to Great-aunt Blythe's house is described as a "narrow green tunnel burrowing uphill through trees and shaggy bushes" (p. 2).
- We "see" Great-aunt Blythe with the words, "The wind ballooned her T-shirt and swirled her gray hair. If she spread her arms, she might fly up into the sky like Mary Poppins" (p. 3).

Figurative language occurs when authors use words "in a nonliteral way, giving them meaning beyond their usual, everyday definitions" (Lukens, 1990, p. 143). Our language is full of multiple meanings and phrases we cannot interpret literally. We need experience with figurative language to fully appreciate many stories.

Personification accentuates human behavior, calling attention to qualities of inanimate objects that might otherwise go unnoticed, as when Drew says, "I walked to the bottom of the steps and peered up into the shadows. Not a sound from the floor above. . . . Like me, the house held its breath and listened" (p. 7).

To accentuate the qualities of an object or person, an author may use a *simile,* a comparative relationship between unlike things. Similes usually include the words *as, like,* or *than* to show the relationship in the comparison, as in, "a spiral of dust and dead leaves danced up the driveway toward us like a miniature cyclone" (p. 5).

Devices of sound appeal to what readers find pleasing to the ear. *Onomatopoeia* uses words for sounds that suggest their meaning, like *crunch, swooosh,* and *r-r-r-ing. Alliteration*, the repetition of consonant or vowel sounds, accentuates particular words and phrases. Try this one: "The wisteria's purple petals speckled the floor like confetti and clung to an old wooden swing" (p. 12). Read the sentence aloud and listen to the repeated *p* and *k* sounds.

What do you notice about Paulsen's writing style and use of language to tell Brian's story in *Hatchet*?

My Turn

Paulsen appeals to my senses with the words he chooses. He uses imagery so that I can "see" Brian in the wilderness and be drawn into his isolation, yet see how he is maturing. It also seems as if Paulsen deliberately structures some sentences to "punch" certain words, to make me take special notice. For example, in Chapter 1, we hear Brian's thoughts:

> The burning eyes did not come back, but memories did, came flooding in. The words. Always the words.
>
> Divorce.
>
> The Secret.
>
> Fights.

> Split.
> The big split. . . . (pp. 5–6)

"Punching" words use the rhythm of short sentences and single words to demand my attention.

Paulsen uses words to help me make mental images of Brian's surroundings. Fire is very important to Brian's existence. He describes one fire-making episode as follows:

> The sparks grew with his gentle breath. The red glow moved from the sparks themselves into the bark, moved and grew and became worms, glowing red worms that crawled up the bark hairs and caught other threads of bark and grew until there was a pocket of red as big as a quarter, a glowing red coal of heat. (p. 92)

Paulsen uses simile for comparison. When the moose is charging Brian at the edge of the lake, Paulsen writes that "he saw a brown wall of fur detach itself from the forest to his rear and come down on him like a runaway truck" (p. 150).

In this past section we have been thinking about literary elements in narrative texts. In a middle grade curriculum, however, students also spend a good deal of time being expected to engage with information texts. How do information texts compare to narrative? Do authors write them in the same manner as narrative texts? Do we read these two types of texts in the same way?

Informational Writing: Becoming Aware of Text Structures

Rosenblatt (1985) reminds us that readers have different expectations for narrative and information texts and, consequently, approach the texts in different ways, for different purposes. In narrative texts, a reader has a great deal of latitude for interpreting an author's ideas in light of the reader's experiences. A reader's purpose for reading narrative may be purely aesthetic, for the pleasure of the experience. In contrast, readers usually approach information texts with different expectations. Because readers expect to need to retain, use, or act on the information in such texts, they must inspect the author's ideas and intentions much more closely.

Narrative writers describe life situations and problems by skillfully using literary elements to develop believable settings, plots, and characters that will touch our emotions and draw us into the story. Informational writers also arrange ideas to serve their purpose(s) for writing. The possibilities for arranging information are many and varied. For example, to inform us about the dangers of pollution, an information text writer may identify its causes and inform us about the harmful effects or potential harm for man and nature. In contrast, a writer whose purpose is to teach us how to determine if water is polluted will need to organize ideas differently, to list the procedure for us to go through to test samples of water.

Thinking in Information Texts

Moore, Moore, Cunningham, and Cunningham (1994) suggest that nine thinking processes account for a large portion of the cognitive activity involved in reading, writing and learning information. Several of these thinking processes may be used simultaneously in a learning experience:

- *Call up* what we already know.
- *Connect* new ideas to what we already know.

- *Predict or anticipate* what is to come.
- *Organize* information into a useful framework.
- *Generalize* information into similar groupings after noting patterns or commonalities.
- *Form an image* using sensory information.
- *Monitor internally* to determine how well learning or thinking is progressing and to repair breakdowns in understanding.
- *Evaluate or judge* contents of passages and the author's writing style.
- *Apply* knowledge or select the most appropriate response from all those acquired.

As we discuss how we make meaning with what we read, consider how ideas in information texts are organized and what you must know to make sense of the author's ideas. Look carefully at how well the author helps the reader make sense of the ideas. Your students deserve informational writing that is considerate of their background as readers and that supports them as they try to learn.

In a balanced reading program, learning to think in literature must be balanced with learning to think in information texts if students are to be equally adept at making meaning in both types of text. As you consider the texts you will use to engage students in meaningful literacy experiences, you also must be concerned about the difficulty levels of texts and their match with students' reading ability.

Matching Readers and Texts

Select any text and ask several students in the same grade level to read it. What is almost effortless for some readers provides some challenge for others, and is clearly too much of a challenge for still other readers. If different students read the same text in different ways, how will you know when a text is appropriate for a particular student? We can describe the match between students and texts as occurring at the independent, instructional, frustration, or listening level:

- *Independent level* reading provides very little challenge and can be understood without support.
- *Instructional level* reading is the level at which help from a more knowledgeable other is needed to make adequate meaning.
- *Frustration level* text is challenging, and without high motivation may be too difficult for a reader to make meaning.
- *Listening level* text is written at the highest level at which a listener can hear and make adequate meaning from the text read aloud by another.

The level of challenge that students experience in text should be related to their purposes for reading. If text is too difficult and the reader is not highly motivated to learn from the text, then the only learning that may occur is that of frustration and defeat. If text is always too easy, there is little reason to learn. There must be a balance between challenge and motivation in the selection of texts for reading.

You must also remember that all readers do not have the same background of instructional experience. Not all readers have had the benefit of instruction by more knowledgeable others, who modeled and encouraged the use of effective reading strategies.

Students find it easier to engage in sustained silent reading when texts are at their independent reading level.

Independent Reading

Text that is independent for a reader requires very little effort for success. Extensive reading at this level builds confidence in readers, habituates decoding, increases fluency, moves many competencies to an automatic level, and builds stamina to persevere in more difficult text. When students read text that is at their independent level, their comprehension and word knowledge are almost completely accurate. They know enough of the text to fill in missing understandings without the aid of more knowledgeable readers. Developmentally, students need opportunities each day to read for relaxation and enjoyment in independent level text.

Instructional Reading

When students have support as they work with a text, they can tolerate more error than when reading at an independent level. Instructional level text presents sufficient challenge to motivate learning, but is not too easy nor too difficult. Students working at this level know enough of the text that, with the support of a more knowledgeable reader, they are able to fill in from their own background to make sufficient meaning. The assistance of the more able reader, usually the teacher, provides support at key points to help students use their knowledge appropriately. Working at instructional level, with appropriate guidance, allows readers to learn from their errors. A general rule of thumb at this level is 90 to 95 percent word recognition and 75 to 90 percent comprehension prior to instruction. With mediated support, the reading then resembles independent reading.

Frustration Level Text

In contrast to independent level reading, which is very easy, frustration level text is too difficult for students to learn from unless personal motivation to read is extremely high. Students may be able to partially read text at this level, but require great effort to sustain themselves. Unless they are highly motivated to learn from the text, sustained effort can be harmful to students' confidence and sense of themselves as readers, and may even lead to students forming misconceptions from the reading. If placement in frustration level text comes from a source outside the child, such as the teacher, motivation to deal with the text may not be high enough to avoid harmful effects. Even though students' comprehension of a text is at a frustration level, they still want the text to make sense. As a result, students may fill "slots" of missing information with logical, but inappropriate, ideas and may form misconceptions.

Listening Level Text

Students are typically able to listen to and understand text that is more difficult than text they can read by themselves. Children's *listening capacity* is the highest level at which they can hear and understand the majority of a text, the level at which they should be able to function as readers if decoding is not required. The support needed to assist students to make meaning from a read-aloud text should be similar to the support needed at the instructional reading level.

Comparing Levels of Text

Different levels of text serve different purposes for readers and require differing levels of motivation for successful use. We may summarize the match between readers and texts as follows:

Text Level	*Purpose*	*Motivation Required*
Independent	Practice, teach self	Low challenge
Instructional	Learn with help	Medium challenge
Frustration	Stretch, test self	High challenge
Listening	Potential as a reader	Medium challenge

Students need the opportunity each day to read texts of varying levels of difficulty. The amount of time that students spend in each level of difficulty should be determined by their development and confidence as readers. Try to provide a balance in the levels of text in which students work.

Emerging readers are making the transition from oral to written language and read with support from a more knowledgeable other. Students in this stage spend much of their time reading predictable text, which begins as frustration level but becomes instructional or somewhat independent through repeated readings. Language experience charts and books, which are students' own dictations, can also be quite independent and offer ease for practice. During quiet reading times emerging readers may select frustration level library books, which they may have heard read aloud, to challenge themselves.

Developing readers are working to gain control over print and need the confidence with text to be willing to persevere. These readers need some instructional level challenge, but should spend the majority of their day reading independent level materials. Students may self-select frustration level text during quiet reading times, but it will not be very helpful for them in gaining control of reading processes.

Transitional readers know quite a lot about print and are ready to sustain more challenge with teacher guidance or in highly motivating self-selected materials. To help them solidify silent reading, be sure they continue to read in independent materials that offer "controlled challenge." Transitional children will be able to learn new skills and to refine old ones when the amount of challenge is monitored.

Mature readers are able to judge their needs as readers fairly well. They should maintain a balance between independent and instructional materials. However, their experience as readers enables them to sustain their reading in difficult texts, particularly if they are highly motivated to read. Mature readers have a repertoire of self-monitoring strategies they can call on to make meaning in difficult texts.

Monitoring Students' Growth as Readers

As students move toward maturity as readers, we must understand the quality of thinking and the processes each student uses to make meaning. This requires collecting data that demonstrates the following:

- What is understood about the types and purposes of written language.
- How a student thinks as a reader, including strategic thinking.
- How a student handles text of varying levels of difficulty, independently and with support.
- The levels of meaning making a student uses independently and with support.

How can we document what a student is thinking, what meaning a student makes of a reading experience? Through observing and conferring with students, we can begin to see patterns in their reading behaviors and responses to reading experiences. We can collect samples of work they write in response to their reading. These forms of assessment data begin to paint a picture of a student's process of making meaning with written language.

Observations

> Observing the process a student uses provides the teacher with a window or view on how students arrive at products. . . . This allows the teacher to make good decisions about how she or he might assist during the process or restructure the process in order to best support more effective use of strategies and students' development as readers and writers (Rhodes & Nathenson-Mejia, 1992, p. 502).

Learning to watch students is not an easy task with the amount of activity that goes on in a classroom. You must begin by asking yourself, "What do I know about this student as a meaning maker and how did I gain that knowledge?" This question should make you think about the following:

- Your purposes for instruction
- The activities that grow out of those purposes
- Your observations of students during instruction

You will interpret your observations based on your knowledge of students' development and on your goals for instruction. Make notes about what you observe so that, over time, your notes serve as more detailed reminders of responses than do your recollections of the events.

Anecdotal Records. As you identify behaviors that should develop from the instructional opportunities you provide, you will need to develop a system for recording your observations. "Anecdotal records can be written about products or can include information about both process and product" (Rhodes & Nathenson-Mejia, 1992, p. 502).

Dated anecdotal records are essential in a process classroom, and provide more detail than a mere checklist. While a checklist is quick and may show a variety of behaviors, it usually does not provide illustrations of those behaviors. Checklists also have predetermined skills. Anecdotal records allow you, the student, and the context for learning to determine the focus for what you record.

Over time, you will use these anecdotal records to make inferences about student behaviors, to identify patterns of behavior, and to identify strengths and weaknesses. You will use anecdotal records for instructional planning, for discussing growth with students and parents, and for generating new questions about teaching, learning, and assessment (Rhodes & Nathenson-Mejia, 1992).

Written Observations of Reading Strategy. An accurate way to observe students' reading strategies is by taking a running record (Clay, 1979) or administering an informal reading inventory (IRI). Running records and IRIs result in written records that reflect the strategies a reader uses to monitor meaning while reading orally. To make a written record, observe a student's oral reading, record what the student actually says while reading, and later, analyze any *miscues,* words that differ from those in the actual text (Goodman, 1972). You may take running records on any piece of text, but they are most beneficial with those that students are using in the classroom.

You also may use informal reading inventories to document reading strategies, but historically IRIs have been used to determine instructional, independent, and frustration reading levels. Published IRIs typically include multiple passages at each level of difficulty, along with questions to ask about students' comprehension of text. Students read a variety of passages, orally and silently, increasing in difficulty, until reaching frustration level.

Whether you use text that is familiar to students or the preselected passages of an IRI, observing and documenting students' reading is necessary for accurately monitoring progress. In Chapter 8, we discuss running records in depth.

Conferring about Reading

In addition to observation, you also learn about the ways that readers make meaning by talking with them. When you confer with students, your primary purpose is to listen to what students can teach you about the way they think and make meaning. You may focus the talk or probe for more information, but you cannot learn from them unless you listen.

As you move about a classroom while students are working, you might stop beside students and ask how the reading is going, giving them the opportunity to communicate their perceptions of a text and their ability to make meaning from that text. Students' comments may range from an explicit retelling to insightful, creative, or critical responses to the text. They may even read aloud as a way of sharing their response.

During a quiet reading time, you might sit in the library area with a student and share a reading. As naturally as possible, inquire about the student's responses to the text. Conferring in this context appears much like an informal conversation.

You create opportunities during small-group reading experiences to let students inform you about their thinking if, in response to a student's comments, you ask, "What makes you think that?" Small groups also provide opportunity for students to confer with one another.

Conferring can also place students in a position to read for you to demonstrate the level of text they can handle comfortably, or the levels of thinking they use to make meaning. The text may or may not be familiar. Discuss the reading to allow students to explain their thinking and response to reading situations. To gather data for assessment, you must ask students about their thinking.

Collecting Samples of Work

Written work also provides data about students' thinking and meaning making. Through illustrations and writing, students indicate their responses to texts read both aloud and independently. Over time, these responses can show a growing depth of understanding about types and purposes of written language and levels of making meaning that might not be represented in anecdotal or conference records. Date all samples and save them regularly in a "work folder." You may wish to save particular samples because they represent specific growth that either you or a student desires to preserve. Samples from the work folder may then become part of a literacy assessment portfolio.

To document meaning making in reading, video- or audiotape students' reading and responses three or four times per school year. You will need a separate cassette or videotape for each student. These recordings, combined with written samples collected over time, will form a rich, comprehensive picture of students' growth as competent readers.

Respecting Diversity in Making Meaning

From our discussion in this chapter, you should understand that students make meaning in different ways and at different levels. To respect students' diversity in making meaning, you must consider the impact of at least three issues in your reading and writing program:

- Language knowledge
- Experience with literature
- Personal strategies for making meaning

Impact of Language Knowledge

Acquiring language differs from student to student (Jaggar, 1975). The students in your classroom will possess a range of words in their listening and speaking vocabularies. Some students will know more than one language, some will be acquiring English as a second language (ESL). You must consider this range of language acquisition and knowledge as you plan for learning experiences.

Students have expectations for how language is used and the purposes it serves based on its use in their familiar environments. Students' understanding of language is the basis for meaningful classroom reading and writing activities. You must consider both background content and language structures.

For example, if you are considering using *Hatchet* as a class text, what language issues would arise? You might realize that some students have had limited experiences with flying or survival in a wilderness and the language that surrounds such experiences. For other students, the structure of Paulsen's sentences and descriptive techniques will prove to be a barrier to meaning.

You know that language knowledge is related to one's background experiences. As you re-examine *Hatchet,* thinking about both the content of the plot and the language, you realize that your students will relate to the book in different ways. Your plans will be focused on enabling all students to make meaning at some level. You think about ways to make the story and the language seem more concrete and accessible for both students who have life experiences that are different from those depicted in the book and those who have different language backgrounds.

You might select drama as a teaching strategy because it creates a physical bridge between a student's language and the language of the story. Students might act out Brian's actions and the mood of the story. Drama helps to make the language more concrete for ESL students, may be motivating to students who see little purpose for print, and allows students who have a strong language background to help tell the story verbally. This is only one example of what could be done to involve all students, respecting and enhancing their language background. I will present other examples of adapting instruction for the diverse needs of students in chapters 5–12.

Impact of Literary Experiences

In addition to their individual life experiences, middle grade students differ in the quality and quantity of their literary experience (Irvin, 1990). Some students read extensively and become deeply engaged with literature, others struggle with required reading, and some choose not to read for school *or* for pleasure. Students who read extensively have greater opportunities than students who are not committed readers to learn about the ways authors use literary elements and information structures to engage us and to influence our thinking. They also practice more at using personal meaning-making strategies as they evolve into mature readers.

You must be keenly aware of your students' diverse reading experience as you plan your classroom activities. For example, if you are using *Hatchet* in a whole-class literature study, your plans must account for students' differing familiarity with chapter books and with a writing style such as Paulsen's, as well as with their varied life experience with such personal issues as parental divorce, being alone, and being put in a situation that requires self-reliance. Your students will react to such events with differing amounts of courage, denial, tenacity, and problem-solving skill, and you must allow for both the presence and the expression of a range of student response.

Impact of Personal Strategies For Making Meaning

Language background and print experience will have an impact on students' expectations for print and, possibly, on their drive to make sense out of print. Students have strategies for coping with print. You must discover what those strategies are and if they are useful in more complex reading tasks. Be especially conscious of ESL students. Remember that students who are acquiring a second language may feel very uncertain about their ability to transfer what they know and use in their first language as they try to learn in a second language. They may demonstrate very little of what they actually know.

When I think about respecting diversity in students, I often think of Mei Mei, the young Chinese protagonist of *I Hate English!* (Levine, 1989). English seemed very strange to her, and she feared that if she learned to speak English she might forget Chinese. Her teacher was sensitive to what Mei Mei was experiencing and searched for meaningful experiences, experiences that would let Mei Mei see that she could value both Chinese and English.

TAKE A MOMENT AND REFLECT

- Reading is a high-speed, automatic, simultaneous operation of complex linguistic and cognitive processes.
- To make meaning, readers must use:
  story and sentence meaning
  sentence syntax or structure
  words, word parts, and punctuation
  metacognitive awareness of how these pieces fit together
- Readers go through identifiable stages of development:
  emerging
  developing
  transitional
  mature
- Emerging readers:
  learn that print has meaning, purpose, and function
  "read" familiar contexts and patterns
  range from preschool to middle first-grade reading level
- Developing readers:
  are "glued to print" and consciously try to match visual cues to meaning
  are oral, word-by-word readers
  are learning to monitor their own reading and self-correct miscues
  move toward silent reading late in this stage
  range from middle first-grade through early third-grade reading level
- Transitional readers:
  experience some difficulty moving between oral and silent reading early in this stage
  are learning how to monitor silent reading
  can begin to sense their style of reading as they sink into silent reading
  begin to be more flexible, and are able to adjust their reading to the task and text in the later part of the stage
  range from early third-grade through sixth-grade reading level
- Mature readers:
  develop learning strategies that allow for extension and development of new skills or refinement of known skills to meet changing life purposes
  read rapidly, especially in familiar content areas
  are interest- and vocation-centered readers
  range from sixth-grade to adult reading level, and continue reading throughout adult life
- Readers monitor meaning making by:
  using prior knowledge
  anticipating or making predictions
  self-correcting miscues
  adjusting reading to meet different purposes in a variety of texts
- Readers think in different ways while they read:
  explicit thinking—knowing what the author actually said
  implicit thinking—using knowledge to fill in around the author's ideas
  critical thinking—judging the value of the author's ideas
  creative/personal thinking—going beyond the author's ideas and valuing their own ideas
- Literary experience is influenced by:
  the reader's level of engagement with a text
  the stance, efferent (information) to aesthetic (beauty), that the reader takes
- Readers respond to literature through their:
  level of engagement with a text
  conceptions or perceptions of text
  connections with related experiences or texts
  question asking or problem solving to make meaning
  explanations of personal responses
  interpretations of texts and responses
  critical judgments about text
- Narrative writing is woven around literary elements:
  settings give us a real sense of place and character
  character actions help us see the development of the plot
  themes help us bring real meaning to characters' actions
  plot develops out of characters' actions and reactions
  point of view provides one interpretation, readers can provide another
  the author's style pulls all the elements together

- Settings can:
  be merely a backdrop or integral to the plot
  set the mood
  show us more about a character
  actually be an antagonist or opposing character
  symbolize other meanings
- Characters:
  serve different functions/purposes
  can be round or flat, dynamic or static
  can be a protagonist or antagonist
  can be a foil, serving a limited purpose
  can be anthropomorphic (nonhuman characters with human qualities)
  should have traits consistent with their actions
- Plots:
  can be progressive or episodic
  can be chronological
  may include flashbacks
  have patterns of action that include suspense, climax, and resolution
  can be cliffhangers, ending with a climax and no resolution
  can be resolved in either open or closed ways
  are driven by character conflicts with self, others, nature, and/or society
- Point of view:
  can be objective (narrator)
  can be influenced by the thinking of one character (omniscient)
  can be controlled by one character (first person)
- Theme:
  can be explicitly stated and clear to the reader
  can be implied by the author and interpreted by the reader
- Style:
  authors affect readers through the style of their writing
  how they structure sentences
  how they use language, including imagery, figurative language, personification, simile, onomatopoeia, and alliteration
- Informational writing is structured differently from narrative writing and requires different types of thinking.
- While reading an information text, readers must:
  call up what is already known
  connect new ideas to what is known
  predict or anticipate what is yet to come
  organize information into a useful framework
  generalize information into similar groupings after noting patterns or commonalities
  form an image using sensory information
  monitor internally to determine how well learning or thinking is progressing and to repair breakdowns in understanding
  evaluate or judge contents of passage and author's writing style
  apply knowledge or select the most appropriate response from all those acquired
- Children will process text at one of four levels, depending on their stage of reading development and the complexity of the text:
  independent
  instructional
  frustration
  listening
- Assessment and evaluation of meaning making includes:
  observation and anecdotal records
  conferring with students
  collecting samples of work
- Expecting and respecting diversity among meaning makers in the classroom can promote meaningful instruction when teachers consider students':
  language background
  experience with literature
  personal meaning-making strategies

REFERENCES

Adams, J., & Collins, A. (1985). A schema-theoretic view of reading. In H. Singer & R. B. Ruddell (Eds.), *Theoretical models and processes of reading* (3rd. ed.) (pp. 404–425). Newark, DE: International Reading Association.

Anderson, R. A., and Pearson, P. D. (1984). A schema-theoretic view of reading comprehension, In P. D. Pearson (Ed.), *Handbook of reading research* (Vol. 1, pp. 255–291). New York: Longman.

Beach, R., (1987). *Reader-response theories.* Urbana, IL: National Council of Teachers of English.

Beach, R., & Hynds, S. (1991). Research on response to literature. In R. Barr, M. Kamil, P. B. Mosenthal, and P. D. Pearson (Eds.), *Handbook of reading research* (Vol. 2, pp. 453–489). New York: Longman.

Black, J., & Seifert, C. (1985). The psychological study of story understanding. In C. Cooper (Ed.), *Research response to literature and the teaching of literature* (pp. 190–211). Norwood, NJ: Ablex.

Bloome, D., & Bailey, F. M. (1992). Studying language and literacy through events, particularity, and intertextuality. In R. Beach, J. L. Green, M. L. Kamil, & T. Shanahan (Ed.), *Multidisciplinary perspectives on literacy research* (pp. 181–210). Urbana, IL: National Conference on Research in English and National Council of Teachers of English.

Britton, J. (1984). Viewpoints: The distinction between participant and spectator role language in research and practice. *Research in the Teaching of English, 18,* 320–331.

Bruner, J. (1986). *Actual minds, possible worlds.* Cambridge, MA: Harvard University Press.

Clay, M. (1979, 1985). *The early detection of reading difficulties.* Portsmouth, NH: Heinemann.

Golden, J. M., & Guthrie, J. T. (1986). Convergence and divergence in reader response to literature. *Reading Research Quarterly, 21,* 408–421.

Goodman, Y. (1972). Qualitative reading miscue analysis for teacher training. In R. Hodges & E. H. Rudorf (Eds.), *Language and learning to read: What teachers should know about language* (pp. 160–166). Boston: Houghton Mifflin.

Harste, J. C. (1986). What it means to be strategic: Good readers as informants. Paper presented at the National Reading Conference, Austin, TX.

Heath, S. (1985). Being literate in America: A sociohistorical perspective. In J. Niles & R. Lalik (Eds.), *Issues in literacy: A research perspective* (pp. 1–18). Rochester, NY: National Reading Conference.

Holdaway. D. (1980). *Independence in reading.* Portsmouth, NH: Heinemann.

Hunt, R., & Vipond, D. (1985). Crash-testing a transactional model of literary learning. *Reader, 14,* 23–39.

Hunt, R., & Vipond, D. (1986). Evaluations in literary reading. *Text, 6,* 53–71.

Hynds, S. (1985). Interpersonal cognitive complexity and the literary response processes of adolescent readers. *Research in the Teaching of English, 19,* 386–404.

Irvin, J. L. (1990). *Reading and the middle school student: Strategies to enhance learning.* Boston: Allyn & Bacon.

Jaggar, A. (1975). Allowing for language difference. In G.S. Pinnell (Ed.), *Discovering language with children.* (pp. 18–29). Urbana, IL: National Council of Teachers of English.

Jones, N. K. (1995). Learning to read: Insights from reading recovery. *Literacy, Teaching and Learning, 1*(2), 41–56.

Juel, C. (1991). Beginning reading. In R. Barr, M. L. Kamil, P. B. Mosenthal, & P. D. Pearson (Eds.), *Handbook of reading research* (Vol. 2, pp. 325–353). New York: Longman.

Lewis, C. S. (1978). The reader and all kinds of stories. In M. Meek, A. Warlow, & G. Brown (Eds.), *The cool web: The pattern of children's reading* (pp. 76–90). New York: Atheneum.

Lukens, R. J. (1990). *A critical handbook of children's literature.* New York: HarperCollins.

Martinez, M. F. (1983). Young children's verbal responses to literature in parent-child storytime interactions (Doctoral dissertation, University of Texas at Austin, 1983). *Dissertation Abstracts International, 44,* 1044A.

Miall, D. (1985). The structure of response: A repertory grid study of a poem. *Research in the Teaching of Literature, 19,* 254–268.

Moore, D. W., Moore, S. A., Cunningham, P. M., & Cunningham, J. W. (1994). *Developing readers & writers in the content areas K–12.* New York: Longman.

Mullis, I. V. S., Campbell, J. R., and Farstrup, A. E. (1993). *NAEP 1992 reading report card for the nation and states.* Washington, DC: Office of Education Research and Improvement.

Newkirk, T. (1984). Looking for trouble: A way to unmask our readings. *College English, 46,* 756–766.

Paris, S. G., Wasik, B. A., and Turner, J. C. (1991). The development of strategic readers. In R. Barr, M. Kamil, P. B. Mosenthal, & P. D. Pearson (Eds.), *Handbook of reading research* (Vol. 2, pp. 401–432). New York: Longman.

Rhodes, L. K., & Nathenson-Mejia, S. (1992). Anecdotal records: A powerful tool for ongoing literacy assessment. *The Reading Teacher, 45,* 502–509.

Rosenblatt, L. (1978). *The reader, the text, the poem: The transactional theory of the literary work.* Carbondale, IL: Southern Illinois University Press.

Rosenblatt, L. (1985). Viewpoints: Transaction versus interaction—A terminological rescue operation. *Research in the Teaching of English, 19,* 96–107.

Schank, R., & Abelson, R. (1975). *Knowledge structures.* Hillsdale, NJ: Lawrence Erlbaum Associates.

Schanklin, N. K. (1982). Relating reading and writing: Developing a transitional model of the writing process. *Monographs in Teaching and Learning.* Bloomington, IN: Indiana University School of Education.

Schon, D. (1983). *The reflective practitioner: How professionals think in action.* New York: Basic Books.

Slatoff, W. (1970). *With respect to readers.* Ithaca, NY: Cornel University Press.

Svensson, C. (1985). *The construction of poetic meaning: A cultural-developmental study of symbolic and nonsymbolic strategies in the interpretation of contemporary poetry.* Lund, Sweden: Liber Forlag.

Teale, W. H. (1986). Home background and children's literacy development. In W. H. Teale & E. Sulzby (Eds.) *Emergent literacy: Writing and reading* (pp. 173–206). Norwood, NJ: Ablex.

Thomson, J. (1987). *Understanding teenager's reading.* Urbana, IL: National Council of Teachers of English.

Vygotsky, L. S. (1978). *Mind in society* (M. Cole, V. John-Steiner, S. Scribner, & E. Sounerman, Eds. & Trans.). Cambridge, MA: Harvard University Press.

CHILDREN'S LITERATURE

Hahn, M. D. (1994). *Time for Andrew: A ghost story*. New York: Houghton Mifflin.

Levine, E. (1989). *I hate English!* New York: Scholastic.

Paulsen, G. (1987). *Hatchet*. New York: Viking Penguin.

3

Growing Toward Maturity as Writers

In this chapter . . .

We explore:

- four views of writing—as a code, a medium, a product, and a process,
- thinking with written language, to retain, re-collect, re-create, re-construct, and re-present ideas,
- types of informal writing, bursts of writing to capture thinking for later use, such as lists, clusters, annotated drawings, and notes,
- journals and learning logs used as teaching tools, helping students to capture their thinking and learn from what they write,
- the process approach to writing, exploring writing as a recursive process including:
  rehearsal or prewriting
  composing or drafting
  revising for meaning
  editing for correctness
  sharing or publishing
- applying a process approach in writer's workshop,
- issues in maintaining legible handwriting, and
- monitoring students' growth in writing through collecting samples of writing, observing, and conferring with students about their writing.

Pat D'Arcy (1989), a British educator, writes, "We must not, at any stage, allow ourselves to forget that the act of writing is an act of making sense and of shaping meaning" (p. 1). *Writing to make sense. Writing to shape meaning.* As readers we know what these phrases mean. From our earliest encounters with print, we have been influenced, even shaped, by the words of others.

We may think, however, that we cannot influence and shape others with our words. Our experiences with writing in school may have left us with little confidence that we can write like the authors we read. But writing is much more than the print we find in books. Look at the print that is around us today, and you will find examples of the ways writing shapes meaning, to influence, to inform, to organize, and to persuade.

In this chapter we explore the range of writing experiences that can and should be a part of a middle grade reading and writing program. This chapter introduces the methods suggested in Part Two and especially in Chapter 9, "Writer's Workshop and Beyond: Learning to Write and Writing to Learn." To set the stage for this exploration we first consider ways that we may view writing, including the relationship between writing and thinking.

VIEWS OF WRITING

Students in middle grade classrooms learn about writing by the ways they are taught to use it and by the things that teachers emphasize about it. D'Arcy (1989) states, "The writing we require from our pupils and the ways in which we respond to that writing will in their turn, influence the pupils' expectations and consequently their approach to and performance in writing, possibly for life" (p. 19).

Calkins (1994) comments, "What our students do as writers will largely depend on what we expect them to do and on what they've done in the past" (p. 113). Will students in your classroom see writing as a symbolic code that they must master, a medium through which they may communicate, an end product to achieve, an active process, or as a combination of these? As we consider different views of writing in the sections that follow, reflect on your own background as a writer. Which view(s) will students find at work in your classroom?

Writing as a Code

If we view writing as a code, we give a great deal of attention to the correct use of language symbols. Most of us have firsthand experience with writing as a code. As students, we spent endless hours completing exercises that focused on grammar, sentence structures, spelling, and so on. We received feedback on our writing in the form of red marks on compositions. We were given specific formats into which we fit our ideas about a topic. While these practices were intended to focus our attention on the details of written language, we also learned that there was a "right" way to write.

Research in writing (Clay, 1975; Graves, 1983, 1994; Calkins, 1986, 1994) has helped us realize that overemphasis on code, at the expense of meaning, can lead students not only to see writing as a tedious task, but may also lead to their becoming inadequate writers. From our discussion about making meaning in Chapter 2, you know that concepts about written language are best acquired in the context of meaningful activity. Writing in the middle grades should emphasize the code of written language within the context of making and shaping meaning.

Writing as a Medium

If we consider writing as a medium, we view it as "verbal play dough" (D'Arcy, 1989), out of which writers may make something useful. Just as an artist uses a medium as a vehicle of expression, so writers use words. Just as an artist experiments with a medium to see what it can do, a writer experiments with language without being quite sure where it will lead. An artist knows that while the medium is visible, its meaning lies within its creator and the individuals who observe it. So too the meaning of writing lies within its creator and observers.

By the way that we engage middle grade students with written language we can help them see language as a flexible and responsive medium, able to be manipulated or reshaped to meet different intentions. Students' experiences with written language affect their views about the possibilities of language. Middle grade students will come to us with a range of experiences in writing. Unfortunately, many of those experiences may have fostered negative feelings. You must be patient and provide many models that enable students to experience the flexibility and responsiveness of writing.

Writing as a Product

The completion of projects or tasks is important to our sense of satisfaction in our work and our lives, and is often the way that we measure our personal success. However, when completion becomes more important than the task itself, our work may become personally meaningless and unsatisfactory.

In writing, we want students to experience the self-satisfaction of finished products. We can encourage their writing to move in certain directions, but what will ultimately be most important is the direction that students think their work should take. If we expect to convince middle grade students that writing is a purposeful and satisfying tool for communication, we must remember that simply producing a written product should never become more important than the meaning that the product holds for the writer.

Writing as an Active Process

Research in writing over the past decade has led us to realize that writing is an active, not a passive, process. Perhaps your own experiences with writing have taught you about this process. Writing is full of mental and physical activity that enables us to move our thinking out of our heads, down our arms, and out our fingers via pen or keyboard. The process of writing makes visible our thinking, our feelings, and the images in our heads.

Thinking of writing as an active process is tied to viewing writing as a responsive and flexible medium. For students to recognize the existence of this process, we must help them become aware of their thinking, then show them how they can capture that thinking with words. Providing varied writing experiences will help students see that writing can serve different purposes, take different forms, and be directed to different audiences.

Calkins (1994) pushes our thoughts about writing as a process even further. Her experiences with writing have taught her that "Writing does not begin with deskwork but with lifework . . . living with a sense of awareness" (p. 3). Cynthia Rylant, a children's book author, describes her own writing process as "being an artist every single day of one's life" (cited in Calkins, 1994, p. 3).

Writing enables us to capture our thinking in words for future use.

What views do you presently hold about writing? What past experiences have influenced your view?

Students must have opportunities not only to experience writing as a process, but must also come to place their own importance on writing as a medium for expression using a code that allows others to understand, and as a product that represents their thinking. Any writing program should provide a balanced view of writing. We must support students as they begin to understand that possibilities for writing exist beyond "completing tasks for the teacher."

Thinking with Written Language

As we write, we think with written language (D'Arcy, 1989; Graves, 1994; Smith, 1982). Our thinking can take several forms depending on our purposes for writing (D'Arcy, 1989): Throughout our lives, we *retain* memories of our experiences with the world. At times we *re-collect*, or call up, these stored experiences in order to use them for some purpose. Some situations in which we find ourselves require us to *re-create* memories from our firsthand experiences, revisiting or even revising our thinking. We can also use writing to *re-construct* our ideas, arriving at new perceptions of knowledge gained through secondhand experience. Finally, writing enables us to *re-present* our thinking so that it can be seen and shared by others. (Note that D'Arcy deliberately hyphenates the terms to call attention to the fact that as we arrive at new knowledge and new understandings through writing, we draw on what we have already collected, constructed, or created.)

Our students will write by drawing on both their experiences and their knowledge of language. A writing program that encourages and supports thinking focuses on what students have retained in memory, enabling them to re-collect, re-construct, re-create, and re-present their thinking.

Retaining Experiences

Through our senses we are constantly taking in new experiences, or "memories" as D'Arcy (1989) refers to them. Processing information through our senses is a natural way of learning (Piaget & Inhelder, 1969). Our senses influence how we interpret and retain experiences. As we *retain* experiences, we construct new schema or adapt existing schema. This process of retaining experience, especially meaningful experience, is virtually effortless and we may not realize all that we know. Talking about experience may be the first step for many students. Engaging in whole-class, small-group, and partner discussions brings ideas to the verbal level. Then, writing to explore thinking becomes a possibility.

Re-collecting Experience

"None of us are in a position to 'know what we know' until we are given opportunity to re-collect what we have retained" (D'Arcy, 1989, p. 4). *Re-collecting*, calling up past experiences or knowledge, gives us opportunity to think about what we know. The more we re-collect what we know, the easier it is to use our experience and reshape our thinking. Experienced writers know this and write from what they know, re-collecting experiences to create believable stories.

Planning activities that enable students to re-collect what they have retained will be an essential step for successful and satisfying writing. Students can re-collect their ideas in many forms of informal writing such as notes, idea clusters, diagrams, lists, and short descriptions. The more that students use writing to see their thinking, the more confident they are that they have something to say.

Re-creating Experience

Our firsthand experiences with the world are usually easier for us to recall than vicarious, or secondhand, experiences. When we sift through the incredible amount of detail we have retained from personal experience, certain memories stand out as significant to us. We *re-create* those experiences in our mind, perhaps highlighting some aspect differently than we had on previous occasions.

We re-create our responses to literature when we identify with the triumphs and struggles of characters. We use literature as a mirror. In its reflection, we use our own life experience combined with our literary experience to look closely at some particularly relevant event.

Writing in your classroom should enable students to re-create their lived experience and write about what they know best. Students who struggle with what to write about may be students who do not value their own lived experience. Carefully selecting for your reading program literature that connects with their lives can extend opportunities for re-creating experiences through writing.

Re-constructing Experience

With each new experience, we gather re-collections of the past to understand the proper connections to make with the present. We adjust our ideas in light of what we know, *re-constructing*, or revising, previously held views. Much of the knowledge we gain in life is through secondhand experience, which can be more difficult to manipulate or reshape than firsthand knowledge.

Almost daily we ask students to re-construct their previous knowledge in light of new information. We introduce new concepts for which they lack firsthand experience. To enable students to use this new knowledge effectively we should help them first re-collect what they already know. Writing, especially informal writing, can be instrumental in helping students see what they know in preparation for re-constructing their knowledge.

Re-presenting Experience

Sharing what we think connects us to the lived experience of others. The forms that such sharing takes depends in large part on our audience and our intentions for sharing. Audience and purpose shape the form and function of the writing.

To reinforce students' sense of what they know, they need many opportunities to share their thinking, considering the form that best fits their intended purpose and will make the strongest connections to their intended audience. *Re-presenting* thinking assumes that students are engaged in meaningful communication and have a vested interest in the outcome.

Your Turn

How will you treat writing in your classroom? How will you ask students to think with written language?

If I treat writing as an active process, students will have numerous opportunities to re-present their thinking. Informal writing, captured over time in logs or journals, provides students with opportunities to see their ideas change as they gather new information. During the process of developing a piece of writing to completion, students may see a change in their ability to clearly re-present their thinking. By re-presenting their thinking in writing at different points in their learning, students focus on their new knowledge. Seeing their own growth leads to self-satisfaction as writers and learners.

Informal Writing Experiences

To help students re-collect, re-create, and re-construct their experience as a tool for learning in the middle grades, we must engage them in continuous writing experiences. Certainly, they will produce many formal, well-developed pieces of writing; but the most valuable experiences may be those that are informal and that occur daily.

Tompkins (1993) suggests that informal writing helps students capture ideas and experiences and organize their thinking. Informal writings are "bursts" of writing that can take many forms and that do not necessarily go through the phases of the writing process (discussed later in this chapter). Informal writing includes the following:

lists	clusters or brainstorms
annotated drawings	charts

graphs	story maps
graphic organizers	Venn diagrams
descriptions	notes
recorded events	explanations

Informal writing gives students the opportunity to record spontaneous thinking in a familiar form. Through such opportunities, students come to see writing as a medium that is flexible and useful for thinking. Informal writing does not emphasize code or product; its primary purpose is to capture thinking in a way that the writer sees as useful. Informal writing may be edited for conventions and may or may not be published.

Informal writing should be an integral part of a middle grade literacy program in which students routinely make written records to capture their thinking and preserve it for future use, as shown in Figures 3.1 and 3.2. We process so much information in today's world that we need mechanisms to retain, re-collect, re-create, and re-construct that information. Formal writing, thinking that gets fully developed, is not always feasible or the most desirable type of writing to accomplish a goal (Calkins, 1994).

Figure 3.1 Goal setting—Fourth grade

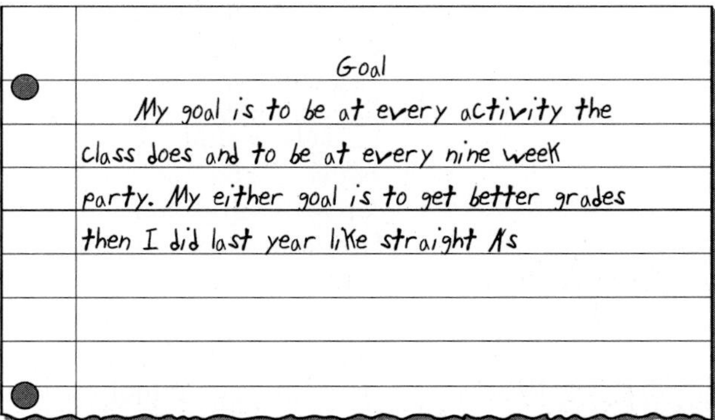

Figure 3.2 Data chart for science—Seventh grade

Micro Organism

Sample	Location
A	Caughlin Ranch Pond ①
B	Sparks ditch
C	Parr Pond
D	Caughlin Ranch Pond ②
E	Panda's fish Tank
F	Miller's ditch ①
G	Caughlin Ranch Stream
H	Miller's ditch ②

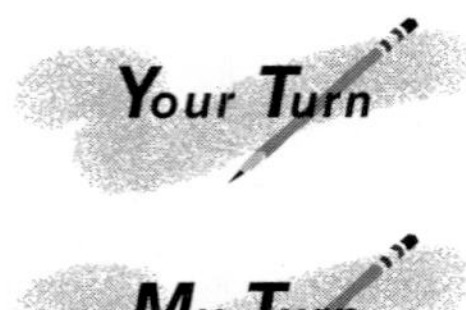

List the variety of ways that you use writing throughout your day.

My Turn

I leave notes for others, make notes for myself, take phone messages, make shopping lists or lists of things to do, sketch and label drawings to explain my thinking to someone, such as when giving directions, and the like. These are all examples of informal writing. In our daily lives, informal writing is the dominant type of writing that we do and should become an integral form of writing in your middle grade classroom. (See Chapter 9 for a discussion and examples of informal writing possibilities.)

Journals and Logs

Students often collect informal writings in a journal or learning log, tools for helping students retain, re-collect, re-create, and re-construct their thinking as informal writing. Journals and logs that utilize a variety of informal writings are the most practical way to bring students into formal writing.

Many people make written records of the everyday events in their lives in some form of journal. While the form may differ, the intention is often similar—to capture feelings and experiences for personal, not public, use. You will often wish to use journals to provide both an outlet for students' personal thoughts and a daily writing opportunity. Journals may be personal or may be a dialogue between you and your students. The purpose, however, remains as a personal outlet for each writer.

Other types of written records might be called "working journals" because writers record observations and information they will use for another purpose (Tompkins, 1993). In this text, we will refer to such working journals as *learning logs* to differentiate them from journals. Learning logs are intended to be a vehicle for helping students use writing as a tool for learning, particularly in content areas such as science, social studies, and mathematics.

Personal Journals

Writers usually choose their own topics for their personal journals. Contents typically focus on events in the writer's life and on personal concerns. The personal journal serves as an outlet and should not be made public, except at the writer's choosing. You may choose to write responses to students' entries to stimulate writing and to model elements of language.

Dialogue Journals

Personal journals can become dialogue journals when the writer addresses the writing to another who is expected to respond. This exchange is a private conversation through writing (Bode, 1989; Gambrell, 1985; Staton, 1987). Students should set the direction for the conversation. Your role is that of encourager and supporter, and to nudge or stretch thinking. Your goal should be for students to become the questioners (Tompkins, 1993). Dialogue journals can be of great value in bridging the gap between talking and writing (Kreeft, 1984), helping students work out nonacademic school problems (Staton, 1980), and supporting students as they think and talk about books (Barone, 1990).

Response Journals

As part of your reading program, you may choose to ask students to write their responses to books they are reading. Tompkins's (1993) review of research reveals that students' responses may include the following:

- Retellings and summaries
- Questions related to understanding the text
- Interaction or empathy with characters
- Predictions of what will happen and validation after reading
- Personal experiences, feelings, and opinions related to the reading
- Simple and elaborated evaluations
- Philosophical reflections

Double-Entry Journals

Students' responses can also be evoked by specific statements made by authors. A double-entry journal (Barone, 1990) combines a quote from a text with the student's response. The journal page is divided into two columns with a quote from the text (noting chapter and page numbers for future reference) on the left and the student's response on the right (Figure 3.3). Because the quote is provided, double-entry responses are focused and interpretable. Double-entry journals may contain the following variations (quotations are from Tompkins, 1993, p. 92):

- "Reading Notes" on the left; response or "Discussion Notes" on the right
- "Predictions" on the left; validation or "What Happened " on the right

Learning Logs

Learning logs can help children record and react to their learning in mathematics, science, and social studies (Fulwiler, 1985), and you can extend this benefit to include literature study. Think of a learning log as a collection of journal responses and informal writings that, when taken together, can help students see growth in their thinking.

Figure 3.3 Log entry—Double-entry log

Double-entry Log

In the text. . . . (give page number)	My response. . . . (what I think)
The sun exploded the sky just blew it up with the setting color. page 170	It reminds me of the sunset, with all the pink blue purple and orange.
Had flashes of color in his brain, esplosians of color. page 177	It made me think of just paint splattered
It was sweet and tangy-almost too sweet. 189	It made me think of Island Twists Mar-O-MangoBerry Kool-Aid

For example, while participating in a whole-class literature study of *Hatchet*, by Gary Paulsen (1987), students might do the following:

- Write a response to the text using a particular journal style.
- Draw and label different kinds of survival equipment.
- Cluster what they know about survival or the wilderness and add to the cluster as they gain new knowledge.
- List interesting words in the text and add related words that could be used to describe the setting.
- Write a description of the setting around the lake as they interpret it from their reading.

Learning logs provide great versatility. In practice, learning logs can combine the formats and intentions of the journals described earlier, as well as a variety of informal writing formats. Learning logs can stimulate writing through such variety, meeting the needs and preferences of individual students.

Our experiences with writing help us decide what thoughts we need to re-collect and what form would best re-present our thinking. In a writing program, informal writing may help students see that writing is beneficial and within their reach. Take a few moments to think about the types of informal writing situations that often occur in a middle grade classroom.

Your Turn

Have you ever kept a journal or log for yourself? What purposes did it serve? How did it help you as a writer?

My Turn

The diary that I kept in junior high school was my first experience with a journal. Rereading it helped remind me of past experiences and how I had handled them. The most important learning log I ever had was when I was conducting research for my doctoral dissertation. Since I had never before conducted a project of this nature, I wasn't sure what to expect. In the log I collected everything that I thought might be remotely useful. In the end, I used some information that I had not anticipated and was glad that I had captured it when I did.

In Part Two I present suggestions for informal writing experiences that grow out of students' interactions with literature and ideas about the world. There will be times when further development of informal writing is appropriate and/or necessary. Professional writers have taught us that worthwhile writing takes time to develop. Longer and more complex pieces of writing should become journeys in thinking, developed through a process approach to writing.

Process Approach to Writing—A Journey in Thinking

Engaging in the process of writing should be like taking a journey:

> All journeys take time, and when the going is tough some will take longer than others. It is possible on a journey to have a rest along the way—several rests, if the journey is an extended trek over unfamiliar ground. It is possible to look back over ground already covered and to look forward at least as far as the next bend. It is useful to be able to call on help if you get stuck, and it can be reassuring to have company at least from time to time, as the journey progresses. (D'Arcy, 1989, pp. 27–28)

In a writing program built on the process approach, pieces of writing emerge over time through a recursive, or flexible, process (D'Arcy, 1989; Calkins, 1986, 1994; Graves, 1983, 1994). To develop an idea fully, writers go through different phases with their thinking and writing, each phase serving a different purpose:

- rehearsal or prewriting
- composing or drafting
- revising
- editing
- publishing or sharing

The process is considered *recursive* because writers move between phases of writing as it suits their need. Earlier we discussed different views of writing: as code, medium, product, and process. In a process approach to writing, you will give attention to all four views of writing. For example, during editing, knowledge of writing as a code is very important. Writing as a medium comes into play as students consider their options for shaping ideas. Writing as a product is realized during the publishing phase. Student perceptions of writing as a *process* will undergird their efforts from start to finish.

Rehearsal or Prewriting

Getting started with a piece, knowing what we want to write, having confidence that an idea is worthwhile or that anyone else might be interested are dilemmas that all writers face. Conscious rehearsal accompanies the decision to write (Graves, 1994).

Getting Started. If informal writing is an integral part of a literacy program, students will already be recognizing, examining, questioning, and exploring their thinking. They will be ready to extend their thinking in more depth. If, however, your students are not used to daily writing, you should provide many informal writing opportunities before introducing a process approach.

To get started, students do such things as the following:

- Daydream or write in their heads
- Sketch or doodle, often labeling or making annotations
- Brainstorm lists of words or ideas
- Cluster or outline ideas or sequences of thought
- Read more about a topic
- Talk with a friend
- Free write
- Make charts, graphs, Venn diagrams, or other graphic organizers for ideas
- Review notes made previously

When students have had experience as "informal" writers, this phase is familiar. It is a way of thinking they have experienced many times and feel comfortable and confident with as they begin to plan a piece. Students' work during this phase should show great variety because they use different strategies as they get started. Encouraging only one strategy for all students, such as idea clustering (Figure 3.4), is limiting for those who find it easier to plan through other means, such as by making lists (Figure 3.5). Experience with informal writing helps students know many different forms that their thinking can take as they prepare to develop an idea into a piece of formal writing. Observing students during informal writing also will help you know more about their preferred writing styles.

Don't hurry students through this planning phase. If you do, you may find they will continue to struggle with a piece that never really meets their expectations. Exploring ideas during this phase is essential if students are to find a focus.

Finding a Focus. At some point during the "getting started" phase, students will be ready to clarify their topic and direction. At this point response from another writer can be very helpful, affirming or clarifying thinking. A responsive listener must try to listen for the writer's intention, what they are hoping to accomplish with the writing.

Students can be trained to become responsive listeners. Notice the word *trained.* You must model what responsive listening looks and sounds like, then coach partners as they practice. You can also be one of these responsive listeners, as you confer with students about the focus of their writing. D'Arcy (1989) suggests that we must look through children's writing, rather than at the writing itself. We must try to see the student's intention for the writing. Once students find their focus, sustained writing will usually follow.

Composing or Drafting

Sustained writing is the goal of this stage. When students have a clear sense of where they are trying to go with a piece of writing, sustaining their effort is not so difficult. Students who continue to struggle with their writing during this phase usually have not truly found their focus.

Your role during this phase is to get out of the way. As long as students are sustaining the writing, let them go. They can use this phase to build their stamina as

Figure 3.4 Idea cluster for "Cinderella's Revenge"—Fourth grade

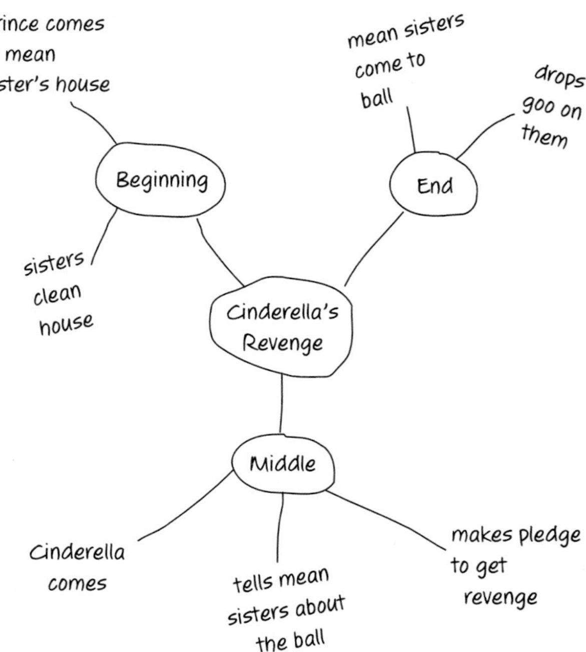

Figure 3.5 Word list for poem, *My Family Is a Rose"—Eighth grade*

person		flower part
mother	keeps peace taxi *always making things	leaf
father	*protects fixes stuff works hard	thorn
sister	strong smart *stable	stem
dog	always happy *joy quiet	petals
me	friendly *gets everyone together	roots

writers. Remember, informal writing does not usually require sustained effort. Composing becomes the first time for many students that writing continues beyond short bursts.

During the composing phase, you begin to see something of the recursive nature of writing. Some writers move back to the strategies used during prewriting, especially when they find that they need to clarify what they know about their topic. Some writers, on occasion, move ahead into the editing phase. For others, moving back and forth between composing and revising/editing is a natural way for them to check their thinking.

One of the reasons you should step back when students are composing is to let them become more aware of their own style as writers. Each of us benefits by knowing how we write and what processes we go through, by knowing what works for us as writers. Students can't learn about their own style if someone else is always intruding into the process.

Revising

Revision refers to making changes for meaning and requires a writer to become a reader, rereading for meaning. A writer who recognizes a gap between intention and execution while rereading may be motivated to rework that particular part of the text.

Making meaning can involve more than just changing words. Students may have to make major changes in meaning, such as restructuring sentences or rearranging the order of the whole piece. They may make minor changes such as adding punctuation to clarify meaning, and also may attend to the grammar or syntax of the language.

Graves (1994) suggests that most writers follow a simple composing pattern: select, write, read; select, write, read. Over time, revision becomes an added step in the pattern as "each line emerges through a select, write, read, write, reread, and rewrite sequence" (p. 81). Revision occurs when writers are monitoring their composing phase, with the focus of their writing in mind. This sequence, however, is not automatic.

Writers learn to revise through their struggle to communicate, and by understanding the possibilities inherent in the writing process.

Being able to revise requires that the writer sense other possible options in the writing. All students need guidance as they learn to look again at their writing. In fact, you may find yourself saying to students, "Take another look at your words. What are you trying to say? Is it doing want you want? Perhaps you might consider . . ."

To some degree, a student's decisions to revise her own work is developmental. Graves (1994) suggests a rough developmental sequence in revision. Students typically add to a piece before they are able to sense where to insert new ideas or information. After insertions, finding and writing the main idea of a piece, instead of a "bed to bed" story that tells all, becomes possible. Finally, lining out words, rather than erasing, is a sign that students see the words as flexible and open to revision.

If students lack sufficient knowledge of their topic or the genre in which they are writing, revision will be difficult. Similarly, if students lack a sense of audience, the focus of the writing will be unclear and revision may not target the ideas that most need reworking. Finally, two issues that plague writers and block revision are lack of time to write and writing too much.

Sometimes students make a poor choice of topic and the writing does not develop. At that point, they need to know that abandoning a piece of writing is appropriate and something that writers may choose to do. The draft should be kept in the writing folder in case the writer decides to give the topic another try later.

Editing

Editing requires a writer to become a reader and read for details, so that other readers are able to interpret the writing as intended. This phase will usually focus on conventions of writing such as grammar, capitalization, and spelling. Your expectations for students' level of use of conventions depends on their stage of word knowledge and spelling development. Here is where you must use your knowledge of students, so that you do not have unrealistic expectations for their ability, for example, to use correct spelling in their finished pieces. If we know that a student is in the early syllable juncture stage, we should not expect to see all schwa (***a**-bout'*) sounds represented conventionally, because that student is not fully aware of the effect of syllable accents on single vowels (late syllable juncture).

You can assist students in achieving a satisfactory level of convention in their writing by helping them to work in editing groups. Here again, you should model for students how to read someone's writing and help them find details that might need attention. During your modeling, you must emphasize that the purpose of giving attention to correctly using the code is to be able to communicate clearly with others. For example, all writers spell words in certain ways because we have agreed, as users of American English, that we will all use the same spellings so we will know what others have written. If each of us chose our own spellings, or our own grammatical structures, we might not be able to make meaning from each other's writing.

Publishing or Sharing

As students move their writing toward completion, form may again become an issue. The best form for a piece of writing may not be evident until the draft of ideas has been completed. Between drafting and publishing, the student may realize a need to change form. For example, what began as a descriptive piece may become a poem because

Cinderella's Revenge
By Aubrey

Once upon a time like usual Cinderella was living happily ever after like in the first Cinderella, but only this time she's getting revenge. So this is how the story goes . . .

One day the prince came along to Pupil, Dupil, and Fupil's house. These are the mean people that Cinderella worked for.

They were there in their aprons cleaning house when the Prince knocked on their door and said, "This is your royal highness." The mean girls ran to get their best clothes on but the Prince knocked down the door with them in their aprons running to their rooms.

This upset them so that they screamed, "Ahhhhhh!"

The Prince looked at them just standing in their aprons. "Oh," said the Prince, "too bad!"

"Well," said Pupil, "you have no right to walk into someone's else's house without them answering. And look at us just standing here in our aprons."

There was suddenly a loud noise. Boom!!! It was the mother knocking down the door.

"Now look, Mom's mad," said Dupil.

" I am so sorry," said the Prince.

"You had better be sorry," said the sisters.

"I like you Prince," said Dupil.

"I don't like you," said the Prince.

"Well, why not?" asked Pupil with her big mean dark eyes.

"Because you are the people who are mean to Cinderella and I love her," said the Prince.

Suddenly Cinderella's guardian picked up the door that the Prince had knocked down, threw it in the air and walked into the room. The guardian said, "Here is your royal queen, Cinderella." (The girls were in shock!)

Cinderella walked into the room with a nice outfit on and said, "Prince I am waiting for you."

"Oh, yes," said Cinderella, "I have something to tell you. We are having a Ball this Saturday night and you are all invited to attend as my guests."

"So . . ." says the Prince "what will we do to them at the ball?" "We could plan where they stand, put three jugs of goo above where they stand and dump it on them," said the Prince.

"Oh what sweet revenge" said Cinderella as she smiled to herself with pleasure.

AT THE BALL . . .

"They're here," yelled Cinderella.

"Go place them in their spots," said the Prince.

"Okay," said Cinderella. Cinderella took them to their places and yelled at the Prince so he would drop the goo on their heads. And this is exactly what he did, the goo fell from the ceiling landed smack dab on the mean girl's heads! Maybe next time the girls will get revenge, but for now it was Cinderella's turn. And once again Cinderella lived happily ever after unlike the mean girls with the goo in their hair.

THE END!

Figure 3.6 Published story—Fourth grade

the student discovers that the message of the writing is better suited to poetry. In such a case, the student moves back to the drafting and editing phases.

During the publishing, or sharing, phase, students have opportunities to publicize their writing. In an author's chair (Graves, 1983, 1994) a student reads aloud a piece of writing to which other students respond. You also may prominently display writing in the classroom or publish it in books that are available for all to read (Figures 3.6 and 3.7). Students learn about writing from the writing of their classmates.

Before we leave this discussion of process, I must make one final comment: The purpose of teaching writing as a process is to help each student find his or her own

My Family Is a Rose

My Family is a rose.

My mother is a leaf, always making something.

My father is a thorn, protecting always.

My sister is a stem, trying hard to keep us stable.

My dog, Goldie, is the petals, always spreading joy.

And I am the roots, trying hard to hold us down from the rushing wind.

Bailey

Figure 3.7 Published poem—Eighth grade

voice, and to learn to express that voice clearly. Graves (1994) adamantly states that voice is the driving force of the writing process. "Voice is the imprint of ourselves in our writing. . . . It's the writer's voice that gives me the best sense of his or her potential" (pp. 81–82). When students have selected a topic they know about and have a vested interest in, their voice is clearly heard. "Voice should breathe through the entire process: rehearsal, topic choice, selection of information, composing, reading, and rewriting" (Graves, 1994, p. 82).

Think about the last piece of formal writing you completed. What do you know about your own writing process? What type of journey did you take with your writing?

In my own writing I have found that rehearsal consists of thinking for a long time about what I will write before I actually put anything on paper (or on disk). When I finally begin to compose, ideas come rapidly. Then I have to let it sit for a few days. I revise best when I step away for a few days and rethink what I want my audience to think or feel. Editing for conventions is relatively easy with a computer, but I find that I tend to edit as I go so there isn't much to correct with the spellcheck program.

Writer's Workshop

As stated, developing a piece of writing is like a journey, with opportunities for the writer to determine how the journey will take shape. The process enables the writer to monitor and pace the writing, with help from more knowledgeable others as needed. Your students will need support to learn that writing can be more than informal bursts of thinking. Writer's workshop is one excellent way to organize your classroom for formal writing experiences.

Writer's workshop is a formal application of the process approach to writing. Students compose, edit, revise, and publish their writing, working as partners or in groups to give each other feedback, conferring with you as necessary. The workshop provides students with blocks of time to write, allows them to choose their subjects, and gives students chances throughout the process to share their writing, to see writing demon-

Students need to know that teachers are genuinely interested in the ideas they share through their writing.

strated, and to evaluate both their own work and the work of others. We discuss writer's workshop fully in Chapter 9.

MAINTAINING LEGIBLE HANDWRITING

"The goal of handwriting instruction is to develop fluent and legible handwriting" (Tompkins, 1993, p. 315). By the middle grades, students have been introduced to both manuscript and cursive handwriting formation. Your focus now should be on helping students develop a personal style of handwriting that is both legible and functional for the individual.

With the focus of attention on the process of writing, as it has been for the past decade, you must not lose sight of handwriting's real purpose. Graves (1994) states that "handwriting is the vehicle carrying information on its way to a destination. If it is illegible the journey may not be completed. Handwriting, like skin, shows the outside of a person. But beneath the skin beats the living organism, the life's blood, the ideas, the information" (p. 241).

To increase the legibility and function of students' handwriting, you must take care not to overemphasize its surface aspects, or how the writing looks on the paper. If you do, you may inadvertently be telling students that handwriting is more important than thinking.

Your purposes in handwriting instruction should be twofold: (1) to provide instruction in patterns of formation that will allow handwriting to become fluid and eventually unconscious, and (2) to help students see the purpose of legibility as a vehicle to clear communication.

Developing Fluent Handwriting

The elements of fluent handwriting are letter formation, size and proportion, spacing, slant, alignment, and line quality (Barbe, Wasylyk, Hackney, & Braun, 1994). If the formation of letters is tedious, students will soon tire in their attempts to communicate. Handwriting instruction should help students see that some methods of letter formation are less tiring for their hands. Learning to be consistent in letter formation will, in general, lead students toward fluid hand motions. To this end, some directed handwriting instruction and practice is warranted, especially when first introducing a pattern (Farris, 1991). Carefully supervise instruction and practice so that you can provide students feedback as a more knowledgeable other about the progressions they follow to make letters.

Fluency in the formation of letters becomes a factor when students are composing. As Graves (1994) reminds us:

> If the familiar motor pathways are not built up through regular writing about topics the writer knows, then slowness can hamper the expression of content. The writing goes down on the page so slowly that the writer pokes along word-by-word on the page. That is, each word takes so long to write down that the next word, or even the rest of the sentence, cannot be contemplated at the same time as the one under construction. (p. 251)

The manner in which students hold a writing implement can also be a positive or negative factor in the physical exertion of writing. Some students have taught themselves to hold the pen or pencil in what appears to be an awkward position. Before you attempt to change a student's grip, observe the student during writing to see if the grip is functional and that the student's hand does not tire easily.

Legibility for Communication

The real purpose of writing is for communication. Therefore, handwriting's true purpose is as a vehicle for communication. Handwriting instruction must emphasize the need for legibility as a vehicle for communication. A writer cannot communicate on paper using handwriting no one can read.

The most appropriate place to reinforce this idea will be in the midst of writing experiences that students will share with others. When students gather together in response pairs or editing groups it will become apparent when someone cannot respond because the writing is not legible. The more you engage students in the sharing of their writing, the more functional opportunities you have to reinforce real reasons for legibility. When students care about communicating, they have more interest in legibility.

Monitoring Students' Growth as Writers

Students develop as writers through both informal and process writing experiences. Understanding the quality of thinking and processes each student uses to produce meaningful print requires the collection of data that demonstrates the following:

- What a student understands about writing as a code, a medium, a product, and a process.
- How a student uses writing as a form of thinking to re-collect, re-create, or re-construct ideas.

- How a student uses various forms of informal writing to communicate.
- How a student uses the phases of the writing process to explore and develop personal understandings of a topic and/or for communicating that topic to others.

In many respects, monitoring growth in writing is easier than in reading because the results of writing are more visible. However, it is still important to go beyond the product to understand students' thinking processes and response to writing as a means of communication.

Samples of Writing

Samples of writing serve as a starting point for assessment and evaluation. What can samples of writing show us? Over time, samples can be compared for growth in the following areas:

- Overall organization
- Quality and appropriateness of content
- Expression of ideas
- Development of personal voice
- Quality and appropriateness of word choices
- Sentence fluency
- Appropriate use of conventions

The elements listed are called *writing traits* (see Chapter 9 for more detailed explanation). While evaluating a student's writing traits may allow us to talk about the writing in more detail, traits may not reveal aspects of the "student as writer" that we ought to know. The traits view writing as a code, a medium, and a product. What about writing as an active process?

To understand the "journey" of the ideas from the writer's mind, flowing down the arm and out of the hand, we must carefully observe the writer in different writing situations and confer with the writer about knowledge of personal writing processes.

We analyze writing traits, such as ideas/content, organization, use of conventions, and so on, in formal writing produced through the writing process. Yet much of the writing students will do in school will be informal writing. Observation and conferring with students will be essential to our understanding their thinking.

Observing Writers at Work

When you watch someone writing, what can you observe? Do you get a glimpse of their "style"? In a room full of writers, will you see different styles, different levels of understanding about how one writes and why one writes, or different levels of confidence and experience as writers? What should you watch for as students write?

As you observe, you should ask yourself, "What do I know about this student as a writer and how did I gain that knowledge?" To answer this question, you must return to your instructional purposes in writing, the writing activities that have grown out of those purposes, and your observations of the student during the activities. Did you watch the student based on your knowledge of development and your goals for instruction? Did you make anecdotal records of your observations so that, over time, your notes would serve as more detailed reminders of the student's responses than would your recollections of the events?

Conferring with Writers

Providing a forum for students to talk about their writing is essential to understanding their motivations and intentions as writers. The writing process has response built into it through student-teacher conferences, response partners and groups, and editing partners and groups. Conferring during informal writing also provides a window into students' thinking. Talk can focus on how students organized their thinking, why they chose a particular format, whether they considered other forms, and on explaining the content of the writing. Assessment and evaluation must begin with and build on what students see in their own writing.

What types of things will you want to know about your students as writers?

____ ■

Respecting Diversity in Writing Development

If students come to school with different experiences, then we can assume that their knowledge of and interest in communicating through writing will also differ. Like reading, writing is very personal. Writers develop through a personal desire to communicate with themselves and others. In your classroom, you can support diversity by (1) honoring students' thinking, and (2) supporting their independent development as writers.

Honor Students' Thinking

When you ask students to put their ideas on paper so that they and others can see them, you are asking them to trust you with their thoughts and feelings. How you treat their ideas will tell students a great deal about how you see them as human beings, how you value them as individuals. If you view writing as an extension of the self, you will treat students' writing with respect.

It will be very easy for you, as an adult, to see things that are missing from students' writing, things that you would like to have seen them put into the writing, things that you think they know and should use. When you see missing pieces, you might be inclined to impose your own ideas on the writing.

Your response to their writing should be to help them accomplish their own intentions. As you do this, you can "nudge" their writing, offering suggestions that might be helpful, but not imposing your ideas on them.

Support Independence

Observing developmental learning environments has taught us that students want to be independent. By supporting their independence as writers we value students' ideas as individuals, providing many opportunities for them to show who they are. When you demonstrate various forms of writing and talk about how you make decisions as a writer, you show students how competent writers think. Modeling thinking processes supports students and reduces the "hidden curriculum" of writing.

TAKE A MOMENT AND REFLECT

Writing can be viewed in at least four ways:

- as a code using language as its symbols
- as a medium to be manipulated and shaped
- as a product to be completed
- as an active process of creating or constructing

Writing is a form of thinking that is done with written language and involves:

- retaining memories and experiences
- re-collecting those memories and experiences
- re-creating memories from firsthand experiences
- re-constructing knowledge from vicarious or secondhand experiences
- re-presenting what is known that was not originally known

Informal writing is made up of bursts of writing that are not taken through the writing process and may not be edited for meaning or conventions. Informal writing includes:

- lists, brainstorms, and clusters
- annotated drawings
- charts and graphs
- graphic organizers
- Venn diagrams
- descriptions
- notes
- records of events
- explanations

Informal writing is often recorded in varying types of journals or logs:

- personal journal
- dialogue journal
- response journal
- double-entry journal
- learning logs

Learning logs typically include many different types of informal writing that is related by subject area or theme.

The writing process is like a journey that includes:

- getting started with an idea for a piece of writing
- exploring the idea to find a focus
- composing ideas in sustained writing
- revising for meaning
- editing for conventions
- sharing the new thinking that has emerged as a result of the writing process

Writer's workshop can put the writing process to work in a classroom by providing predictable blocks of writing time, demonstrations of various aspects of writing, assistance with revision or editing at the time it is most needed, and opportunities to celebrate writing with peers.

Attention should be given to helping students maintain fluency and legibility in handwriting.

Monitoring students' growth as writers involves:

- focusing on samples of writing over time
- anecdotal records of observations of writing behavior
- conferring with students about their thinking while writing and about their writing processes

Writing development should:

- respect diversity in students' thinking
- support independence in development

REFERENCES

Barbe, W. B., Wasylyk, T. M., Hackney, C. S., & Braun, L. A. (1994). *Zaner-Bloser creative growth in handwriting (grades K–8)*. Columbus, OH: Zaner-Bloser.

Barone, D. (1990). The written responses of young children: Beyond comprehension to story understanding. *The New Advocate*, 3, 49–56.

Bode, B. A. (1989). Dialogue journal writing. *The Reading Teacher*, *42*, 568–571.

Calkins, L. M. (1986, 1994). *The art of teaching writing*. Portsmouth, NH: Heinemann.

Clay, M. (1975). *What did I write? Beginning writing behaviour*. Portsmouth, NH: Heinemann.

D'Arcy, P. (1989). *Making sense, shaping meaning: Writing in the context of a capacity-based approach to learning*. Portsmouth, NH: Heinemann.

Farris, P. J. (1991). Handwriting instruction should not be extinct. *Language Arts, 68,* 312–314.

Fulwiler, T. (1985). Writing and learning, grade 3. *Language Arts, 62,* 55-59.

Gambrell, L. B. (1985). Dialogue journals: Reading-writing interaction. *The Reading Teacher, 38,* 512–515.

Graves, D. (1983). *Teaching writing*. Portsmouth, NH: Heinemann.

Graves, D. (1994). *A fresh look at writing*. Portsmouth, NH: Heinemann.

Kreeft, J. (1984). Dialogue writing—Bridge from talk to essay writing. *Language Arts*, 61, 141–150.

Piaget, J., & Inhelder, B. (1969). *The psychology of the child*. New York: Basic Books.

Smith, F. (1982). *Writing and the writer*. London: Heinemann.

Staton, J. (1980). Writing and counseling: Using a dialogue journal. *Language Arts, 57,* 514–518.

Staton, J. (1987). The power of responding in dialogue journals. In T. Fulwiler (Ed.), *The journal book* (pp. 47–63). Portsmouth, NH: Heinemann.

Tompkins, G. E. (1993). *Teaching writing: Balancing process and product*. Upper Saddle River, NJ: Merrill/Prentice Hall.

4

Growing Toward Maturity in Word Knowledge

In this chapter . . .

We explore issues related to reading and writing words and the importance of helping students develop confidence and competence in their knowledge of words, including:

- issues that surround learning words:
  - developing sight vocabulary
  - contextual meaning
  - phonics patterns
  - structural patterns
- developmental stages of word knowledge:
  - letter-name stage
  - within-word pattern stage
  - syllable juncture stage
  - derivational constancy stage
- monitoring students' growth in word knowledge
- respecting students' diversity in word knowledge development

Learning Words

Learning words and then learning to use them effectively are essential to our becoming competent readers and writers. As we explore word knowledge and how it evolves, you must remember that reading development typically leads writing development. As writers, we draw on our knowledge of written language that we learned as readers.

Adults who read competently often assume that mere knowledge of words is the essential element in reading. However, we know that reading is more than understanding words alone. It is a complex system of skills and knowledge. Within this system, knowledge and activities involved in visually recognizing individual printed words are useless by themselves and are possible only as they are guided and received by complementary knowledge and activities of language comprehension. On the other hand, if the individual word recognition processes do not operate properly, the system itself cannot function (Adams, 1990, p. 3).

Adding to and refining our knowledge of words is challenging. "The vocabulary of written English consists of a relatively small number of words that occur frequently and an extremely large number of words that occur only infrequently" (Winsor, Nagy, Osborn, & O'Flahavan, 1993, p. 5).

Consider the following example. Anderson, Wilson, and Fielding (1988) estimate that the average fifth-grade student reads about one million words in a year, counting both in- and out-of-school reading. At least 10 percent, or 10,000, of these million words will be seen only once during that year. Winsor et al. (1993) estimate the composition of those 10,000 words:

- 40 percent (4000) derivatives of more frequent words (*debt* to *indebtedness*)
- 13 percent (1300) inflections of more frequent words (*merge* to *merges, merit* to *merited*)
- 15 percent (1500) proper nouns
- 22 percent (2200) in several categories (capitalizations, numbers, deliberate misspellings, mathematical expressions)
- 10 percent (1000) truly new words

Middle grade students need a range of strategies for learning new words and for refining their knowledge of words, processes they will continue all their lives. As adults, we know words today that we did not know even a few months ago. The more we read and the more varied subjects and writing styles we explore, the greater our chances of encountering unfamiliar words.

In addition to reading new words, our knowledge must include the ability to write a wide range of words. As writers, we must recognize relationships among sound, symbols, and meaning to form words conventionally. Writing draws on knowledge learned through reading. When we read widely, and consider the words chosen by other authors, we acquire models of spelling and usage.

As competent readers and writers, we have internalized our knowledge of words we know on sight, our use of context to derive meaning, and our knowledge of letter/sound patterns (phonics) and of meaningful parts of words (structural analysis). We use this knowledge to help us make meaning. To help middle grade students become increasingly competent readers and writers, we must gain conscious control over our own knowledge of these components.

Sight Vocabulary

We recognize many words instantly, without needing to study distinguishing details. Such words are called *sight words* or our *sight vocabulary*. Meaningful words are easier for us to remember. Familiar words in our environment, words we see over and over, are usually the first ones we learn to read. To be fluent readers, we need a range of stored sight words (Holdaway, 1980). To build this storehouse, we notice features of familiar words that help us distinguish them from other words, then store these features and words in memory for later use. As we work over time to make meaning with print, the distinguishing visual features we notice become more and more refined. With the help of more knowledgeable readers, we also begin to make associations between symbols and sounds. In our memory, we link the *phonological,* or sound, structure of words with their distinctive visual features (Ehri, 1991).

We develop our large storehouse of sight words by both extensive and intensive reading. Extensive reading, across different genres and topics and for different purposes, exposes us to many different words. Intensive reading gives us opportunity to distinguish the details in words and to link new words to words and word parts that we already know.

Contextual Meaning

We must learn to use the context that other words provide to discern the meaning of unfamiliar words. *Context* involves using the *meaning cues* we derive from surrounding familiar words, phrases, and sentences, and the *structure cues* of grammar and syntax to provide clues to the meaning of words that seem unfamiliar. Context should also be our main way of checking the accuracy of the visual cues we use to pronounce unfamiliar words.

We have already processed the meaning of the text up to the point of our encounter with an unfamiliar word. Using that meaning, we look at the unfamiliar word for clues to letter-sound patterns and ask, "What word do I know that looks like this word (visual) and fits in this phrase/sentence/paragraph?" We then check context by asking, "Does that sound right (structure) and make sense (meaning)?"

Our ability to use contextual meaning relies both on our understanding of reading as a process and on our effective use of meaning-making strategies. If reading instruction has focused our attention on visual cues more than on meaning and structure cues, we may not know how to use context adequately. Successful use of context to make meaning assumes that we balance our use of all three cues as needed.

Phonics Patterns

Phonics is the component of word knowledge that relies on letter–sound relationships within syllables. While knowledge of phonics is highly correlated with success in reading and spelling, it is important to remember that knowledge of phonics alone does not constitute reading.

When we speak of phonics, we typically mean the *visual cues* to sounds represented by the left-to-right arrangement of consonants and vowels within syllables. To use our phonics knowledge, we must be able to match letter patterns with the possible *phonemes*, or sound units, stored in memory from oral language.

Phonics has been a widely debated issue in reading instruction in the United States. English is primarily an alphabetic system, in which symbols represent the speech sounds of oral language. In an ideal alphabetic system each speech sound has its own distinctive graphic representation. Herein lies the problem with English. Sometimes the phonemic significance of a letter is modified by the following:

- The letter(s) that come immediately after (*lit*/*light*)
- One or more nonadjacent letters (*can*/*cane*)

- The identity of the word or its constituent syllables as wholes (*father/fathead*)
- The absence of stress or accent on a syllable (***a**-bout'*).

Because English is not a perfect alphabetic system, we must look for the patterns that do exist, patterns that we can emphasize with our students. We must look for letter patterns within syllables and consider the types of thinking used to identify sound patterns. In this chapter we discuss the full range of phonic elements so that you are prepared to meet the range of readers you may find in your middle grade classroom.

Consonants and vowels form patterns of single and double letters within a syllable that we come to recognize in familiar words and generalize to unfamiliar words to predict pronunciation (Figure 4.1). In general, it is best to help students develop phonics knowledge by moving from the simple to the complex, engaging students in thinking about the following patterns, in order:

- Single-letter patterns before double
- Consistent patterns before variant
- Sounded patterns before silent

To be useful, instruction in phonics should focus on elements that appear in students' reading materials. Notice the organization of patterns in Figure 4.1.

Consonant Patterns

Consonants, of which there are 21 in the alphabet, are fairly stable in the sounds they represent. Consonants fall into two basic categories, single and double. What do we know about these categories?

Single-consonant patterns include the following:

- Consonants that are consistent in the sounds they represent.

Figure 4.1 Overview of phonics patterns

Consonants		**Vowels**	
Single	**Double**	**Single**	**Double**
Consistent	**2 Consonants—2 Sounds**	**Long**	**Long—consistent**
letter names sound letter does *not* name sound	Blends/clusters initial & final	CV, CVCe	vowel digraphs
Vary	**2 Consonants—1 Sound**	**Short**	**Long and Short—vary**
vary by position vary by vowel that follows	double consonants consonant digraph *h* digraphs silent letter	CVC	vowel digraphs
		Neither long nor short *r*-controlled	**Neither long nor short** diphthongs *r*-controlled

- Those that vary depending upon the placement of the consonant(s) within a syllable and/or the letters that follow the consonant(s).

Double-consonant patterns include the following:

- Blends or clusters, combinations of two or three consonant letters in which each letter represents a sound, as in ***bread***, ***clap***, and ***street***. Within the syllable, blends/clusters work as a unit.
- Double consonants, two of the same consonant letters together, such as *egg* or *dre**ss***, that represent one sound. One consonant is sounded and one is silent.
- Consonant digraphs, units of two consonants that represent one sound, either a new sound not represented by either of the letters in the unit, such as ***sh*** in *ship*, or the sound of one of the letters in the unit, with the other letter being silent, such as ***wr*** in *write*.

Single Consonants. Single consonants often represent the sound we hear when we say the name of the letter. For example, when we say the name of the letter *b*, we make a "buh" sound that represents the sound of the consonant within a syllable. The letter *b* not only names its sound but also is fairly consistent in the sound it represents at both the beginning and end of a syllable.

Single consonants that name their sound will usually be the easiest letter–sound correspondences for children to distinguish. Figure 4.2 identifies the consonants that name their sound. When children first begin to notice letter sounds, they are also learning about the names of the letters of the alphabet. Children give so much attention to naming letters that it makes sense to them that the sounds of the letters should relate to their names. Working to make sense out of the abstract nature of written language, children tend to generalize from naming letters to naming consonant sounds. Early spelling attempts also focus on letter-naming strategies. Effective early consonant instruction thus will focus on the letters whose name and sound are similar.

Some single consonants also represent sounds that vary depending on their placement in the syllable. Looking at Figure 4.2, we see that the letter *s* can represent the sounds of /s/, /z/, or /sh/ depending on position.

Pronunciation of some consonants is influenced by the letters that immediately follow. As shown in Figure 4.2, the letters *c* and *g* can each represent two different sounds depending on the vowel that follows. The sound represented is described as a *hard* sound when followed by the letters *a* (*cane/gate*), *o* (*cone/gone*), or *u* (*cute/gun*) and as a *soft* sound when followed by *e* (*cent/gem*), *i* (*city/giant*), or *y* (*cycle/gym*). The terms *hard* and *soft* refer the formation of the sound in the mouth.

Double Consonants. After students know single consonants fairly well, you may introduce *blends* or *clusters*. Blends and clusters do not require new consonant knowledge, but do require that students understand that letters can work as a unit. Teaching blends in *r, l, s,* and *w* families, as shown in Figure 4.2, facilitates generalizations about the sounds represented. Knowing how to think of the blend *br* as a unit facilitates knowing *cr, dr, fr, gr, pr,* and *tr* as sound units.

Double consonants, which usually appear at the end of a syllable (*ball*) or are divided between two syllables (*supper*), may be children's first introduction to the concept of silent letters. The concept of a silent letter is very abstract and children may initially find it confusing.

Figure 4.2 Overview of consonant patterns

Single Consonants

Consistent sound

letter names sound

b bat, cab
d dot, mad
f fan, leaf
g bag
j jam
k kid, peek
l lid, pail
m man, ham
n nut, bun
p pin, map
r rug, car
t tag, cat
v van, love
z zoo, quiz

letter doesn't name sound

h hat
w win
y yes

Variant sound

vary by position & vowel that follows

c (hard *c* = /k/)
cage
cone
cut

c (soft *c* = /s/)
cent, face
city
cycle

g (hard *g* = /g/)
gate, bag
girl
gone
gum

g (soft *g* = /j/)
gem, cage
giant
gym

s sand, bus
sure—
—his

x x-ray, fox
xylophone

Double Consonants

Two consonants-Two sounds

initial blends
***r* family**

br break
cr crown
dr drop
fr frog
gr grapes
pr prize
tr tree

***l* family**

bl blue
cl clown
fl flag
gl glass
pl play

***s* family**

sc scarf
scr scrap
sk skip
sl slide
sm smile
sn snap
sp spoon
spr spray
st stop
str street

***w* family**

dw dwell
sw swim
tw twin
qu quick (/kw/)
squ squirrel

final blends

lb bulb
ld hold
lk milk
lt belt
nd hand
nk pink
nt went

Two consonants-One sound

double consonants (one silent letter)

bb rabbit
dd add
ff cuff
gg egg
ll ball
nn inn
ss dress
zz fuzz

***h* digraphs (*new* sound)**

ch chip, each
chef
school
gh —, laugh
ph phone, graph
sh ship, dish
th this, breathe
thin, breath

digraph with silent letters

ck duck
dge —, fudge
gh ghost
gn gnat, sign
kn knock
ng ring
tch —, match
wr write
wh what
who

In a *consonant digraph*, two consonant letters typically represent one sound. The digraph may represent either a new or a familiar consonant sound. For example, digraphs made with the letter *h*, such as *sh*, do not represent the common sounds of *s* or *h*, but instead is a new phoneme. In contrast, silent letter digraphs, such as *kn* or *ck* (***knock***), include a familiar consonant sound and a silent letter (in *kn*, the *k* is silent and the *n* is sounded).

Onsets. Syllables divide into two parts: *onsets* and *rimes*. The consonant(s) found at the beginning of a syllable, preceding the vowel, is called the *onset*. In the word *bake*, the letter *b* is the onset of the syllable and occurs before *ake*, which is the *rime*, the rhyming portion of the syllable. Working with onsets and rimes can be a productive way to help children learn phonics at the syllable level and see letter patterns as units of sound.

Onsets can be single or double consonants, but they always occur before the vowel in the syllable. What letters represent the onsets in the following words?

mail street bump when

The onsets are ***m**-ail*, ***str**-eet*, ***b**-ump*, and ***wh**-en*. The onsets are the same single and double initial consonant patterns we have been discussing. We will return to onsets as we discuss the development of students' knowledge about vowels and vowel patterns.

Vowel Patterns

Students must know the following to understand vowel patterns in words:

- Vowels are letters that vary and represent phonemes that are long (sound names the vowel letter), short (as in *bag, beg, big, bog, bug*), or neither.
- The position of letters in words influences the vowel's sound. For example, in the word *cane* we cannot know the sound of the letter *a* until we look past it and see the letter *e* at the end that indicates the possibility of a long vowel pattern.
- Some vowel patterns represent a consistent sound (*ai* is usually always long *a*), while other patterns (*ea* in *meat, head, steak*) may represent one of several sounds.
- In multisyllable words the sounds that vowels represent in unstressed syllables are often not the expected sounds. For example, the *e* in *pen'-cil* has the expected sound of short *e*, but the *i* in the unstressed syllable is sounded like short *u* instead of short *i*.

Like consonants, vowels can be divided into two basic categories, single and double, as shown in Figures 4.1 and 4.3. Within each category there are short vowel patterns, long vowel patterns, and patterns that are neither short nor long (Figure 4.3).

Single Vowels. Single vowels can represent a variety of phonemes:

- *Short vowel* patterns are often found in closed syllables that end with a consonant, such as ***u**p*, *b**i**g*, *and st**a**mp*.
- *Long vowel* patterns are often found in open syllables that end with a vowel, such as *m**e*** or *g**a**me*.
- *R-controlled single vowel* patterns are found in syllables in which the letter *r* follows a single long or short vowel and modifies its sound, such as *c**ar***, *c**are***, *b**ir**d*, *st**ore***, *f**ur***.

Figure 4.3 Overview of vowel patterns

Single Vowels			Double Vowels		
Short	**Long**	**Neither long nor short**	**Long— consistent**	**Long–short vary**	**Neither long nor short**
vc cvc	**cv, vce**	***r*-controlled**	***vowel digraph***	***vowel diphthong***	***diphthong***
a at bag	*a* cake	*ar* car	*ai* rain	*ea* meat	*au* haul
e egg, bed	*e* me	*er* her	*ay* may	bread	*aw* saw
i in, hit	*i* hide	*ir* bird	*ee* feet	great	*oi* oil
o on, log	*o* go, rope	*or* for	*igh* night	*ei* vein	*oy* boy
u up, sun	*u* cute	*ur* fur	*oa* boat	ceiling	*oo* boot
	rude	*are* care		*ey* key	foot
	y fly (/i/)	*ere* here		they	*ou* through
	baby (/e/)	there		*ie* pie	round
		ire fire		chief	*ow* grow
		ore horse		*ou* soul	cow
		ure sure		young	*ui* fruit
					ue blue
					ew flew
					***r*-controlled**
					air fair
					ear hear
					bear
					learn
					eer peer
					oar roar

Double Vowels. Double vowels can represent a variety of phonemes:

- *Vowel digraphs* are two vowels or a vowel plus a semi-vowel (a consonant that takes on the characteristics of a vowel, usually *w* or *y*) that represent one phoneme that is usually either a long or short vowel sound, such as ***rain**, **they**, **pie**, **boat**, or **soul**.*
- *Diphthongs* are two vowels or one vowel with a semi-vowel in which one vowel sound slides into another, producing a phoneme that is often neither long nor short, as in ***saw** and **tool**.*
- *R-controlled double vowel* patterns are vowel digraphs and diphthongs followed by the letter *r* that modify the vowel sound, such as ***fair**, **steer**, or **oar**.*

Rimes. The rime portion of a syllable, such as *ake* in **bake,** provides more stable and predictable vowel patterns. Adams (1990) suggests that vowel sounds are more stable and predictable when they are a part of rimes than when they are viewed in isolation, and that of the 286 phonograms that appear in primary grade texts, 95 percent were pronounced the same in every word in which they appeared.

To support word learning for less experienced readers, nearly 500 words can be made from 37 rimes (Wylie & Durrell, 1970; Stahl, 1992):

	a		***e***		***i***		***o***	***u***
-ack	*-ame*	*-ash*	*-eat*	*-ice*	*-ill*	*-ink*	*-ock*	*-uck*
-ail	*-an*	*-at*	*-ell*	*-ick*	*-in*	*-ip*	*-oke*	*-ug*
-ain	*-ank*	*-ate*	*-est*	*-ide*	*-ine*	*-ir*	*-op*	*-ump*
-ale	*-ap*	*-aw*		*-ight*	*-ing*		*-or*	*-unk*
-ake		*-ay*					*-ore*	

In contrast to the great variability that Clymer (1963) found in vowel generalizations used in vocabulary in basal reading materials, rimes offer promise for helping students see vowel patterns as more predictable and useful in unfamiliar words. Using rimes, students learn to work from syllables to phonemes and to see the importance of the position of letters within a syllable. Rimes also offer a means of teaching spelling patterns that correspond to frequent, coherent, syllabic units needed in writing.

STRUCTURAL PATTERNS

Structural patterns, along with phonics patterns, are the visual cues that we use to read words. While phonics patterns enable us to understand letter–sound relationships within syllables, structural patterns enable us to break apart multisyllable words to find units of meaning and to more efficiently apply our knowledge of phonics. Structural words are made from combinations of base words and affixes, as shown in Figure 4.4.

Morphemes, such as base words, roots, and affixes, are the meaningful units that contribute to the overall meaning of multisyllable words. Morphemes are either free or bound. *Free* morphemes function as words without needing to be attached to other morphemes, while *bound* morphemes must be attached to at least one other morpheme to make a recognizable word.

Working with the structure of words helps us enlarge both our sight vocabulary and our meaning vocabulary. Vocabulary is learned best when we see how words are related to one another (Beck, Perfetti, & McKeown, 1982). Focusing on the structure of words requires us to consider the meaning of word parts as we also consider the sound of those parts.

Studying structural patterns, such as those shown in Figure 4.5, helps us see that multisyllable words are made from combinations of base words/roots and affixes, as in the following examples:

Figure 4.4 Overview of structural patterns

Structural Patterns			
Base + Base		**Base + Affix**	
Compound Words	Contractions	Prefixes	Suffixes
		Independent Dependent	Inflectional Derivational

base + base	= *over* + *drawn* or *shouldn't*
base + affix	= *jump* + *ing* or *care* + *ful*
affix + base/root	= *dis* + *obey* or *com* + *bine*
affix + base + affix	= *dis* + *loyal* + *ty*
base + affix + affix	= *care* + *ful* + *ly*
affix + base + affix + affix	= *un* + *self* + *ish* + *ly*

Multisyllabic words contain a base word or a root. *Base words* are free morphemes and can function as words by themselves or may have affixes attached to create words with related meanings. A *root* can also form the base of a word, but will be a bound morpheme, such as "bine" rather than a free morpheme such as *obey*. To understand the meaning of a multisyllabic word, we must be able to identify the meaning of the base word or root.

Affixes are bound morphemes that can be divided into two categories, prefixes and suffixes. *Prefixes* are morphemes added before a base word or root, while *suffixes* are morphemes that are added after. Prefixes are either independent or dependent. A prefix is independent if it is attached to a word, as in ***dis****obey*. A prefix is dependent if it is attached to a morpheme, as in ***com****bine.*

The terms *independent* and *dependent* actually refer to the base word or root being able to function without the prefix, as shown in Figure 4.5. This is an important distinction for readers who are trying to use knowledge of structural patterns to determine the pronunciation and meaning of new words. The meaning of *disobey* can be found by combining the meaning of the base word *obey* with the meaning of the independent prefix *dis*. In contrast, the meaning of words with dependent prefixes cannot be determined by the same structural thinking strategy. We know the meaning of *combine* as a whole word that we have used in meaningful contexts, and not by relating the meanings of *com* + *bine.*

Suffixes can be inflectional or derivational. *Inflectional* suffixes do not change the essential meaning or usage of a base word, but rather affect number or possession of nouns, tense of verbs, or comparison or degree of adjectives. For example, in Figure 4.5, *dog* + *s* changes the number of dogs, *jump* + *ed* changes the time of the action, and *tall* + *er* describes a comparison of height. Adding the inflectional suffix did not change the part of speech or usage of the base word, so determining the overall meaning is relatively easy.

In comparison, *derivational* suffixes do affect the meaning and usage of base words, and add greatly to the richness of language. Adding a derivational suffix will usually change the part of speech of a base word, thereby changing the way that the word may be used. If we know the meaning of the base word and the suffix, we are able to use a strategy similar to the one used with independent prefixes. For example, if we know the meaning of *pain* and *less,* we can determine the meaning of *painless.* Notice how the usage of the base word changes: *pain* is a noun, while *painless* is an adjective. The use of derivational suffixes gives writers and speakers power to describe situations more clearly.

The components of word knowledge—sight words, context clues, phonics patterns, and structural patterns—enable readers to interact with the ideas and images of others. During the middle grades, students must become successful and confident users of these components to be able to make meaning with words and to continually add to their knowledge of words. Being able to unlock words in print that are already in one's speaking vocabulary opens the door for students to become powerful users of language.

Figure 4.5 Structural patterns

Base + Base		Base + Affix(es)	
Compound Words	**Contractions**	**Prefixes**	**Suffixes**
literal meaning concrete object *dog + house* *bed + room* *gold + fish* *police + man* *play + ground* **literal meaning, not concrete** *bed + time* *after + noon* *play + time* *eye + sight* *wild + life* **known words, implied/accepted meaning** *every + one* *out + side* *run + away* *over + drawn* *fall + out* *soft + ware* *butter + fly*	***not* family** *are + not = aren't* *can + not = can't* *have + not = haven't* *do + not = don't* *will + not = won't* *would + not = wouldn't* *could + not = couldn't* *should + not = shouldn't* ***are* family** *you + are = you're* *they + are = they're* *we + are = we're* ***will* family** *I + will = I'll* *you + will = you'll* *we + will = we'll* *they + will = they'll* ***is* family** *he + is = he's* *she + is = she's* *it + is = it's* *I + am = I'm* **have family** *I + have = I've* *you + have = you've* *we + have = we've* *they + have = they've*	***independent— not bound to base*** *dis* — *dis*obey *en* — *en*joy *for* — *for*give *fore* — *fore*told *im* — *im*pure *in* — *in*active *inter* — *inter*view *mis* — *mis*lead *non* — *non*stop *pre** — *pre*view *re* — *re*pay *un* — *un*do **dependent— bound to base/root** *com* — *com*bine *con* — *con*cern *de* — *de*cide *ex* — *ex*cuse *pre** — *pre*fer *pro* — *pro*cess *can be both independent and dependent	**inflectional nouns** *s* — *dog + s* *es* — *dish + es* *horse + es* *'s* — one *boy's* two *boys'* ***verbs*** *s* — *jump + s* *ed* — *jump + ed* *bat + t + ed* *bak + ed* *ing* — *jump + ing* *hit + t + ing* *bake + ing* **adjective** *er* — *tall + er* *big + g + er* *pretty + er* *nice + er* *est* — *tall + est* *big + g + est* *pretty + est* *nice + est* ***derivational*** *able* — comfort*able* *ance* — allow*ance* *ess* — princ*ess* *ful* — care*ful* *ify* — class*ify* *ion* — addit*ion*, divis*ion* *ish* — fool*ish* *ism* — critic*ism* *ist* — final*ist* *ity* — abil*ity* *ive* — product*ive* *ize* — organ*ize* *less* — pain*less* *ly* — friend*ly* *ment* — pay*ment* *ness* — kind*ness* *ogy* — biol*ogy* *ous* — joy*ous*

We will now use our knowledge of sight words, context, phonics, and structural patterns to see how each fits into students' development, exploring when we might expect them to acquire, absorb, and successfully work with these components. One focus of Part Two will be instructional approaches for teaching each component.

Developmental Stages of Word Knowledge

Knowledge about words develops in identifiable stages that we may correlate with the stages of reading development introduced in Chapter 2 (Henderson & Beers, 1980; Morris, 1981; Bear & Barone, 1989; Henderson, 1985; Templeton, 1991; Temple, Nathan, Temple, and Burris, 1993):

Reading Stages	*Correlated Word Knowledge Stages*
Emerging	Prephonemic Phonemic
Developing	Letter-name Within-word pattern
Transitional	Syllable juncture Derivational constancy
Mature	Derivational constancy

Each stage of word knowledge is characterized by the development of progressively refined concepts about written language.

Emerging readers and writers in the prephonemic stage learn the following:

- Print has meaning.
- Print is made of symbols.
- Symbols can be used to represent spoken words.

Emerging readers and writers in the phonemic stage learn the following:

- Sounds in words can be segmented and heard.
- Letters can represent the beginning and ending sounds in words.
- English is read and written from left to right.

Developing readers and writers in the letter-name stage learn the following:

- Each sound part in a word can be represented by one or more letters.
- Names of letters contain clues to the sounds they represent.

Developing readers and writers in the within-word pattern stage learn the following:

- Certain letters, especially vowel letters, can represent more than one sound.
- Some letter patterns include silent letters that can serve as visual clues to vowel sounds.
- The placement of letters within a syllable can be a clue to the sounds they represent.

Transitional readers and writers in the syllable juncture stage learn the following:

- Longer words have syllables, or units of sound and meaning, and each syllable includes a vowel sound.
- Multisyllable words can be segmented into the syllable patterns learned in letter-name and within-word pattern stages.

- Multisyllable words can have parts, such as prefixes and suffixes, that contribute to meaning.
- Multisyllable words can be made of meaning units, sound units, or a combination of both.
- Joining syllables to make words can cause the spelling of the base word/root to change through dropping, doubling, or changing letters.
- Joining syllables to make words can cause changes in the pronunciation of vowels within some syllables.

Transitional and mature readers and writers in the derivational constancy stage learn the following:

- Words related in meaning are often related in spelling.
- The joining of some syllables can cause a change in the pronunciation of the base word/root.
- Combining the meaning of word parts contributes to the overall meaning of words.

In a typical middle grade classroom, reading and writing levels will range several years above and below the official grade level. For example, fourth-grade students may range from second-grade to sixth-grade reading levels; eighth-grade students may range from fourth grade to twelfth. It is possible to have a few students outside of these ranges of development due to second language or other learning challenges. We focus here on the stages of word knowledge development in which we are likely to find most middle grade students: within-word pattern, syllable juncture, and derivational constancy. We discuss the letter-name stage for background knowledge in the early development of vowels. For a more in-depth treatment of earlier stages, see my *Developing Competent Readers and Writers in the Primary Grades* (Merrill/Prentice Hall, 1996).

Figure 4.6 provides an overview of the early stages of word knowledge development. Phonic and structural elements presented in Figures 4.2, 4.3, and 4.5 have been sequenced for instruction within appropriate stages. It may be helpful for you to refer to these figures as we consider development of word knowledge during each stage.

One thing to keep in mind in each stage is the difference between reading vocabulary and writing vocabulary. Students will usually be able to read letter-sound or structural patterns before they will be able to accurately write the same patterns from memory. The patterns that are used frequently in instructional reading materials will soon be the patterns that you can analyze and practice in writing.

Letter-Name Stage

Letter-name readers and writers focus intently on graphic (letter) information. Chall (1979, 1983) describes this stage as being "glued to print" because of the energy devoted to word recognition. In this stage, students begin to recognize words out of context (Mason, 1980). In addition, they begin to use knowledge of letter-sound correspondences to read and write words (Chall, 1979; Ehri, 1987) and discover that there is a fairly systematic relationship between letters and sounds (Gough & Hillinger, 1980).

During the letter-name stage students discover that there are more phonemes in words than just beginning and ending consonant sounds, and they search for letters to represent each sound as they hear. During this stage students turn to the initial consonant knowledge gained during the phonemic stage and try to use the correspondence

Figure 4.6 Early stages of word knowledge development

Word knowledge stages	Focus during the stage
Prephonemic (birth–pre-K)	print has meaning, such as environmental print writing is not connected to letter–sound patterns
Phonemic (pre-K–early 1st) read—meaningful context high meaning (names) write—letter strings, initial and/or final consonants for words	print has rules early concept of word in print letters have names words contain separate sounds letters represent sounds in words (*b, bd = bed*)
Letter-name (early/mid 1st –late 1st) read—one-syllable and some two-syllable words "glued to print" word-by-word oral readers write—one-syllable words with short vowels	all sounds in a word can be represented by letters letter names can be clues to sounds initial and final consonants short vowels (*a, i, o, u, e*) initial consonant blend families (*br, cl, st*) initial and final consonant digraphs with *h* (*sh, th, ch*) begin to notice long vowel markers

between letter names and some phonemes to represent all phonemes in words, including vowels. For example, when a letter-name child is searching for a way to represent the middle of ***bed*** (they already know /b/ and /d/) the letter name that most closely matches the sound of /e/ in *bed* is the letter name *a*, so they write ***bad***.

Temple et al. (1993) explain this phenomenon, called *substitutions:*

> When children seek to spell a long or tense vowel, they have no trouble finding a letter to represent it . . . because the names of the vowel letters, A, E, I, O, U are long or tense themselves. But when they want to spell a short or lax vowel trouble ensues because there are no short or lax letter names. *The strategy most children employ in such a case is to find the long (tense) letter name that is made in the same place in the mouth as the short (lax) vowel they wish to spell.* (p. 73)

Other common vowel associations during this stage, influenced by letter names and the location of specific vowels in the mouth, are as follows:

- *red* (short *e*) may be written as *rad*
- *bit* (short *i*) may be written as *bet*
- *hot* (short *o*) may be written as *hit*
- *nut* (short *u*) may be written as *not*

If we isolate the sound of a short vowel, such as the *i* in ***bit,*** we hear the *name* (not the sound) of the letter *e*. Remember, a student in the letter-name stage is trying to use the names of letters as a clue to the sounds in writing.

Independent writing during the letter-name stage shows awareness of single short vowels, but not necessarily conventional spellings of all short vowel words. Long vowel patterns, such as a silent vowel marker, are usually absent. For example, the word *make* typically is written as *mak*. Single consonants are used more consistently than in the phonemic stage. Double consonants, however, are used consistently only at the onset of a syllable. Letter-name spellers are not sure how to represent more than one syllable. For example, letter-name writers might spell in the following ways (see Bear & Barone, 1989). The representative spellings are shown in general order as they might occur from early to late letter-name stage:

bed—*bad, bed*
ship—*sep, shep, ship*
drive—*griv, driv*
bump—*bop, bup, bomp*
when—*wan, win, wen, whan*
train—*chran, tan, tran, teran*
closet—*clast, clost, clozt*
chase—*tas, cas, chas, chass*
float—*fot, flot, flott*
beaches—*bechs, becis, behis*

Your Turn

As you look at the preceding spelling samples, what do you notice? What letter–sound relationships are under students' control and represented conventionally? What patterns have they noticed in reading and are attempting in writing?

Early in the stage single consonants, beginning and ending, are used fairly consistently and conventionally. This is knowledge that students bring from the phonemic stage. Double consonant patterns, such as *h* digraphs and blends, begin to appear during the later part of the stage and move toward convention. Short vowels are also represented and move toward convention as the stage progresses. Long vowel markers are typically absent, causing long vowel words to look like short vowel patterns.

■

Within-Word Pattern Stage

As the name of this stage suggests, the focus is on letter-sound patterns within words, particularly long vowel and varying vowel patterns. By the time that students begin to focus on within-word patterns they are well into the developing reader stage and becoming proficient at reading single-syllable words with short vowels. An overview of the stage is shown in Figure 4.7.

Vowel patterns are the focus of the within-word pattern stage:

- Single long vowels with a silent *e* as a visual signal to a long vowel
- Vowel digraphs that represent one vowel sound
- Diphthongs that represent a vowel sound that is neither long nor short
- Vowels that are modified by consonants, especially *r*-controlled

The concept of silent letters, both vowels and consonants, is one focus of this stage. In the previous stages emphasis was on the concept that letters represented sounds. Now students learn that letters can also represent silence, or no sound.

Figure 4.7 Overview of within-word pattern stage

Word Knowledge Stage	Focus of Learning in the Stage
Within-word pattern (late 1st–early 3rd) read—one-, two-, and some three-syllable words moving toward silent reading some difficulty moving between oral and silent write—one-syllable words with long and varying vowels	silent *e* (*a_e, i_e, o_e, u_e, e_e*) consistent long double vowels (*ai, ay, ee, igh, oa*) double and variant consonants (*dd, ff, gg, ll, ss, zz, c, g, s*) final blends (*nt, lk, mp*) *r*-controlled, single vowel (*ar, er, ir, or, ur*) long and short double vowels (*ea, ei, ey, ie, ou*) digraphs with silent letters (*wr, kn, wh*) *r*-controlled, single long vowel (*are, ere, ire, ore, ure*) double vowels, variant (*au, aw, oi, oy, oo, oe, ow, ou, ui, ue, ew*) *r*-controlled, double vowel (*air, ear, eer, oar*)

While vowel mastery will occupy much of the instructional time in this stage, we also begin to emphasize seeing structural patterns in words. Students in this stage do the following:

- Begin to use structural units to identify words
- Recognize contractions as the combination of two base words (*can* + *not* = *can't*)
- Become more proficient at using inflected suffixes that do not change base words (*jump* + *ing*)
- Become aware of the meaning of some derivational suffixes attached to base words
- Become aware of the meaning of some independent prefixes attached to base words

With the strides made in knowledge of phonics and structural patterns, within-word pattern readers are better at self-monitoring and their using context to confirm word identification is becoming more automatic. During this stage students often move from oral to silent reading.

Independent writing during the within-word pattern stage should show consistency with short vowels and a growing awareness of long vowel patterns. Single consonants should be mastered and double consonants become more consistent. Within-word pattern spellers are more consistent in representing vowels in each syllable, but spelling changes to base words (*popping*) are typically not represented. The following words represent writing characteristic of students in the within-word pattern stage (see Bear & Barone, 1989):

bed—*bed*	***train***—*trane, traen, train*
ship—*ship*	***closet***—*clozit, closit*
drive—*drive, drieve*	***chase***—*chais, chase*
bump—*bump*	***float***—*flowt, flote, float*
when—*wen, when*	***beaches***—*bechis, beechis, beaches*

Your Turn

As you look at the preceding spelling samples, what do you notice? What letter–sound relationships are under students' control and represented conventionally? What patterns have they noticed in reading and are attempting in writing? What new knowledge is represented that was not present during the letter-name stage?

My Turn

As we look across the within-word pattern writing samples, note that single and double consonants become consistent and conventional. What about the vowels? Short vowels are used conventionally and long vowels either consistently have some type of vowel marker or are spelled conventionally in one-syllable words but not as consistently in two-syllable words. Within-word pattern writers continue to have some difficulty crossing the division between syllables.

Syllable Juncture Stage

As the name implies, the focus of this stage is on joining syllables to make complex words. Students come to the syllable juncture stage knowing how to read and write fairly proficiently at the syllable level. Instruction during this stage must focus on helping students transfer what they know about single syllables to multisyllable words, particularly words in which bases and affixes are altered in the joining of syllables. Figure 4.8 presents an overview of this stage. Becoming comfortable with multisyllable words is absolutely essential if students are ever to break into rapid mature reading.

During this stage, the emphasis on combining structural units to form related words enables students to rapidly expand their reading and writing vocabularies. Students read and write words that represent different parts of speech but have related meanings. For example, the spelling of the base word *joy* is examined in within-word pattern stage. During the syllable juncture stage, students explore words and meanings by adding affixes to base words, such as *en**joy**, **joy**ous, **joy**ful, en**joy**able,* and *en**joy**ment.*

Spelling during the syllable juncture stage should show mastery of most single-syllable spellings from the letter-name and within-word pattern stages and greater control over multisyllable spellings. One focus of this stage is noticing the difference between words in which base words remain the same when adding affixes and words in which base words change. For example, in Figure 4.5, find the inflectional suffixes in the righthand column. Notice that when suffixes are added to base words that end with a vowel, that vowel is dropped. Notice also that when the base word has a short vowel sound and ends with a single consonant, the single consonant is doubled to preserve

Figure 4.8 Overview of syllable juncture stage

Word Knowledge Stage	Focus of Learning in the Stage
Syllable juncture (early 3rd–6th) read—multisyllable words, phonetic and structural solidifying silent reading becoming flexible readers write—two- and some three-syllable words, structural and phonetic	base + base (compound words, contractions) base + inflected suffix, no change to base (*s, es, ed, ing*) independent prefix + base (*untie*) base + inflected suffix, base changes (consonant double, *e* drop, *y* to *i*) base + derivational suffix (no pronunciation change) complex phonetic patterns (*caught*) phonetic syllable patterns, including schwa V/CV—*ci/der* VC/CV—*mar/ket* VC/V—*riv/er* c + le—wig/gle tri/ple prefix + base + suffix (no pronunciation change)

the short vowel sound. These are examples of changes to base words that students learn to write conventionally during this stage.

Students also begin to discriminate between words that are made primarily of structural units and words that are made of phonic units. Students learn how to generalize their knowledge of one-syllable phonic patterns to words of more than one syllable. For example, *river* is a two-syllable phonic word, made of two closed syllables *riv* + *er*. The first syllable, *riv*, is a CVC pattern with a short vowel between two consonants. The second syllable, *er*, is an *r*-controlled vowel pattern. The first syllable pattern is learned during the letter-name stage and the second syllable pattern is learned during the within-word pattern stage.

Toward the later part of this stage students must be guided to examine multisyllable words for phonic patterns they already know, to use these patterns effectively when unfamiliar words are encountered. In a multisyllable phonic pattern the emphasis that each syllable receives influences the vowel sound produced. A single vowel in an unaccented syllable often is sounded as a *schwa*, an "uh" sound similar to short *u* regardless of the letter used to spell the sound. Each of the following words has a schwa sound in the unaccented syllable: ***a**-bout', pen'-**ci**l, and sec'-**o**nd.*

The following words represent writing that is characteristic of students in the syllable juncture stage (see Bear & Barone, 1989):

closet—*clozet, closet*

beaches—*beachis, beaches*

preparing—*praparing, prepairing, preparing*

popping—*poping, popping*
cattle—*catle, catel, cattel, cattle*
caught—*caut, caught*
inspection—*inspecshun, inspecsion, inspection*
puncture—*punksher, punture, puncture*
cellar—*seller, celler, cellar*
pleasure—*plesher, plesour, plesure, pleasure*
squirrel—*scqoril, sqarel, squirle, squirrel*
fortunate—*forchenut, fortunet, fortunate*

As you look at the preceding spelling samples, what do you notice? What letter-sound relationships are under students' control and represented conventionally? What patterns have they noticed in reading and are attempting in writing? What new knowledge is represented in this stage that was not represented during the letter-name or within-word pattern stages?

Let's look first at the spelling of structural words. When base words can be clearly heard, as in *beaches,* the base is often spelled conventionally before the affixes. Prefixes that can be clearly heard typically are spelled conventionally before suffixes (*inspection*). Words without a change to the base (*beaches*) are spelled conventionally before words with a change to the base word (*pop-p-ing, pre-par(e)-ing*).

In phonic words, the location of letters within each syllable influences the sounds represented. For example, the syllables in *closet* and *pleasure* are *clos'-et* and *pleas'-ure.* Students must remember from the within-word pattern stage that when the letter *s* occurs at the end of the syllable it can have a *z* sound.

In addition, a single vowel in an unaccented syllable typically represents a schwa, or short *u* sound, regardless of the vowel letter. Words such as *cattle, cellar,* and *squirrel* present challenges to writers because the vowel in the unaccented syllable is not written the way that it sounds. The second syllables of *cat'-tle, cel'-lar,* and *squir'-rel* are unaccented. The vowel in the second syllable takes on the sound of short *u,* giving us the following pronunciation: cat'_l, sel'_r, and squer'_l.

Derivational Constancy Stage

The final stage of word knowledge development focuses on structural meaning of words, giving students greater flexibility as readers and writers. Figure 4.9 presents an overview of this stage.

In this stage, students encounter more words with prefixes, particularly dependent prefixes. Remember, independent prefixes are attached to bases that are words and have meaning when they stand alone, without the prefix (*re* + *view*). In contrast, dependent prefixes must be attached to the base to make a meaningful word (*con* + *cern*).

The main difference between these two types of prefixes is the thinking strategies that we as readers must use to find meaning. With independent prefixes, we simply need to think about how the meaning of the prefix changes the meaning of the familiar base word:

Figure 4.9 Overview of derivational constancy stage

Word Knowledge Stage	Focus of Learning in the Stage
Derivational constancy (6th–adult) read—multisyllable words mature flexible reading read for personal and vocational purposes write—multisyllable words	dependent prefix + root (con + cern) Pronunciation changes change in stressed syllable *com pose', com' po si tion* *met' al, me tal' lic* change in syllable division *sign, sig' nal, sig' na ture* *grave, grav' i ty* Greek combining forms number prefixes (*mono, bi, tri*) scientific forms (*tele-, -meter, thermo-, astro-, -graph*) Latin roots and related words spect (to look)—spectator, inspection, spectacles Assimilated prefixe *ad + tract = attract* *in + mobile = immobile*

re—again + *view*—to look =

review—to look again

With a dependent prefix, the meaning of the base word is not merely combined with the prefix. The base of a dependent prefix often has little meaning to us in isolation:

con—with + *cern*—to regard =

concern—to relate or belong to

We usually know the meaning of words with dependent prefixes because we know the meaning of the prefix and root combined, and not the separate parts.

In this stage students also study the relationship among pronunciation, spelling, and meaning of words. When affixes are added to base words and roots, a number of phenomena occur that result in pronunciation and spelling changes. Notice what happens to the base of each of the following words:

exclaim	*flame*	*define*
exclamation	*flammable*	*definition*

At least three things can occur when a suffix is added: a spelling change occurs, different syllable(s) are stressed, and vowel or consonant sounds change. Consider the preceding word pairs again. What changes occurred when suffixes were added?

ex-claim'	*flame*	*de-fine'*
ex'-cla-ma'-tion	*flam'-ma-ble*	*def'-i-ni'-tion*

In each word, the long vowel markers are gone. There is also a change in the syllable that is stressed. In English, when a single vowel is not stressed with the voice, the vowel in that syllable can change its pronunciation and becomes a schwa.

Compare the changes in the preceding words to the following word pairs. Notice the changes in spelling and pronunciation.

justice	*mercy*	*tense*
justify	*merciful*	*tension*

Check your thinking:

jus'-tice	*mer'-cy*	*tense'*
jus'-ti-fy	*mer'-ci-ful*	*ten'-sion*

Each pair retains its pronunciation of the first vowel, which is the strongest clue to spelling the affixed word. The first syllable retains the stress, so the pronunciation of the first vowel is unchanged. The spelling change in *mer**ci**ful* retains the soft *c* sound (*cy–ci*). The spelling change in *ten**si**on* (*se–si*) shifts the *s* sound to *sh*.

In addition to the preceding examples, the following patterns merit study when adding affixes:

- Silent letters become sounded when they begin or end a syllable:

*si**g**n*	*si**g**'-na-ture*
*bom**b***	*bom-**b**ard'*

- Long vowels become short when the silent *e* is dropped:

*s**a**ne*	*s**a**n'-i-ty*
*c**o**ne*	*c**o**n'-ic*
*di-v**i**ne'*	*di-v**i**n'-i-ty*

- Long vowels become a schwa when *e* is dropped and the syllable is not stressed:

*com-p**o**se'*	*com-p**o**-si'-tion*
*de-f**i**ne'*	*de-f**i**-ni'-tion*

- A schwa becomes a short vowel in a stressed syllable

*lo'-c**a**l*	*lo-c**a**l'-i-ty*
*im'-**a**ge*	*im-**a**g'-ine*

Greek combining forms and Latin roots add richness to our language and should be studied during the middle grades. Greek combining forms are easily recognized and their meaning inferred. The Greek number prefixes (*mono, bi, tri, quad*) are usually familiar to students. Analysis of familiar words can show students their usefulness. For example, *mono* combines with other bases and roots to form such words as *monologue, monopoly, monorail, monotone,* and *monotonous.* Science exposes readers to other Greek forms such as *thermo, photo, tele, meter, graph,* and *astro* that appear frequently in middle grade texts. The principles of pronunciation–spelling relationships discussed earlier provide a base for students to study Greek combining forms in such words as *telegraph, telegraphy,* and *telegraphic.*

Latin roots are not always as clearly identifiable. Their study should be in groupings of words related by their root. For example, one grouping might be words with the root *spect*—*in***spect**, **spect***ator,* **spect***acles, in***spect***ion, and re***spect.** Examining related words can lead students to more sophisticated study of assimilated prefixes, such as *in + luminate = illuminate.* To ease pronunciation, certain prefixes have become assimilated into the beginning of the root. For example, the prefix *ad* (to, toward) takes on the beginning sound of the root in the words *account, approve,* and *assume.* In the word *immobile,* the prefix *in* becomes *im* to facilitate pronunciation.

Derivational constancy is the stage in which mature readers and writers will remain throughout life. As we encounter varied forms of written language, we learn to read and write many new words. In addition, new words are added to our spoken language as society continues to change. The more that we notice the meaningful units, or morphemes, in these new words, the more likely we are to build mental relationships between new words and words we already know. Such relationships help us add to our storehouse of words for communicating with others.

Monitoring Growth in Word Knowledge

Studying growth in students' developmental knowledge of words provides a frame of reference for assessment and evaluation. What we intend to evaluate will guide the data we collect for assessment. Careful observation of reading and writing behavior, along with samples of reading and writing, enable us to ask important questions about students' growth in word knowledge.

Questions to Guide Evaluation of Word Knowledge

The questions that we might ask about students' growth in word knowledge will change across stages of development. The answers to these questions come as we consider word knowledge instruction in Part II, particularly in Chapter 10.

In the within-word pattern stage, we want to ask the following questions:

- Do students' sight vocabularies show marked increase over the letter-name stage?
- Do students' reading and writing reflect a growing knowledge of single- and double-vowel patterns? What behaviors suggest that students understand that some letters in English will be silent and may serve as markers for a vowel in the same syllable?
- How consistently are students able to use context plus consonant, vowel, or structural knowledge to read unfamiliar words?
- How consistently are students able to read base words within structural patterns in which the base does not change?

In the syllable juncture stage, we want to ask the following questions:

- Does each student have a large enough sight vocabulary to read fluently in appropriate text?
- Are students able to use structural knowledge with words in which the base has been changed by the joining of syllables? What behaviors have we observed?
- Are students beginning to integrate phonics and structural patterns to decode unfamiliar multisyllable words?
- Are students becoming more consistent in conventionally representing familiar syllables in two- and three-syllable words?

In the derivational constancy stage, we want to ask the following questions:

- What behaviors suggest that students are ready to break into mature reading?

- What behaviors suggest that students are developing power with words and have developed independent learning strategies?
- What behaviors suggest that students relate meaning, spelling, and pronunciation when reading and writing unfamiliar words?

We gather data to address these questions by observing students' behavior during reading and writing activities, conferring with students about their reading and writing, and collecting samples of reading and writing over time.

Samples of Word Recognition in Context

To evaluate a student's knowledge of words in the context of text, we may make a running record (Clay, 1979, 1985) of each student's oral reading. As a student reads orally, we use a variety of symbols to show the various strategies the student uses in a variety of familiar and unfamiliar texts. The running record shows patterns of reading behavior, particularly the strategies on which a student relies most often to make meaning. The running record also shows which texts are independent, instructional and frustration level for a student (running records are discussed in Chapter 8).

Samples of Word Recognition in Isolation

Another check of growth in word recognition is to present words in isolation for students to read. When students read words in isolation, they may use only one of the three cuing systems as a check for accuracy, the visual. Meaning (context) and structure (grammar), the cuing systems most used by proficient readers, cannot aid them in reading words in isolation. Remember also that accurate use of visual cues constitutes only the accurate recognition of words, and is not in itself reading. In reading, recognized words must be linked together into cohesive thoughts through the use of meaning and structure cues.

To check a student's proficiency in word recognition, we use both phonemes (*b*) and words (*bath*) in isolation. Having students read words in isolation can provide clues to students' knowledge of phonic and structural patterns.

Samples of Word Knowledge through Focused Writing

To complement what running records and word recognition assessments may show about students' growth in reading words, we ask individual students to write a carefully selected sample of words that represent various stages of word knowledge development. When students write the same words several times over the course of a school year, we may easily compare samples and see clearly any growth in word knowledge.

In a student's focused writing sample, we evaluate each word for the stage of word knowledge it represents. It is important also to determine what the overall sample shows about a student's knowledge of words. As we discuss the stages of development, remember that all concepts within a stage may not develop evenly or in an exact sequence.

Respecting Diversity in Word Knowledge

Experiences in and out of school set students apart from one another (Allington, 1994). By the middle grades, students have a great many experiences that contribute both positively and negatively to their success, or lack of success, in reading and writing. Students who come to the classroom with less experience with English will have had less opportunity to think in ways that are necessary for learning words and thinking about text in the language.

One of the most significant differences between students who are successful in reading and writing and those who are not is time—the time spent practicing word knowledge in meaningful reading and writing. As with other endeavors, students who practice more frequently are likely to get better at using their skills. To help all students be successful, we should consider ways to increase the time students spend actually reading and writing both inside and outside of school.

TAKE A MOMENT AND REFLECT

Knowledge of words develops in identifiable stages.

The basic components of word knowledge development are:

sight words
context clues
phonics patterns
structural patterns

Sight words are:

- words that are recognized automatically
- stored in memory by linking distinctive spelling features to the phonological (speech sound) structure of words in memory
- necessary for fluent reading
- gained through extensive and intensive reading

Using context:

- is deriving meaning from surrounding text
- should be the main checking system for decoding
- is a thinking strategy already known in spoken language

Phonics patterns include consonant and vowel elements.

- Consonants can be:
  1. single—consistent and variant
  2. double—blends/clusters, double consonants, digraphs with new sounds or silent letters
- Vowels can be:
  1. single—long, short, or neither
  2. double—long, long and short, or neither
- Understanding phonics patterns requires an understanding of the importance of directionality in print
- Students' reading, writing, and questions show independent and emerging knowledge.
- Phonics instruction should:
  1. be developmentally appropriate
  2. build on well-formed concepts about print
  3. be taught in meaningful context
  4. demonstrate thinking with print
  5. include onsets and rimes
  6. develop automatic recognition
  7. use invented spelling for added practice
- Order of phonics instruction should emphasize
  1. single before double
  2. consistent before variant
  3. sounded before silent

Structural patterns include morphemes or units of meaning.

- Meaning of base words/roots can be changed by adding or changing affixes
- Base words can function without affixes, roots usually need an affix.
  - affixes include:
    1. prefixes—independent and dependent
    2. suffixes—inflected and derivational
- Structural patterns are made from combinations of base words/roots and affixes:
  1. base + base
  2. affix + base
  3. base + affix

Stages of reading correlate with stages of word knowledge development.

- Emerging correlates with prephonemic and phonemic stages.
- Developing correlates with letter-name and within-word pattern stages.
- Transitional correlates with syllable juncture and derivational constancy stages.
- Mature correlates with derivational constancy stage.

In the letter-name stage, students:

- are developing a sight vocabulary
- solidify single initial and final consonants
- strive to represent all phonemes in a syllable
- use letter names as a strategy for identifying phonemes
- consistently represent single short vowels
- represent consistent double consonants
- begin to read structural patterns
  1. inflected suffix with no change to base word
  2. compound words that are sight words
- use context plus letters to confirm word identification

In the within-word pattern stage, students:

- are broadening their sight vocabulary
- solidify consonant knowledge
- develop understanding of function of silent letters
- focus on vowels
  1. single long vowels
  2. vowel digraphs
  3. diphthongs
- use structural patterns
  1. compound words, contractions
  2. more inflected suffixes
  3. independent prefixes
- begin to use context plus syllables to confirm word identification

In the syllable juncture stage, students:

- have an extensive sight vocabulary
- focus on changes that occur with the joining of syllables, such as dropping or adding of letters
- begin to focus on syllabication and apply phonics and structural patterns to multisyllable words

In the derivational constancy stage, students:

- are ready to break into mature reading
- focus on how spelling and pronunciation of words relate to meanings
- expand vocabulary through the study of dependent prefixes, Greek combining forms, and Latin roots

REFERENCES

Adams, M. J. (1990). *Beginning to read: Thinking and learning about print.* Cambridge, MA: MIT Press.

Allington, R. L. (1994). The schools we have. The schools we need. *The Reading Teacher, 48,* 14–29.

Anderson, R. C., Wilson, P. T., & Fielding, L. G. (1988). Growth in reading and how children spend their time outside of school. *Reading Research Quarterly, 23,* 285–303.

Bear, D. R., & Barone, D. (1989). Using children's spellings to group for word study and directed reading in the primary classroom. *Reading Psychology, 10,* 275–292.

Beck, I., Perfetti, C., & McKeown, M. (1982). Effects of long-term vocabulary instruction on lexical access and reading comprehension. *Journal of Educational Psychology 74,* 506–521.

Chall, J. S. (1979). The great debate: Ten years later, with a modest proposal for reading stages. In L. B. Resnick & P. A. Weaver (Eds.), *Theory and practice of early reading* (Vol. 1, pp. 29–55). Hillsdale, NJ: Erlbaum.

Chall, J. S. (1983). *Stages of reading development.* New York: McGraw-Hill.

Clay, M. (1979, 1985). *The early detection of reading difficulties.* Portsmouth, NH: Heinemann.

Clymer, T. (1963). The utility of phonic generalizations in the primary grades. *The Reading Teacher, 16,* 252–258.

Ehri, L. C. (1987). Learning to read and spell words. *Journal of Reading Behavior 19,* 5–31.

Ehri, L. (1991). The development of the ability to read words. In R. Barr, M. L. Kamil, P. B. Mosenthal, & P. D. Pearson (Eds.), *Handbook of reading research* (Vol. 2, pp. 354–376). New York: Longman.

Gough, P. B., & Hillinger, M. L. (1980). Learning to read: An unnatural act. *Bulletin of the Orton Society, 30,* 179–196.

Henderson, E. H. (1985). *Teaching spelling.* Boston: Houghton Mifflin.

Henderson, E. H., & Beers, J. W. (1980). *Developmental and cognitive aspects of learning to spell: A reflection of word knowledge.* Newark, DE: International Reading Association.

Holdaway, D. (1980). *Independence in reading.* Portsmouth, NH: Heinemann.

Mason, J. M. (1980). When do children begin to read?: An exploration of four year old children's letter and word reading competencies. *Reading Research Quarterly, 15,* 203–227.

Morris, D. (1981). Concept of words: A developmental phenomenon in the beginning reading and writing processes. *Language Arts, 58,* 659–668.

Stahl, S. A. (1992). Saying the "p" word: Nine guidelines for exemplary phonics instruction. *The Reading Teacher, 45,* 618–625.

Temple, C., Nathan, R., Temple, F., & Burris, N. (1993). *The beginnings of writing* (2nd ed.). Boston: Allyn & Bacon.

Templeton, S. (1991). Teaching and learning the English spelling system: Reconceptualizing method and purpose. *Elementary School Journal, 92*(2), 185–201.

Winsor, P., Nagy, W. E., Osborn, J., & O'Flahavan, J. (1993). *Structural analysis: Toward an evaluation of instruction.* Center for the Study of Reading, Technical Report No. 581. (ERIC Document Reproduction Service No. ED 360 625.)

Wylie, R. R., & Durrell, D. D. (1970). Word recognition and beginning reading. *Elementary English, 47,* 787–791.

Part II

Applying Methods and Strategies

As teachers, we must offer learning experiences to our students from an informed perspective. Part Two provides you the opportunity to gain such a perspective. In each chapter, you will draw on your knowledge of reading, writing, and early adolescent development gained from Part One as you learn to make effective instructional decisions.

Chapter 5 focuses on issues that are basic to all reading and writing instruction. Reading aloud to students and providing time for self-selected independent reading should be daily occurrences for all students in the middle grades. Reading aloud, especially, should not end when students leave the primary grades. You must always remember that the amount of experience students have with literature, both narrative and information, is a key factor in success in reading and writing.

In Chapters 6, 7, and 8 we explore in depth your options for teaching reading with authentic literature. These three chapters present a range of instructional approaches. Which you will choose will depend on your comfort with literature-based reading instruction and your students' experience with literature study.

We begin in Chapter 6 with teacher-mediated instruction. Whole-class study is an excellent way to both learn and teach about literature-based reading. In Chapter 7, we move away from whole-class teacher-mediated instruction toward small-group experiences that progressively give students more responsibility to direct their own learning. In Chapter 8 we explore student self-regulated reading instruction.

In Chapter 9 we discuss writer's workshop and using informal writing across the curriculum. We focus on these aspects of writing to help you understand the potential that writing has for supporting students' learning.

In Chapter 10, we bring reading and writing together, exploring how the study of words supports learning. We consider the specific phonic and structural elements essential to learning in each stage of word knowledge.

Chapter 11 surveys a commercial reading/language arts program. We discuss how you might use your knowledge of literature-based reading, writing, and word study to teach with such materials.

Finally, in Chapter 12, we step back to consider how to integrate students' literacy learning into other areas of the curriculum. After defining *integration* itself, we discuss how it might appear in a middle grade curriculum.

5

Read-Aloud and Independent Reading

Supporting Continued Growth

In this chapter . . .

We consider two elements that are absolutely essential to developing competent readers and writers: reading aloud to students and students reading independently to themselves. To help you develop a classroom environment that supports and encourages these elements, we explore:

- the value of reading aloud to middle grade students,
- tips for good read-alouds,
- using read-aloud to close the gap between readers in a middle grade classroom,
- using mediated listening thinking activities (MLTAs) to extend read-alouds,
- the value of independent reading,
- ways to encourage independence in reading, and
- establishing an environment that fosters independent reading.

Before you get started . . .

Hatchet by Gary Paulsen (1987) is featured in the mediated reading examples and in the Your Turn/My Turn activities.

In addition . . .

Appendix B contains lists of suggested books for reading aloud and for independent reading.

Last year, I didn't like reading very much. But this year I like it a lot. Mr. Liston reads to us every day. He reads great books and we talk about them. He read us Hatchet. *It was like I could see the main character, Brian, in my mind, like when he had to get the survival pack from the plane and the plane was deep in the lake. It's really scary to think you can't survive on your own. But he did! I like to read Gary Paulsen books now. He's written some really great ones! (Brad, 6th grade)* ■

THE VALUE OF READ-ALOUD

Reading aloud to students should not be just for the primary grades. Reading aloud to middle grade students who are reluctant readers may be your "most direct way of communicating the special qualities of written language" (Holdaway, 1980, p. 17) and may be the single most important thing you can do to add to their knowledge of reading in both narrative and information texts (Anderson, Hiebert, Scott, & Wilkinson, 1985; Routman, 1991). Reading aloud to students, especially in the middle grades, should be thought of as the "centerpiece of the curriculum from which all else flows" (Kristo, 1993, p. 54).

When you read aloud to students, you bring print to life, awakening the sounds and rhythms of our language. You provide a model of skillful oral reading that demonstrates that even competent readers continue to monitor for meaning. And perhaps most important of all, you demonstrate that reading is both worthwhile and pleasurable.

Middle grade students are intent on understanding themselves and their world. Reading aloud lets them experience literature as a "window" through which they can engage with the world, or as a "mirror" in which they see reflections of themselves (Cullinan, 1989, p. 390). Through listening to literature, "students come to find themselves, imagine others, value difference, and search for justice" (Langer, 1995, p. 1). Reading aloud to students promotes engagement with text that is essential for meaningful literature study.

Read-aloud is also your opportunity to engage students in literate thinking. You cannot assume that middle grade students are committed readers or that they know how to think their way through challenging text. Thinking about the meaning of print is a difficult task that requires a great deal of mental energy on the part of the reader. When you read aloud to students, you serve as the "decoder," enabling students to concentrate on thinking about a text's meaning.

TIPS FOR GOOD READ-ALOUDS

Reading aloud to students requires much thought and practice. The following teaching suggestions are drawn from Freeman (1992), Trelease (1989), myself, and many teachers I have watched bring books to life with students.

Pick books that you like or are old favorites. When you "love" a book you are more likely to share that book with genuine enthusiasm. Students will know when books are special to you.

Preview the book. Become thoroughly acquainted with a new book's language and ideas before sharing it with your class. Then decide what to emphasize during the read-aloud.

Allow ample time. Don't start a read-aloud session unless you have time to do it justice. Filling a 10-minute space in the school day by reading aloud is generally not a good idea.

Reading aloud to students enables them to focus on the meaning of a text.

Connect with your audience. To let your listeners know they are involved in the reading with you, make frequent eye contact with students as you read.

Read with expression. Try to maintain good pitch, volume, and expression while you read. You can practice reading aloud by tape recording yourself to hear your expression and pacing. When you actually do read-aloud you may be so preoccupied with other details that you cannot evaluate your reading.

If you read a picture book, students need to see the illustrations. Be sure students sit close enough to see the detail in illustrations. Much of the plot, character development, and setting is told through them.

If you read a chapter book, help students make connections to previous chapters. Following the storyline of a chapter book requires a different type of thinking than with picture books. Students with limited experience in chapter books will especially need help connecting the chapters as you read from day to day.

Read in your own style. Your read-aloud style should fit your personality. Creating voices for every character is not necessary. If you are comfortable with your style, you may be more likely to relax and enjoy the experience with your students.

Adjust the pace as you read. When you reach parts of the story that are complex or that require careful mental processing, slow down the pace of your reading to give listeners time to process the ideas. When the writing is primarily descriptive, allow your listeners ample time to build mental pictures.

Don't read above students' emotional level. Consider students' emotional maturity, as well as their background knowledge, when you select books. Students may not always be ready for the emotional demands of specific events or themes, especially in some chapter books.

It's okay to abandon a book. Sometimes, even when you preview and thoughtfully select books, you find that your choice may be a poor match for a particular group of students. In such cases abandoning the book may be the best solution.

Make read-aloud books available to students. As you finish a read-aloud, give the book a "place of honor" in the classroom library area. Some students will want to revisit the book and select it for their independent reading.

Award winners are no guarantee. Just because a book has won an award doesn't guarantee it to be a good read-aloud for your students. Be sure that you preview all books with an ear for the way that the story sounds when read aloud and an eye to its appropriateness.

Share information and anecdotes about authors and illustrators to help students make personal connections with books. People write and illustrate books! Resources such as *Something About the Author* (Telgen, 1971–1994) and *Children's Literature Review* (Selnick, 1976–1995) provide personal and professional information about the people who write and illustrate the texts you share with students.

Prepare one of your favorite books for a read-aloud. Start small, with just a few students. Having a small group will allow you to focus both on students' responses and your feelings about sharing the book. If possible, tape record your session. This will allow you to go back and listen to your expression, pacing of the reading, and ease of interaction with the students.

What book did you select? Why did you choose it? As you previewed the book, what decisions did you make about the following:

How to hold the book?

How to pace the book?

What might hinder expressive reading?

The appropriateness of the book?

How did the reading go? Would you change anything the next time?

You should continue to practice reading aloud to students until you notice that you no longer feel self-conscious and you focus on *your* ability to read aloud. Instead, you should focus on the interaction *between the students and the text.*

Closing Gaps Between Readers

Students come to the middle grades with varied reading experience and ability to make meaning with text. In any middle grade classroom, the range in reading levels may be as much as two-thirds the age of the students. For example, in sixth grade, when students are typically about 12 years old, the range of reading levels may span eight years or more, from first or second grade to high school.

Students' experience with fluent reading, their ability to instantly recognize a large number of words, and their attitudes toward themselves as readers account for much of this variance in reading levels. Reading aloud to students removes word recognition and lack of fluency as barriers to making meaning, providing students with more equal access to the ideas and emotions in a text. Students are more likely to engage with a text when not hindered by the physical aspects of reading.

Reading aloud, then, has the potential to close the reading gap between students, fostering a sense of community in the classroom. Think of it as an instructional technique that treats reading as a responsive process, involving both emotion and thought.

If your students are to become more competent readers, they must learn to respond effectively to written language. Reading aloud can teach students to respond to literature before you ask them to read and respond on their own. You can support and enhance students' responses during read-aloud by providing an environment that encourages "book talk" (Roser & Martinez, 1995), and by serving as a mediator or bridge between students and texts (Dixon-Krauss, 1995).

Encouraging Book Talk

All students, regardless of their literary experiences, have thoughts and insights about the stories they hear and read. Unfortunately, some students may not believe that their thoughts and insights are worthy of being voiced. They may not have had many opportunities in school to really "talk" about books and their meanings. In the middle grades, when students are searching for meaning in their own lives, it is vitally important to provide a "book talk" environment that enables students to unlock and share their thoughts and insights. *Book talk* in this context refers to engaging students in literary talk or discussions. The term can also refer to summaries or teasers that you provide about books to encourage and broaden students' choices of reading material.

Good book talk occurs when students "grapple with core issues, compare insightfully, observe closely, question profoundly, and relate life experiences to story situations" (Roser & Martinez, 1995, p. 33). How can this happen in our classrooms? Roser and Martinez (1995) state that good book talks are likely to occur when the following are true:

- The teacher has a *plan* for the talk.
- A *conversational setting* exists in the classroom.
- Experienced readers share their *genuine responses* to stories.
- Listeners/readers *return to stories* for a closer look.
- Books are drawn together into instructional units that share a focus, topic, or theme.
- Listeners/readers have opportunities to explore their thinking through writing.

Mediating Between Readers and Texts

When you read aloud to students you serve as a more knowledgeable reader who provides support for their thinking and interactions with both narrative and information text. Helping students focus their attention on the salient aspects of a text during read-aloud has been shown to improve their understanding of it (Morrow, 1993). As a more knowledgeable other, you can support and encourage book talk among your students.

Through your understanding of making meaning and responding to texts (see Chapter 2) you know that teachers should be mediators, adjusting the amount of assistance provided during students' interaction with texts and providing feedback about their response. One valuable technique, a mediated listening thinking activity (MLTA), supports students' thinking and responses before, during, and after the reading of a text. Over time, students internalize the strategies they learn for responding to text for independent use in new reading situations.

Planning a Mediated Listening Thinking Activity (MLTA)

As you prepare a read-aloud that assists middle grade students in making meaning with text, you should think about your *purpose(s)* for engaging students with a particular text and the *strategies* you will use to assist students as they make meaning before, during, and after the reading. In addition, you should *reflect* on how you will adjust your support to students as they give feedback about their thinking during discussion.

These steps, purpose-strategy-reflection, form an instructional cycle for mediated learning (Dixon-Krauss, 1995) that repeats throughout the reading of a text. You will adjust your level of assistance as student feedback tells you how much support they need to move toward being self-regulated learners.

You plan an MLTA in three segments: before, during, and after reading. In each segment, consider the purpose(s) for using the selected text, the strategy(ies) you will use to support students and how you might use their feedback to adjust instruction. Figure 5.1 presents an overview of an MLTA. Review this figure before reading further.

Your purposes and strategies for supporting students during an MLTA should focus on the following:

- How competent readers monitor their thinking while reading a text, especially an unfamiliar one
- The content of the new text
- The style it is written in
- Students' needs as readers

For example, imagine that you are preparing to read *Hatchet* by Gary Paulsen (1987) to a class of middle grade students. *Hatchet* is the engaging story of 13-year-old Brian, who survives a plane crash and must learn to survive on his own in the Canadian wilderness. During the read-aloud, you want to provide support for students' thinking so that all students will successfully make meaning during the experience. Beyond enjoyment, your overall purposes for reading *Hatchet* might be to explore the following:

- Readers' response to a dynamic character—the main character, Brian, exhibits significant change as he learns to survive in the wilderness.
- Coming to know a character through an omniscient narrator—Brian is alone in the wilderness. The narrator shares Brian's thoughts, in addition to describing his actions and speech, to help the reader know Brian more completely.
- The setting—Elements of the wilderness, such as wild animals, weather, and isolation, act as antagonists (opposing characters) and help to reveal Brian's character.
- Themes as revealed through a character—Paulsen dramatizes the themes of survival and inner strength through his narrative description of Brian and his behavior.

You begin an MLTA by introducting the text, and by asking open-ended questions. Encourage students to use what they know as readers to anticipate both the book and the opening chapter as an introduction to the author's style of sharing plot, characters, setting, and theme. During the read-aloud, encourage students to do the following:

1. *Predict*, anticipate, or wonder about what might happen (as needed).
2. *Listen* to the text being read aloud.
3. *Respond* to what is happening.
4. *Connect* new ideas to what they already know (as needed).

After the reading, give students the opportunity to reflect on the chapter and consider their engagement with the text.

Figure 5.1 Mediated listening thinking activity (MLTA)

Before reading

Teacher should:

- Establish clear purpose(s) for reading a particular text.
- Identify strategies for meeting that purpose.
- Consider how to adjust support during the reading to help students move toward independent thinking.
- Encourage students to anticipate reading, using text and background knowledge.
- Focus reading for identified purposes (e.g., authors can use point of view and setting to help the reader get to know a character).

Students should:

- Predict what might come in the reading using available information.
- Connect the prediction to current background knowledge.
- Prepare to meet the purpose(s) of the reading.

During reading

Teacher should:

- Read aloud in a fluid and lively manner.
- Stop the reading at appropriate places to assist students in making meaning and meeting reading purposes.
- Encourage students' use of identified strategies.
- Encourage responses, listening thoughtfully.
- Adjust support for making meaning according to need reflected in students' responses.

Students should:

- Use listening–thinking strategies to meet reading purpose(s).
- Give feedback to teacher about their thinking during the reading.
- Meet the purpose(s) of reading.
- Use background knowledge and text to understand essential vocabulary.

After reading

Teacher should:

- Encourage response through open-ended questions, such as "What did you think of what we read today?"
- Elicit retelling, first unaided through open-ended questions, then aided by probing for specific points.
- Based on response, determine which essential words may warrant further discussion.
- Reaffirm strategies used to meet reading purposes.

Students should:

- Share responses to the reading (creative/personal meanings).
- Retell most important points (explicit/implied meanings).
- Discuss understanding of essential vocabulary (explicit/implied meanings).
- Explore understanding of essential story elements (implied/critical meaning).

The following sample MLTA, for Chapter 1 of *Hatchet,* illustrates the process of mediating students' thinking and responses during read-aloud. As you think about the content of Chapter 1, try to be sensitive to ways in which you may use your own responses to the text to support students' engagement with it. However, remember that as an adult reader, your responses are often more complete and sophisticated than are those of most middle grade readers.

Sample MLTA—Hatchet

Before Reading.

Share information that is available to any reader who picks up the book—the title and front cover illustration, and any information on the back cover that introduces the author or describes the plot, such as the following:

> Sitting next to the pilot in a single-engine plane headed for the Canadian wilderness, where he will visit his father for the first time since his parents' divorce, thirteen-year-old Brian Robeson is haunted by thoughts of that divorce and his knowledge of the Secret that caused it.
>
> When the plane crashes, Brian is the sole survivor. Left with only the clothes on his back, and a hatchet his mother gave him as a parting gift, Brian must face the devastating truth: "Right now I'm all I've got. I have to do something." He must learn to survive. (cover of Trumpet Club edition, 1988)

Predict: "What ideas do you have so far about this story?" (pause for responses) "What clues do we have for the meaning of the title, *Hatchet*?" (pause) "Let's begin the chapter and see what else we find."

During Reading.

Listen: Read pp. 1 and 2. Set the scene in the small plane and introduce the limited omniscient point of view from which the story is told, using the example on p. 2, "The thinking started. . . . Divorce. It was an ugly word, he thought."

Respond: (think aloud) "I guess that Gary Paulsen is going to let us know what Brian's thinking."

Predict: "Could this be a way that we will learn more about Brian? What do you think?" (pause for comments)

Listen: Read p. 3, introducing the "Secret" surrounding the divorce, mentioned on the back cover.

Respond: (pause reading to think aloud) "I wonder why Gary Paulsen capitalizes that word, *Secret,* each time he writes it?" (show text to students who are close by or have students look at own text; briefly pause for responses)

Listen: Read pp. 3–7, in which the pilot shows Brian a few things about steering the plane. You may read this section aloud without interruption unless students need help with airplane terms, such as *rudder,* or to imagine the setup of a cockpit. It will be important to recall this section during the reading of Chapter 2 when Brian must handle the plane by himself. The first foreshadowing of the pilot's impending heart attack comes on p. 5: "He (pilot) took the controls back, then reached up and rubbed his left shoulder. 'Aches and pains—must be getting old.'"

Pause if students comment; if not, defer discussion until pp. 6–7, where there is more information about the pilot's condition. On p. 7, Paulsen also mentions a "survival pack," filled with emergency supplies.

Respond: "What do we know about Brian so far?" (responses to Brian's thinking about his parents' divorce and visitation rights) "What do you think is happening with the pilot?" (responses to clues about the impending heart attack)

Connect: "How does this connect to the information on the back cover of the book?" (pause for responses)

Predict: "What do you expect in the remainder of this chapter?" (pause) "Let's find out."

Listen: Read from the bottom of p. 7 through p. 12 (end of chapter). Brian thinks back to when his mother had driven him to the airport and given him a hatchet. This section reveals information about Brian's relationship with his mother, and also describes the pilot's heart attack.

After Reading.

Respond: (encourage open response) "What do you think about Brian's situation?"

Connect: (encourage students to think back over the events in the chapter [retelling] as they explore their responses) "What do we know so far?" (pause) "What would you do if you were Brian?"

Predict: "Based on what we know, what do you expect might happen in Chapter 2?"

In addition to the information covered in the preceding sample MLTA, most texts contain essential words that you should discuss with students to support their understanding and enjoyment of the text. To decide how to handle any given essential word in a text, ask the following questions:

- Is the word in students' listening vocabulary?
- Is the word used in a context that helps readers figure out the meaning?

If a word is essential to understanding, is in the students' listening vocabulary and appears in a helping context, give students the opportunity to figure out the word(s) with clues from the text. If students' experiences or the context are insufficient, provide support for word meaning during reading and discussion.

Your Turn

To practice mediating between students and books, take the time now to prepare an MLTA using Chapter 2 of *Hatchet*. Use the format shown in the sample MLTA for Chapter 1, structuring the predict-listen-respond-connect sequence to meet your specific needs. What will you try to help students notice and think about while they listen to you read Chapter 2 aloud?

Chapter 2 of *Hatchet* describes Brian's actions following the pilot's death. I would begin my MLTA by recalling our predictions at the end of Chapter 1. Then I would break the reading into three sections:

- Coming to grips with the dead pilot (pp. 13–mid 17)
- Developing a plan of action (pp. mid 17–24)
- The last two paragraphs, when the engine stops (p. 25)

After reading the first section, ending with, "The plane flew on normally, smoothly," I would ask students to retell and respond to Brian's actions to get control of the plane. This discussion should lead to predictions of what might happen in the remainder of the chapter.

After reading the second section, I would encourage students to respond to Brian's actions, asking, "What do you think about Brian's actions and his plans for landing the plane?"

After pausing for responses, I would read the last two paragraphs of the chapter and again ask for responses.

This is a moving chapter. Students typically have strong responses to Brian's situation and have little difficulty sharing. Reflecting back on portions that showed how Brian tried to use what he knew from reading and prior experience sets students up for later chapters, when they must anticipate how Brian will be able to survive on his own. Connecting chapters 1 and 2 helps students be aware of what they know about Brian to this point. To end the MLTA, I would reread the last sentence in the chapter, which provides an excellent point for students' predictions about Chapter 3.

To review, a mediated listening thinking activity (MLTA) helps students to make meaning during a read-aloud, supporting their thinking before, during, and after reading. Using an MLTA as an assisted reading experience can help you understand the meanings your students are finding in texts read aloud to them. Making meaning is the essence of reading and many students need help to develop their ability to understand more complex texts. Some lack both extensive and intensive experiences with literature, and need repeated opportunities to explore text to make meaningful connections with the important ideas.

When you are learning new techniques or approaches for teaching, such as the MLTA, you must practice for the technique to feel comfortable and under control. Be patient! With adequate preparation and practice, you will become less concerned about your own success in conducting an MLTA and more focused on your role in mediating between students and the text.

A read-aloud that includes an MLTA is an excellent beginning to literature study with middle grade students. With careful planning, a daily read-aloud can become a literature workshop, providing an inclusive experience for all readers. You may extend the daily read-aloud time into a whole-class literature experience that you enhance with student-led small-group discussions, literature logs, and other extension activities. In Chapter 6 we discuss using read-aloud in whole-class literature study with *Hatchet* (Paulsen, 1987). Appendix A also contains a complete sample study, using *A Taste of Blackberries* (Smith, 1973).

Middle grade students may know how to read, but their knowledge is of little value if they choose not to read. Daily read-alouds enable students to use their knowledge of reading to think about ideas in texts within the structure of written language.

Daily read-aloud engages students' minds and encourages their desire to read independently.

The Value of Independent Reading

In addition to read-alouds, independent reading is one of the most important ways that students can spend their time if they are to become fluent, competent readers (Center for the Study of Reading, 1990). Regardless of your approach to reading instruction, your students should have time to read independently every day, for the following reasons:

- The more that words pass in front of a reader's eyes, the greater the opportunity that individual has to become a better reader (Allington, 1977).
- One-third or more of vocabulary growth can be accounted for by independent reading (Center for the Study of Reading, 1990).
- Reading strategies improve significantly if students read independently for at least 10 minutes per day or one hour per week (Anderson et al., 1985).
- Students' attitudes toward reading improve through self-selected independent reading (Tunnell & Jacobs, 1989).

Independent reading may occur in the classroom or at home, but it must occur!

Encouraging Independence in Reading

As a middle grade teacher, you can encourage independent reading in the following ways:

- Provide blocks of time for independent reading.
- Use your knowledge of what motivates students.
- Support self-monitoring behaviors.

Independence and Time to Read

Although students in the middle grades have participated in reading instruction for four to eight years, many are not yet fluent, independent readers. To become independent, students must frequently practice reading strategies. Some middle grade students read only when it is assigned and, even then, may still not complete the assignment. Some students may never have experienced "reading time" in school as a connected block of time devoted just to reading. For some students, "reading" has meant a number of short periods of instruction, each filled with a different activity.

To encourage independent reading, then, your first step must be to provide ample blocks of reading time, encouraging students to sink into meaningful independent reading:

- *Provide time each day for recreational reading.* Also called SSR (sustained silent reading) or DEAR (drop everything and read), everyone in the classroom reads silently for a specified period of time in books of their own choice. If you are teaching in a content area in middle school, you may provide independent reading time in books related to topics the class is studying. The advisory period in the middle school also can frequently be devoted to independent reading.
- *Provide time for self-selected independent reading during periods of "work time" in the classroom.* Encourage independent reading in topics of interest or units of study, rather than assigning additional paper and pencil activities.

- *Establish a reading program with independent reading at the center of instruction.* In literature circles (Chapter 7) and reader's workshop (Chapter 8), students select books for reading and spend large amounts of time reading independently each day.

Independence and Personal Motivation

To become independent readers, students must be motivated to read (Holdaway, 1980). When middle grade students look at school reading tasks, do they see tasks that are worthy of their sustained effort? Can they see themselves moving toward independence as readers?

Students who are highly motivated to learn a task have an incredible internal drive that is often able to overcome any initial setbacks encountered in new learning experiences (Holdaway, 1980). Students can sustain themselves when they see that the desired task is worth learning and can see themselves making progress toward independence.

What choices concerning independent reading would motivate middle grade students? To answer this question, we must consider the nature of middle grade students in general (see Chapter 1), and in particular, their individual needs and interests. Your students must be able to see that their needs and interests are at the heart of classroom activities.

First, and most important, students should freely choose the texts they will read. The most motivating aspect of reading is certainly the personal meaning that individuals construct. Students are likely to find more meaning in books they choose themselves. Second, you should allow your students to choose whether and how they share with others their personal responses to books read for pleasure. As adults, we are able to choose whether we will share our response to independent reading. Students should have a similar choice. If they must always be accountable to someone other than themselves for their reading, when will their reading behavior be under their control or totally for pleasure?

Independence and Self-Monitoring

To become independent readers, students must learn to develop their natural desire to monitor and critique their own reading performance (Holdaway, 1980). Students are able to independently monitor their own reading when their ability to make meaning is high. This is most likely to occur when reading materials are suited to a student's level of performance and desire to read. If texts are difficult, learning how to monitor one's own reading is too great a challenge and becomes self-defeating.

Your classroom reading program can support both students' sense of gaining independence, and their drive to be more independent by providing interesting low-challenge material (material at student's independent reading level—see Chapter 2—in which their word recognition and understanding of the material is almost perfect) to build students' sense of confidence and independence.

PROVIDING AN ENVIRONMENT FOR INDEPENDENT READING

Independent reading will not happen automatically in your classroom. You must plan for it just as you plan other parts of the language arts program. Students know whether or not independent reading is really important by the way that you do the following:

- Establish a "reading" environment in the classroom.
- Provide a consistent and predictable time for reading.

- Make available a variety of reading materials to meet student needs and interests.
- Provide an attractive and functional place where students can have access to reading materials.
- Promote independence through self-selection.

Establish a Reading Environment

When someone sees your classroom for the first time, do they see a room that says, "Readers live here"? The classroom environment in which students live for a good part of their day should promote reading. Will a visitor see a class library that houses a variety of reading materials? Inviting displays that promote reading? Displays of student work that show the types of reading experiences they are having?

When students watch you, will they see someone who cares about reading? Will you encourage students to share their reading? Will you share your own reading with students? The reading atmosphere in your classroom shows the way that you value reading.

To promote interest, you will need to sell books to some of your students. Just because you find great books and display them in the classroom doesn't mean that students will become independent readers. You can help students be interested in books by making special introductions for new books. As a part of each read-aloud time, give a short talk about a new book, telling a few highlights or a summary, or pose an interesting situation that students may explore by reading the book. For chapter books, read part of an exciting event aloud as an enticement.

You may wish to place somewhere in the classroom a display of books around special topics being studied. You can then introduce the display and highlight a few books each day. Students can share what they are finding in the books in the display.

Provide Consistent and Predictable Time to Read

Acquiring competence is a matter of practice over time. How much practice do middle grade students need to develop as independent readers? It will vary. Some students will read outside of school. Some students will not require as much reading practice as others. Some students may slow their own progress because they continue to select books that are almost too challenging so they can "look" like their peers.

You can respond to students' varying needs for reading time by doing the following:

- Provide a set time each day for everyone to read independently, such as silent sustained reading (SSR), drop everything and read (DEAR), stop talking and read (STAR).
- Provide flexible time for choosing independent reading during work periods.
- Encourage at-home reading as a part of homework assignments.

By the middle grades, students should easily be able to sustain their reading for 30 to 45 minutes. Sustained reading, however, requires students to build stamina. Students who have not had the opportunity for sustained reading will need time and patient guidance in learning how readers keep their own reading going.

You can also build independent reading time each day by making it a choice during such instructional blocks as reading/language arts or content area activities. Devoting instructional time to independent reading, including books about a current topic of study, allows students more practice time.

Students become better readers by reading!

Teachers who use a reader's workshop approach (Chapter 8), have a great deal of instructional time devoted to independent reading. Reader's workshops often combine SSR with instructional reading time to have longer blocks for student-selected independent reading.

In the hustle and bustle of the school day it is easy to let independent reading time slip away. If you want to begin to equalize differences between students' background experiences with books, you must provide time for students to read.

Provide a Variety of Reading Materials

If you want students to value their independent reading time, you need to build a varied collection of books and magazines. Students bring a variety of interests into the classroom. Will they find books to feed those interests in the classroom and/or school library? Students have varied reading abilities. Will they find materials to fit their levels of independence? If you believe that reading is important and you want students to read, then you must provide interesting and varied materials.

In the classroom library, you need a minimum of 10 books per student. To build your library, check out class sets from both the school and public libraries. Class sets, typically 30 to 40 books, can be kept for three to four weeks. For students who are reading primarily picture books, you may need to circulate books more frequently. When it is time for new books, involve students in deciding which books to recycle.

School book clubs are another good source of inexpensive books. As a suggestion, at the beginning of each school year you may wish to ask parents if they would be willing to buy three or four books from book clubs for the class library, during the school year, or one book every two or three months. Many parents will be willing to do this. Book club prices are usually lower than those of bookstores. Your class may also conduct fundraisers to buy books with the consent of the school administration.

In your class library, consider acquiring duplicate copies of some books. Some students enjoy reading the same book a friend is reading. Duplicate copies provide an opportunity for students to initiate their own literature discussions with someone who has read or is reading the same book.

Provide Easy Access to Reading Materials

The classroom library should invite students to want to read. The area doesn't have to be large, but it does need to be inviting. My preference was usually to have the class library near a wall area or bulletin board where we could make a display about a featured author, a special day like Earth Day, or other topics of study for which books were available. Books were featured in other areas of the room also, but I gave particular emphasis to books in the library area.

In the early part of the school year and throughout, students can help you decide how to make the library area an attractive place they like to visit. Students' involvement in planning increases their sense of ownership in the classroom.

Teach Self-Selection

You cannot assume that middle grade students are proficient at selecting appropriate reading materials just because they have been in school for a number of years. To know your students as independent readers, it is wise to discuss their interests and to observe their processes of selecting reading materials.

You can also learn about students' interests through interest inventories, interviews, and journal entries. Interest inventories are helpful in gathering initial personal information about students. Students can individually respond in writing on a form such as the one shown in Figure 5.2. If time is available, you may prefer to use the items from the interest inventory and interview students or have students interview each other. Face-to-face interactions typically provide opportunities for clarifying responses or probing other areas of interest indicated by a student's response.

Figure 5.2 Interest inventory

Name________________________________Age_______Grade_______Date_______

1. When you are at school, what are your favorite things to do?

2. When you are at home, what are your favorite things to do?

3. Do you have special hobbies or interests?

4. What things do you prefer to do by yourself?

5. What things do you prefer to do with your friends?

6. What things do you prefer to do with your family?

7. Do you like to read? __________. What are your favorite books?

8. How do you know if someone is a good reader?

9. Are you a good reader? __________. Why or why not?

When you know students' interests, you can suggest particular books or authors, and may order class reading materials targeted to those interests. Book displays and sharing opportunities can also highlight books of interest to particular students.

You can also make better use of the school library by providing the media specialist/librarian a list of students' interests. The librarian may then highlight a variety of relevant books during library visits.

The difficulty level of books is another issue in selection. Ideally, students should read books that are "just right" for them. When a student selects a book she thinks she would like to read, encourage her to try it out first to see how well it suits her. Consider the "five finger test": While the student is reading the first page or two (approximately 100 words) ask her to tuck away a finger every time she comes to an unknown word. If she bends enough fingers to drop the book, it might be too difficult for her. Then she must decide if she is willing to "work" at reading the book. Students who want to read particular books badly enough, even if they might be difficult, should be allowed to try. How will students become independent if we always select their books or try to control their choices?

Setting up and periodically restocking the classroom library presents an excellent opportunity to discuss selecting books and to practice with support. You may discuss with students about reading easy, just right, and hard books. Students should consider the amount of energy it takes to read a hard book. You can have students browse and select a book they think is "easy" for them, one that is "just right," and another that is "hard." Students can discuss how they came to that conclusion and teach each other about how they select books. The success of independent reading rests heavily on students being able to self-select appropriately.

How will you establish an environment that encourages independent reading in your classroom?

______________________________ ▪

Monitoring Students' Growth as Readers

Both read-aloud and independent reading periods provide opportunities for students to teach you about who they are as readers. As students spend time being read to, they demonstrate attitudes toward reading and how they use meaning-making strategies in a listening–thinking situation. As students read independently, they demonstrate both their attitudes toward themselves as readers and their use of self-sustaining reading strategies.

Teacher's Assessment Portfolio

You should systematically collect data about your students and reflect on what they suggest about each of them as a reader, writer, and learner. You may collect data for each student and place them in an assessment portfolio to show growth over time. The items selected for this portfolio should create a broad picture both of a student's strengths and of areas that may need attention.

Assessing and Evaluating Read-Aloud. When read-aloud is an interactive activity, as in an MLTA, students share their general attitudes about reading as well as their attitudes about the particular text being read. By the middle grades, students who do not engage during a read-aloud are less likely to benefit from whole-class instruction. It is important to notice students' behavior during read-aloud and to consider what such behaviors suggest about students as readers.

An MLTA enables students to share their attitudes and thinking about a text before, during, and after the reading. During each phase of an MLTA you have the opportunity to observe their reactions and interactions. As you observe behaviors that help you better understand a student, make records. To help focus your observations, list behaviors you believe are important for middle grade students to demonstrate during read-aloud and use it as a checklist to guide your observations. Figure 5.3 shows a sample observation checklist and anecdotal record form.

To observe read-aloud behaviors, begin by asking yourself these questions:

- Do I know the text I am reading well enough to allow me to observe students' responses rather than think about my ability to read aloud well?
- What do I notice most about students during a read-aloud?
- Do I use my observations to adjust instruction during the read-aloud?

Figure 5.3 Sample observation checklist and anecdotal record

Name ______________________________ Date ____________________

Response to read-aloud:	**Usually**	**Sometimes**	**Rarely**
1. Shows positive response.	_____	_____	_____
2. Participates in discussion.	_____	_____	_____

Comments:

Shares thinking through discussion:			
1. Makes meaning by using:			
oral context	_____	_____	_____
background knowledge	_____	_____	_____
2. Monitors own thinking about text.	_____	_____	_____
3. Uses knowledge of story elements:			
plot development	_____	_____	_____
character traits	_____	_____	_____
setting	_____	_____	_____
point of view	_____	_____	_____
themes	_____	_____	_____
author's style	_____	_____	_____
4. Makes connections between texts to enhance meaning.	_____	_____	_____

Comments:

To improve your observation skill, do the following:

- Focus your attention on a few students, rather than the class as a whole, and record observations as soon after the read-aloud as possible.
- Select only one main purpose to accomplish before, during, and after the read-aloud, enabling you to focus on observing a limited number of types of student responses.

In your initial observations, it is a good idea to focus attention on a few students who most need support during the read-aloud to become engaged or to make meaning. They are your best gauge of how the read-aloud is going. To prepare to share the chosen text, set one main instructional objective for the reading, such as noticing character traits by listening to dialogue. Your interactions with students should focus on your objective.

Assessing and Evaluating Independent Reading. What independent reading behaviors should you expect? Appropriate self-selection? Sustained silent reading? Engagement with texts? By the middle grades, students should have had many opportunities to read independently, including selecting appropriate books and shifting from oral to efficient silent reading behavior. You may not see such independence, however, in all of your students.

To provide an environment that supports independent reading, you must carefully observe students to see how effectively they use their opportunities to read, and identify students who need your guidance and support. Do students seem to be engaged with the texts they have selected? For how long do individuals sustain their reading? When engagement appears to wane, what seems to be the reason? You will combine your observations and students' self-evaluations to determine what you must adjust in the classroom environment and in students' background knowledge and reading strategies to enable them to become effective independent readers. You must decide which independent reading behaviors are important and systematically observe students for occurrences. Figure 5.4 shows a sample observation form.

Student Learning Portfolio

Students should also develop a learning portfolio that will illustrate who they are as learners. Students place items in the portfolio that, when taken together, provide a picture of how they evaluate themselves as readers and writers.

Student Self-Evaluation of Read-Aloud. In addition to your evaluation of read-aloud, students should have the opportunity to evaluate their own responses. Middle grade students are able to monitor their listening–thinking processes. The more you ask students to be aware of and evaluate their own thinking and responses, the more sensitive they become to the listener's role during read-aloud. You may ask for both verbal and written self-evaluations.

Verbal self-evaluation can take place during read-aloud discussions and individual conferences. You may model self-evaluation by talking aloud about your thinking as you prepare for the reading. Encourage students to evaluate their own thinking and responses during the reading by sharing first with a partner, then with the class as a whole.

You can make written self-evaluation easier for students by developing a response form that queries them about their thinking and responses during the read-aloud. The form of the evaluation can be either focused or open. A focused evaluation may be a

Figure 5.4 Sample independent reading observation form

Name ______________________________ Date ________________

Independent Reading:	**Usually**	**Sometimes**	**Rarely**
1. Self-selects appropriate materials.	_____	_____	_____
2. Engages in sustained reading appropriate to development and experience.	_____	_____	_____
3. Abandons books that are inappropriate.	_____	_____	_____
4. Is establishing personal preferences for content, style, authors, genre.	_____	_____	_____
5. Displays positive attitudes toward personal reading.	_____	_____	_____
6. Seeks advice about selecting reading materials when needed.	_____	_____	_____
7. Uses library effectively.	_____	_____	_____

Comments:

checklist for students to complete (Figure 5.5), while an open-ended response may take the form of a sentence completion or short answer task (Figure 5.6). Still another way to encourage self-evaluation is to have students discuss their response to read-aloud in their literature logs or journals. You may choose to keep these self-evaluations in either the student's learning portfolio or your assessment portfolio.

Student Self-Evaluation of Independent Reading. Students can keep records of their independent reading. The level of detail in the record should reflect how you will use the information in the classroom. Figure 5.7 shows a sample daily recordkeeping form that includes the number of pages read and, when expanded appropriately, allows for recording the reading of a one chapter book over several weeks. Daily records are helpful if we are trying to encourage students to evaluate the consistency of their independent reading. In contrast, it may be sufficient to have students merely make one record of each book, as shown in Figure 5.8. The information we ask students to record should serve a purpose that students understand, such as noting reading preferences or recording how long students spend with each book or how often they abandon books. Students can help decide what to include on the record form.

Figure 5.5 Focused student self-evaluation of read-aloud

Name ______________________________ Date ____________________

	Usually	Sometimes	Rarely
When the teacher reads stories aloud:			
1. I enjoy listening.	_____	_____	_____
2. I get involved in the story.	_____	_____	_____
3. I participate in discussions.	_____	_____	_____
4. I learn new words and phrases.	_____	_____	_____
5. I use what I already know to anticipate and follow the story.	_____	_____	_____
6. I use what I know about stories to understand:	_____	_____	_____
• the development of the plot	_____	_____	_____
• the development and actions of the characters	_____	_____	_____
• the role of the setting	_____	_____	_____
• how the point of view influences the story	_____	_____	_____
• the way the author uses language to tell the story	_____	_____	_____
7. I use the meaning of other words in the story to figure out words I'm unsure about.	_____	_____	_____
8. If I listen carefully, I learn ways to understand more about stories or information books.	_____	_____	_____

Comments:

Figure 5.6 Open-ended student self-evaluation of read-aloud

Name ______________________________ Date ________________

1. When the teacher reads aloud to the class, I like to ________________

____

____

____

2. When we discuss books the teacher reads aloud, I ________________

____

____

3. During a read-aloud, I learn about the development of plot by ____________

____

____

4. I learn about the development of the characters by ________________

____

____

____

5. I learn about the role of the setting by ________________________

____

____

6. I learn about the author's style of writing by ____________________

____

____

7. I learn more about thinking like a reader when the teacher ____________

____

____

Figure 5.7 Daily reading record

Name ______________________		Daily Independent Reading Record
Date Started:		**Title:** **Author:**
Date:	Pages read:	Comment:
Date:	Pages read:	Comment:
Date:	Pages read:	Comment:

Figure 5.8 Independent reading record

Name ______________________		Independent Reading Record
Date Started & Date Completed or Abandoned	**Title & Author**	**Comments**

You also should encourage your students to monitor and evaluate their own independent reading. Figure 5.9 shows a sample self-evaluation form that combines both focused and open response items.

In the middle grades, independent reading takes on much greater importance as students are expected to use reading and writing for independent learning and to contribute to collaborative projects. As a base for other assessment data and forms of evaluation, read-aloud and independent reading provide valuable insights into students' attitudes about reading and about themselves as readers.

Figure 5.9 Student self-evaluation of independent reading

Name ______________________________ Date ________________

	Usually	Sometimes	Rarely
1. When given a choice of things to do, I choose to read.	_____	_____	_____
2. When I read independently:			
I know how to select books that are right for me.	_____	_____	_____
I can read for 20 minutes or more.	_____	_____	_____
I abandon books that are not right for me.	_____	_____	_____
I am learning what types of books and authors I like best.	_____	_____	_____
I monitor my own reading to be sure it's making sense to me.	_____	_____	_____
3. When I go to a library, I know how to find what I need.	_____	_____	_____

4. As an independent reader, I am ______________________________

____

____

____

____

5. The way I can tell a book is just right for me is ______________________________

____

____

____

____

6. To be a better independent reader, I need to ______________________________

____

____

____

____

Respecting Diversity Through Read-Aloud and Independent Reading

The students in your classroom bring a richness of diverse experiences that you should acknowledge, support, and enhance through read-aloud and independent reading. As you engage students with books, you must take into account students' interests, world knowledge, and cultural experiences, and their experience with book language.

Your selection of books for read-aloud experiences and the classroom library should reflect the variety of students' interests. When you select a text for read-aloud, typically a whole-class activity, you *must* consider students' interests. Include students as appropriate in making decisions about the books to be read aloud.

Providing a well-stocked classroom library and encouraging frequent browsing trips to school and public libraries tells students that you recognize the diversity of interests in the classroom and value them individually. When you provide independent reading time with self-selected materials, you tell students that you realize that they may prefer to read something other than classroom instructional materials.

Regardless of socioeconomic levels and background experiences, what students already know should be the starting point for reading in your classroom. In this way you validate students' lived experience. Balancing narrative and information text also provides opportunity for students with specialized knowledge to share what they know with you and with their peers. If their uniqueness is to be an asset, then you must challenge yourself to use students' knowledge as the starting point of the curriculum.

Historically, people of different cultures have shared their values, beliefs, and experiences with others through oral and written stories. In addition, an increasing number of contemporary writers are sharing the life stories of multicultural characters, both real and fictional. Gathering quality multicultural literature for the classroom library and read-aloud program shows students that people they identify with are worthy of being central characters in books. Each of us needs cultural models that validate us as worthy human beings.

Ramirez and Ramirez (1994) state that, for any cultural group, quality multiethnic books contain text that reflects an authentic, sincere, and accurate portrayal of individuals and the way of life. Quality books also reflect the language of the group in natural usage (see Appendix B for suggested titles).

The fewer experiences your students have with the formality of book language, the more conscious you must be in providing sustained exposure through read-aloud and independent reading. During read-aloud you are a language bridge, mediating between students and book language. In independent reading, help students make selections that engage them in fluent reading of low-challenge text, in which they are more likely to be able to sustain their engagement with book language for longer periods of time.

TAKE A MOMENT AND REFLECT

When planning for read-aloud:

- Pick books you like.
- Preview before reading, because even award winners are no guarantee.
- Allow ample time to pace the book appropriately for your students.
- Share information about authors and illustrators.
- Be conscious of how you position the book if there are relevant illustrations.
- Connect with the audience through expression and eye contact.
- Help students make connections with the reading.
- Abandon books that are above students' emotional level or are otherwise inappropriate.
- Make read-aloud books available for independent reading.

Close the gap between readers through read-aloud:

- Give all students access to a text.
- Encourage "book talk" during the read-aloud.

Mediate between students and books:

- Use MLTA strategies before, during, and after the reading of a book to support students' interactions with a new book.

Independent self-selected reading:

- Should happen every day
- Helps students become fluent readers
- Increases vocabulary
- Improves reading skill
- Improves attitude toward reading

Encourage independence with books:

- Provide a consistent predictable time to read.
- Provide adequate time for independent practice.
- Provide a well-stocked library with easy access.
- Provide a comfortable reading environment.
- Introduce new books.
- Help students learn how to select appropriate books.

SSR and DEAR are forms of independent reading:

- Use self-selected materials
- Sustained effort is a goal, 30 or more minutes per day

Reader's workshop uses independent reading as the main source of instruction (see Chapter 8).

Monitor students progress in reading by considering:

- Developing positive attitudes toward reading through read-aloud
- Developing knowledge about reading through read-aloud
- Developing independent reading behaviors
- Provide opportunities for student self-evaluation

Respect reading diversity among students through providing for varied

- interests
- abilities
- styles

REFERENCES

Allington, R. (1977). If they don't read much, how they ever gonna get good? *Journal of Reading, 21*(2), 57–61.

Anderson, R. C., Hiebert, E. H., Scott, J., & Wilkinson, I. A. G. (1985). *Becoming a nation of readers.* Champaign-Urbana, IL: Center for the Study of Reading.

Center for the Study of Reading (1990). *Teachers and independent reading: Suggestions for the classroom.* Champaign-Urbana, IL: Author.

Cullinan, B. E. (1989). *Literature and the child* (2nd ed.). San Diego: Harcourt Brace Jovanovich.

Dixon-Krauss, L. A. (1995). Lev Semyonovich Vygotsky: The scholar/teacher. In L. A. Dixon-Krauss (Ed.), *Vygotsky in the classroom: Mediated literacy instruction and assessment* (pp. 1–5). New York: Longman.

Freeman, J. (1992). Reading aloud: A few tricks of the trade. *School Library Journal, 38*(7), 26–29.

Holdaway, D. (1980). *Independence in reading.* Portsmouth, NH: Heinemann.

Kristo, J. (1993). Reading aloud in a primary classroom: Reaching and teaching young readers. In K. E. Holland, R. A. Hungerford, and S. B., Ernst (Eds.), *Journeying: Students responding to literature* (pp. 54–71). Portsmouth, NH: Heinemann.

Langer, J. A. (1995). *Envisioning literature: Literary understanding and literature instruction.* New York: Teachers College Press.

Morrow, L. (1993). *Literacy development in the early years* (2nd ed.) Boston: Allyn & Bacon.

Ramirez, G., & Ramirez, J. L. (1994). *Multiethnic children's literature.* Albany, NY: Delmar.

Roser, N. L., & Martinez, M. G. (1995). *Book talk and beyond: Children and teachers respond to literature.* Newark, DE: International Reading Association.

Routman, R. (1991). *Invitations: Changing as teachers and learners K–12.* Portsmouth, NH: Heinemann.

Selnick, G. J. (Ed.). (1976–1995). *Children's literature review* (Vols. 1–34). New York: Gale Research.

Telgen, D. (Ed.). (1971–1994). *Something about the author.* (Vols. 1–76). Detroit, MI: Gale Research.

Trelease, J. (1989). *The new read-aloud handbook.* New York: Viking Penguin.

Tunnel, M. O., & Jacobs, J. S. (1989). Using "real" books: Research findings on literature based reading instruction. *The Reading Teacher, 42,* 470–477.

CHILDREN'S LITERATURE

Paulsen, G. (1987). *Hatchet.* New York: Viking Penguin.

Smith, D. B. (1973). *A taste of blackberries.* New York: Thomas Y. Crowell.

6

Introduction to Whole-Class Literature Study

In this chapter . . .

We examine how a class of middle grade students engages in the study of one text to explore their understandings of the author's craft, thinking like readers, and making personal connections. We consider:

- how to organize whole-class literature study,
- providing instruction through
  whole-class minilessons
  mediated listening thinking activities (MLTA)
  mediated reading thinking activities (MRTA)
- engaging students in small-group discussions, and
- using writing to support and extend literature study.

Before you get started . . .

Hatchet by Gary Paulsen (1987) is featured in this chapter's classroom scenarios and Your Turn/My Turn activities.

In addition . . .

Appendix A contains a complete sample whole-class literature study for *A Taste of Blackberries* (Smith, 1973). Appendix B lists suggested books for whole-class literature study.

Whole-Class Literature Study

Students in the middle grades need many opportunities to explore their ideas about themselves, others, and their world. Using high-quality literature is an excellent way to engage students in personal and group exploration. While middle grade students have five or more years of school behind them, they may have little experience participating in the *study* of literature. Their expectations for books may come more from reading as skills work and as assigned tasks than from reading literature.

To encourage literate thinking among students, you may choose to begin with whole-class literature study. The advantage of whole-class experiences is that you are able to help students realize that readers make meaning in different ways with the same text. Whole-class studies also enable you to focus on how your role is changing from director to mediator or facilitator.

Introductory experiences in literature study should focus students' attention more on literary thinking and response than on the mechanics of reading. Through read-along and silent reading, students are supported by a more knowledgeable other (Vygotsky, 1962) as they think and respond, preparing for more independent approaches to literature study.

In this chapter, we explore two ways to introduce middle grades students to whole-class literature study through mediated approaches. The first is read-along, in which the teacher reads aloud as students read along in their own copies of a text. The second approach is to assist students while they read portions of a text silently. To illustrate both of these approaches, we visit Lou's sixth-grade classroom as he engages his students in studying *Hatchet* (Paulsen, 1987).

On this particular day the students retrieve their copies of *Hatchet* and settle in their desks for the day's literature study. Lou begins by saying, "Yesterday, as we ended our reading of Chapter 2, the plane appeared to run out of fuel and the engine stopped. Brian [the protagonist] had been thinking about what he would do when that happened. What were some of the things Brian had been thinking?" Lou takes responses, then the class launches into an hour composed of reading along as Lou reads aloud, small-group discussions, and whole-class discussion of Brian and his struggle to survive.

Lou is introducing his students to literature study. By reading *Hatchet* aloud, he serves as the class "decoder" and leads a study in which all students can think about and respond to the text. The students in Lou's class vary widely in their experiences as readers. By reading aloud to students, Lou closes the gaps in the range of readers in his classroom.

Lou encourages students to silently read along in their copies with him as he reads aloud. Initially, Lou takes the lead and encourages students to notice particular passages, sometimes rereading those passages, enabling students to both hear and see the text. Having a personal copy allows students to study the text with Lou's assistance as a more knowledgeable reader. Students also are able to refer to the text during followup or extension activities.

Lou is using *Hatchet*, along with other works, in a study of author Gary Paulsen. He hopes to help his sixth-grade students understand how the characters in Paulsen's books use their life experiences to learn more about themselves and their world. Through this unit, Lou will extend students' literary understanding by focusing attention on the techniques that authors such as Paulsen use to reveal the personal growth of their characters.

Having students read along in their own texts is an excellent way to initiate a unit or theme study, focusing the attention of all students on the unit theme or concept. With Lou as a guide, students will study *Hatchet* as the core book (Zarrillo, 1989), or main text, of a "Gary Paulsen—Author" unit. The literature in such whole-class studies is typically teacher selected and whole-group activities are typically teacher led (Heibert & Colt, 1989). When the class has completed its study of *Hatchet*, Lou uses literature groups or self-selected independent reading with related texts to extend the author study. During this time he provides for student choice of reading materials and student-led discussion groups.

From Reading Aloud to Literature Workshop

Lou plans to use reading aloud for whole-class literature study. To do so, he coordinates reading aloud, students reading along, whole-class strategy instruction, opportunities for students to explore their own responses to the reading, and times for group sharing to create a literature workshop.

You may use read-along in literature study in either whole-class or small-group discussion formats (Figure 6.1). Note the differences in work time structure for whole-class (A) and small-group (B) discussions. Note, too, that the flow of activity in both formats moves from whole-group read-along, to either individual response activities or small-group discussions, then back to the whole group for closure.

When Lou first began to teach reading through a literature-based approach he used a whole-class format, keeping the class together for discussions but providing some opportunity for independent and small-group response activities. Lou now realizes that in whole-group activities it is difficult to actively involve all students in the discussion, so he tries to provide opportunities for small-group discussions whenever possible.

Planning a Literature Workshop

The instructional experiences Lou provides during whole-class literature study are drawn from (1) the reading/language arts curriculum that his school district expects him to teach, (2) the piece(s) of literature that he has selected for study, and (3) what he has determined through assessment and previous instruction that his students are ready to learn.

Reading to students as they follow along in texts is an effective way to introduce the study of literature.

Figure 6.1 Literature workshop components

Whole Group (30–35 minutes):	• Community opening • Whole-class minilesson workshop procedures literary elements listening/thinking strategies • Guided listening/read-along (MLTA) prediction read-along response connecting ideas • Whole-class discussion following MLTA response connecting ideas
A. Whole Class Work Time (15–20 minutes):	• Literature logs • Projects (art, drama, writing, etc)
B. Small-Group Work Time (10–15 minutes):	• Meet in student-led small groups use teacher-made discussion guides for responses, connecting ideas students record personal and/or group responses • Literature log followup (optional)
Whole Group (10–15 minutes):	• Community sharing session (whole class) personal reflections/responses from literature logs projects • Community sharing session (small group) small-group discussions discussion guides • Connect with previous readings • Evaluate the day • Anticipate next reading

Selecting Objectives

Each school district develops curriculum guides that identify what students should know at each grade level or developmental stage. Figure 6.2 presents a sample of the sixth-grade reading and literature objectives for Lou's school district.

You are familiar with *Hatchet*, the text Lou has selected for study. Now look at the district teaching objectives shown in Figure 6.2. Which objectives do you think Lou might emphasize as his class studies *Hatchet*?

Figure 6.2 Instructional objectives for reading and literature, sixth grade

1. Read for pleasure and information.
2. Read silently.
3. Read and distinguish among types of literature.
4. Identify components of prose writing: theme, plot, setting, point of view, and character.
5. Recognize literary devices and figures of speech, such as idioms, similes, metaphors.
6. Identify valid generalizations, appropriate summaries, inferences, and conclusions.
7. Identify propaganda devices.
8. Interpret information from charts, tables, and cutaway diagrams.
9. Follow written directions.
10. Identify base words, suffixes, and prefixes.
11. Identify analogous relations between two pairs of words.
12. Identify the connotation of a word or phrase.
13. Use context clues to determine time relationships.
14. Use a dictionary, card catalog, and other resource and reference materials.
15. Use skimming, close reading, and light reading as appropriate strategies.

As Lou plans for the study of *Hatchet,* his main purpose(s) for students are as follows:

- Reading for pleasure
- Becoming aware of techniques authors use to reveal character growth (the main character of *Hatchet*, Brian, is a dynamic character)
- Exploring ways that readers learn about their strengths and weaknesses while studying the characters in Paulsen's books
- Making inferences about a character through an omniscient narrator
- Using a discussion guide in student-led small-group discussion to help students become more independent in their study of literature
- Using close reading as an appropriate strategy in the study of a chapter book

According to his school district's curriculum, Lou emphasizes objectives number 1 (reading for pleasure and information), 4 (identify components of prose writing), 6 (make inferences), and 15 (use close reading as an appropriate strategy).

■

Developing a Reading Plan

When Lou selects a book for a literature workshop, he carefully reads the text, and considers the content and length of each chapter and the amount of time he has for instruction each day. Then, he makes an initial plan for grouping chapters for the read-aloud. *Hatchet* has 19 chapters and an epilogue. Most chapters are 8 to 12 pages long, and it takes Lou from 1 to 1½ minutes to read aloud one page. He wants to read about 15 pages per day, allowing time for a few stops to help students clarify their initial understanding of the text, so typically he plans 20 to 25 minutes for the read-aloud portion of the workshop.

Based on the required reading time, Lou then groups chapters that fit together. His reading plan requires at least 14 class meetings to complete the book, plus additional sessions to bring closure to the study. He also realizes that interruptions in the school schedule and his students' needs and interests may require him to revise his plans. Lou's initial reading plan will take 15 days (Figure 6.3). As the read-along progresses, Lou adjusts his plan to accommodate the needs and interests of his students.

Figure 6.3 Reading plan for *Hatchet*

Reading Plan for Literature Workshop— Hatchet (Paulsen, 1987)		
Day	**Chapter**	**# of Pages**
1	1	12
2	2	13
3	3 & 4	16
4	5	12
5	6	10
6	7	12
7	8 & 9	14
8	10 & 11	15
9	12 & 13	17
10	14 & 15	18
11	16	14
12	17	11
13	18	10
14	19 & Epilogue	11
15	Closure	

Planning Lessons

As a part of his planning, Lou considers how he will help students develop the literary knowledge and thinking strategies they need to engage with author Gary Paulsen, as he shares Brian's story in *Hatchet*. In a literature workshop, Lou provides instruction through the following:

- mediated listening thinking activities (MLTA)
- whole-class discussions
- whole-class minilessons

As he reads each chapter, Lou marks places in his copy where he anticipates needing to help his students think through the ideas in the text so they might meet his instructional goals of (1) exploring personal traits, such as believing in ourselves and making effective decisions, and (2) understanding the techniques Paulsen uses to reveal character growth. He also makes notes about possible instruction to help his students extend and refine their general understanding of literature and use of effective reading-thinking strategies.

From this reading, Lou plans an MLTA for each chapter (see Chapter 5). In each MLTA, Lou supports students in their interactions through his use of the predict-listen-respond-connect cycle. Depending on student feedback, Lou adjusts the amount of support he provides to enable them to make meaning with the text.

From his notes for each chapter, Lou also plans minilessons to make students aware of particular knowledge or strategies that could make their reading more pleasurable or effective. Samples of Lou's notes for the first two chapters of *Hatchet* are shown in Figure 6.4.

Implementing a Literature Workshop

When Lou is familiar with his chosen texts and is clear about his educational objectives, he begins to implement the literature workshop. Early in the school year Lou follows a whole-class format similar to that shown in Figure 6.1, keeping the class together for discussion, then allowing time for students' personal responses to the text. After the class has studied one or two chapter books together, Lou encourages students to guide discussions by using small groups (see Figure 6.1) before the whole class discusses the reading in much depth.

In the next sections, we follow Lou as he implements each part of a literature workshop:

- Whole-class minilessons
- Using an MLTA to engage readers
- Whole-class and small-group discussions

Whole-Class Minilessons

Before Lou reads to students, he begins his instruction with a minilesson. A *minilesson* is a short, 5- to 10-minute lesson that provides students with a useful "tip" for upcoming reading activities (Five, 1988; Hagerty, 1992). Lou thinks aloud about using reading or literary knowledge (skills) or a specific reading strategy. This thinking aloud helps students learn how good readers make their decisions, what information they consider, and why some possibilities get discarded (Davey, 1983).

Lou plans minilessons to teach procedures and strategies that will help students make the literature workshop successful. For procedural minilessons, Lou mentally

Figure 6.4 Chapter notes for planning

Chapter 1

* omniscient narrator point of view
  - hear Brian's thinking
  - introduced to Brian's character
  - the Divorce, the Secret
  - how Brian came to be on plane
* The "hatchet" is introduced (foreshadowing) p. 8
* pilot's heart attack introduces problem, pp. 10-12
* language
  - banked, p. 3
  - rudder, p. 3
  - hot white hate of his anger at her, p. 9
  - bushplane, p. 7

Chapter 2

* good description
  - coming to terms with pilot's death
  - needing to fly the plane
  - using the radio
* language
  - turbulence, p. 13
  - horizon, p. 14
  - altimeter, transmitter, p. 16
  - throttle, p. 21
  - altitude, p. 22
* powerful ending, last sentence, p. 25

walks through the daily workshop routine and tries to anticipate what may be new to his students. For strategic and literary minilessons, Lou draws examples from the book being studied or books that are familiar to all of the students. Following are two of Lou's lists of minilesson topics that he uses during the reading of *Hatchet*.

Literature Workshop Procedures

- How is listening to a book like reading a book? (emphasizing thinking skills and strategies)
- Yes, I need to check my own thinking when I'm listening, just like when I'm reading.
- What do I do to help myself listen during read-aloud?
- Making predictions helps me listen and read.
- Making predictions, anticipating, thinking ahead, wondering, . . . show I am engaged with the reading.

- How does connecting back to what I already know help me make meaning?
- Why should I give the teacher feedback about my thinking during the read-aloud?
- What should I do during small-group discussions?
- How can I help our group have a good discussion?
- How can we use a discussion guide to help us in our small-group discussions?
- How do we share our group's ideas with the whole class?

Use of Literary Elements

- Who's telling Brian's story? Why do we get to hear what Brian thinks?
- Learning about Brian by listening to his thoughts.
- What is a flashback? Why do authors use flashback?
- How does Gary Paulsen use flashback to fill us in on Brian's story?
- Is description really important?
- How does Gary Paulsen use description?
- When is a setting also a character? In *Hatchet*!
- How does Gary Paulsen use the setting to show us more about Brian?
- Is Brian changing? How can we tell?

At this particular time in the school year, the students in Lou's classroom are participating in student-led small-group discussions for the first time. To help students learn to participate in, and eventually lead, their own discussions, Lou has prepared discussion guides for each chapter of *Hatchet*. After Lou has read aloud Chapter 1, he teaches a minilesson that introduces using the discussion guides in the small groups (Figure 6.5). Typically a minilesson would precede the reading, but in this case students needed to know the content of Chapter 1 for the lesson to be effective.

Through this minilesson, students in the class are able to hear and see their peers take the first steps toward student-led discussions. Throughout the reading of *Hatchet*, Lou repeats and reinforces instruction about discussion skills to help his students become more confident and independent in their ability to lead discussions.

Your Turn

Imagine that you are leading a literature workshop using *Hatchet* and you want to plan minilessons to help students develop their use of literary knowledge and reading strategies that will be relevant to this text. What minilesson topics might you select? Why? It may help you to think back to the sample MLTA in Chapter 5 and Lou's planning for Chapter 1 and 2 shown in Figure 6.4.

Chapters 1 and 2 in *Hatchet* introduce the main character, Brian, the problem the plot will develop around, the limited omniscient point of view used to tell the story, and the author's style of using language. What other topics did you identify? Any of these topics can be developed into useful minilessons:

- How does Paulsen use an omniscient narrator to help us get to know Brian as a person and draw us into the potential problems that he faces? This point of view requires the reader to make interpretations about the character. A minilesson on this topic should use text from *Hatchet* and encourage students to discuss and support their interpretations.

Figure 6.5 Sample minilesson—First day using discussion guides for small groups

Lou has just finished an MLTA with Chapter 1 of *Hatchet* and has the students move into groups, saying, "Today is our first day to break up into small groups as a followup to our reading of *Hatchet*. To help us decide *what* ideas to share in the small group, I have made a discussion guide for each of you to use in your meetings." (Lou places a transparency of the discussion guide on the overhead projector as copies are distributed to the students.)

"A discussion guide has ideas and questions about the book we are reading. Your small group can use them to help you learn to share your own ideas about the reading."

"To make this discussion guide, I read Chapter 1 and tried to think about the parts where you might say, 'Why did Brian do that?', or where you might wonder, 'Now, what's going to happen?', or where you might say to yourself, 'If that was me, I would. . . .'

"I have asked one of the small groups to help me today by being part of a small-group discussion. We are going to model how your group can use the discussion guide to help you talk about Chapter 1." Lou joins the group, who are seated near the front of the classroom. Each child has a copy of the guide. The other groups can see the guide on the overhead projector.

"Pretend that I'm one of you and this is our small group. I'll begin today by reading the first question. Then each of us will share our ideas about it. We'll go around the circle, taking turns, and listening to what each other has to say. I, for one, want to know if the other members of my group have ideas that are the same or different from mine. As we share, we'll also make notes on our guide sheets to help us remember important ideas."

Lou reads the first question aloud, "What do you think about Brian's situation at the end of the chapter? What makes you think that?" Then he shares his ideas, saying, "Brian is in a pretty bad situation. He doesn't know how to fly. He's probably really nervous to be all alone. But Brian seems like a thinker. He's always thinking about things that are happening. Maybe he'll keep thinking and not let himself get so scared that he can't do something. Now, will each of you take a turn and share your ideas?"

Danny says, "I'll bet he's really nervous, too. No, I'll bet he's petrified. Nothing this scary has ever happened to me. I don't know what he will do." (As Danny speaks, Lou makes notes on his guide sheet.)

Brad adds, "If I were Brian, I'd be scared and excited. I'd want to figure it out so I could live. I would want to live so much that I *would* figure it out. Brian watched the pilot. I'll bet he'll think of something."

Trina offers, "Brian doesn't seem like a chicken. I'd be scared, sure, but if I didn't do something, I would die. Brian has got to do something. What good will it do to just get scared or cry? He'll die anyway. He did fly the plane for a little while. Maybe he'll figure something out."

Jodie says, "It said that Brian felt a white-flash of horror or terror, I can't remember which, and he couldn't breathe. That's really being scared. But he's 13. He'll do something. I'm like Trina. I think he'll try to fly the plane. He did that once already."

Lou turns to the class and says, "Think for a moment about what you saw us do. Who can tell us what you saw and heard?" Several students retell the events. Lou then says, "Now, I want you to do the same thing with the members of your small group. Each of you has a copy of the discussion guide. For today, I would like you to do what you saw this group do: read a question and give each person in the group time to share their ideas about it. When everyone has had an opportunity to share, go on to the next question. Again, go around the group and take turns. Be sure that you talk about each question.

"If you finish before I call the class back together, take the time to record any other questions and ideas you have about this chapter. When we get back together as a class I'll ask you to share ideas from your small groups."

- Since one of Lou's objectives is to explore dynamic characters, a minilesson on this topic might engage students in brainstorming strategies they already use to learn about characters. Sharing such information not only helps students learn from each other, but also enables them to teach us about what they already know and do as readers.

Encouraging Students to Read Along

As stated, most minilessons precede, rather than follow, a read-along. After each minilesson, Lou introduces the chapter he will read aloud. He plans an MLTA for each read-aloud/read-along, keeping in mind the following literary and pedagogical aspects:

- The natural breaks between events within a chapter
- Where his students might need support to clarify actions or connect with previous events
- How he can encourage students to become more engaged with the character and use their engagement to better understand their own struggles with life

Lou uses MLTAs to support students' thinking and encourage response from chapter to chapter, adjusting as necessary the amount of support he provides during the read-along. If, for example, Lou notices during discussions that many students are having difficulty adjusting to the point of view of the book, he makes more frequent stops than he originally planned to help students follow the way the narrator uses Brian's thoughts to tell the story.

As Lou plans for MLTAs, he uses the *predict-listen-respond-connect* cycle. (Refer to the sample MLTA in Chapter 5 and notice how the cycle is adapted to the way that Paulsen presents ideas in *Hatchet*.) Lou uses the *listen-respond* phase of the MLTA cycle

Discussion is an essential part of whole-class literature study.

consistently while reading aloud, encouraging his listeners to share their understanding and responses. During this portion of the cycle, Lou must listen intently to student feedback so he knows how much support students need for the text to be meaningful.

He adds the *predict* phase when his listeners might anticipate upcoming events, such as by using clues about the impending heart attack to anticipate the question of who will fly the plane.

Lou uses the *connect* phase when recalling past events that might help listeners clarify meaning, such as by connecting the clues about the heart attack with information about the plane crash from the back cover of the book.

Thinking about reading aloud as phases of a *predict-listen-respond-connect* cycle provides a framework for teacher planning. The cycle calls attention to how readers think when responding to text and to where the "listeners" in a class may need support to have more meaningful interaction with the text.

Engaging Students in Whole-Class Discussions

After the read-along, students usually engage in some type of discussion, either whole-class or small group. At the beginning of the school year, Lou begins with whole-class discussion rather than small groups. He intends to move into more independent reading but first wants students to feel confident at thinking about and verbalizing responses to text.

In a literature workshop that relies on whole-class discussions to help students reflect on and clarify their understanding of text, the "After Reading" portion of the MLTA occurs immediately following the read-along. In Chapter 5 we presented a sample MLTA for Chapter 1 of *Hatchet*. The "After Reading" section of that MLTA is reproduced following this paragraph. Notice how the questions focus on having students respond to the reading, retell important events, and make predictions for the next chapter. These prompts are intended to promote a well-rounded discussion of the text.

Respond: (encourage open response) "What do you think about Brian's situation?"

Connect: (encourage students to think back over the events in the chapter [retelling] as they explore their responses) "What do we know so far?" (pause) "What would you do if you were Brian?"

Predict: "Based on what we know, what do you expect might happen in Chapter 2?"

Engaging Students in Small-Group Discussions

After introducing his students to literature study through teacher-led whole-class discussions, Lou moves to student-led small-group discussions following the read-along. The students submit the names of three others with whom they would like to talk about the reading. Using these choices, Lou creates heterogeneous groups of four or five. Groups typically remain together for the duration of a unit of study.

When small-group discussion is new for Lou's students, he provides a discussion guide to help students focus their talk. Through a whole-class minilesson (see Figure 6.5) Lou models using the guides. Students use the guides until they have enough experience with small-group discussions to monitor them on their own.

Figure 6.6 presents a sample discussion guide for Chapter 1 of *Hatchet*. Notice that the items closely parallel the "After Reading" discussion suggested in the Chapter 1 MLTA. When Lou uses small-group discussions in whole-class literature study, he delays in-depth discussion of the reading until after students have had an opportunity to explore their ideas in the small groups.

Figure 6.6 Small-group discussion guide—*Hatchet,* chapter 1

Discuss each item with the members of your group. Record important ideas on this think-sheet for use in the whole-class discussion that will follow. Place the completed guide in your literature log.

1. What do you think about Brian's situation at the end of the chapter? What makes you think that?
2. Thinking that the pilot is dead, what would you do if you were Brian?
3. Look back in Chapter 1 to find parts of the story that are told through Brian's thoughts. Reread several parts to members of your group. As a reader, how do you respond to a story that is told through someone's thoughts?

Even though Lou is working with sixth-grade students, many have limited experience in reading responsively or critically or in leading their own discussions of books. To promote personal engagement, the discussion guide has open-ended questions that query students for their personal opinions and responses. Lou encourages students to provide support for their thinking from the text whenever applicable.

As Lou moves through the chapters of *Hatchet,* he makes the questions on the discussion guides more and more open. By broadening the questions, he encourages students to provide more direction for discussions. Figure 6.7 shows a sample discussion guide for Chapter 16, near the end of *Hatchet,* when Lou is encouraging students to take more control of the small-group discussions.

Figure 6.7 Small-group discussion guide—*Hatchet,* chapter 16

Discuss each item with the members of your group. Record important ideas on this think-sheet for use in the whole-class discussion that will follow. Place the completed guide in your literature log.

1. On pages 157–158, Gary Paulsen writes,

> ". . . inside of one day, just one day, he [Brian] had been run over by a moose and a tornado, had lost everything and was back to square one. . . .
>
> But there is a difference now, he thought—there really is a difference. I might be hit but I'm not done. . . .
>
> . . . . He had changed, and he was tough. I'm tough where it counts—tough in the head."

Question: Do you think Brian has changed? When you think back on all that has happened to Brian, what *clues* do you see to his change?

2. What other ideas did your group think were important to discuss today? Would you be willing to share these ideas in the whole-class discussion?

In the early stages of using small groups, students usually talk about each item on the discussion guide in turn. Students' responses typically focus on simply answering the questions and not much more, and are often shallow, not the insightful thinking we hope to have as response to good literature. But this is just what Lou expects because his students do not have much experience with student-led discussions. From their prior experience with reading groups, students often expect Lou to take the lead, so they wait to see what he thinks they need to know. As the small-group process becomes more familiar, the "question-answering" begins to sound more like a conversation.

Lou leaves space on the discussion guides for students to record responses as appropriate. During Lou's first small-group minilesson, he suggested that students focus on discussion. They wrote responses in their guides after the discussion as a way of remembering what they wanted to share with the class. This illustrates an important point: When you begin to use discussion guides, you must carefully consider your purpose(s). If one purpose is getting students to talk, you can't let filling in the discussion guide become so important that students stop discussing in order to write answers.

Lou circulates among the groups during the small-group discussions. He listens, but does not answer questions or tell students what responses to make. Lou believes that his students need to begin to make decisions for themselves. Their questions typically seek affirmation that they are doing the "right things." Lou responds with, "What do *you* think about . . . ?" When the students see that Lou really wants to know what they think, they stop asking and begin to trust themselves.

Also during discussions, Lou makes notes about students' responses. He studies these responses to do the following:

- Learn about students' thinking
- Prepare for the possible directions that class discussions might take
- Plan for the next day's read-along
- Monitor students' growth as literate thinkers

Lou thinks of the small groups as a rehearsal for whole-class discussions. In the small groups, each student has the opportunity to reflect on and share personal thoughts and responses. As a result, there is greater diversity of thinking, and more students' ideas are included in the whole-class discussion.

By the time students participate in discussions of two or three chapter books in whole-class study, Lou hopes that students will direct their own discussions in the small groups. Student-led book talks should be the goal in the middle grades.

Your Turn

Discussion guides focus students' attention on the aspects of each chapter that would be beneficial to discuss at the close of a literature workshop, when the whole class comes together. Try developing a discussion guide for Chapter 2 of *Hatchet*. What aspects of the chapter will you call to students' attention? Develop three open-ended discussion questions, one that encourages the reader to look back at the text, one that allows the reader to take a personal stance, and one of your own choosing.

My Turn

To develop a discussion guide for Chapter 2, I looked back at the sample MLTA for that chapter (see Chapter 5). The MLTA for Chapter 2 is divided into three parts: Brian coming to grips with the death of the pilot, his developing a plan of action, and his reaction when the engine stops. I would use these same points to extend students' thinking as they prepare for whole-class discussion, using the following three questions:

1. (look back) Reread the opening paragraph for Chapter 2. Have someone in your group read the paragraph aloud. What do you think Gary Paulsen meant by this description of Brian? Why do you think he described Brian this way?
2. (personal response) What would you have done to figure out how to fly the airplane and communicate using the radio?
3. (open—prediction) What do you think Brian will do now that the engine has stopped? What do you think you would do?

Moving Along with Whole-Class Literature Study

Literature Workshops with Silent Reading

After students gain some experience with thinking and talking about literature, they should be able to share the responsibility for reading the text as well. To accomplish this, Lou changes the read-along portion of the literature workshop to an assisted silent reading experience.

In the middle grades, a literature workshop using silent reading is most effective when students meet the following conditions:

- Students' reading ability is near the difficulty level of the selected text.
- They desire to read the selected text.
- They have past experience in literature study.

While Lou helps students to prepare for the silent reading, he no longer reads the text for them. He is careful, however, to be sure that students do not find themselves frustrated during the reading.

To support his students, Lou plans minilessons that will help them develop strategies for effective silent reading. He realizes that he may need to teach reading strategies that he did not emphasize in the read-along literature workshop.

In the minilessons, Lou emphasizes the use of text and models how competent readers think while they read silently. For example, as the class prepares to read Chapter 3, Lou uses a strategy minilesson to demonstrate using context and background knowledge to think about words that have multiple meanings. He places excerpts from *Hatchet* on the overhead projector, then thinks aloud so that his students will realize that good readers often must use their reasoning abilities to make meaning in their reading (Figure 6.8).

Planning a Mediated Reading Thinking Activity (MRTA)

The essential difference between a literature workshop using read-along and one using silent reading is in the way that the text is read. Look back at Figure 6.1, which shows two basic types of literature workshops. You may emphasize silent reading by changing the MLTA in each to a mediated *reading* thinking activity (MRTA).

Like an MLTA, an MRTA includes predicting, responding, and connecting. However, instead of listening to text read aloud, you support students as they read the text silently to themselves. When planning an MRTA for *Hatchet,* for example, divide the text into manageable chunks, just as when you read aloud. Then, help students use their ability to read silently as they learn to think more critically and responsively about literature.

In your planning, consider the type of support students might need to interact successfully with the text. During discussion, listen to students' feedback to learn whether they are handling the silent reading effectively. Students reading a year or more below

Figure 6.8 Sample minilesson—Using context and background knowledge to determine word meaning.

"When I'm reading, sometimes I think I know the meaning of a word, but the way it's used in the story doesn't seem to fit. Then I remember that in English words can have more than one meaning. So I have to look carefully at how the author used the word.

"Two days ago, we started reading *Hatchet*. When we got to page 5, we came across the word *banked* and some of you questioned whether it had anything to do with money. Let's look at that part of the text again.

"Remember, we were reading about Brian trying his hand at flying a plane for the first time." Lou places a copy of the text on the overhead with the word *banked* highlighted:

> Brian turned the wheel slightly and the plane immediately *banked* to the right, and when he pressed on the right rudder pedal the nose slid across the horizon to the right. He left off on the pressure and straightened the wheel and the plane righted itself.

Lou says, "I'm thinking that the meaning of *banked* that I usually think of, as something to do with money, doesn't seem to fit in this story about flying an airplane. There must be another meaning for this word. So I look past the word, because I know that clues to word meaning can come after a word, as well as before it. I read that the nose of the plane went to the right, then, with less pressure, the plane righted itself. I think about planes I have seen flying and I get an image in my mind of what this plane might be doing. If a plane makes a turn, the wings are usually tipped. *Tipped*—maybe that fits. So I try *tipped* in place of *banked.*" Lou places another sheet on the overhead with the sentence rewritten:

> Brian turned the wheel slightly and the plane immediately *tipped* to the right,

"That makes sense to me and seems to fit with the other sentences. I know from this that *banked* must have more than one meaning. In our reading today, if you come to a word where your meaning doesn't fit with the way the author is using it, let's stop and see if we can figure it out by looking at the other words around it."

the level of text being studied may experience some frustration during silent reading periods, unless they are highly motivated to read the selected text.

To prepare for the silent reading in an MRTA, think about your purpose(s) for engaging students with a text such as *Hatchet*, and the *strategies* you will use to assist students to make meaning before, during, and after each silent reading. In addition, *reflect* on how you will adjust support to students as indicated by their feedback during discussion. Review what you know about how competent readers monitor their thinking while reading, especially in unfamiliar text. Then, think about the content and writing style of *Hatchet,* and use what you know about your students to anticipate the needs they might have when reading.

As with the MLTA, you begin the MRTA by introducing the text and asking open-ended questions that encourage students to use what they know as readers to anticipate both the book as a whole and the opening chapter as an introduction to the author's style of sharing plot, characters, setting, and theme. During the MRTA, encourage students to do the following:

1. *Predict*, anticipate, or wonder about what might happen (as needed).
2. *Read* a selected part of the text silently.
3. *Respond* to the text.
4. *Connect* new ideas to what they already know (as needed).

Following the reading, give students the opportunity to reflect on the chapter, considering their own engagement with the text.

The sample MRTA for Chapter 1 of *Hatchet* that follows is one example for mediating students' thinking and responses during silent reading. We use Chapter 1 at this time so we may more effectively compare and contrast this MRTA with the sample MLTA in Chapter 5.

Sample MRTA—Hatchet

Before Reading.

Share the information that is available to any reader who picks up the book—the title and front cover illustration, information on the back cover introducing the author and briefly describing the plot, just as in the MLTA. Then prepare for the first segment of silent reading.

Predict: "What ideas do you have so far about this story?" (pause for responses) "What clues do we have for the meaning of the title, *Hatchet*?" (pause for responses) "Let's begin the reading to see what else we find."

During Reading.

Read: "Let's each read silently to the middle of page 3, to the paragraph that ends with '. . . he hadn't noticed the burning tears.'" (students read)

Respond: "What do we know so far?" (wait for responses) "How did we find out?"

Connect: "Did you notice how the author tells us what Brian is thinking? Remember on page 2 it said, 'The thinking started.' Why do you think Gary Paulsen wants us to know what Brian is thinking?" (wait for responses) "Could this be a way that we will learn more about Brian? What do you think?" (brief pause for comments, and to think aloud) "I wonder why Gary Paulsen capitalizes that word, *Secret,* each time he writes it?" (briefly pause for responses)

Predict: "Notice how the next paragraph takes us back to the pilot and the plane. What do you think might happen now?" (listen for connections with information on the back cover of the book)

Read: Read silently to the middle of p. 5. Stop with the paragraph that ends with Brian saying, "Thank you."

Respond: "How would you feel about flying the plane?" (wait for responses)

Predict: "When you read the last two sentences on p. 5—'The words. Always the words,' what does it make you think might happen next in the story?" (pause)

Read: Read silently from the top of p. 6, beginning with "Divorce . . .", to the bottom of p. 7, ending, "Probably something he ate, Brian thought."

Respond: "What did we find out in this section?" (pause for responses) "What makes you think that?"

Connect: Sometimes authors give us clues to something that is going to happen, making us curious, wanting to read on to find out. Did you notice any clues?" (note survival pack and pilot's discomfort) "From the back cover we know there will be a crash, so we think the survival pack could be important. We also know the pilot has some type of problem."

Predict: "The last sentence we read said, 'Probably something he ate, Brian thought.' What do you think the problem might be? What makes you think that?" (pause for responses) "Let's read to find out."

Read: Read silently from the last paragraph on p. 7, beginning, "His mother had driven him from the city . . . ," to the paragraph near the top of p. 10 ending with, "Brian forgot it as they took off and began flying."

Respond: "How do you think Brian feels about his mother? What leads you to believe that?" (pause)

Connect: "Brian's mother gave him a hatchet. Could this be another clue for us to think about? What do you think might be important about the hatchet?" (pause)

Predict: "The next paragraph on p. 10 begins, 'More smell now.' What do you think we might find out?" (pause for responses) "Let's read to the end of the chapter and find out."

Read: Read silently the remainder of the chapter.

After Reading.

Respond: "What do you think about Brian's situation?" (brief pause for initial responses)

(If you are using a whole-class format, discussion continues. If you are using small groups, place the connecting and predicting questions on a discussion guide along with other items appropriate for discussion.)

Connect: "Take a few minutes to look back at the chapter. What do we know so far? What parts of the chapter are important for us to think about and remember? Be ready to share those parts with the class." (after sufficient time return to whole-class discussion of important parts)

Predict: "Chapter 1 ends with these words, 'He was alone. In the roaring plane with no pilot he was alone. Alone.' What do you think will happen in Chapter 2? What do you think Brian will do?" (pause) "If you were Brian, what would you do?" (prediction could also be a literature log entry)

The MRTA provides a framework for mediating between students and a text they are reading silently. Use comments and open-ended questions to encourage response and help students make connections among ideas presented in the text. How you probe student responses depends entirely on the depth of thinking in the feedback students provide.

Using Logs in Literature Workshops

Some teachers choose to add a literature log to their workshop to give students opportunities to focus on personal responses. After whole-class or small-group discussions, students record their responses to the text in a literature or reading log. You may then contrast these personal responses with the small-group and whole-class discussions to better understand the growth of individual students.

In a literature workshop that uses small-group discussions, I suggest that a significant portion of the literature log entries be student's choice. Other opportunities for student response are already influenced by the questions/comments that you select for the MLTA/MRTA and discussion guides. Students in the middle grades should have many opportunities to explore their own thinking as well as the thinking of peers and teachers.

As we discussed in Chapter 3, there are many format options for logs or journals (Figures 6.9 through 6.11, and see Figure 3.3). Introduce students to these various ways to structure their log or journal responses, and let them make choices about the nature of their entries.

In addition to personal responses, students can also record ideas and information pertinent to the literature study. For example, Lou asks students to dedicate a few pages in their logs for noting interesting and/or troublesome words. He also encourages them to illustrate, cluster, or chart their ideas as needed.

If you use logs or journals for personal response, provide opportunities for sharing responses during the literature workshop. Sharing not only provides additional purpose for making the entries, but also enriches group discussions.

Whole-class literature workshop is an excellent way to get started in literature study. Read-along involves all students initially, regardless of their reading level. Engaging students in silent reading later on provides challenge. In addition, beginning whole-class literature study by using one text can help you develop the confidence to try more challenging organizations, such as book clubs, literature circles, and individualized reader's workshops, discussed in chapters 7 and 8.

As one example, Appendix A contains a complete whole-class literature study for *A Taste of Blackberries* (Smith, 1973). In this short chapter book, Doris Buchanan Smith shares a powerful story of two boys, Jamie and an unnamed narrator, whose friendship

Figure 6.9 Log entry—Making predictions

Predictions

4/1 Ch 7 I think he's going to start on his shelter and thinking about his mom

After —wasn't even close he didn't do anything to his shelter

Ch8 I think he'll get more food and take a bath in the lake

Ch9 I think his fire will get started and he will be warm and get some more stuff like twigs & branches

After —right on! his fire got started and he got warm

Ch10 I think he'll stay by the fire and eat his berries and fall asleep

After —not even close His hunger took over he was starving

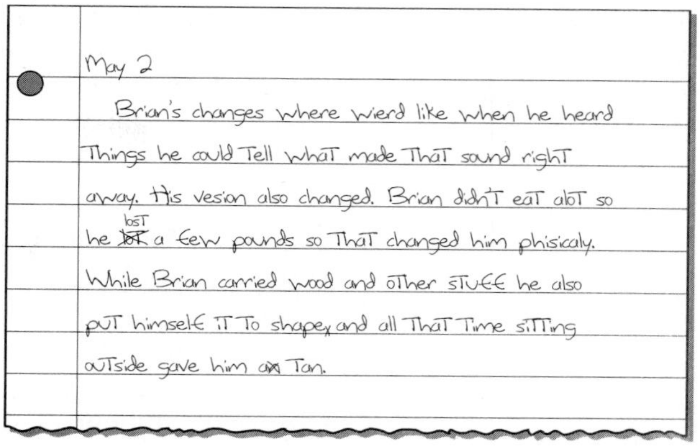

Figure 6.10 Log entry—Personal commentary on text

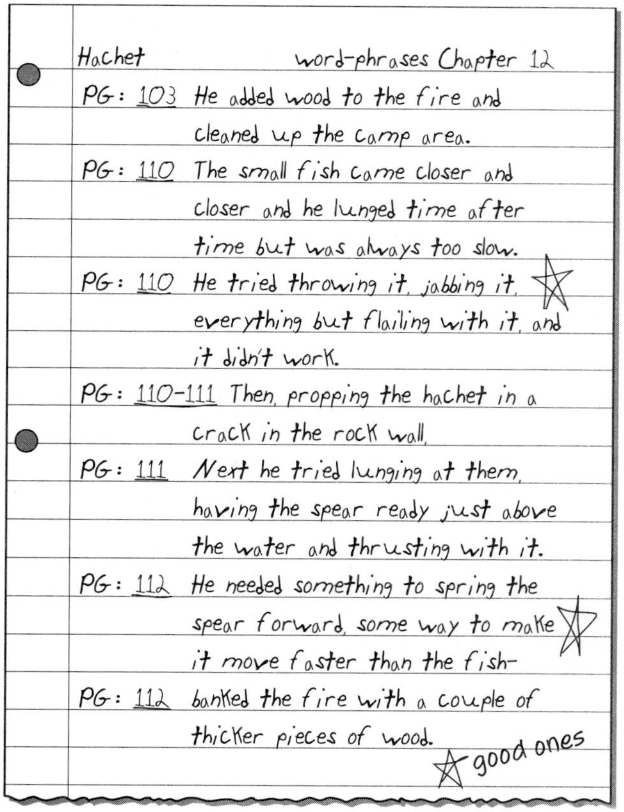

May 2

Brian's changes where wierd like when he heard things he could tell what made that sound right away. His vesion also changed. Brian didn't eat alot so he ~~lot~~ lost a few pounds so that changed him phisicaly. While Brian carried wood and other stuff he also put himself it to shape, and all that time sitting outside gave him a tan.

Figure 6.11 Log entry—Picture phrases

Hachet word-phrases Chapter 12

PG: 103 He added wood to the fire and cleaned up the camp area.

PG: 110 The small fish came closer and closer and he lunged time after time but was always too slow.

PG: 110 He tried throwing it, jabbing it, everything but flailing with it, and it didn't work. ☆

PG: 110–111 Then, propping the hachet in a crack in the rock wall,

PG: 111 Next he tried lunging at them, having the spear ready just above the water and thrusting with it.

PG: 112 He needed something to spring the spear forward, some way to make it move faster than the fish- ☆

PG: 112 banked the fire with a couple of thicker pieces of wood.

☆ good ones

is challenged by Jamie's accidental death. Through the first person voice we are able to feel children's struggles to understand the workings of the world. Smith's use of language is a rich, creative strength of this book. This literature study was developed by a group of teachers who enjoy meeting to talk about books. The study guide includes suggested lesson plans for each chapter, sample discussion guides, and suggested literature log prompts. With more experienced students, you would revise the focus of the MLTAs/MRTAs and discussion guides to encourage students to be more self-directed.

Monitoring Students' Growth in Literature Study

To evaluate individual students' growth in a literature-based reading program, you will observe their reading and writing behaviors, record observations that demonstrate effective use of strategies for making meaning in authentic literature, and sample their actual reading and writing. To monitor students, you will continue to develop the teacher and student portfolios begun in Chapter 5.

Teacher's Assessment Portfolio

Multiple opportunities exist for documenting student growth during whole-class literature study through observation and samples of work. Evaluation of the data will depend on your purposes for instruction and the strategies you emphasize.

Observing Students. What does Lou watch for when his students are engaged in literature study? During read-along, Lou observes students' responses while he reads aloud, using observation forms such as those presented in Chapter 5. During silent reading, he observes how effectively students are able to sustain their reading, beginning with information learned through observations of independent reading (see Chapter 5). In addition, Lou carefully notes the nature of the interaction during whole-class discussions and how students attend to response activities.

As we found earlier in this chapter, Lou's purposes for the study of *Hatchet* are as follows:

- Reading for pleasure
- Becoming aware of techniques authors use to reveal character growth, because the main character, Brian, is a dynamic character
- Exploring ways that readers learn about their strengths and weaknesses while studying the characters in Gary Paulsen's books
- Making inferences about a character through an omniscient narrator
- Using a discussion guide in student-led small-group discussion to help students become more independent in their study of literature
- Using close reading as an appropriate strategy in the study of a chapter book

From these purposes, Lou creates an open-ended form to record observations during the study of *Hatchet* (see Figure 6.12). The form also includes reading and writing behaviors that he emphasizes in MLTAs and MRTAs.

While Lou does not formally confer with students during whole-class literature study, he speaks with them informally as a way of clarifying what he observes, recording the highlights on his observations forms.

Samples of Student Work. Lou places selected samples of work completed during whole-class literature study in his assessment portfolio. Students will have completed discussion guides, literature log entries, and other selected activities. Lou selects one discussion guide and/or log entry that represents growth for a student in a particular reading or writing behavior, often conferring with the student about the piece selected. Lou notes on the piece why he is including it in the portfolio.

At the end of a grading period, usually either 6 or 9 weeks, Lou uses the items in the assessment portfolio in an overall evaluation of student growth in the language arts. Instead of placing a numerical or letter grade on each piece as it is completed, Lou prefers to evaluate student growth over the entire grading period. He feels that a long-term view provides a more accurate picture of what a student has accomplished.

Figure 6.12 Observation form for *Hatchet*

Literature Study: *Hatchet* **Name** ______________________

1. Reads for pleasure:
   - Shows positive response to reading.
   - Uses strategies effectively to enhance enjoyment.
2. Character:
   - Aware of ways authors reveal character growth.
   - Uses knowledge to learn about main character.
   - Learns about character through omniscient narrator.
   - Makes inferences about character through omniscient narrator.
3. Workshop procedures:
   - Uses discussion guide in small groups.
   - Takes turns, listens to others in discussions.
   - Makes written responses to text.
4. Increases reading effectiveness:
   - Learns new vocabulary in and out of context.
   - Uses text and personal knowledge to make predictions.
   - Retells and responds to important events.
   - Makes connections within text, between texts.
   - Uses a variety of strategies to make meaning.
   - Sustains silent reading.
5. Increases writing effectiveness:
   - Communicates clearly, concisely.
   - Uses new vocabulary in appropriate context.
   - Spelling appropriate for development.
   - Makes personal connections with text.
6. Unit theme:
   - Explores personal traits through reading.

Student Learning Portfolio

Throughout a whole-class literature study, such as *Hatchet*, students are either reading along or reading silently in the text, participating in discussions, recording their responses on discussion guides and/or literature logs, and performing other tasks.

Student Self-Evaluation. At the midpoint and at completion of a literature study, you will want to ask students to "step back" and view their own progress as readers, writers, and thinkers. Using the purposes identified for the "Gary Paulsen—Author" unit, Lou develops an open-ended self-assessment (Figure 6.13) to help his students consider their development of specific attitudes and behaviors. Students place completed forms in their learning portfolios.

Lou also uses the literature log throughout the literature study as a tool for finding out what individuals are thinking about the book. Periodically, Lou asks for specific feedback from students about the small groups, their ability to handle the silent reading, or any other area in which students may need support. Students are always free to use the log for comments, questions, or concerns that they want Lou to know about. In this sense, the literature log becomes a personal dialogue between Lou and a student. It is a way for Lou to respond individually to students.

At the end of a literature study, students select one or more log entries that show something about themselves as a reader or writer that they want represented in their learning portfolio. Students indicate on blank paper or a specially prepared form (Figure 6.14) their reasons for selecting specific items.

Respecting Diversity in Whole-Class Literature Study

Using a whole-class approach to literature study, you should become particularly sensitive to your selection of literature and your interactions with students. It is easy in a whole group to lose contact with some students. We must become "kid-watchers" (Goodman, 1985; Pappas, Kiefer, & Levstik, 1994). You must challenge yourself to carefully observe each student, and make anecdotal records that chronicle individual growth.

Over the school year, try to select literature in which all students see "people like themselves." Multicultural literature and writing reflecting a variety of lifestyles and

Figure 6.13 Student self-evaluation for whole-class literature study

Name ______________________________ **Self-Evaluation for *Hatchet* & "Gary Paulsen—Author" Unit**

Evaluate Your Reading:

Gary Paulsen lets you hear Brian's thoughts. How does this help you as the reader?

What does the author do to help you see how Brian's character changes?

While reading *Hatchet*—

What did you learn about yourself as a PERSON?

What did you learn about yourself as a READER?

Evaluate Your Small-Group Discussions:

How did using the discussion guides help you learn to talk about *Hatchet* without having a teacher in your group?

What did YOU do to help your group have good discussions?

What can make the discussions more helpful and interesting?

Figure 6.14 Open-ended student self-evaluation

Date ____________________

I chose this piece for my Learning Portfolio because it shows . . . ____________

____

____

Signed ____________________________

family structures should figure prominently in your selections (see Appendix B for suggestions). In addition, the main characters with whom students interact should be both male and female, and should reflect different types of personalities and ways of solving life's problems.

During whole-class literature study, you must be aware of the choices you provide for students. Students need many opportunities to share their knowledge and strategies as well as their needs. A balance between guided activities and choice provides the flexibility you need to meet the range of interests and needs in your classroom.

TAKE A MOMENT AND REFLECT . . .

Whole-class literature study provides introductory literature experiences for middle grade students.

Reading aloud to students removes decoding as an obstacle to literature study.

Reading aloud becomes reading along when students have personal copies of the text being studied.

Organizing instruction into a workshop framework brings cohesion to literary experiences.

Literature workshops move from:

- Whole-group instruction
- To small-group and independent work time
- Back to whole-group for closure

Instruction is drawn from:

- School district curriculum and objectives
- The literature being studied
- Student needs and interests

Whole-class literature workshop uses techniques to guide student thinking:

- Mediated listening thinking activity (MLTA)
- Mediated reading thinking activity (MRTA)

MLTA uses whole-class read-along to guide thinking.

MRTA uses whole-class silent reading to guide student thinking.

MLTA and MRTA are built on a thinking cycle of:

- predict
- listen or read
- respond
- connect

To implement a literature workshop:

- Analyze the text in light of student needs and school district curriculum
- Develop a plan for reading and study of the text
- Plan whole-class minilessons to support both the study of the text and workshop procedures
- Provide students with copies of the text
- Guide student thinking using either MLTA or MRTA
- Engage students in small-group and/or whole-class discussions about the text

Small group discussions are student-led, but are structured by teacher-made discussion guides.

Discussion guides:

- Encourage student response and connections within and across texts
- Become less structured as students are able to direct their own talk

Teachers monitor growth through assessment portfolios that contain:

- Documented observation of student performance
- Selected samples of student work that show strengths and areas of need

Students monitor their own growth through learning portfolios that contain:

- Selected samples of work with justification for selection
- Self-evaluation of progress in literature workshop activities

REFERENCES

Davey, B. (1983). Think-aloud—Modeling the cognitive processes of reading comprehension. *Journal of Reading, 27,* 44–47.

Five, C. L. (1988, Spring). From workbook to workshop: Increasing children's involvement in the reading process. *The New Advocate*, 103–113.

Goodman, Y. (1985). Kidwatching: Observing children in the classroom. In A. Jaggar & M. T. Smith-Burke (Eds.), *Observing the language learner* (pp. 9–18). Newark, DE: International Reading Association.

Hagerty, P. (1992). *Reader's workshop: Real reading*. Ontario: Scholastic Canada Ltd.

Heibert, E. H., & Colt, J. (1989). Patterns of literature-based reading instruction. *The Reading Teacher, 43,* 14–20.

Pappas, C. C., Kiefer, B. Z., & Levstik, L. S. (1994). *An integrated language perspective in the elementary school* (2nd ed.). New York: Longman.

Vygotsky, L. S. (1962). *Thought and language*. (E. Hanfmann & G. Vakar, Eds. & Trans.). Cambridge, MA: MIT Press.

Zarrillo, J. (1989). Teacher's interpretations of literature-based reading. *The Reading Teacher, 43,* 22–28.

CHILDREN'S LITERATURE

Paulsen, G. (1987). *Hatchet*. New York: Viking Penguin.

Smith, D. B. (1973). *A taste of blackberries*. New York: Thomas Y. Crowell.

7

Moving Toward Student-Led Literature Study

Book Clubs and Literature Circles

In this chapter . . .

We consider how to move from whole-class to small-group literature study, providing opportunities for students to assume greater responsibility for their talk about books. This chapter introduces you to book clubs and literature circles, exploring:

- planning for book clubs and literature circles,
- providing instruction in both approaches,
- reading and writing to prepare for book club and literature circle meetings,
- discussion in book clubs and literature circles, and
- effectively using community sharing sessions.

Before you begin . . .

Hatchet by Gary Paulsen (1987) and *The Sign of the Beaver* by Elizabeth George Speare (1983) are featured in the classroom scenarios and Your Turn/My Turn activities.

In addition. . .

Appendix B contains a listing of suggested books for book club and literature circle study.

Book clubs and literature circles offer students increased opportunity to participate in and direct their conversations about books. Students take the role of knowledgeable other in student-led discussions, sharing their thinking and supporting one another as they explore new ideas. Book clubs and literature circles move students toward independence and mature reading.

Avid readers, especially adults, typically have opportunities to participate in "book clubs," both formal and informal, that enable them to gather with others to converse about literature of personal interest (Raphael, McMahon, et al., 1992). It is such "grand conversations" about books that brings many readers back to the page (Peterson & Eeds, 1990). Through their research in literacy, McMahon, Raphael, and their colleagues (McMahon, 1991; Raphael, Goately, McMahon, & Woodman, 1992; Raphael & McMahon, 1994; Goatley, Brock, & Raphael, 1995) have developed an approach to literature-based reading that uses student-led book clubs in the classroom.

Literature circles, a term coined by Kathy Short (1986), grew out of her research in literature-based reading with Jerome Harste and Carolyn Burke in the mid 1980s. Literature circles are part of the authoring cycle (Short, 1986), a curricular framework that brings together the writing process, students' life experiences, and quality literature.

Book clubs and literature circles provide curricular frameworks that encourage middle grade students "to expand and critique their understandings about their reading through dialogue with other readers" (Short, 1995, p. x), and help them develop the ability to decide *what* to share about the literature they read and *how* to share it (Raphael, Goatley, et al., 1992).

What can we learn from each of these frameworks that will help us engage middle grade students in meaningful literature study? Our interest is in developing approaches that you can apply to classrooms in which students have experience with studying literature and are ready to accept more responsibility for structuring their work.

Book Clubs

A book club (McMahon, 1991; Raphael & McMahon, 1994) is an approach to literature-based reading that provides balance between teacher-led and student-led opportunities for learning. Raphael and McMahon developed the idea to answer the question, "How might literature-based instruction be created to encompass instruction in both comprehension and literature response?"(Raphael, McMahon, et al., 1992, p. 55).

In a book club, a classroom of students breaks into small student-led groups to talk about books. Unlike whole-class literature study, described in Chapter 6, book club discussions are directed by student interests and concerns rather than teacher-made discussion guides. The teacher, however, continues to have a significant role in text selection, group instruction, and facilitating whole-class discussions.

A book club approach is most effective when students are engaged in a unit or theme that includes the study of a series of related texts. Students' study and discussion lead to making connections within and across texts, potentially deepening their engagement with the books.

A book club approach has four components: reading, writing, discussion, and instruction. The amount of time devoted to each component varies daily, depending on the text being studied, students' familiarity with book club routines, and what occurred on the previous day:

- *Reading*—Through silent reading, partner reading, choral reading, oral reading/listening, and reading at home, students receive ample reading opportunities to be ready for sharing when the clubs meet.

- *Writing*—Students reflect on their reading, then write and/or draw in their literature logs in preparation for sharing ideas with their peers in club meetings.
- *Discussion*—Students have opportunities to interact with and learn from others in both book clubs and community sharing sessions as they internalize their ideas about literature and life.
- *Instruction*—Teachers provide opportunities for students to learn what and how to share their literary thinking with others.

The components in the book club approach are similar to those in whole-class literature study (Chapter 6). The essential difference is that book clubs provide students more responsibility for directing their own reading, writing, and talking about books.

Getting Started with Book Clubs

To dramatize our discussion of book clubs, we visit Lou's sixth-grade classroom once again. Lou is interested in moving his students toward more independent reading and book discussions. He decides this time to try a book club approach using *Hatchet* (Paulsen, 1987) instead of the whole-class literature study he used before. For this approach, Lou organizes instructional time as shown in Figure 7.1. Notice that he

Figure 7.1 Book club components

Teacher-led Whole Group (10–15 minutes):	• Community opening • Whole-class instruction (what and how to share) • Plans for the day (students share plans for preparing for book clubs)
Student-led Work Time (40–50 minutes):	• Reading (to prepare for book club meetings) silent partner reading choral reading oral reading/listening • Writing/drawing in literature log (to prepare for book club meetings) represent ideas reflect about story literature elements pose questions • Book club meetings student-led discussion share log entries
Teacher-led Whole Group (10–15 minutes):	• Community sharing session book club discussions • Evaluate the day • Plans for tomorrow

begins with a whole-class meeting, moves to various forms of student-led reading and writing, then to book club meetings in which students share their reading and writing, and finally back to the whole class for sharing the outcomes of the book clubs. Lou schedules additional reading time as needed, including SSR and time for reading at home, to help all students be prepared for book club meetings.

Compare the structure of whole-class literature study (Chapter 6, Figure 6.1) with that of book clubs, shown in Figure 7.1. Are any differences apparent to you?

My Turn

The one difference I hope you notice is that the responsibility for the reading shifts from the teacher to the student. You share the responsibility for instruction as students show you they are ready for more independence. In whole-class literature workshops, you moved from using only whole-class discussion (Figure 6.1, part A) to including small-group discussion with discussion guides (Figure 6.1, part B), while continuing to guide the reading. In a book club approach, you will share responsibility with students for the reading, as well as the content of the small-group discussions.

Planning for Book Clubs

As Lou plans for book clubs in his classroom, he considers three things:

1. The language arts curriculum he is required to teach
2. What *Hatchet* (or other selected texts) offers to the reader
3. The level of development of his students as readers and writers

While the required curriculum and the selected text(s) are important, Lou knows that the actual topics he selects for instruction depend on the feedback he gets from students during community sharing sessions and his observations during club meetings.

As Lou did for his literature workshop, he must develop a plan for reading *Hatchet;* a plan that will enable each student to be prepared to meet with their book club group. Lou will not read the text aloud to the class; instead the students will read the text themselves. As he plans, Lou must consider the amount and type of support each student might need to successfully complete the reading:

- Which students will need extended reading time at school, such as during SSR?
- Which students will need to have a copy of the book for reading at home?
- Which students will need to be matched with a more able partner to share the reading, or join a small group that will read the text orally?

For book clubs to be effective, each student must have adequate access to the ideas in the text.

To form each "club," or small group, Lou has students suggest the names of three others with whom they wish to work. Student choices typically lead to heterogeneous groups. If not, Lou makes some of the choices to be sure the groups are diverse, yet balanced by personality and reading experience. His class has seven book club groups, six with four members each and one with five.

With *Hatchet,* Lou's class begins the unit of study, considered in Chapter 6, "Gary Paulsen—Author." After completing *Hatchet,* Lou will extend the theme study by adding other Paulsen books, which students study in their book clubs. Studying related books enables students to make connections not only within a text but also between texts. Intertextual connections strengthen students' understanding of author's craft and their own flexibility in making meaning. Appendix B contains a listing of suggested books for literature study.

Instruction in Book Clubs

Each day Lou gathers the class together to begin their literature study and provides whole-class instruction, similar to the minilessons in the literature workshops. He focuses on the following:

- Book club procedures and how to share (taking turns, listening to others, etc.)
- Making decisions about what to share (personal responses, unresolved questions, relationships of the current text to other texts, etc.)
- Expanding students' knowledge of literary possibilities (author's craft, development and use of particular literary elements, etc.)

Lou's decisions to provide specific instruction depend on what students already know and what support they must receive. Whenever possible, Lou demonstrates and shows concrete examples to support students' learning.

As Hill (1995) suggests, Lou keeps a running list of the instructional lessons he has developed and presented to the class, which enables him to see patterns in his instruction. The list also serves to document the skill and strategy instruction that occurs in his classroom. Lou's list includes lessons on book club procedures, effective reading and writing strategies, and on deciding what thoughts to share and how best to share them.

Book Club Procedures

- What does it mean to be responsible for my own reading?
- Choosing the best way to get my reading done for a book club meeting.
- Making my learning log work for me:

  Choosing the best time to record my ideas.

  Choosing what ideas to record.

  Choosing the best way to record my ideas.
- What do we do during a book club meeting?
- How is a book club different from a reading group?
- What is a community sharing session?
- How does discussion in book club compare to discussion in a community sharing session?

Effective Reading and Writing Strategies

- What do I do when I *monitor* my own reading?
- How do I *know* when reading is making sense?
- Sometimes I get confused when I read. What should I do?
- What can I do about words I don't know?
- When should I use context clues?
- When should I use phonics clues?

- How can I tell if I should try phonics or structure?
- What happens if I don't agree with what the author is saying?
- Why do I get different ideas from reading than my friends do?
- When should I listen to the author? When should I listen to myself?

Deciding What to Share

- What seems important to me about this book?
- What do I notice about the way the author has put ideas together?
- Am I responding to particular ways that the author used story elements (plot, setting, character, theme, point of view, style) to tell the story? If so, what elements do I really notice?
- What questions do I ask myself as I read? Could others in my book club be asking themselves the same questions?
- When I finish reading, which of my questions are still unanswered?
- How does this story relate to me?
- How does this story relate to what I already know?
- Does this story remind me of other books I have read or know about?
- What does this book really have to say to me about life?
- I can add to the discussion by sharing things in my log (clusters or mapping, timelines, lists, charts, annotated drawings, etc.) and explaining my thinking.
- How can I learn from what I contributed to the group discussion?

Deciding How to Share

- How can I help others understand what is important to me about this book?
- People take turns in a discussion. How should I do that?
- What does it mean to really listen to other people's ideas?
- How can I help myself be a better listener?
- How do I show others that I really care about what they say?
- I can contribute to discussion by doing the following:

  Telling others what I think.

  Commenting on an idea shared by another student.
- When I want to know more, I can ask a question about another person's ideas.
- What can I learn from looking at my own participation in the group?

Considering what you know about the development of middle grade students, what ideas do you have for helping them think about *how* to share their ideas with others in student-led discussions? Discuss your ideas with a peer.

My Turn

I especially would like for students to *show respect for each other's ideas.* For respect to be present in book club discussions, I must develop it in all aspects of classroom life. I cannot expect attentive listening, turn taking, or thoughtful responses in the book clubs only. Throughout the school day I, as the adult model, must show students that the behaviors I expect of them are the same behaviors that I demonstrate with them. Secondly, I must help students get to know each other in social, as well as academic, situations so they are comfortable with one another and can trust others with their thoughts. Finally, the tasks I ask students to engage in and the quality of the books I ask them to read must be worthy of their attention.

Reading to Prepare for Book Clubs

When Lou introduces *Hatchet* to the students, he provides a copy of a day-by-day reading plan that he has developed, shown in Figure 7.2. Students place the plan in their literature log for reference and will use it to pace their reading in preparation for book club meetings. Students typically meet with members of their book club every day.

To set the tone for the whole-class study, Lou reads aloud Chapter 1 as students follow along in their own copies. As he reads aloud, Lou uses an MLTA, just as he did in the literature workshop. He talks aloud and thinks aloud to emphasize his own thinking and questioning, modeling the way proficient readers might prepare for a book club discussion. On subsequent days, students will read on their own. Lou encourages class discussion of the reading plan, including evaluation of the decisions that each student makes to accomplish the reading (silent, partners, choral, etc.). Lou encourages students to use this opportunity to discover more about their own needs as they pace their reading and to record their observations in the comments section of their plan (see Figure 7.2).

Figure 7.2 Sample reading plan for book club

Name ______________________			**Reading Plan for *Hatchet***
Date	**Chapter**	**Pages**	**Comments**
	1	12	
	2	13	
	3 & 4	16	
	5	12	
	6	10	
	7	12	
	8 & 9	14	
	10 & 11	15	
	12 & 13	17	
	14 & 15	18	
	16	14	
	17	11	
	18	10	
	19 & Epilogue	11	

Students independently read and write as they prepare for book club meetings.

Students often read ahead when they are interested in a story. When they do, Lou asks them to reread the section to be discussed that day so that it will be fresh and they will be able to make significant contributions to the discussion.

Writing to Prepare for Book Clubs

Students' writing in a book club approach focuses their attention on the impending discussion and helps them to take relevant stances that lead to literary understanding (Langer, 1994). Lou notices that often his students use the writing to make links between different parts of a text or across texts in the same unit of study.

At the beginning of the study, Lou models how he uses his literature log. After introducing *Hatchet* by reading Chapter 1 aloud, he places a page of his own log on the overhead projector and makes his entry in response to the chapter (Figure 7.3).

Lou then encourages students to make entries in their own logs in preparation for the book club meetings. He reminds them of the many types of entries the class has used in the past (see also Raphael & McMahon, 1994), including the following:

- *Personal comparisons or connections* the reader makes with some particular aspect of the book
- *Questions or unresolved issues* that the reader wants to share with/get response from group members
- *Important events or parts* of the book that the reader wants to remember
- *Character charts or maps* that show physical features, actions, interactions with other characters, or any personal interest in a character that the reader explores or wants to remember

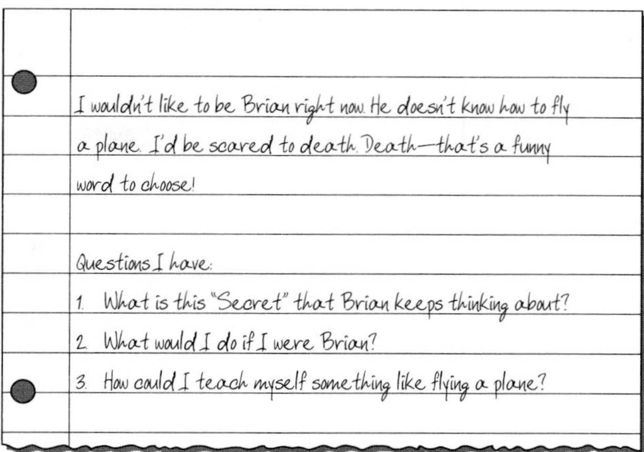

Figure 7.3 Literature log entry—*Hatchet,* chapter 1

- *Illustrations* of pictures in the reader's head (artistic and written description) in response to author's description or reader's personal experience, along with explanation of their importance
- *Words and phrases* that interest the reader or that the reader wants to learn more about
- *Something in particular that the author does* that engages the reader
- *Personal commentary or critique* of the story or the author's style

The log is an excellent source of information for evaluating students' engagement with books and in book club discussions. Laura Pardo (1992), a fifth-grade teacher, has her students brainstorm an idea list for reading logs and makes it a permanent bulletin board. As her students discover new possibilities for the literature log, Laura provides opportunity for students to teach their peers.

Book Club Meetings

When the members of book clubs meet, discussions are intended to be a natural outgrowth of their reading and writing about books. Unlike the literature workshop, students are not given a teacher-made discussion guide. Instead, students share responses from their literature logs as the starting point for small-group discussions. The direction that the discussion takes then depends on the interests of the group members.

In their research with book clubs, Raphael, McMahon, et al. (1992) identify a number of purposes for student talk in book clubs:

- Share responses from reading logs.
- Discuss process of making responses.
- Discuss main points of a text.
- Clarify points of confusion.
- Make connections within and across texts.
- Relate ideas from text to personal feelings, experiences, and prior knowledge.
- Identify author's purposes and critique success at achieving those purposes.

These purposes demonstrate that, when provided opportunity to direct their own discussions, students can achieve significant understanding about literature and make connections between themselves and texts.

Read the beginning of one group's discussion after reading Chapter 1 of *Hatchet.* This book club has four members, Travis, Jessie, Brad, and T. C.:

Travis: OK, I'll start. In my log I wrote, "Right now I just want to keep reading to find out what's going to happen to Brian."

Jessie: I wrote, "I'd be too scared to do anything. I wouldn't be able to remember what the pilot had shown me."

Brad: Hey, Brian can't die now, this is only Chapter 1.

Travis: I can't believe the pilot had a heart attack! I didn't know that when someone has a heart attack, they, ya' know, the smell.

Brad: Maybe when you're in all that pain, you can't help what your body does, you can't keep gas in.

Jessie: I have a question. What do you think the "Secret" is?

T. C.: It must be something that made his parents break up.

Travis: Maybe one of his parents went with someone else, ya' know, like one of them fell in love with someone else.

T. C.: Or maybe one of them did something really embarrassing.

Brad: Well Brian knows what it is and it sure does bother him!

T. C.: I want to know what it is!

Jessie: Well, I have another question then. What do you think Brian is going to do now? . . .

This discussion begins with students reading from their logs. At first the talk is somewhat stilted, then begins to sound a little more like natural conversation. In conversational groups such as this, members often take on different roles. Notice that Jessie takes the role of the "question-asker" and Brad seems to be the "clarifier."

What purposes do we see in the preceding conversation? If we consider the purposes that Raphael and her colleagues identified, we might say the following:

- Travis and Jessie share responses from their logs.
- Jessie makes a personal connection with her own feelings.
- Travis and Brad discuss main points of the text (heart attack) and attempt to clarify their own confusion between the text and personal background knowledge of heart attacks.
- T. C., Travis, and Brad try to clarify their confusion about the "Secret."

How do the topics raised compare to the questions on the discussion guide used during the literature workshop in Chapter 6? (See Figures 6.6 and 6.7.) Is student-led discussion a potential learning opportunity in Lou's classroom? Remember that developmental learning theory (Holdaway, 1980) suggests that learners need many opportunities to monitor, pace, and evaluate their own work as they make approximations toward more mature reading and writing. Book clubs provide such opportunity.

Community Sharing Sessions

After about 15 minutes, Lou asks the book clubs to bring their discussion to closure for that day by deciding on an idea or question to discuss with the whole class in a community sharing session. Club members know their discussion will continue tomorrow, after they have read Chapter 2.

As the class settles into a configuration for face-to-face discussion, Lou begins by asking, "What are some of the ideas that your group thinks are most interesting or important in this chapter?" Listening to the views of others and taking turns in discussion become extremely important in this whole-class sharing session. All members do not have to participate, but all must be attentive to their classmates.

Lou has tried having one student begin the session, progressing around the circle letting students who wish to make initial comments do so, then opening up for whole-class discussion. He has found, however, that this approach leads to a rather stilted discussion and actually keeps the class from moving from discussion to conversation. Now he opens with a general question or asks if any student would like to begin.

Community sharing should be an inclusive activity. All students have participated in book clubs and have valuable ideas, comments, and questions to share with the class. Lou sees his role as facilitator and encourager, helping all students feel that their thinking will be valued. He must be sure that the ideas of all students receive respect through attentive listening and polite response by their peers.

To support students as they learn self-direction, Lou includes evaluative discussion at the end of each sharing session. The class spends a few minutes "debriefing" the day (Redman, 1995), discussing what went well and addressing possible solutions for problems. The class also looks ahead to the next day of book clubs and anticipates what will occur.

As Lou's sixth-grade class progresses through *Hatchet,* the daily book club routine will become opening, student-led reading, student-led writing, student-led book clubs, and joint student- and teacher-led sharing sessions. Book clubs are an excellent way to move students toward independence as learners.

Now that we have discussed the book club approach, what benefits do you see in it? When might book clubs be more appropriate than whole-class studies?

The benefits I see are increased opportunity for self-direction and independence for students, while I continue to provide support through whole-class instruction, community sharing sessions, and assessment of student progress. By the time that students are in the middle grades, they should have many opportunities for self-direction, but often their reading and writing experiences have not prepared them for such independence. Book clubs allow me to gradually release control of instruction by providing a predictable structure in which students learn to prepare for and monitor their own discussions.

LITERATURE CIRCLES

Kathy Short (1995) captures the essence of literature circles when she says, "Literature circles provide a curricular structure to support children in exploring their rough draft understandings of literature with other readers" (p. x). The term *rough draft* reminds us of writing processes. In literature circles, students share their "rough draft" ideas about their reading and receive response from others, causing them to reflect on their ideas and consider the ideas of others, and perhaps revise their own ideas in some way, just as they revise their writing.

Since the mid 1980s, teachers have talked about and experimented with literature circles in middle grade classrooms. While interpretations vary, many commonalities exist. The following are characteristics of most literature circles:

- Four to six students gather together to talk about books they are reading.
- Groups are formed by students who choose the same book to read.
- Groups are heterogeneous, representing a range of interests and abilities.
- Groups may focus on one core book or on a number of related books.
- Books are typically related by author, genre, topic, or the study of a particular literary element.
- Students determine the pace of the reading and when the groups will meet.
- The teacher may or may not be present during the literature circles.
- In addition to discussions, students typically respond to texts through journals, logs, and/or projects.

Why do teachers choose literature circles? Owens (1995) cites several reasons, stating that literature circles do all of the following:

- Promote a love for literature and positive attitudes toward reading.
- Reflect a constructivist, student-centered model of literacy.
- Encourage extensive and intensive reading.
- Invite natural discussions that lead to student inquiry and critical thinking.
- Support diverse response to text.
- Foster interaction and collaboration, provide choice, and encourage responsibility.
- Expose students to literature from multiple perspectives.
- Nurture reflection and self-evaluation.

As you can see, a number of these reasons are similar to those for using literature workshops and book clubs. Literature circles, however, typically offer more opportunities for student choice and decision making.

What influences the success of literature circles? Kary Brown (1995), a fifth-grade teacher, suggests that the success of literature circles (and this applies to book clubs also) is influenced by a number of factors:

- The variety and quality of books selected for study
- The degree of choice and ownership students have
- Students' motivation and interest in reading and talking about their chosen books
- Students' previous experiences with literature circles
- The amount of modeling by the teacher and other students to demonstrate aspects of literature circles such as deciding what and how to share
- Group dynamics

Students' ability to work effectively in literature circles and book clubs improves over time. You will want to provide initial guidance and direction for students, reducing support in later stages.

Getting Started with Literature Circles

Meet Melodia, a sixth- and seventh-grade middle school reading teacher. After introducing a unit called, "Meeting the Challenge," through whole-class literature study with *Hatchet* (Paulsen, 1987), Melodia moves to literature circles so that students have the opportunity to make choices about the texts they read and become more independent in directing how their reading and writing about text will occur. She organizes rotating 75-minute blocks for literature circles, as shown in Figure 7.4. Note that the opening and closing activities resemble whole-class literature workshops and book clubs, while the central work time is a flexible block of activity. Herein lies the real difference between literature circles and book clubs. In literature circles, students not only choose the books they will read, but they also choose when they will read, when their groups will meet to talk about the books, and how they wish to respond to their text.

Your Turn

Compare the structure of a literature circle with the book club earlier in this chapter, referring to Figures 7.1 and 7.4. What similarities do you see? Are any differences apparent to you?

My Turn

Both approaches open and close with what appear to be similar teacher-led whole group activities. Even the elements in the student-led work time seem very similar, with the exception of flexible strategy grouping and informal conferences added to the literature circle approach. The literature circle structure identifies the reading, writing, and group meetings as self-paced, which suggests more student control than in book clubs. Let's see!

■

Melodia often uses literature circles to extend whole-class literature study. After her students' whole-class study of *Hatchet,* Melodia selects five books (multiple copies

Figure 7.4 Literature circle components

Teacher-led Whole Group (10–15 minutes):	• Community opening • Whole-class minilessons—applicable to all students or texts • Plans for the day
Student-led Work Time (40–60 minutes):	• Self-paced reading according to group plan • Self-paced response literature log projects • Literature circles meet according to group plan • Flexible strategy groups by invitation specific practice • Informal conferences
Teacher-led Whole Group (10–20 minutes):	• Community sharing session literature circle discussions book talks response projects • Evaluate the day • Plans for tomorrow

of each text are available) that reflect the unit theme, "Meeting the Challenge." In each text the characters learn something about themselves and others as a result of a challenging situation:

- *The Sign of the Beaver* (Speare, 1983). Twelve-year-old Matt is left alone in the Maine wilderness, among the Beaver tribe and wild animals, to tend the cabin for at least six weeks until his father returns with the rest of the family.
- *Felita* (Mohr, 1979). Felita must leave her friends when her Puerto Rican family decides to move to a better neighborhood, only to face discrimination in the new neighborhood.
- *The Great Gilly Hopkins* (Paterson, 1978). Giladrial Hopkins, facing her third foster home in as many years, must come to terms with who she is, a mother who does not want her, and her need for a place to call home.
- *Time for Andrew: A Ghost Story* (Hahn, 1994). Andrew moves through time, switching places with an ancestor, only to discover family life and values that challenge the person he is and wants to become.
- *Thunder Rolling in the Mountains* (O'Dell & Hall, 1992). Sound of Running Feet, daughter of Chief Joseph of the Nez Perce, must help her people escape to Canada or be forced to live on a reservation.

The books represent a variety of genres (contemporary realistic fiction, historical fiction, and a time-travel fantasy) and a range of reading levels. They also contain strong female and male roles; illustrations of Native American, Puerto Rican, and Caucasian cultures; and family configurations that include extended, two-parent, and foster families.

Just before the class completes *Hatchet,* Melodia introduces the five books. She indicates the level of challenge of each book and makes them available for browsing. She urges students to "check the fit" of any book they think they might choose by reading several pages. During the class session before the literature circles begin, students submit a first and second book choice. Melodia tries to give students their first choice, while keeping the groups balanced by reading experience and personality.

Planning for Literature Circles

Developing a Reading Plan. On the first day of literature circles the students develop a reading plan for their selected book. Melodia asks each group to try to set up a plan they can complete within three weeks. She also reminds the groups to be sure that their plan will meet the needs of each group member and enable everyone in the group to feel successful. Melodia works with each literature circle to be sure that less experienced students allow ample time to complete the reading and select the most effective way to do so. She also provides blank forms, similar to Lou's form (see Figure 7.2), for students to complete when their circle develops a reading plan.

Students often refer to the pacing of previous whole-class studies to help them decide on a reading plan. Having just completed *Hatchet,* students use that reading plan to help them decide how much to read before scheduling a literature circle. They also think about their own interactions with the text.

The group reading *The Sign of the Beaver* (Speare, 1983—25 chapters, 135 pages, sixth-grade reading level) decides to read twice the number of pages as they did in *Hatchet* before they meet in their circles, and plans to meet every other day. Throughout their reading of *Hatchet,* group members found themselves wanting to read ahead, so they decide that reading more text at one time might be more satisfying. They also decide that over a weekend they can read a few extra pages. The group plans to complete the reading in two weeks, then plans a week to enjoy response activities and to prepare to share the book in the community session. Figure 7.5 shows the group's reading plan.

In contrast, the group that chose to read *Felita* (Mohr, 1979—7 chapters, 112 pages, fourth-grade reading level), feels uncertain about determining their own reading schedule. They call Melodia over to their group meeting and discuss their feelings with her. She asks them how they felt about the daily reading schedule they followed for *Hatchet,* and suggests they might consider such a schedule if it feels comfortable. Melodia also reminds the group that they are free to change the schedule if they gain confidence and do not need to meet each day. The group decides to follow a daily schedule, reading a chapter each day, with the exception of Chapter 2 (the group discovers that Chapter 2 is much longer than the others, so they decide to give it two days rather than one). Their reading plan is shown in Figure 7.6.

Figure 7.5 Student-developed reading plan for *The Sign of the Beaver*

Name Darren Reading Plan for The Sign of the Beaver

Circle meets on	Chapter	No. of Pages to read	Comments
Tues.	1-4	21	
Thurs.	5-9	22	
Mon.	10-15	30	
Wed.	16-19	29	
Fri.	20-25	29	
3rd Week			prepare to share with class

My plan is . . . to get my reading done in class and at home. I tried the book when we were choosing. It's pretty easy for me. I know most of the words. If I don't get done at school I'll take it home. My group will help me if I need it.

Figure 7.6 Student-developed reading plan for *Felita*

Name: Zeena Reading Plan for: FeliTa

Circle meets on	Chapter	No. of Pages to read	Comments
Tues.	1	14	
Wed.	2 (1/2)	12	
Thurs.	2 (1/2)	12	
Fri.	3	9	
Mon.	4	14	
Tues.	5	10	
Wed.	6	11	
Thurs.	7	11	
Fri.-Fri.			projecT for sharing

My plan is . . . To read every day aT school (when I geT exTra Time) and every nighT aT home. I Take my Time when I read. Irene is going To help me by checking my reading every day and reminding me To find a quieT place. SomeTimes we will read TogeTher.

Helping Students Accept Responsibility. Melodia asks each group to give her a copy of their reading plan. She also asks students to indicate how they will accomplish the reading. She encourages each literature circle also to talk about how they can help each other get the reading completed if necessary.

Melodia wants her students to be responsible for their decisions, but she is well aware that many lack the experience. When she knows what they are trying to accomplish, Melodia is better able to adjust both her individual and whole-class instruction. As the literature circles begin, Melodia will combine what she knows about her students with observations of their independent and group work to anticipate when and how she might help them move toward independence.

Instruction in Literature Circles

Literature circles are intended to foster independence among students. Melodia provides instruction through whole-class minilessons, flexible strategy groups, informal individual conferences, and discussion during community sharing sessions. She engages students in thinking about new literature circle procedures, continues to "nudge" their understanding of literary possibilities, and encourages them to practice strategies that competent, independent learners use to make their reading and writing satisfying.

Whole-Class Minilessons. You already know of many possibilities for minilessons. We have considered lists of possible topics in whole-class instruction and have viewed examples of actual minilessons and group instruction. We can draw on what we know:

- *General knowledge* of literature and reading *background* (Chapter 2)
- *Procedures* for book clubs (Chapter 7) and reader's workshop (to be discussed in Chapter 8)
- *Literary lessons* for literature workshop (Chapter 6)
- *Strategy lessons* for book clubs (Chapter 7)

Flexible Strategy Groups. During student-led work time, Melodia invites groups of students who have specific needs to meet with her in small groups. Typically the groups focus on strategies for effective reading and writing. Melodia emphasizes monitoring and pacing of silent reading, two areas that she observes challenge her students. These small groups also provide additional practice with selected issues raised in whole-class minilessons.

Melodia encourages students to become aware of their own needs as learners. When the class begins the unit, "Meeting the Challenge," Melodia mounts a poster titled, "Invitations" on the wall near the library corner and asks students to use the poster to indicate when they need particular types of strategy groups. When three or more students indicate a similar need, Melodia offers a small-group session, or may invite students to join a strategy group. Otherwise, Melodia confers with individuals or pairs of students.

Informal Conferences. During the work time, Melodia moves about the classroom, observing students and stopping periodically to chat with them about their work. Students also initiate informal conferences with Melodia to share log entries, raise questions about a text, seek support for project plans, settle disputes in literature circles (which she mediates when appropriate), and the like. As she circulates she is careful not to disturb any student who is deeply engaged in reading, writing, or worthy conversation. Melodia makes mental notes about her interactions, and later records essential observations for ongoing student evaluation.

Whole-Class Discussions. The class draws together for whole-class instruction at the beginning and end of each literature circle day. Minilessons are the focus of the opening class session, sharing and book talks are the focus of the closing session. Melodia plans whole-class instruction to focus on issues that the majority of students need, such as literature circle procedures and reading or writing strategies that lead to independence. She saves more specialized or individual issues for informal conferences or strategy groups.

Plans for the Day. During each opening class meeting, Melodia checks the "status of the class" (Atwell, 1987). She asks students to tell her about their plans for the work time. They come to expect Melodia's query and focus their attention on what they intend to accomplish during the work time. Responses range from silent reading in readiness for the literature circle to putting the final touches on a project to share during the community session. From these responses, Melodia has a better idea of the role(s) she must take during work time.

Reading to Prepare for Literature Circles

Each group develops a plan to guide their reading, which helps students learn to focus their attention during the work time, to set goals for themselves, and to pace their reading. Middle grade students benefit from this organizational tool. Melodia's role is one of support: When the reading is going well, she pulls back and lets students remain in control. When it is not going well, she moves in to help students evaluate the situation and refocus, then pulls back once again. Her goal is for students to learn to monitor their own progress.

Reading for literature circles requires greater amounts of time as books become longer and more complex. Melodia's students must increase their reading time at home or use the "free" time available during other class periods or in advisory. If Melodia was in a self-contained classroom and had the entire day with one class of students, she could also use the time typically devoted to independent reading (SSR) to read literature circle books.

During the middle grades, students should sink into silent reading and become flexible readers, able to move easily between silent and oral reading. However, some students will have spent far too much time in oral reading and will not be very proficient silent readers. In addition, they may not have consolidated the skills needed to move between oral and silent reading. You will need to carefully observe students during periods of independent reading for evidence that they understand how to sustain themselves during silent reading. This may be an area for instruction during flexible strategy groups.

Writing to Prepare for Literature Circles

Literature circles typically allow a great deal of choice. With book clubs, students prepare for club meetings by making entries in their literature logs. When Melodia moves to literature circles, she does not require her students to make log entries each day. Her purpose for the log does not change, but her goal changes for students. Now Melodia is working for student independence!

Melodia wants students to view writing as relevant and satisfying and to decide the appropriate times to use writing for pleasure and writing to learn. If she continues to require daily log entries, then she retains control and students will have little decision-making experience. Melodia tries to expand their knowledge of the possibilities for written response. Throughout the literature circle workshop, Melodia (1) models a variety of ways to use the log, discussing formats and purposes for entries, (2) encourages students to share the ways they use their logs, (3) displays log entries that show how writing helps to support thinking, and (4) encourages using logs in whole-class meetings, literature circles, strategy groups, and conferences.

The one request that Melodia makes of her students is to come to the literature circle meetings prepared with notes, questions, and/or specific places in their reading that warrant discussion, and prepared to share a particularly interesting portion of text with their group.

One tool that Melodia has found useful to encourage writing is the use of "sticky" notes (such as Post-it™ notes). Students place a large sticky note on the front of their

Middle grade students should have many opportunities to direct their own book discussions.

book, on which they collect interesting words and phrases and use smaller sticky notes to mark places in the text for sharing, questioning, or commenting. Students are eager to use the notes, which they sometimes refer to as their "sticky note log."

Melodia wants her students to understand writing as a purposeful act. Throughout the day, she emphasizes ways that writing captures thinking, helping readers remember details and notice changes in their ideas and feelings.

Literature Circle Meetings

Circles meet according to the reading plans that each group develops, and may range from each class session (typically three per week) to only once a week. One or two meetings per week is typical, depending upon the amount of text students are able to be responsible for.

Today, the group that chose *The Sign of the Beaver* (Speare, 1983) is having its first meeting. Darren, Oswaldo, Rachel, Paul, and Breann have each read chapters 1 through 4 (21 pages) according to their plan, and gather at a table in the back corner of the room with their books, literature logs, and pencils.

One member assumes responsibility at each group meeting for checking to be sure that each person is prepared and ready for discussion, then gets the discussion started. Today is Breann's turn. She asks each member if they have completed the day's reading, are prepared for discussion, and noted their work on the reading plan. Paul says he would like to share first. Breann agrees and the conversation begins.

Paul: Matt sure is learning a lot about living by himself. In Chapter 3 he kept having the feeling that he shouldn't trust that stranger. Then the stranger took his father's gun. I started wondering why Matt let that happen. He didn't trust him. Then I remembered a part on page 15:

> Then he [Matt] felt ashamed. What would his father say about begrudging a stranger a meal and a night's rest? [Speare, 1983, p. 15]

He was trying to do what he thought was right, but I would have hidden the gun too, just to be safe.

Darren: He fell asleep and the guy took off. He really needed that gun! That cabin is pretty small. Where could he have hidden the gun?

Paul: He was thinking he should have kept it in his hands. That's not smart. The guy would see it and maybe hurt Matt. Since there's no people around, I'd hide it in the woods. It would be hard to find. But Matt didn't think of that.

Rachel: Nothing like that had happened to him before. This is all new. Sometimes you don't know what to do until after something happens to you. You don't expect it.

Oswaldo: He didn't expect the bear either. He forgot to bar the door.

Breann: What does that mean—"bar the door"? I wrote that down to ask about.

Oswaldo: It's a piece of wood that you lay across the door like this (makes a sketch on his paper). I think it's because they didn't have locks. The bar is kind of like a lock.

Breann: Why should they have to lock their doors? No one is around there.

Darren: Bears are! I don't think Matt's been on his own before. Six weeks. That's a long time. My parents would never leave me and my brother that long.

Paul: Mine sure wouldn't.

Rachel: Wasn't it cool the way he counted the days, making notches on sticks? Each stick was a week—kind of a calendar.

Breann: I keep wondering when he's going to meet some Indians. It has to happen. The cover gave it away.

Paul: Remember when the stranger said the Indians left for a while because of the bugs but they would be coming back soon? Maybe that was a hint.

The conversation continues in this way for 15 to 20 minutes and ends with students checking the next reading assignment and meeting date. Similar to book club meetings, literature circle talk is influenced by notes that students have made in their literature or sticky note logs. In a book club, students make daily entries before their club meets and use the log to guide the discussion. In a literature circle, students have more freedom to use their log as it fits their purposes as readers. Consequently, topics of discussion may be both in readers' minds and written in their logs. When discussion reaches this level, it becomes more adultlike and natural.

After the circle meeting, Melodia asks students to evaluate their preparation and participation. Students use a simple form the class developed when literature circles were first introduced (see Figure 7.9). With independence as a goal, students must learn to evaluate and correct their own behavior.

Community Sharing Sessions

To bring closure each day, the class gathers together to share responses to books and new insights as readers and writers. This session is quite similar to the closing session for a book club approach, except that students are reading a variety of books and this session provides opportunity for them to make intertextual connections, especially with any core books they may have in common. In Melodia's class, *Hatchet* is a core book. One of Melodia's tasks is to help students extend their understanding of the theme, "Meeting the Challenge," by making connections between texts.

Orchestrating this session takes planning. Melodia asks students to indicate on a signup sheet when they wish class time to share response projects. She also keeps track of scheduled literature circle meetings and invites groups to share outcomes with the class, encouraging intertextual connections.

You have been introduced to two approaches to small-group literature study, book clubs, and literature circles. What similarities and differences do you find in these two approaches when you compare their components, organization, teacher's role, and students' role? Compare your ideas with a colleague's.

My Turn

The *components* of these two approaches are similar, though they may have different names. Both include some form of reading (silent reading, partner reading, and/or choral reading), writing (literature logs), discussion (small-group and whole-class sessions), and instruction (whole-class and/or flexible groups).

The overall *organization* is also similar. Both begin and end with whole-group meetings, the first usually including instruction that relates to either procedures, literature, or strategies. The final meeting is a sharing session, focused by what occurs in the small-group discussions. Reading, writing, and small-group discussions during work time occur in slightly different ways:

- Literature circles—Work time is flexible. Small groups are not doing the same things each day, and students make more decisions about the pace of their work.
- Book clubs—Each component occurs daily, for varying amounts of time. While the teacher sets up the amount of reading for each day, students decide how they will accomplish it. Writing in the literature log is typically student directed, but occasionally the teacher may provide a writing prompt. Students direct book club discussions with the aid of literature log entries.

The *teacher's role* in both book clubs and literature circles is as a facilitator who structures the environment for learning, then steps back to let children learn how to take control of their learning. There is a slightly higher degree of teacher-initiated structure in a book club approach than with literature circles.

The *students' role* is more self-directed in a literature circle approach than in book clubs. Both approaches encourage independence, and structure the learning environment for students to take control of their learning.

■

Monitoring Students' Growth as Readers and Writers

In Chapter 6 we considered evaluation issues that are central to any form of literature-based reading and writing instruction. In this section we add to that discussion your purposes for evaluation in literature study that emphasizes small groups and increased independence.

Teacher's Assessment Portfolio

You may document student growth during small-group literature study through observation, informal conferences, and samples of student work. Hill (1995), who works with teachers using a literature circle approach, suggests that monitoring student progress in small groups makes it possible for teachers to do the following:

- Provide immediate feedback to students.
- Plan for instruction.
- Assess students' as readers and writers.

- Prepare progress reports for parents and students.
- Document student performance and growth.

Your purposes for instruction will ultimately determine how you choose to evaluate your students.

Observation and Informal Conferences. A primary purpose for moving from whole-class literature study to book clubs and literature circles is to provide opportunities for students to make more decisions about their own reading and discussion of texts. These are the two areas on which you will focus as you make anecdotal notes.

In Lou's and Melodia's classrooms, students spend a great deal of time reading to prepare for book club and literature circle discussions. After whole-class lessons on selecting appropriate reading materials, developing group reading plans, and becoming aware of pacing one's own reading, Lou and Melodia must observe to see which behaviors students are able to use effectively and which require more development and support.

During reading time, Melodia and Lou observe how students choose to complete their daily reading. They encourage silent reading and provide additional support to students who have difficulty.

Lou joins one or two book club groups each day as an observer and note taker. As Lou listens in on discussions, he gathers ideas about students' engagement with the text and sees areas in which they might need support. He looks for behaviors such as sharing personal feelings and connections, discussing main points in a text, sharing contents of literature logs, responding to others' ideas, consulting the text to support thinking, helping to clarify points of confusion, and making connections within and across texts or with the author.

He jots notes on a group grid (Figure 7.7) which allows him to see trends across members of a group. (The form he uses has space for four students across because most of the book clubs in his classroom have four members.) Melodia uses a similar procedure with literature circles.

When students select a literature circle text, Melodia observes the level of student engagement and watches for body language that suggests students' attitudes toward reading. In addition, Melodia visits with students about their choice of text and how the

Figure 7.7 Recording observations

Date:_____ Text:_______________________________

Date:_____ Text:_______________________________

reading is progressing. She initially writes her observations on a grid similar to Lou's, but eventually transfers them to individual forms (Figure 7.8) and places them in her assessment portfolio.

Figure 7.8 Book club/Literature circle evaluation form

Literature Study: Hatchet **Name**____________________

Reading:	**Usually**	**Sometimes**	**Rarely**
• Shows positive attitude toward reading	____	____	____
• Completes reading for group meetings	____	____	____
• Is learning to self-pace reading	____	____	____
• Shows improvement in sustained silent reading	____	____	____

Comments:

Writing:			
• Shows positive attitude toward written response	____	____	____
• Completes written response for group meetings	____	____	____
• Responds in a variety of ways	____	____	____

Comments:

Discussion:			
• Shares personal responses	____	____	____
• Discusses main points of text	____	____	____
• Shares responses in literature log	____	____	____
• Consults text for support	____	____	____
• Responds to ideas of others	____	____	____
• Clarifies points of confusion	____	____	____
• Makes connections within and across texts	____	____	____
• Makes connections with author	____	____	____
• Responds to ideas of others	____	____	____
• Uses self-evaluation to improve participation	____	____	____

Comments:

Samples of Student Work. At the end of each literature study, Melodia and Lou select at least two pieces of student work to copy and place in the assessment portfolio that they keep for each student. They select work that shows an area of strength and an area that warrants attention. Literature logs, along with a list of what students have read in literature circles, serve to chronicle day-to-day work. Samples of response projects in the form of photos, creative writing, artwork, and audio- or videotapes broaden understanding of what is possible for a student. Samples of work are excellent ways to document progress that you can share with parents and administrators.

With each sample that Lou and Melodia select for placement in the assessment portfolio, they write a brief note stating their reasons for selecting the piece, emphasizing what they believe it shows about the student's progress.

Student Learning Portfolio

Just as teachers select pieces of work to represent a range of what they feel a student knows and can do during each grading period, students also select work they feel represents their learning. Students select samples of work from their literature logs, response projects, and a variety of self-evaluation forms. Lou and Melodia urge students to select samples of work that show different kinds of growth.

Student Self-Evaluation. Throughout small-group literature study in Lou's sixth-grade and Melodia's sixth- and seventh-grade classrooms, students engage in a variety of activities in which they make decisions about their own behavior and performance. Even though middle grade students have several years of experience in school, these teachers do not assume that students have had much experience in self-evaluation. They realize that students need continuous guidance in this area. Students can learn how to evaluate themselves by considering criteria appropriate for their tasks and by learning to set goals for themselves.

There are numerous opportunities for goal setting and self-evaluation in both the book club and literature circle approaches.

- After small-group meetings, Melodia asks each student to take a few moments to reflect on the dynamics of the group and whether it functions effectively. During one of the whole-class instruction sessions, Melodia and the students developed an open-ended form for recording each person's ideas (Figure 7.9). Over the course of the school year the class uses the form to consider the need for revisions.
- To help students learn from their own behavior, Lou periodically audiotapes or videotapes small-group discussions. Students use the tapes during a small-group meeting or community sharing session to critique the effectiveness of their own behaviors. With Lou's help, each student in the group sets a goal of one behavior to focus on for the next several weeks. The group also talks about what their discussions will look and sound like when they reach their goal(s). As a reminder to themselves, students write their goals in their literature logs. Each time the small group meets, members remind each other of their goals and support one another during group activities.
- Each group paces its reading using a reading plan. In book clubs this plan is teacher developed; in literature circles the group develops it with some teacher guidance. In either case, students must then learn to pace their reading so they are ready for small-group meetings at the appointed times. Lou works with students to help them realize how they can best pace their reading.

Figure 7.9 Evaluation of small-group discussions

Name______________________________ **Date**____________________

Book Title:____

Overall our discussion today was ____

My participation in the group was ____

Something I learned in our discussion is ____

The best part of our discussion was ____

To help our discussion be more effective and interesting, I should____

and our group should____

I would also like to say that ____

Respecting Diversity in Book Clubs and Literature Circles

Book clubs and literature circles provide opportunities for students to demonstrate their independence in learning. What will independence look like in a middle grade classroom? With varying backgrounds of experience both in and out of school, students are certain to bring diversity in the ways they practice their independence.

Teach Decision Making

When given choice, students will not always choose in ways that you might wish. You must be prepared to respect their choices, help them consider both the basis for their choices and the possibilities they did not select. Your instruction and interaction with students should help them learn that choice is a matter of identifying possibilities, considering the viability of each possibility, and making effective decisions.

When you set the pacing of group reading, you must allow for students' ability to successfully meet that pace. Sufficient reading time for each individual must be the top priority, even if it means reducing time spent on other supporting activities. Students who need extra time should have the choice of reading the literature study book during SSR or DEAR, if available. In addition, providing extra copies of books for out-of-class reading supports those students who need extended reading time. You must also plan to help group members learn to support one another.

Select a Variety of Literature

As you select books for small-group study, you should be aware of student interests and reading levels, offering if possible something of interest for everyone. While personal reading interests are provided for during independent reading, instructional materials should also have appeal for students to sustain their reading. This is particularly true for chapter books.

The manner in which you prepare students for selecting a book for small-group study is also important. Book talks and making books available beforehand for examination can help students choose books that will meet their needs and interests.

TAKE A MOMENT AND REFLECT . . .

Book clubs and literature circles move students toward independence and mature reading.

Book clubs:

- Provide balance between teacher-led and student-led reading and writing
- Include four components that occur daily in varying amounts
  1. Reading—teacher planned, student paced
  2. Writing—to prepare for book club meetings
  3. Discussion—student-led small groups and teacher-led whole group
  4. Instruction—whole-class lessons to support book clubs

In book clubs, a class typically studies one book at a time, but may study several related books over a period of several weeks.

Book club groups are heterogeneous, with four to five students.

Book club whole-class instruction focuses on:

- club procedures
- helping students decide what to share
- helping students decide how to share it
- developing effective reading and writing strategies

The teacher makes a book club reading plan and provides support for students to successfully complete the reading.

Students make decisions about the most effective way to complete the daily reading, including using SSR/DEAR and "at home" reading time.

Writing in literature log focuses on items to share and questions to ask small-group members.

Book club meetings are student led and begin with sharing log entries.

Talk in book club meetings serves several purposes:

- share responses
- discuss process of making responses

- discuss main points of text
- clarify confusions
- make connections within and across texts
- relate to personal feelings, experiences, and knowledge
- connect with or critique author

Community sharing sessions follow book club meetings and provide opportunity for all students to share their thinking about a text.

Literature circles are small-group discussions that allow students to explore their "rough draft" thinking about a book.

In literature circles, heterogeneous groups of four to six students read different, but related, texts:

- Student choice of text determines group membership.

Literature circle whole-class minilessons provide instruction:

- literature circle procedures
- reading and writing strategies
- literary knowledge needed across related texts

Students determine the pace of the chosen reading and develop a reading plan that all group members can accomplish, with support of the group.

Students decide what, when, and how much to write in response to their reading and for group sharing.

Literature circles meet according to group plan, students consult logs and texts as they develop their discussion.

Flexible strategy groups occur as needed to address specific needs for individuals and small groups.

Informal conferences occur as needed for teachers to monitor student progress.

Community sharing sessions occur at the end of a work time and provide opportunity for students to share responses to texts.

To monitor each student's progress teachers document observed behaviors and select representative samples of work showing strengths and needs for an assessment portfolio.

Students evaluate their own growth and performance, select samples of work, provide justification for the selection, and place items in their learning portfolio.

Students bring varying levels of independence to the middle grades.

Teachers respect diversity by teaching decision making with a variety of literature that appeals to needs and interests of all students.

REFERENCES

Atwell, N. (1987). *In the middle: Writing, reading and learning with adolescents.* Portsmouth, NH: Heinemann.

Brown, K. (1995). Going with the flow: Getting back on course when literature circles flounder. In B. C. Hill, N. J. Johnson, & K. L. S. Noe (Eds.), *Literature circles and response* (pp. 85–93). Norwood, MA: Christopher-Gordon.

Goatley, V. J., Brock, C. H., & Raphael, T. E. (1995). Diverse learners participating in regular education "book clubs." *Reading Research Quarterly, 30,* 352–380.

Hill, B. C. (1995). Literature circles: Assessment and evaluation. In B. C. Hill, N. J. Johnson, & K. L. S. Noe (Eds.), *Literature circles and response* (pp. 167–198). Norwood, MA: Christopher-Gordon.

Holdaway, D. (1980). *Independence in reading.* Portsmouth, NH: Heinemann.

Langer, J. A. (1994). *Envisioning literature: Literary understanding and literature instruction.* New York: Teachers College Press.

McMahon, S. I. (1991, April). *Book club: How written and oral discourse influence the development of ideas as children respond to literature.* Paper presented at the annual meeting of the American Educational Research Association, Chicago.

Owens, S. (1995). Treasures in the attic: Building the foundation for literature circles. In B. C. Hill, N. J. Johnson, & K. L. S. Noe (Eds.), *Literature circles and response* (pp. 1–12). Norwood, MA: Christopher-Gordon.

Pardo, L. S. (1992, December). *Accommodating diversity in the elementary classroom: A look at literature-based instruction in an inner city school.* Paper presented at the meeting of the National Reading Conference, San Antonio, TX.

Peterson, R. & Eeds, M. (1990). *Grand conversations: Literature groups in action.* Richmond Hill, ON: Scholastic-TAB.

Raphael, T. E., Goatley, V. J., McMahon, S. I., & Woodman, D. A. (1992). Teaching literacy through student book clubs: A first year teacher's experience. In B. E. Cullinan (Ed.), *Literature across the curriculum: Making it happen* (pp. 137–152). Newark, DE: International Reading Association.

Raphael, T. E., & McMahon, S. I. (1994). "Book Clubs": An alternative framework for reading instruction. *The Reading Teacher, 48,* 102–116.

Raphael, T. E., McMahon, S. I., Goatley, V. J., Bentley, J. L., Boyd, F. B., Pardo, L. S., & Woodman, D. A. (1992). Research directions: Literature and discussion in the reading program. *Language Arts, 69,* 55–61.

Redman, P. (1995). Finding a balance: Literature circles and "teaching reading." In B. C. Hill, N. J. Johnson, & K. L. S. Noe (Eds.), *Literature circles and response.* (pp. 55-70). Norwood, MA: Christopher-Gordon.

Short, K. (1986). *Literacy as a collaborative experience.* Unpublished doctoral dissertation, Indiana University, Bloomington, IN.

Short, K. (1995). Foreword. In B. C. Hill, N. J. Johnson, & K. L. S. Noe (Eds.), *Literature circles and response.* (pp. ix–xii). Norwood, MA: Christopher-Gordon.

CHILDREN'S LITERATURE

Hahn, M. D. (1994). *Time for Andrew: A ghost story.* New York: Clarion.

Mohr, N. (1979). *Felita.* New York: Bantam Doubleday Dell.

O'Dell, S., & Hall, E. (1992). *Thunder rolling in the mountains.* New York: Bantam Doubleday Dell.

Paterson, K. (1978). *The great Gilly Hopkins.* New York: Harper & Row.

Paulsen, Gary (1987). *Hatchet.* New York: Viking Penguin.

Speare, E. G. (1983). *The sign of the beaver.* New York: Houghton Mifflin.

8

Reader's Workshop

Individualizing Literature Study

In this chapter . . .

We consider ways in which self-selected independent reading and writing help middle grade students mature as readers. Our study will include:

- visiting two classrooms that practice reader's workshop, a self-contained fifth grade, and a seventh- and eighth-grade middle school reading class
- the components of reader's workshop: time, choice, structure, response, and community
- what teachers must do to prepare for reader's workshop, and
- how to organize the classroom, including

  book selection

  independent reading

  conferencing

  response activities

  adequate instructional support

Before you begin . . .

Time for Andrew: A Ghost Story by Mary Downing Hahn (1994) is featured in one of the classroom scenarios.

Eavesdropping on a Reader's Workshop

Kristen is a first-year developmental reading teacher. On most any day, if we visited one of her seventh- or eighth-grade reading classes at a local middle school, we would notice a hush fall over the room as students settle into the quiet reading period that is part of her reader's workshop. On this particular day in early November, the students are immersed in a study of mysteries . . .

As the students enter the classroom, they retrieve their literature logs from the orange bin near the door and visit with classmates as they settle into their desks. Bell tones on the intercom signal the beginning of second period. Kristen waits for the students to settle, then asks, "How does a mystery writer create a mysterious mood?" She takes responses, then says, "We have been reading mysteries for the past three weeks. As I confer with you and listen to your comments about your books, you seem to be noticing that one thing mystery writers do is create a mood that, as Brandon said the other day, 'has MYSTERY written all over it.' "

Kristen places a text sample on the overhead projector and continues, "The mystery I am reading is Time for Andrew, by Mary Downing Hahn. It's a time warp mystery where two boys trade places in time. In the very first chapter though, on pages 5 and 6, I already have the feeling that the mystery is starting. Look at what the author writes and listen to her words. Can you feel the mysterious mood she is creating?" Kristen reads the passage aloud in a mysterious tone. Following the reading, the class has a brief discussion about the text that Kristen shared.

Kristen ends the minilesson by saying, "Each of you is reading your own mystery. How is the writer of your mystery creating a mysterious mood? When we come together for our sharing time at the end of the period, I would like for some of you to share examples of what your author is doing to create a mysterious mood.

"I see that Jeff, April, Marta, and Oscar are signed up for conferences today. Which of you would like to be first? April. Okay. After I finish the four conferences, the group that is working with decoding three- and four-syllable words will meet in our group area. Is there any other business that we need to take care of as a class? Are we ready to begin the quiet reading period? Well, then let's begin. You have two minutes to get settled with your books." ■

Today's reader's workshop in Kristen's classroom is similar to those on most other days. Students choose books they want to read, Kristen confers regularly with students, minilessons focus students' attention on important reading issues, silent reading is the mainstay of the program, and students are encouraged to share their responses to literature in a variety of ways (see Atwell, 1987; Five, 1988; Hagerty, 1992; Hansen, 1987).

Through self-selection of reading material, it is possible that each student in Kristen's reader's workshop is reading a different book. They also may be beginning and/or ending books at different times. Self-selected reading has been used successfully with students of all ages for many years (Ducker, 1968; Veatch, 1959; Holdaway, 1980). In times past we have referred to this approach as individualized reading, but today we refer to it as reader's workshop. Regardless of its name, student choice of reading material is its central focus.

Reader's Workshop Components

The term *reader's workshop* currently describes a range of literature-based reading programs. In this text, however, we use the term's original meaning as a reading program based on the following components: time, choice, structure, response, and community (Atwell, 1987; Five, 1988; Hagerty, 1992; Hansen, 1987; Hornsby & Sukarna, 1986).

Time

Teachers who use reader's workshop commit consistent blocks of time to reading, particularly silent reading, because of their belief that students learn to read by reading (Holdaway, 1980). Independent reading time is no longer recreational, as with SSR or DEAR time, it is the center of the reading program. When time for daily independent reading is predictable, students realize that they will not be hurried and can read in more natural ways, just as adults do who enjoy pleasure reading (Hagerty, 1992). Ample time for browsing and selecting books also is provided. Personal reflection is also an important part of the time devoted to reading.

In Kristen's classroom, each class period is devoted to reader's workshop. Students in this middle school meet four of their seven classes each day for 75 minutes. With the rotating block schedule, Kristen usually sees her second period students three days per week. Time to read remains predictable because students know that each second period will be a reader's workshop. In self-contained middle grade classrooms, teachers are usually able to have reader's workshop daily, for one hour or more.

Choice

Advocates of reader's workshop recognize the role of personal motivation in the process of making meaning with print (Hagerty, 1992; Holdaway, 1980). Learning to make appropriate personal reading choices requires practice and knowledge of the literature possibilities. Choice is a joint responsibility of both student and teacher. Students must come to know both themselves as readers and their personal preferences for topic and style. Teachers must come to know their students' interests, make quality literature readily available, and introduce students to the possibilities in that literature.

Before Kristen began the study of mysteries, she collected 117 mysteries from her personal book collection, the school library, and each public library branch, representing a range of subgenres (mostly contemporary, historical, and fantasy), writing styles, and reading levels. Kristen managed to find multiple copies of a few books, knowing that many of her students enjoy reading the same book as a friend.

Her students' reading interests and experiences vary widely. Their reading levels range from third to eleventh grade, with most students falling somewhere between sixth and ninth-grade level. Since the beginning of the year, Kristen and the students have talked about making good book choices and knowing when a choice is "right" for the individual. In addition, students have completed interest inventories (see Chapter 5) and talk often with Kristen about their reading interests.

Structure

Reader's workshop requires a well-planned organization and consistency that students can count on (Hagerty, 1992). The teacher's role is that of guide and facilitator, anticipating the type and degree of support students will need to become independent readers. Reader's workshop moves from whole-group sessions to a work time, then back to the whole group for sharing. Teachers provide mediated instruction both to the class and to small groups. Unlike the previous workshop formats we have discussed, teachers also schedule individual conferences with students to monitor and evaluate their progress.

Kristen uses a predictable structure for reader's workshop. A large wall chart shows how the blocks of time are allocated. Each day Kristen posts a workshop agenda on the board. Students know who is in conference, if there are small-group meetings, if someone is presenting a project, and so on. The class uses planning sessions during each whole-group meeting to clarify agenda items. Kristen provides instructional support through minilessons and small-group strategy instruction, individual conferences and help sessions, and whole-class discussions.

Response

Reader's workshop encourages readers to explore and extend their individual responses to literature as a part of becoming independent readers. Research on reader-response theories (Beach, 1993; Rosenblatt, 1978) has shown that it is a reader's personal response to literature that encourages that reader to return to literature experiences. Response comes from the reader, and cannot be controlled by an outside force. (For further discussion of reader response, refer to Chapter 2.)

Kristen's students have opportunities for response through conferences, literature logs, projects, and group sharing. Students meet regularly with Kristen to share response to their reading. She uses this time to let students teach her about their views of the literature.

Literature logs are typically open responses that the student directs. Occasionally, Kristen will ask students to focus their response on an issue that the class is studying. During the mystery unit, students critique their mystery according to criteria that the class decides are important. In open responses, students usually choose to direct their responses toward issues in class discussions and minilessons.

Students may choose to complete an individual or group project as a response to a text. While Kristen requires two projects each nine weeks, the students decide when, and which books they will do projects for. Projects may be rehearsed readings, reader's theater, a model or other art, a book talk, an innovation of the author's writing style, or the like.

A final form of response available for Kristen's students is group sharing. In this classroom, groups may be a few peers or the entire class. Students often choose to read the same book as a friend. Kristen encourages those students to get together and share their responses to the text. Another form of small-group sharing comes when students read different books but get together to discuss a common characteristic, such as plot development or writing style. During the mystery unit, students who read different books were able to share their ideas about the qualities of a good mystery. Finally, each reader's workshop ends with a community sharing session, giving students a forum for sharing both completed projects and responses to their current reading.

Community

In a reader's workshop, students will teach each other what they know if given the opportunity and an environment that supports interaction, collaboration, and risk taking. We are well aware of the power of interaction and collaboration in learning (Johnson, 1981; Slavin, Madden, Karweit, Dolan, & Wasik, 1991; Vygotsky, 1962). Sharing sessions and cooperative work time encourage students to learn to depend on and learn from each other. The teacher is a model for how to listen to and respect the ideas of others. A sense of community in a classroom creates the feeling that everyone in the room is both teacher and learner, with knowledge to share (Hagerty, 1992). Remember, everything we know as individuals was not taught directly to us. Much of what we know we taught ourselves or learned by observing and interacting informally with more knowledgeable others. Reader's workshop encourages students to become teachers, teaching themselves and each other.

Students clearly feel the open and accepting atmosphere in Kristen's classroom. Throughout each class period, students encourage and support one another, just as Kristen provides support to each of them. Multiple opportunities for sharing their ideas encourages students to be both learners and teachers, and Kristen fosters this community atmosphere.

Time, choice, structure, response, and community—five components needed to make reader's workshop successful. But the most important element is *you*, the teacher! A successful reader's workshop is not possible unless you have a clear understanding of your students and of the possibilities of literature.

Putting the Components to Work: Reader's Workshop in Fifth Grade

To illustrate the possibilities of reader's workshop, teacher Kim Muncy describes its operation in her fifth-grade class. Kim ventured into student-selected reading for the first time during the 1995–1996 school year. As you read Kim's story, consider the organizational issues involved in this individualized approach to literature-based reading and writing.

Kim narrates:

During the first 10 minutes of reader's workshop we meet as a class and I provide a minilesson, either on a reading strategy or something I want the students to notice about the book they are reading. This is also the time I give book talks on new books I've purchased for the class library.

For the next 20 minutes everyone reads silently in the book of their choice. I let the students choose their own books because they know best what they can and want to read. (I did an interest inventory at the beginning of the year to find out what their interests were and to get to know my students. This was a big help when I added books to the class library.) During this time I don't allow any commotion or talking because I know many students are like I am and are easily distracted by the smallest noise.

For the first 10 minutes of the silent reading time, I also read. This is my opportunity to become more familiar with children's literature, and I can model what a good reader looks like, since many of my students don't have a consistent model elsewhere.

After these first 10 minutes, I begin conferring (one at a time) with three students who had scheduled the time the day before. Each conference lasts about five minutes. The students bring their book, reading record, and reading. I keep running notes on our conference.

I usually open the conference by looking at their reading log and asking them how they're doing with it. The students know how important it is to keep their log up to date. When we discussed the reading log in class, these were some of their reasons why:

"So we know where we left off the day before."

"So we can see how many pages we read each day."

"So we have a place to keep interesting words if we want to use them in our writing."

"So we can remember what authors wrote which books and we can look for another book by that author in the library."

Next, I review what we conferred about the last time we met by looking at the notes in my folder. Sometimes the students are really impressed that I remember the details of their story and what we talked about. I ask them to tell me about what they are reading now. If they haven't finished the book yet and need a bit more nudging, I might ask some questions:

What do you like best about your book so far?

What can you tell me about what you've read so far?

What is happening where you are reading right now?

What do you think will happen next? Why do you think that?

How do you think the story will end?

How does the author hold your attention?

Can you relate to any of the characters? Which ones? Why?

Why do you think the author chose this particular title?

If they have finished the book, I ask different questions:

What else have you read by this author or about this subject?

What reaction(s) did you have to the book? Why do you think you reacted that way?

What reaction do you think the author intended for the reader?

What problems or confusion did you have while reading? How did you solve them?

What surprised you about this book? Why did it surprise you?

How does this book compare to other books you have read?

What are you planning to read next?

At some point in the conference, the student orally reads a rehearsed part of the book, and then we discuss why they chose that part and what's happening in it. I take notes the entire time and continue even after they leave. My notes are on what the book is about and how I feel they are understanding what they are reading, as well as how capably they answer my nudging questions.

I just started being aware of the compliments I give the students after they read. I noticed that they leave the conference with smiles on their faces! I try to be specific, and compliment students appropriately:

I noticed how you self-corrected when you realized the reading didn't make sense. Good readers do that.

You use great voice when you read, and it's interesting to listen to you read. Good readers do that.

I noticed you emphasized important words in your story. Good readers do that.

Sometimes I make a suggestion that seems appropriate for that particular student:

As you finish this book, you might think about or try to . . .

As you write in your reading log, you might think about or try to . . .

When you come to words that you're not sure about, you might think about or try to . . .

When you're ready to choose another book, you might think about or try to . . .

After about 20 minutes of silent reading, the students have the option of working on a reading activity of their choice for the next 10 minutes. They may also continue to read silently, which is what most of my students choose. I don't force an activity after every book because I believe that students will read more if they know they have the freedom to read without having to do an activity. Isn't that really the point of reading, anyway? I believe they learn to read more by reading, not by doing extension activities. Plus, they might feel that some books are not worth the time involved in doing an extension activity.

After the activity time, I ask them to fill out their reading logs for the day. On a form that I provide [see Figure 8.5], they record the dates they began and completed the book, pages read, its title, author, and genre, interesting words, comments, and their future plans for activities or reading. At this time I do not ask for a great deal of written response because I want students to spend more time reading, enough to really get absorbed in their books. Response comes in conferences and group discussions.

The next 10 minutes or so is share time. It brings closure to the day's workshop activities. The three students I confer with have the opportunity to share with their peers anything related to their books. This time helps them become independent readers because they are encouraged to have their own thoughts, feelings, and ideas about a particular book without anyone judging their reasons for expressing a particular idea. The audience has the chance to respond, which helps form a sense of community in this classroom.

It seems that lately students are challenging the ideas of those who are sharing by asking them why they feel a certain way about a book. Many students' answers are so direct and confident that they really make me believe they are becoming stronger readers.

If there is extra time during the share session I'll ask if anyone tried something new or learned something new that day. I also ask if anyone found an interesting word. Lately, the interesting words are quite abundant. If the students want to share an interesting word or a word that they don't understand, they must have written it in their reading log along with the page number they found it on. They share the word with the group in what I call "before, during, and after" context. They have to read the sentence that comes before the word, the sentence the word is in, and the sentence that comes after. The audience tries to figure out what the word means in context, and most of the time, they do. When someone is able to come up with the definition, we discuss how they figured it out.

There are now so many people who want to share an interesting word that I had to limit it to five a day. Some of the kids now write their interesting words on a piece of sentence strip paper and staple it up on our word wall to share with others who might want to use it in writer's workshop.

For evaluation, I check their reading logs periodically, looking for effort as far as keeping it complete and up to date. What I'm finding out, though, is how many times I have to go over how to properly fill out the record form. I'm attributing this to the fact that maybe those students truly don't understand the reason for even having a reading log, and therefore they don't feel it is important.

I also ask that they complete four projects of their choice on the book of their choice each 12 weeks. If they don't complete four books in 12 weeks, and I have some students who don't, I modify the evaluation to suit their needs and let them know that it's more important for them to read than to do projects. Students need to know they can pace themselves. They need to find the rhythm and speed that is best for them as readers.

Organizing a Reader's Workshop

Like other workshop approaches (see chapters 6 and 7), a reader's workshop is a cohesive block of instructional time that includes both whole-group and independent/small-group work periods. It requires a (preferably continuous, uninterrupted) block of time, usually of an hour or more, to allow students ample time for sustained silent reading.

Figure 8.1 outlines the components of a reader's workshop. Compare this outline to Kristen's and Kim's programs, described earlier in this chapter. Although reader's workshop practice will vary from classroom to classroom, the five components—time, choice, structure, response, and community—must form the foundation of all decisions teachers make as they modify the workshop to fit their students.

Preparing for Reader's Workshop

From reading the accounts of Kristen's and Kim's classrooms, you know that teachers who implement reader's workshop must be very familiar with the following:

- Their students needs and interests
- A variety of appropriate literature
- The required reading/language arts curriculum
- Successful reading behaviors and attitudes

Students' Needs and Interests

You must be keenly aware of your students for your reader's workshop to be successful. You should know about their interests inside and outside school, and know them as readers. Using an interest inventory, as Kim did with her fifth-grade class, is a start (see

Figure 8.1 Reader's workshop components

Whole Group (10–15 minutes):	• Community opening • Whole-class minilessons workshop procedures literary knowledge reading strategies • Book talks • Plans for the day
Work Time (35–50 minutes):	• Quiet reading period • Scheduled conferences • Response activities literature log small-group sharing of same text or related texts independent projects (art, drama, writing, readings) • Flexible strategy groups • Individual help/questions • Making new selections
Whole Group (10–20 minutes):	• Community sharing session projects small-group discussions book talks • Evaluate the day • Plans for tomorrow

Chapter 5). Observing students during silent reading, response, sharing, and conference activities also provides you with assessment information that will help you make your group and individual instructional decisions. To truly individualize literature instruction, you must be able to document each student's progress. Careful record-keeping can help you feel confident of your knowledge of students as individuals and of their growth as readers. You document students' knowledge and skill levels by using informal reading inventories or running records, conference notes, and students' reading/writing portfolios, projects, and other responses.

A Variety of Appropriate Literature

You will need a broad knowledge of children's and young adult literature. You must read widely across genres and topics, and consider various authors' writing styles. Three thousand to five thousand children's and young adult books are published each year. To stay current, call on the help of experts who review literature in magazines such as *Horn Book, Booklinks, The ALAN Review, School Library Journal,* and *Voices of Youth Advocates.* In addition, most professional journals, such as *The Reading Teacher, Language Arts, The New Advocate, Teaching Children Mathematics, Social Studies and the Young Learner, Social Education,* and *Science and Children*, have regular columns that review and evaluate literature.

Reader's workshop requires a collection of quality literature that meets the varied needs and interests of middle grade students.

You should maintain a classroom library stocked with quality literature. In addition the school librarian should be a key person in your literature program. Enlist the librarian's help in selecting and acquiring quality literature. Books can be acquired through school district instructional material budgets, student book clubs, the school library, the public library, garage sales, and donations from parents and community.

Try to acquire books that provide a balance among genres and topics that appeal to both boys and girls, and whose reading levels span at least three to four years above and below each grade level you teach. Your school librarian can help you become familiar with school district policies that might affect your selections. Some school districts have published lists of books approved for student use.

The Required Reading/Language Arts Curriculum

You must be familiar with the reading and language arts curriculum in your school district. Each school district develops curriculum guides that identify what students should know at each grade level. We can obtain copies of curriculum guides for local school districts and become familiar with the types of goals and objectives identified for the middle grades. Figure 8.2 shows an example of one school district's instructional objectives for seventh- and eighth-grade reading and literature.

If you are teaching seventh or eighth grade in the district whose instructional objectives appear in Figure 8.2, which objectives would you include in the instruction you provide during reader's workshop? Why?

I could incorporate each of the district's instructional objectives into a reader's workshop. Any workshop's overall objective is to have personal purposes for reading, which include reading for pleasure and information (3a–d, 4a–d). As my students read silently (3c), they would also have to use strategies to monitor their meaning making and for sustaining their reading over longer periods of time (1a). In minilessons, strategy groups, and individual conferences I would use familiar texts to extend their knowledge of a variety of genres (2a) to help them make appropriate choices for reading (3a), their knowledge of literary elements (2a) and author's use of literary devices to enhance their appreciation of texts (2a–d, 4a), and their knowledge of words and word meanings (1b, 4d). This knowledge would then help them select appropriate strategies to suit the purposes for which they are reading (1a).

■

District instructional objectives such as those shown in Figure 8.2, may not identify specific procedural and strategy knowledge needed for reader's workshop. You must add those objectives to your curriculum:

- What ideas to share about students' reading in conferences and share sessions
- How best to share their ideas
- Recognizing students' personal strengths and needs as readers
- When a book is not appropriate and should be abandoned
- How to monitor their own meaning making

Figure 8.2 Instructional objectives for reading and literature, grades 7 and 8

1. Understand that reading is a process that involves active construction of meaning:
   - **a.** Use appropriate strategies to make meaning while reading.
     - reasonable predictions
     - logical substitutions
     - monitor and self-correct
     - draw on prior knowledge
   - **b.** Apply knowledge of word structure and phonics to read and understand multisyllable words.
2. Read, analyze, and interpret diverse forms of discourse.
   - **a.** Utilize basic literary elements to explore meaning in a variety of genres.
   - **b.** Explore similar and contrasting points of view.
   - **c.** Analyze characters (personality traits, motivations, connection to self).
   - **d.** Analyze the writer's purpose and intended audience.
   - **e.** Synthesize information from a variety of sources.
3. Recognize the value of reading and literature for lifelong learning, personal growth and enjoyment.
   - **a.** Choose and read own material at their fluency level from classroom, home, or library.
   - **b.** Make connections between reading material and personal life.
   - **c.** Read silently in class a minimum of 30 minutes each week.
   - **d.** Listen to texts read by teacher or professional performer.
4. Understand how language can evoke emotion.
   - **a.** Read/listen to literature that elicits a variety of emotions.
   - **b.** View performances.
   - **c.** Explore persuasive nonfiction.
   - **d.** Recognize and interpret figurative language.

Successful Reading Behaviors and Attitudes

In an individualized program such as reader's workshop, you want to feel confident that your students will continue to grow as readers. Therefore, you must know and understand reading processes and the types of learning environments in which literate behaviors flourish, and must use that knowledge to identify the appropriate reading behaviors and attitudes you expect your students to exhibit. Your expectations guide your decisions as you set up a reader's workshop. Careful and consistent observation of students as they select books, read independently, confer with you, make records of their reading, and share with their peers, will help you identify students' attitudes toward reading and the reading behaviors they are using successfully.

Implementing a Reader's Workshop

Now that you are aware of the basic issues that surround reader's workshop, let's take a closer look at some of the essential elements that lead to successful workshops. As we move along, note that some elements of reader's workshop draw on what we already know about literature workshops, book clubs, and literature circles.

Supporting Independent Reading

Middle grade students need support to mature as readers and to use independent reading time wisely. You must provide an environment that supports quiet reading and must help them learn to select appropriate reading materials.

Providing a Quiet Reading Time. In both Kim's and Kristen's classrooms, silent reading was given priority in the reading period. Both teachers believe that students must have sustained opportunities to read if they are to become proficient silent readers. Middle grade readers must develop "the ability to persevere at a personal pace that makes efficient use of current skills" (Holdaway, 1980, p. 34). As in any activity, perseverance requires sustained practice.

In Kim's classroom, 20 of the 60 minutes devoted to reader's workshop are spent in silent reading. The commitment to this time enables Kim's students to settle into their reading. She allows the independent reading to extend beyond the quiet reading period if students choose, because Kim believes that self-selected reading is also self-paced reading. Kristen has 75-minute periods, which allow for extended blocks of quiet reading when needed.

Some teachers find it difficult to have a large block of time for silent reading, so they combine the time devoted to SSR with reader's workshop. Like silent reading in the workshop, SSR is intended to accomplish self-selected, self-paced reading, thus extending the amount of time available for sustained silent reading in the reader's workshop.

Selecting an Appropriate Book. In reader's workshop students must learn to choose books that are appropriate for their interests and reading level. You support book selection daily by sharing books through read-alouds, book talks, and personal responses. Whole-group meetings in reader's workshop are excellent opportunities for everyone to share their feelings about books. When a sense of community exists in a classroom, students place importance on the views of others and allow those views to influence their selection of new books. Part of your task is to teach students how to determine book difficulty and how to decide when to abandon an inappropriate selection.

For example, Kristen begins the mystery unit by making an inviting display of selected books, and gives book talks to introduce as many books as she can. She also provides browsing time during the week prior to the unit.

Your Turn

Draw on what you know! You would like to start a reader's workshop but your students have little experience selecting their own texts for reading instruction. What could you do?

Your students have little experience pacing their own reading to complete a text. What could you do?

Selecting texts? Students have experience selecting library books and SSR materials. Using what they know, I could talk about and demonstrate how I know a book is easy, just right, or challenging. I could also spend some time in literature circles, which offer text choices, before beginning reader's workshop.

Self-paced reading? Here again, literature circles may be my first step before reader's workshop. Then my students will gain experience in self-pacing while they have the support of a group of students who are reading the same text and can help with pacing decisions.

Conferring with Students

Conferring with individual students is one of the most difficult and time-consuming parts of reader's workshop, but it also is one of the most valuable ways for you to learn about your students. Conferences are often the part of reader's workshop that makes teachers hesitant to try this approach. Kristen tries to confer with four students each day. She encourages students to indicate their readiness by signing up for a conference. Kristen prefers to see students when they are ready. She finds the talk is more productive.

From Kim's description earlier in this chapter, you know that conferences are short private meetings, lasting five to seven minutes, between the teacher and a student. Conferences allow open dialogue about a book the student is reading or has just completed. This time between teacher and student is *not* a time for instruction. Instead, your purpose is to learn how students are handling the books they chose independently. Conferences provide you with opportunities to monitor a student's individual reading progress, to diagnose difficulties, and to encourage the use of particular strategies (Hagerty, 1992; Holdaway, 1980). Figure 8.3 summarizes student's and teacher's roles in conferences. As shown, your role is one of questioning, listening, probing responses, and making notes.

Kim and Kristen keep conference notebooks, with records of their meetings with each student. During and immediately following each conference, they note such student behaviors as the following:

In reader's workshop, students should receive guidance on selecting books that are appropriate for both their interests and reading level.

Figure 8.3 Student and teacher roles in a reader's workshop conference

During a conference—

A student shares . . .	**and the teacher . . .**
• personal responses to a book	• probes the responses
• selected part of a book through oral reading	• probes the responses
• literature log entries for the book	• reviews and discusses the entries • encourages and guides student's efforts throughout • makes a record of conference observations

Figure 8.4 Kim's reader's workshop conference notes

Name *Stacy*	Book Notes	Observation/Comments
10/1 *–fantasy*	*Jeremy Thatcher, Dragon Catcher* *–Jeremy runs to a place he's never seen before* *–gets dinosaur eggs in magic shop* *–has directions on how to hatch eggs* *–dragon sends Jeremy messages*	*–good reading log entries, had none before* *–excellent comprehension* *–realizes story also told through characters thoughts* *–sees foreshadowing* *–not sure how book will end*
10/13 *–historical fiction*	*Under the Blood Red Sun* *–Japanese family moved to Hawaii in 1940s.* *–issues of discrimination, fear*	*–just right, very smooth oral reading* *–good comprehension* *–struggled with Japanese words, doesn't interfere with comprehension* *–read selection because she felt it was most interesting*

- level of response and understanding
- fluency
- word recognition and self-monitoring
- ability to select appropriately
- self-pacing
- self-evaluation

Figure 8.4 shows a sample of Kim's conference notes.

Draw on what you know! You would like to start a reader's workshop, but your students have never participated in one-to-one conferences. What could you do?

I can draw on what I know about teaching small-group discussions in literature workshop (Chapter 7). I could develop a series of minilessons about what conferences are and what happens in a conference, perhaps modeling a conference in front of the class. Then we could discuss as a class what occurred and why.

■

Responding to Literature

How we feel about the literature we read is what draws us back to read again and again. Students in your classroom will have different responses to the same text and will express those responses in different ways. Consequently, you need to provide varied opportunities for students to show their response to the literature they read, including the occasional option of not responding.

Literature or Reading Logs. In reader's workshop, the literature log is a personal record of a student's independent reading. Ultimately, this log should reflect the direction that students are taking with their reading. In the beginning, however, it is important that students understand the purpose for the log, especially to see it as more than a required task they complete for the teacher. Recall Kim's comment about the difficulty some of her students have with the reading log. Purpose and value are very important to middle grade students; they tend not to perform well on tasks that they perceive have little value or an unclear purpose.

Literature logs may take many possible forms (see chapters 3 and 9 for examples). In a reader's workshop, the log might have several sections:

- A daily reading record that includes date, book title, pages read, and space for comments
- A page or more devoted to words of interest and words not easily recognized
- Responses to reading (open, focused, double-entry, story frames, dialogue letters, story map, etc.)

Student and teacher should together decide the number of entries in the log. It may not be necessary to write a response each day. The log should not become tedious, but rather should be a functional record of reading progress.

Daily Reading Record. This record becomes part of a student's history as a reader. You may use it in conferences to help students consider the criteria they use to select books, and to help students evaluate the pace of their reading and their ability to persevere with a book. Note how Kim uses reading records as she discusses students' progress during conferences. Her reading log combines book selection and record of reading (Figure 8.5). You need to decide how much information you want students to put on one record form. Figure 8.6 shows a sample alternate form.

Words and Phrases from Reading. Kim encourages her students to share their interest in words with others in group meetings. By the middle grades students have a great deal of word knowledge, but may not recognize that knowledge as helpful in self-

Figure 8.5 Sample reading log form

Name Valentina					Reading Log	
Date	Pages Read	Genre	Title & Author	Words to Remember	Comments	Future Plans
9-18	32	fiction	Not For a Billion Gazillion Dollars Paula Danziger	———	abandoned	———
9-22	1-21-45-98-123-157	fiction	Words of Stone Kevin Henkes	simultaneous boisterous	voice!	may do an activity
9-30	38	fiction	Slime Lake Tom B. Stone		boring, too easy - abandoned	———
10-1	1-43-67-91-149-end	fiction fantasy	The Cricket in Times Square George Selden	deliberate miraculously menacing	good character believable!	I will do an activity. I liked this book.

Figure 8.6 Sample daily reading record

Date & Book Title	Pages Read	Comments
Nov. 12 Time For Andrew	Ch 1 (pp. 3-11)	I chose this book because Mrs. Felten is reading it too. It sounded spooky.
Nov. 13	Ch 2 & 3 (pp. 12-21) Home- pp. 22-29	This is spooky. Drew found some really old marbles in the attic.

learning. Independence in word recognition means helping students become aware of their ability to work with new words and phrases.

You may review word and phrase lists individually during conferences or in strategy groups, to meet the needs of students who are at similar stages of development of word knowledge. Record page numbers to refer to the use of a word in the text, perhaps using the "before, during, and after" context technique as Kim described. Figure 8.7 shows a sample log entry for words from Kristen's class.

Responses to Reading. It is not necessary to make daily entries. In the early phase of reader's workshop, you may want to offer focused log entries to "nudge" student's interactions with literature. You may also ask students to reflect on a book and make closing comments before they move to a new selection. You and your students should decide together the type and frequency of log entries.

Figure 8.7 Sample word/phrase lists in literature log

Interesting Words/Phrases	Words/Phrases to Study
Time For Andrew p. 2 ancestral home p. 2 his scowling face floated between me and the rows of corn p. 4 dim-witted p. 11 his face was skull-like p. 12 gurgled	Time For Andrew p. 7 art deco p. 9 reminisced p. 11 inarticulate

Your minilessons can focus on how to make different types of entries and how to select a particular type of entry. See Chapter 3 for more detail on particular types of literature log entries.

Your Turn

Draw on what you know! You would like to start a reader's workshop but your students have little experience selecting topics and forms for their literature log responses. What could you do?

I would begin with making daily log entries, mixing focused with open responses (choice). I would couple daily responses with minilessons and flexible strategy groups focusing on types of possible responses and how to decide what to write.

Small-Group Sharing. Middle grade students need opportunities to share their responses to books with others, both formally and informally. After quiet reading periods, students should be able to spontaneously share their ideas with others as they work. Students who have read the same books may elect to form small sharing groups during work time to compare their ideas.

In addition to spontaneous sharing, consider formalizing such small-group meetings. These sharing opportunities will resemble book club and literature circle meetings. As you begin to bring students together, you may want to provide a "discussion guide" that suggests ways to begin the conversation, particularly when students have read different, but related, books whose relationship may not be readily apparent. An open-ended discussion guide, such as Kristen uses when her class studies mysteries (Figure 8.8), helps students make connections across texts.

Independent Projects. The emphasis in reader's workshop is on student choice, rather than on choices the teacher directs. Students do, however, need to be aware of their options. One idea is to make a wall chart of possible extensions, such as those in the following list. Remember, projects should *never* become more important than reading and talking about books.

Figure 8.8 Discussion guide for connecting texts

Mysterious Connections. . .

We are all reading mysteries! This small-group meeting is to explore how mystery writers reveal the "mystery" of their story. Gather 3–5 people together who are far enough in their books that the author has revealed the "mystery."

To get started

1. Share the cover, title, author, and BRIEF summary of what your book is about so far. (BRIEF means one or two sentences, not a "blow-by-blow" description of the plot.)
2. Share what the "mystery" is and how the author let you find out about it.
3. What similarities and differences do you find among the books in your group? Make notes to recall the important points. Be ready to share this information in community sharing.

How Authors Reveal the "Mystery"

Similarities	Differences

Response Projects

- Writing
  letter to or from a character
  character diary or journal
  innovate on or change a story
  newspaper article about a character or event
  write a sequel
  write a "reminder" story, "This story reminds me of . . ."
  write to the author of your book
- Art
  advertisements
  cartoon sequences
  diorama scenes
  wall mural
  family or character "photo" album
  collage of characters, main events, settings

make a wordless book that illustrates main events
make a quilt of favorite events, quotes, characters, etc.

- Reading
  make a display of books, poems, magazines, newspaper articles that relate to the theme of your book
  find and share other books by the same author or topic
  research the "facts" behind your book
- Drama/Speech
  videotape/audiotape a scene
  interview a character
  become a character
  give a book talk
- Maps or Clusters
  physical location (settings or plots)
  character attributes or relationships
  time line of events or character change
  story map (beginning-middle-end, problem-events-resolution)
- Games
  develop a board game about your character or story
  make a card game to match character attributes or story events

Draw on what you know! You want to start a reader's workshop, but your students have had no experience in selecting independent response activities and pacing their completion of the projects. What could you do?

Minilessons on selecting independent projects could certainly be helpful. The planning time that is built into the beginning of each workshop also could be a valuable time to help students think about how they will use their time, especially if they are involved in an independent project. I would not assign projects until other parts of the reader's workshop are familiar and working effectively.

Instruction in Reader's Workshop

Students' need for interaction with a more knowledgeable other does not disappear when their reading and writing become self-directed. They will continue to need teacher guidance in reading and writing processes and strategies. Your instruction can take the form of minilessons, flexible strategy groups, and individual help.

Whole-Class Minilessons. During the opening group meeting, you may provide short focused lessons on the following topics:

- *Procedures to help a reader's workshop run smoothly*
  Steps and expectations of a reader's workshop.

How to pick out a book that's right for you.
Deciding when to abandon a book.
How to fill out a reading record.
Deciding how to respond to a book.
How to decide on an extension activity (project).
How to prepare for a conference.
Giving a book talk.
What to do when you finish your book.
How to share what you read.
What to do in discussion groups.
How to respond as a listener when someone shares.
How to respect books.

- *Use of a particular literary element or technique*
  What are the different genres and their characteristics?
  What are the literary elements in a book?
  How does your author use literary elements?
  How are literary elements important in a story?
  What is the theme of your book? How can you tell?
  How is a plot organized?
  Different types of plots: going forward, going backward.
  Discussing conflict and when it might be good.
  Does there have to be a conflict?
  How does your author let you get to know a character?
  Why are some characters more important than others?
  Why would an author use a foil character?
  Discussing point of view and its importance.
  How do authors begin and end stories?
  How do authors hook your interest?
  How are fiction and information books different?
  Identifying parts of a book and how to use them.
  Fact versus opinion.
  Reality versus fantasy.

- *Appropriate use of a particular reading strategy*
  How to deal with unknown words: pronunciation and meaning.
  How to recognize similes and metaphors.
  How to ask yourself questions while reading.
  How can you sketch for understanding?
  How to make inferences.
  Drawing conclusions.

Recognizing and finding details.

Summarizing.

Finding the main idea.

Thinking ahead (predict), thinking back (connect).

Stopping to reflect on a story.

How can you help yourself read information texts?

You will need to give all three types of minilessons in a truly balanced reading program. Minilesson content is typically drawn from observations of students, knowledge of the books they are reading, and the existing reading/language arts curriculum. Kristen helps students focus on the characteristics of mysteries through her minilesson on how authors reveal the mystery. This minilesson was developed from curriculum objectives, the mysteries her students were reading, and her knowledge of students' experiences with the characteristics of a genre.

You will often use talk-aloud and think-aloud strategies in your minilessons to help students learn how readers think about reading. Minilessons will be most helpful to students if you draw your examples from familiar literature, such as books you have shared in whole class read-aloud. The sample procedural minilesson in Figure 8.9 focuses students' thinking on preparing for a reader's workshop conference.

Flexible Strategy Groups. One concern that teachers often express is, "How can students continue to learn new skills and strategies when they are reading by themselves?" Meeting students in flexible small groups extends the ideas that you emphasize in the whole-group minilessons and provides practice that some, but not all, students may need. Small groups serve a limited purpose, such as to develop a particular strat-

Figure 8.9 Sample procedural minilesson for reader's workshop

Getting ready for a reader's workshop conference

"We've been having reading conferences for several weeks now and I've noticed that you've been remembering to bring your book and literature log to the conference. That's part of getting ready for a conference.

"Another part of getting ready takes place in your head. When I'm going to confer with you, I think back to our last conference. I think about the things you told me about your book, I look at the notes I made about our conference, and I think about the book you were reading. I also think about what I've seen you doing in reading since that last conference, and the minilessons we've had that might help you enjoy reading your books more. Then I anticipate what you might say to me when we meet. That's what I do in my head.

"When you get ready for a conference with me, you should also spend some time thinking about what will happen. Think about what you want to tell me about your book. Since you know that our conference is also to help you be a better reader, you might think about what I can do to help you enjoy your book the most.

"Tomorrow I will be conferring with __________, __________, and __________. Each of you might spend some of your work time today getting ready for our conference tomorrow."

egy, then are disbanded. Present ideas first to the whole group in minilessons. When you notice that a number of students are still not using particular literary knowledge or reading strategies, more extensive small-group work is warranted.

You may select topics for strategy groups from the lists of suggested minilesson topics in this text, your knowledge of reading process and student's literature, from your school district's curriculum, or from a basal reading series, if you are using one. Strategy group instruction is teacher mediated and may resemble small groups used in other literature-based workshops. Holdaway (1980) suggests letting students attend strategy groups if they feel they need help rather than mandating attendance.

- Kristen notices during conferences that some students are having difficulty with multisyllable words, especially words with unusual roots. Over a period of several weeks she offers small-group work in strategies for decoding multisyllable words in context, but only for students who demonstrated need. She draws her examples from her conference notes as well as from books students are currently reading. Following instruction, Kristen observes the students to see whether their decoding of multisyllable words shows improvement.
- Kim notices during conferences and informal talks that a number of students have little to say about the characters in their texts. Probing their responses yields little new information. Kim decides to offer several strategy group sessions on characterization. Using a familiar text, she explores examples of how characters are introduced, how they are slowly developed, and how they may change over time as a result of events and conflicts. Her focus then turns to the books students are currently reading, and to helping them apply characterization strategies. Over the next several conferences, Kim carefully observes the students' sense of character to see whether the strategy sessions are effective.

Individual Help/Questions. When Kim and Kristen are not conferring, they circulate among students, providing support and encouragement. They answer questions, and make suggestions that help students build on previous conferences or whole-class instruction. Kim thinks of this as a time to continue learning about her students as individuals and as readers.

Both teachers make notes to add to their conference records. (They find it helpful to carry a clipboard for this purpose.) Kim transfers her notes to the conference record, while Kristen, because she has many students, prefers to use sheets of computer labels, writing a student's name on each label. When a label is filled, she peels it off and places it in the student's assessment portfolio. Empty labels clue her to who she is *not* watching closely.

Community Sharing Sessions

Formal sharing occurs during group meetings, with book talks or the sharing of projects. You might choose to organize sharing as Kim did, having those students you conferred with each day also be the ones who share responses to books with their peers. Regardless, students will need coaching to decide what to share and how they want to share their responses.

Consider teaching students to use *remembers, reminders,* and *questions* (Graves, 1994) in response to someone who is sharing. After a student has shared his or her response, group members respond with "Remembers," telling the person what they remember about the shared ideas, somewhat like retelling after a story; "reminders," memories and past experiences that are cued by what was shared ("It reminds me of . . ."); and "questions" about what was shared to clarify or to fill in missing information.

Monitoring Students' Growth as Independent Readers

Reread Kim's explanation of the organization of her reader's workshop, noting the references she makes to gathering assessment data and evaluating student progress. Note that her statements require knowledge of students gained through evaluation. Kim makes notes during conferences. She listens to students read aloud and asks them to justify their selection of text. She observes students during minilessons, community sharing, and independent reading times. Reading workshop teachers become keenly aware of how individuals think, act, make decisions, and follow through on tasks.

In a reader's workshop, what might you want to add to your teacher's assessment portfolio that reflects student growth? Where is your greatest potential for interaction with students? Conferences might be your number-one choice. From other literature approaches, you are already aware of the possibilities for observation and gathering samples of work. Because of conferring's unique role in reader's workshop, we will focus here on the value of these face-to-face meetings for monitoring student progress.

Teacher's Assessment Portfolio

Both Kim and Kristen keep a conference notebook with a section for each student. During individual conferences they make notes that include the following types of observations:

- The types of texts students are selecting to read
- Patterns of reading (completed, abandoned)
- How and what they choose to share of the text
- The quality of rehearsed oral reading
- Strategies they use to make meaning
- Students' insights about the author's use of literary elements
- Students' insights about themselves as readers
- Students' general level of engagement with texts

No single conference yields assessment data on each of these points, but, when taken collectively, conference notes can be a valuable source for evaluation.

Self-Selecting Texts. As Kim looks back over her conference notes (see Figure 8.4), along with the student's reading record (see Figures 8.5 and 8.6), she is able to get a clear sense of the types of books students select to read. She can see which types of books they complete in a timely manner, those they complete reluctantly, and those they abandon. Kim feels that students' patterns of selecting texts form a base for her understanding of them as readers. She chooses to have a complete list of all books read during a grading period in each student's assessment portfolio.

Sharing Text in Conferences. To prepare for a conference, students select and rehearse a piece of text that is meaningful in some way and that they wish to share with the teacher. In the conference the student reads the selected text aloud. Kim and Kristen think about the portions of text that students select to share and wonder what those selections suggest about each student's (1) level of engagement, (2) sense of self as a reader, and (3) insights about the author's craft. Both teachers ask students to introduce what they will read and after the reading, probe student's responses and make notes.

Quality of Rehearsed Oral Reading. When students share text in a conference, they typically read aloud text that has been rehearsed. Kim and Kristen listen carefully to the fluency level that students exhibit. After rehearsal, students should read appropriate text in a fluent and expressive manner, much like text at their independent reading level.

Both teachers make running records reflecting a student's strategies for monitoring meaning while they read orally. The teacher observes, records what the student actually says while reading, and later, analyzes any miscues, or words that differ from those in the actual text. Clay (1968) developed this procedure while she studied the reading behavior of young children, but it also is valuable in helping teachers listen carefully to middle grade readers. The procedure is similar to miscue analysis developed by Goodman and Burke (1972).

You may make running records with both familiar and unfamiliar text. When text is familiar, expect fewer errors. When text is unfamiliar, you have your best opportunity to see and hear the self-monitoring strategies that students control and use fairly automatically.

Running records can either be scripted or unscripted. For a scripted running record (see Figures 8.10 and 8.11), you have a typed copy of the student's text. For an unscripted running record, you will make a record of the reading on a blank sheet of paper (see Figure 8.13 for a sample record).

To take a running record, sit beside the student during the conference, but slightly behind so that your recording is less distracting. As the student reads, make a record of the reading. It also is a good idea to tape record the reading, especially when running records are new, to be sure that you recorded accurately. You can also use the tape during student and parent conferences.

Scripted Running Record. Kim typically uses scripted running records early in the school year as a way of learning what self-monitoring strategies her students use in oral reading. She assumes that the way students use strategies in oral reading will be similar to their use in silent reading. Using a variety of texts, Kim is able to determine students' independent, instructional, and frustration reading levels.

Taking a scripted running record is an excellent way to check students' ability to self-select appropriate texts for reader's workshop. Such a record will ensure that students are selecting instructional level text. On the day before Kim plans to make a scripted running record, she borrows the student's chosen book, photocopies a passage of about 250 words, and returns the book to the student. The next day, Kim asks the student to read the photocopied selection of text orally, tape recording the reading to be sure that she marks the running record accurately.

Kim listens carefully for accuracy in the student's reading. She asks if the selected text is familiar, and whether the student has rehearsed the reading. When a student is familiar with the text, especially if he has rehearsed it, she expects the oral reading to sound like independent reading (95–100% accuracy), instead of instructional level reading (90–95% accuracy).

Figure 8.10 shows the codes used to mark a scripted running record. Note the difference between recorded behaviors counted as errors and those recorded but not con-

Figure 8.10 Marking a scripted running record

Correct: Accurate reading is always marked with a check (✓).

Miscues that are counted:

Substitution— Student reads a word differently than the printed text.

✓ ✓ ✓ rose ✓ ✓ ✓ ✓ ✓ ✓
I studied his rosy face, his white hair and mustache.

Omission— Student leaves out a word printed in the text.

✓ ✓ ✓ ✓ ✓ ✓ ✓ ✓ ✓
I studied his (rosy) face, his white hair and mustache.

Insertion— Student adds a word or words that are not in the printed text.

✓ ✓ ✓ ✓ ✓ ✓ ✓ ✓ ✓ his ✓
I studied his rosy face, his white hair and ^ mustache.

Teacher Tells— Student appeals to the teacher for help, teacher first responds, "Try it," student is unable to respond, then teacher tells.

✓ ✓ ✓ ✓ ✓ ✓ ✓ ✓ ✓ T
I studied his rosy face, his white hair and mustache.

Try That Again— Student becomes completely lost in a section of text, teacher brackets passage that has caused the problem and says, "Try that again." The whole passage is coded as TTA and counted as one miscue. Any additional miscues in the rereading are marked with the usual codes. Miscues from the first reading are ignored.

✓ ✓ ✓ ✓ ✓ ✓ ✓ ✓ ✓ ✓
TTA [✓ steadied ✓ round fake —
I studied his rosy face, his white hair and mustache.]

Miscues that are NOT counted:

Repetition— Student repeats a word or phrase. This usually indicates that she has lost the meaning or she is using rereading as a strategy to figure out an unknown word. One underline is used for each repetition.

✓ ✓ ✓ ✓ ✓ ✓ ✓ ✓ ✓ ✓
I studied his rosy face, his white hair and mustache.

Self-Correction— Student corrects own miscue *without* assistance. The original miscue does not count.

sc
✓ steadied ✓ ✓ ✓ ✓ ✓ ✓ ✓ ✓
I studied his rosy face, his white hair and mustache.

Teacher Encourages— Student stops reading at point of unknown word, may or may not appeal for help, teacher encourages but does not tell, saying "Try it," E (Encourage) is recorded, then student response is recorded.

✓ E ✓ ✓ ✓ ✓ ✓ ✓ ✓ ✓ ✓
I studied his rosy face, his white hair and mustache.

sidered errors. Those not counted as errors are miscues that either do not interfere with making meaning or that ultimately result in a correct reading.

For example, Kim listens to a student read a passage from *Time For Andrew* (Hahn, 1994, p. 83). The student has just selected this text. The reading passage is taken from the middle of the text and is fairly representative. A scripted running record of this reading might look like that shown in Figure 8.11.

There are 56 words in the passage in Figure 8.11. Which errors would you count? How accurately does this student read? Is this text appropriate for her? What leads you to that conclusion? (Remember, instructional level text is 90–95% accuracy of word recognition.)

Figure 8.11 Sample scripted running record

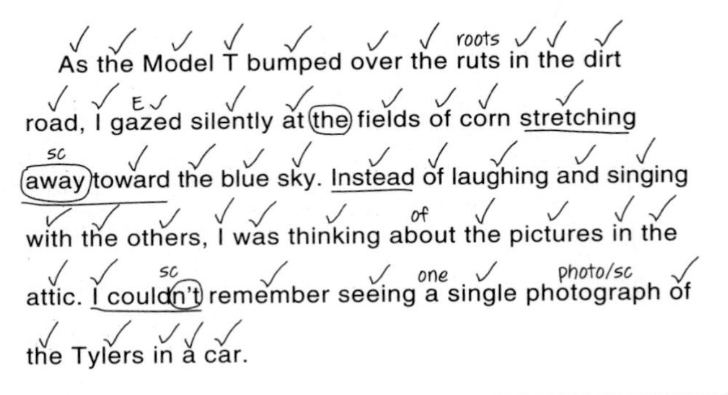
As the Model T bumped over the ruts in the dirt road, I gazed silently at the fields of corn stretching away toward the blue sky. Instead of laughing and singing with the others, I was thinking about the pictures in the attic. I couldn't remember seeing a single photograph of the Tylers in a car.

Four errors would count:

- *roots* for ruts
- omission of *the* in the second line
- substituting *of* for *about* in the fourth line
- substituting *one* for *a* in the fifth line

Seven errors would *not* count:

- encouragement to try *gazed,* which the student then read accurately (notice the check)
- repeating *stretching* ___________ *toward*
- self-correcting the omission of *away*
- repetition of *instead*
- repetition of *I couldn't*
- self-correction of *couldn't*
- self-correction of *photograph*

Calculate the accuracy rate:

Total words	–	number of errors	=	words read correctly
56	–	4	=	52
Words Correct	÷	Total Words	=	Accuracy Rate
52	÷	56	=	.92 = 92%

The accuracy rate tells us that our reader correctly reads 92 percent of the words in this text. This text is at our student's instructional level (90–95%).

How well does this student monitor her own reading? How might you calculate that? Self-corrections and repetitions are signs of self-monitoring. This student uses repetition to check her thinking. If she did not self-correct her errors (*away, couldn't,* and *photograph*), there would have been a total of seven. To calculate her rate of self-correction, compare all possible errors to the number of corrected errors.

$$\frac{\text{Errors + self-corrections}}{\text{self-corrections}}$$

$$\frac{4+3}{3} = \frac{7}{3} = \frac{2.3}{1} = 1{:}2$$

Round off 2.3 to 2, giving a ratio of 1:2. The ratio means that for approxim every two miscues, the reader self-corrects one. That is an excellent self-correct rate. She monitors her own reading quite well.

If the student did not self-correct her errors, her accuracy rate would have droppea to 87.5 percent, or into frustration level:

Total words	–	number of errors	=	words read correctly
56	–	7	=	49
Words Correct	÷	Total Words	=	Accuracy Rate
49	÷	56	=	.875 = 87.5%

When the reader does make an error she does not self-correct, what type is it? What information in the text is our student attending to? Remember from Chapter 2 that three cuing systems influence our reading: meaning (makes sense), structure (sounds right), and visual (looks similar). Look at the reader's errors. Which cuing systems seem to be influencing her miscues?

		Error Type	
Counted Error:	*Meaning*	*Structure*	*Visual*
roots for *ruts*	______	______	______
omissions of *the*	______	______	______
substitute *of* for *about*	______	______	______
substitute *one* for *a*	______	______	______

Visual, meaning, and structure errors all could be influencing the *roots* miscue. *Roots* looks similar to *ruts,* it makes sense, and sounds right in the sentence. The omission of *the* could be influenced by meaning and structure. The sentence still sounds right and makes sense. Substituting *of* for *about* (and *a* for *one*) draws on meaning and structure cues. The sentences still sound right and make sense.

From analyzing responses on the running record, what might you conclude about this student's reading? You can see that she makes meaning through repetition, self-correction, and miscues that preserve structure and meaning. To help her see clearly what her students are doing, Kim uses a form (Figure 8.12) that shows the analysis of cues used for each error and self-correction.

Unscripted Running Record. Sometimes Kim wants to informally assess a student's oral reading. In that case, she takes an *unscripted* running record, which she makes without making a copy of the reading text. While looking at the student's text, she uses marks to show the student's reading accuracy. The advantage of an unscripted record is that you can make one at any time, without advance notice. Unscripted running records can be excellent records of student's oral reading.

Figure 8.12 Form for recording running record showing cuing strategies

Running Record

Name ______________________________ Date ____________

Text ____

Accuracy rate = _______%

Reading level: _______ Ind. (95–100%)
_______ Inst. (90–95%)
_______ Frus. (50–89%)

Counted errors = _______%

Self-correction rate = 1: _______

Cues used: M = meaning
S = structure
V = visual

No. of words in text _______

pg.		E	SC	M	S	V

If Kim is conferring with the previous student, and takes an unscripted running record of the same text from *Time for Andrew,* the record would look like the one shown in Figure 8.13. She would score and analyze the running record in the same manner as she would the scripted version.

Student Learning Portfolio

In reader's workshop, students must learn to keep careful records of their reading. They log each book, including those they decide to abandon. They also decide which books they will write responses for and what types of responses to make.

At the end of each grading period, students in both Kristen's and Kim's classes place copies of their reading records in their portfolios along with selected responses

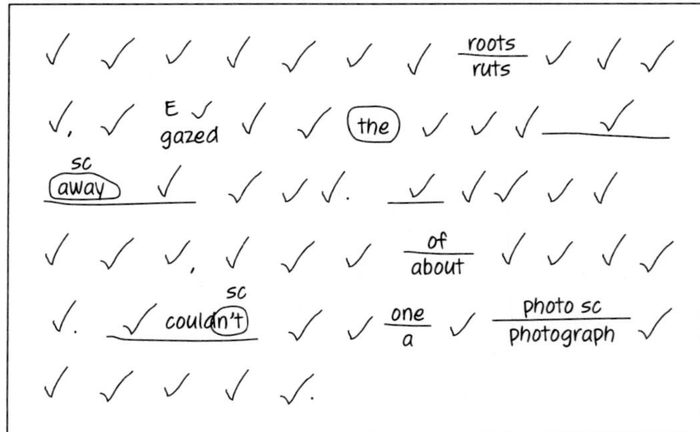

Figure 8.13 Sample unscripted running record

from logs and projects that show their growth as readers. Students also select responses for books that were especially challenging or meaningful. As in whole-class literature study, book clubs, and literature circles, students are expected to justify their choices. See chapters 6 and 7 for further discussion of the possibilities for student learning portfolios.

Respecting Diversity in Reader's Workshop

Provide for Personal Interests

Self-selected reading, as in reader's workshop, provides opportunity for students to pursue personal reading interests in literature of their choice. Of the different literature-based approaches we have considered, reader's workshop is the most responsive to students' needs and desires as readers. In reader's workshop, students are able to pursue passions, as well as develop interests in new areas of literature.

Value Students' Judgment

Providing for self-selection of reading material tells students that you trust their judgment. Just as adults come to know their own taste in literature, so can students. They may make some poor choices, but it is difficult to learn how to choose if we do not have the opportunity.

Conferring face to face provides opportunities to guide students in their personal decision making. Conferences hold students accountable for monitoring their own progress, but also provide them with support to successfully self-monitor.

In reader's workshop, students have a range of choices for log entries. The log represents another decisionmaking opportunity, and helps students learn about their ability to make and follow through on their choices. You will want to discuss these choices in the conferences, focusing on students' rationales for their decisions.

Foster Independence

Your ultimate goal for students as learners should be for them to become independent readers. Reader's workshop allows students to pace their own reading by providing large blocks of time so that, through self-pacing, they can find their own rhythms as readers.

Self-selection helps individual readers learn to effectively monitor their own reading, to recognize levels of comfort with different types of reading material. Strategic readers develop through having opportunities to monitor their own reading. It is not enough to know what a strategy is and how to do it. The real test comes when a student must decide on a particular strategy and know how to activate and use it in real reading. Self-selection can support the development of self-monitoring, and will ideally lead to self-evaluation. Through self-selected reading, students can develop trust in their own judgment and in their ability to evaluate their own reading performance.

TAKE A MOMENT AND REFLECT . . .

Reader's workshop is an individualized reading program based on:

- Predictable blocks of time
- Student choice of reading material
- A consistent structure
- Opportunity for students to respond to their reading
- A sense of community developed through collaboration and sharing

Reader's workshop is set up on a workshop framework that moves from:

- Whole-class instruction and planning
- To a block of independent work time, then
- Back to whole-class sharing and planning

To prepare for a reader's workshop, you must

- Know a great deal about students' needs and interests
- Have access to a range of literature
- Consider how you will meet your school district's required curriculum
- Be able to recognize successful reading behaviors and attitudes

To implement a reader's workshop, you must:

- Provide a quiet reading time each day
- Help students refine their ability to select appropriate reading materials
- Make available consistent time to confer with students about their reading
- Encourage student response to reading by using literature or reading logs
- Build community through small-group and whole-class sharing
- Provide opportunities for individual expression through response projects

Instruction in a reader's workshop is provided through:

- Whole-class minilessons that address workshop procedures, aspects of literature, and the effective use of reading strategies
- Flexible strategy groups that are organized as the need becomes apparent through conferences, teacher observation, and student initiation
- Individual help sessions initiated by students
- Interaction during community sharing sessions

Student progress in independent reading is monitored through:

- Records of texts students select to read
- Patterns that illustrate reading behavior (completed texts, abandoned texts, level of engagement)
- Quality of rehearsed oral reading during conferences
- Personal insights of self as reader
- Taking running records to document effective use of reading strategies

Running records:

- Are scripted or unscripted records of the miscues that students make while reading
- Can be made for any text that students read
- Use a system of markings that show students' reading behavior
- Can reveal patterns of effective and ineffective strategy use
- Should be completed for each middle grade student three or four times each school year

You respect diversity among students in reader's workshop when you:

- Build on their personal interests through reading
- Value the judgments students make about their reading
- Encourage and foster independence in reading

REFERENCES

Atwell, N. (1987). *In the middle: Writing, reading and learning with adolescents.* Portsmouth, NH: Heinemann.

Beach, R. (1993). *Reader-response theories.* Urbana, IL: National Council of Teachers of English.

Clay, M. (1968). A syntactic analysis of reading errors. *Journal of Verbal Learning and Verbal Behavior, 7,* 434–438.

Clay, M. (1979). *The early detection of reading difficulties.* Portsmouth, NH: Heinemann.

Ducker, S. (1968). *Individualized reading: An annotated bibliography.* Metuchen,NJ: Scarecrow.

Five, C. L. (1988, Spring). From workbook to workshop: Increasing children's involvement in the reading process. *The New Advocate,* 103–113.

Goodman, Y. M., & Burke, C. (1972). *The reading miscue inventory.* Upper Saddle River, NJ: Merrill/Prentice Hall.

Graves, D. (1994). *A fresh look at writing.* Portsmouth, NH: Heinemann.

Hagerty, P. (1992). *Reader's workshop: Real reading.* Richmond Hill, ON: Scholastic Canada Ltd.

Hansen, J. (1987). *When writers read.* Portsmouth, NH: Heinemann.

Holdaway, D. (1980). *Independence in reading.* Portsmouth, NH: Heinemann.

Hornsby, D., & Sukarna, D. (1986). *Read on: A conference approach to reading.* Portsmouth, NH: Heinemann.

Johnson, D. M. (1981). The effects of cooperative, competitive and individualistic goal structures on achievement: A meta-analysis. *Psychological Bulletin, 89,* 47–62.

Rosenblatt, L. M. (1978). *The reader, the text, the poem: The transactional theory of the literary work.* Carbondale, IL: Southern Illinois University Press.

Slavin, R. E., Madden, N. A., Karweit, N. L., Dolan, L. J., & Wasik, B. A. (1991). Success for all: Ending reading failure from the beginning. *Language Arts, 68,* 404–409.

Veatch, J. (Ed.). (1959). *Individualizing your reading program: Self-esteem in action.* New York: Putnam.

Vygotsky, L. S. (1962). *Thought and language.* (E. Hanfmann & G. Vakar, Eds. & Trans.). Cambridge, MA: MIT Press.

CHILDREN'S LITERATURE

Hahn, M. D. (1994). *Time for Andrew: A ghost story.* New York: Clarion.

9

Writer's Workshop and Beyond

Learning to Write and Writing to Learn

In this chapter . . .

We explore ways to use your knowledge of writing development to support and enhance students' sense of themselves as writers, including:

- the components of writer's workshop,
- an illustration of writer's workshop in a fifth-grade classroom, as Kim narrates her first year of implementing the approach,
- linking writer's workshop with other areas of study,
- using informal writing across the curriculum to help students learn,
- using learning logs in subject area instruction and units or theme studies, and
- issues that surround writing instruction, such as grammar and usage, mechanics, and conventions.

WRITER'S WORKSHOP

In this chapter, we discuss setting up a classroom environment to support and enhance students' writing competence. We begin with a statement by Calkins (1994) about the power of writing as a tool for learning:

> The powerful thing about writing with words is that we are really working with thoughts. Writing allows us to put our thoughts on the page and in our pockets; writing allows us to pull back and ask questions of our thoughts. It is this dynamic of creation and criticism, of pulling in to put thoughts on the page and pulling back to question, wonder, remember more, organize and rethink that makes writing such a powerful tool for learning. (p. 222)

Students learn to write through many varied experiences, both informal and formal. As they write, they simultaneously learn to capture and organize their thoughts for future use. In a writer's workshop students move through the phases of the writing process to develop formal pieces of writing. In other words, they put writing process to work! These phases are clearly visible in the workshop (Figure 9.1). The order of activity is optional, depending on intended outcome(s), allocated time, and what works best for students. Each part of a writer's workshop has specific purposes for supporting students' growing competence as writers.

Predictable Time to Write

If students are to become competent writers, time for writing must be predictable. The work requires time to plan, to settle in, and to get in one's stride as a writer. You should allocate a sustained block of at least 40 to 60 minutes per day (Graves, 1994; Calkins, 1994). Calkins (1994) stresses the need for consistent blocks of time to write:

> If students are going to become deeply invested in their writing, and if they are going to live toward a piece of writing and let their ideas grow and gather momentum, if they are going to draft and revise, sharing their texts with one another as they write, they need the luxury of time. If our students are going to have the chance to do their best and then to make their best better, they need long blocks of time. Sustained effort and craftsmanship are essential in writing well, yet they run contrary to the modern American way. (p. 186)

Teachers who are committed to developing competent writers look for ways to move instruction related to aspects of writing into the work of the writer's workshop. To

Figure 9.1 Writer's workshop components

Whole-Group Meeting (10–15 minutes):	• Minilesson or shared writing • Plans for the day
Work Time (20–30 minutes):	• Individual writing time • Conferring • Response partners/groups • Editing partners/groups • Publishing
Whole Group (10–15 minutes):	• Share sessions or author's chair • Plans for tomorrow

find consistent blocks of workshop time in an already crowded school day, teachers often do the following:

- Begin the day with students writing while the teacher is occupied with administrative matters such as attendance and lunch counts.
- Complete writing tasks from other subject areas, such as theme studies.
- Merge instruction in aspects of writing, such as handwriting, grammar, and spelling, that might otherwise be taught separately.
- Join reading instruction or literature studies with writing into a reader's/writer's workshop.

Demonstrations of Writing

Some aspects of the writing process are not easily observed as someone writes. Students need to see writing modeled and to hear how writers think about the content and process of their writing. Minilessons and shared writing experiences provide explicit demonstrations of workshop procedures, writing processes, forms of writing, and conventional uses of language.

Minilessons. As discussed previously, minilessons are not full-length lessons. They address knowledge and strategies that are helpful for students to know at a particular time or that students are "using but confusing." Minilessons serve as a "forum for planning a day's work, a time to call writers together . . . for raising a concern, exploring an issue, modeling a technique, reinforcing a strategy" (Calkins, 1994, p. 193).

Minilessons are short and to the point, lasting 5 to 10 minutes, and are intended to "put the idea in the room" so that students can explore whether it is helpful to them and share the idea with each other (Calkins, 1986). Minilessons plant seeds of ideas or expand on students' demonstrated awareness.

In the beginning stages of writing workshops, minilessons can help students learn workshop procedures. Later in the school year minilessons may focus on the use of genres and literary elements, or on strategies for becoming effective writers. The topics you select for minilessons should grow out of what students show through their feedback during opportunities to write.

Shared Writing Lessons. A more direct way to demonstrate writing is through shared writing lessons, in which a "more knowledgeable writer" and students develop a piece of writing together, recording the shared thinking on a large chart or overhead transparency. This has also been referred to as *group writing*, but "shared" is a good description of what should actually occur. The focus of what is written depends on the particular knowledge students need to see modeled.

Shared writing lessons are typically more in depth than minilessons and allow for demonstration, as well as discussion, of particular techniques in a piece of group writing. On days when you schedule shared writing, you will extend whole-group time during the workshop and shorten individual writing time and/or the sharing session.

Sometimes shared writing might actually be shared revising or shared editing, using a piece that the class has written together. Existing pieces can be considered as drafts, then used in a new way, to help students see that sometimes writers decide to change the focus of a piece. Changing the focus can change the way the author's voice sounds, the intended audience, or even the form that the writing takes (such as changing from personal narrative to poetry).

Topic Choice

Professional writers select their own topics for writing. In an effective writer's workshop students, too, choose their topics. "'Ownership' is vital if students are to make a real commitment of time and effort to the task of learning the craft of writing" (Wells, 1986, p. 202). By the time they reach the middle grades, most students are quite capable of selecting their own topics for writing.

When students are able to select their own topics, boys and girls often make very different choices (Douglas, 1988; Graves, 1973). Boys often choose to write about the world outside of themselves with a focus on informational writing, while girls write with a focus toward "I" and personal narratives. The differences between students' self-selected topic choices reflect the diversity that exists in our classrooms.

Response to Writing

Providing opportunity for students to select their own topics requires you to take their choices seriously and respond to their writing based on what individuals are trying to accomplish. Students need the response of others "to discover what they do and do not understand" (Graves, 1994, p. 108) about their topic, the writing process, and their desire to be understood by others.

Response through Conferring. While it can be very helpful for you to confer with students about their writing, your goal is really to help them learn to confer with themselves as writers. "Writing separates our ideas from ourselves in a way that it is easiest for us to examine, explore, and develop them" (Smith, 1982, p. 15). Early on, we must help students learn how to step back from their writing, how to *want* to step back, to see themselves in their words. Conferring with students should help them learn how to ask themselves questions about their piece as they reread and rethink their intentions.

Informal conferences happen as you circulate among students and begin conversations. You schedule *formal conferences* to have an in-depth look at a completed piece of writing or to evaluate a student's growth as a writer. Students need to confer at different points in their writing—getting focused, refocusing a draft, questioning a choice of form, thinking about getting started on a new piece, affirming that their piece is going well, receiving a nudge to take the next step, and so on. Talking with students about their writing enables you to learn who they are as writers and to become more sensitive to their individual needs for instruction.

Response Partners/Groups. Students will probably need response to their writing that goes beyond conferring with you. Helping students learn how to respond to one another's writing will strengthen writing in your classroom, allowing everyone to become a teacher. The procedure you use to enable students to get response to their writing depends on how your classroom functions. In some classrooms, small groups can work effectively. Careful observation of students helps you decide whether partners or groups are most effective.

The success of response in your classroom will closely relate to the overall climate of support and respect you foster.

Editing Partners/Groups. Encourage editing for conventions after students have had response to the meaningful aspects of their writing. While some students do minor editing during writing, many students delay major editing until after completing their initial draft. They may require assistance from a more able writer to notice details in the writing that are unconventional or that need attention. Students can be very helpful to each other, teaching each other strategies for checking spelling and punctuation. Editing partners or groups will need coaching to be sensitive to the varying levels of knowledge that exist in a classroom.

Whether revising for meaning or editing for conventions, you are asking students to let the knowledge they have gained as readers also help them as writers. You should stress this point as you demonstrate revising and editing skills throughout daily writing activities.

Your Turn

Have you observed a writer's workshop in a middle grade classroom? If so, what did you notice most? How did students appear to feel about the workshop?

My Turn

I first observed writers' workshop in a fifth-grade class. In the beginning of the school year the workshop seemed chaotic, but as students learned what Louise, their teacher, expected, they settled into a rhythm of writing. At first I questioned how students could learn about writing by working on their own. Then I began to notice how pairs of students helped each other when there were questions. I was also amazed that students would write for sustained periods of time without the teacher telling them. At first I was very skeptical of writer's workshop, but Louise taught me that through support and experience, teachers can help students become independent and confident writers.

Putting the Components to Work: Writer's Workshop in Fifth Grade

For a close look at how writer's workshop actually functions, we visit with Kim, a fifth-grade teacher in her first year of using writer's workshop as one way of teaching writing skills and strategies. Kim describes a typical day of writer's workshop in her classroom, noting the issues that she has dealt with in this first year.

Getting Started

From 9:15 to 10:15 we have writer's workshop. I've never done this until this year. Now, I can't imagine *not* doing it. Our format for writer's workshop is *very* predictable. We always start out with a minilesson. They are about 10 minutes long, and range from how to incorporate a writing trait, like organization or voice, in a piece of writing, to ways we can help ourselves and others edit papers. I draw my topics from the following list.

Workshop Procedures

- How to do writer's workshop and expectations
- How to confer
- How to fill out a writing log
- Sharing writing
- Being a good listener
- Talking with friends, sharing ideas

- Evaluating your writing
- How to fill out a cover sheet before submitting it
- Understanding a grading rubric
- Publishing ideas and other extension activities

Writing Strategies

- Matching form, purpose, and audience
- Using the phases of the writing process
- How to keep yourself going during writing time
- How to edit your or a friend's paper
- Taking risks
- How/when to revise (adding on, inserting, changing)
- How/when to edit
- When to abandon a piece
- Which resources are best?

Using Writing Traits

- Organization
  narratives—personal, fictional (story)
  expository—research report, explanation, description, compare/contrast
  persuasive—letters, speech
  getting the reader's attention
- Ideas and content
  staying focused on your topic
  knowing enough about your topic
- Voice
  hearing "you" in your writing
  writing in an interesting way
- Word choice
  choosing words that fit your piece
  describing a character, setting, or event
- Sentence structure and fluency
  using a variety of sentence forms
  getting a "flow" to your writing
  using the right words in the right places
- Writing mechanics/conventions
  making your writing easy to read
  using conventions to help the reader

I always base the topic of the minilesson on what students have demonstrated in their work and from what they've shared with me in conferences. For example, in yesterday's minilesson I shared some examples of leads that other authors use to get their writing started (Figure 9.2). Through conferences and other discussions with students it appeared to be a concern. This is also the time when I share my writing, because students need to know what good writing sounds and looks like as a model to draw on when they're writing.

I ask questions after the minilesson to check students' writing plans for the day:

- Who is starting a new piece today?
- Who is continuing a piece?
- Who will be rereading, revising, or reworking their writing today, and do you need any help doing this?
- Who will be editing today, and would you like to be in an editing group?

Daily Writing Time

After I get an idea of who is doing what and jot down notes for myself about responses to my "check" questions, the students begin in their work folders, which hold notes, drafts, finished copies, resources, and so on.

Students choose their own topics during writer's workshop because it gives them a sense of ownership of their work. Sometimes I ask them to make choices within a particular genre, such as mystery, or a theme such as "Survival" or "Ancient Egypt." Even within these areas, students still have ownership over the specific topic and form their writing takes. When I have something specific I want them to write about, we do it outside of writer's workshop.

This writing time lasts 20 to 30 minutes. While the class starts to work, I first go to those students who I know always have a hard time getting focused and started. I make sure they know what they'll be working on that day. I allow students to go to quiet areas in the room with a partner to discuss ideas and to share their work. When everyone is settled, I begin my daily conferences.

Writing conferences are opportunities for students to teach us about who they are as writers.

Figure 9.2 Sample minilesson—Writing a good lead

"I've noticed you enjoy reading books that capture your interest right from the start, in the first sentence or two. In writing we call that 'a good lead.' Did you know there is more than one kind of good lead? To help you think about your options for writing, let's look at the leads for some literature we have read to see what other authors do to get their writing off to a good start.

"Sometimes authors start with a lead that fits the genre and introduces the plot. Do you remember when we studied mysteries and we especially liked *Time for Andrew* by Mary Downing Hahn (1994)? She introduces the mystery with the following words" (places quote on overhead):

> "There it is." Dad slowed the car and pointed to a big brick house standing on a hill above the highway. From a distance, it looked empty, deserted, maybe even haunted. (p. 1)

"Remember that Drew's dad and mom were taking him to his Aunt's house to stay for a few months. Notice how Hahn uses this lead to introduce that situation and create a sense of mystery right from the start. I think this is an example of good mystery lead.

"Sometimes authors choose to start by setting the scene, especially when it is going to play an important part. In *The Star Fisher* by Lawrence Yep (1991) we followed Joan Lee, a Chinese-American girl, as she moved to West Virginia in 1927, hoping to be accepted in the new town" (places quote on the overhead):

> I thought I knew what green was until we went to West Virginia.
>
> As the old locomotive chugged over the pass, I could see nothing but green. Tall, thin, trees covered the slopes, and leafy vines grew around the tree trunks; and surrounding the trees were squat bushes and tall grass.
>
> And as the train rattled down into the valley, the green slopes seemed to rise upward like the waves of an ocean; and I felt as if the train were a ship sinking into a sea of green. (p. 3)

"Yep begins with setting to help you sense what Joan felt when she first saw her new home, West Virginia.

"Sometimes an author leads by introducing us to the main character, to get us interested in that character right away. In the beginning of *Maniac Magee,* Jerry Spinelli (1990) writes the following" (places quote on overhead):

> They say Maniac Magee was born in a dump. They say his stomach was a cereal box and his heart a sofa spring.
>
> They say he kept an eight-inch cockroach on a leash and the rats stood guard over him while he slept.
>
> They say if you knew he was coming and you sprinkled salt on the ground and he ran over it, within two or three blocks he would be as slow as everybody else.
>
> They say. (p. 1)

"Does this description of Maniac Magee capture your interest? Does it make you want to know more about him? If so, then Spinelli wrote a good character lead.

"We have looked at three options that authors used for getting the story started—focusing on plot, setting, or character. What authors choose depends on what they want the reader to notice first. As you are working on your pieces today, look at the way you chose to begin. Do you think your lead will capture the reader's interest? What does your lead have to do with what you want your reader to notice first? Perhaps some of you will be willing to share your lead at the end of today's writer's workshop."

Conferences

I see three or four students, who know it is their turn. (I have a rotating list of names for conferences, so the students always know when they're meeting with me.) When they come to conference, they bring their writing folder and what they are working on or what they would like to discuss. I confer with students to get to know them better, to monitor their progress, and to help them with any problems.

I usually get the conference going by saying, "Tell me about what you're working on." This is usually all it takes to get them talking. If they don't seem willing to share, I might ask "nudging" questions:

How did you begin your piece?

What can you tell me (if it's fiction) about your characters, setting, problem, or . . .?

What is happening in your piece that you're working on right now?

What will happen next?

How will you end your piece?

How did you come up with your ideas?

What are your future plans for this writing?

What do you like best about your piece?

What would you change if you could?

What gave you trouble while writing?

What did you learn as you wrote?

How do you keep your reader interested and focused?

What surprised you about your piece?

How is this piece important to you?

How does this work compare with other pieces you've written?

By asking "nudging" questions, I'm trying to teach students how to think about what they're writing and to evaluate themselves. I believe this leads to greater independence. At the close of the conference, I always mention specific things I liked in their writing or that I noticed that were new or different.

Keeping Records

I keep running progress notes on each student, which I take during and immediately after their conference (Figure 9.3). I keep track of titles, genres, strengths in the writing, problems I see students having, problems they say they are having, whether their log is being kept up, and any future plans they might have for publishing the piece.

In my notebook I also have a list of 5- to 10-minute small-group workshops that students can sign up for, and when each workshop will be or was given. Workshops are my way of offering group instruction based on student need. Workshops follow up minilessons, but are a bit more in depth. I call them *workshops* because the students think it sounds like it will be more fun than work. They sign up for a workshop they think will help them with their writing, such as one on organization, conventions, or word choice. Students can sign up at the end of a conference or any time that I am free.

Figure 9.3 Kim's writing conference notes

Travis
9/1 – friends
– Eric brainwashed by Dan, evil scientist
* described characters
9/11 – wrote sequel, Laughing Waters
– characters (Eric, Dan) show more development
10/2 – Pinball
– man in pinball machine, bouncing around
– needs to make clearer (he feels)
– got idea from Virtual Reality program
* doesn't know how to keep reader interested
wants help here
– used a lot of dialogue incorrectly, so he signed up for "____"
workshop and Zack is also helping him since Zack is a "master"
at quotations

Finding Time to Teach

I learned from Donald Graves (1994) that if students don't recognize they need help with a particular problem, they probably aren't ready to receive help yet. I really found this to be true when I first began my workshops. I used to recommend that students come to specific workshops, and afterwards I would still find the same mistakes in their work. I realized that students may not recognize or find useful the writing ideas that I was sharing. Now I concentrate on helping students get to know themselves as writers so they are able to accept my invitations to workshops.

When I have at least two students signed up for a particular workshop, I send them a special invitation telling them where, when, and what to bring to the workshop. If for some reason a student does not come, I ask the class if anyone else is interested in that particular workshop and schedule an additional time. I always keep track of who comes, and I look to see if they implement workshop ideas in their writing.

During the workshop, we work with pieces the students are either working on or have finished. It seems that all I have to do to get them to search further in their writing is to focus their attention on a particular technique or element. Then they seem to notice it in many different places. By using their own writing for workshop lessons, they are taking charge of what needs to be added, deleted, or revised, and they are the ones who find the areas that need attention. I put our workshop minilessons on chart paper, and hang them on the walls so all students, including those who were not in a particular workshop, can refer to them if they are having difficulty with that skill.

I also keep a list of names of students who have mastered certain workshop lessons. Other students can use these "masters" as a resource if I am not available. One goal I have is to teach some of these "masters" how to teach a workshop on a skill or strategy they have mastered. How valuable it would be for them, their peers, and for me to see how they would communicate one of my workshop lessons to others!

Sharing Writing

After 20 or so minutes of writing time, students choose to continue writing or to work on a publishing project for a finished or nearly finished piece. Publishing or celebrating students' work becomes part of their experiential base, and aids in making it their own while giving it a touch of finality. Our publishing projects have taken the following forms:

- bookmaking
- posters
- cartoon strips
- wordless books with tapes
- greeting cards
- advertisements
- videos
- plays
- pamphlets
- reader's theater
- puppet shows
- physical models
- pop-up books
- postcards
- big books
- dioramas
- newscast interviews
- pantomimes with tape
- flip book with script
- collages
- sculptures
- fact file
- TV productions

Sharing their writing with others enables students to receive feedback about their thinking.

The end of writer's workshop consists of the class coming together for discussion. Some kids share excerpts of what they're writing, some share projects, and some share risks they've taken in their writing. I also ask if anyone tried what was discussed in the minilesson or workshop that day. Students schedule sharing time, and can check a posted list to prepare themselves if it's their share day. I also have emergency open slots for kids who just can't wait until their turn comes up next. The audience then has a chance to respond with what Donald Graves, in his book, *A Fresh Look at Writing* (1994), calls remembers, reminders, questions, and comments. Students tell the author what they remember about the piece, say if it reminds them of anything, and ask questions or make other comments about the writing.

Keeping Track of Student Progress

For evaluation purposes, the students are required to fill out a writing log (Figure 9.4). They know they need to keep logs up to date and that I always check them at conferences. We also continue to discuss as a class the importance of keeping a writing log. My students offer the following reasons for keeping their logs:

> "So we can see what kind of stories we like to write."
>
> "So we'll try something new.
>
> "So if we abandon a piece we can see it in our writing log and have another try at it if we want to."

Figure 9.4 Sample writing log

Name Seiko — Writer's Workshop Log

Begin	Finish	Genre	Title	Strengths	Weaknesses	Future Plans
9/7	9/10	non-fiction	ME	used good word choice	my words were not new	maybe introduce one of my friends?
9/11	I don't want to finish	fiction	Grasshoppers	I used good rhyming	my words don't sound new.	none, right now
9/12	9/12	commercial	Sugar Cola	neat idea	wasn't a good product	Do another commercial?
9/13	9/20	fiction adventure	Thunder Mountain	new types of rides	________	Make more rides?
9/21	9/27	fiction baseball	Giants vs Rockies	I liked it and it's a good story	NO NEW WORDS!	make another story cause it got rained out.
10/1	10/23	fiction adventure	The Home in The Woods	a good camping story	needs more adventure	Write a sequel?
10/26	Dumped	fiction	The Princess and The Frog (my version) →	Tried my ideas	Kind of boring	maybe come back when I have more ideas
10/30	11/4	mystery	We're coming Back To get You	good quotes. never used SAID	no new words	make it more exciting

"We can keep track of how long it takes us to write a whole story."

"We can work on the weaknesses that we have in our 'weaknesses' column."

Students also must turn in a written piece every two weeks. Most students turn in a completed piece, but some turn in longer unfinished pieces. With each piece they turn in, they fill out an evaluation cover sheet that asks the following:

- What type of story did you write?
- What do you like best about your writing?
- What do you like least about your writing?
- What gave you the most difficulty?
- What do you want the reader to notice?

I have them do this so they can begin to evaluate their own work at deeper levels (see "Monitoring Students' Growth as Writers" at the end of this chapter for other examples).

I evaluate the pieces by means of a rubric that I created from a student writing guide. Everyone has copies of the guide, and if they get a low score for a certain area, they can look in their copy to get immediate feedback. If they are unhappy with a score, they know they are welcome to revise, edit, or whatever the problem may be, to try to raise their score.

My students have come to learn that they can count on writer's workshop every day, no matter what the schedule is. On the few days that it has to be cut short, they are very disappointed.

Writer's workshop is working for me with this class of students. I truly believe this because I have seen improvement in all areas of writing traits as well as in the writing strategies of most students, including my least experienced. I have three students who were unwilling to write at the beginning of the school year. They considered a story to consist of a beginning sentence, a middle sentence, and an ending sentence. Through some incredible nudging, and by going to them first when each writing period begins, I have seen growth not only in the length of their pieces, but also in the amount of detail and voice. Now, I am trying to stretch them even further. They struggle and work hard at achieving one self-made goal at a time.

When at the end of the year we choose stories to go into each student's schoolwide portfolio, I am sure the reluctant writers will see a lot of growth. As for my stronger writers, they are learning to take risks and try new things in their writing. I'm also learning a lot as I go.

I'm not sure that my class last year could have done a writer's workshop. They were not very independent. I probably would have needed to make the workshop more structured, especially in my expectations of student roles. I may have had fewer short workshop lessons with more in-depth class lessons, and firmer guidelines for editing partners. This is something I'll have to consider in the future as I meet each new class. It won't be a barrier for me, only more of a challenge.

Writer's workshop will be a challenging approach to use in your classroom. At this point, what aspect do you feel most confident about and why? What aspect do you feel least confident about and why?

When I first tried a writer's workshop in the middle grades, I was teaching sixth grade. I was committed to the daily predictable time block needed for the students to become confident writers. I also believed that the students needed to select their own topics so that their writing would be meaningful. What I didn't feel at all confident about was how students would continue to learn about such conventions of writing as grammar and spelling if I didn't teach them directly. At the time, I didn't know many other teachers who were using a workshop approach, so I searched for articles and books by people who had, in hopes that I could learn from them.

Focusing the Content of Writer's Workshop

Kim chooses to allow free choice of topics in her writer's workshop. Other teachers, particularly those in middle school, choose to focus the writer's workshop on particular types of writing that enhance content area studies. For example, to support a social studies unit on ancient Greece, a teacher may focus students' attention on expository writing, using writer's workshop to teach how to write a research report.

In middle school, teams of teachers often work together on interdisciplinary units. To support a team's unit of study, the English teacher often provides time in writer's workshop to develop pieces around the theme. For example, seventh- and eighth-grade students at a local middle school were studying about political action in their community, in particular how to influence the city parks department to put grass on their barren school grounds for a joint-use park. To make their case, students needed to learn how to write persuasive letters to local government officials. As Duncan, the social studies teacher, helped students research the issues, Carla, the English teacher, devoted writer's workshop time to helping students learn how to develop persuasive arguments.

To support an American History unit on the Civil War, Marie's eighth-grade English teacher provided writer's workshop time for students to develop pieces that displayed their Civil War knowledge. Marie chose to write fiction that was made more believable by historical information, a sample of which is shown in Figure 9.5. Included with a part of Marie's draft are samples of three forms: revision and editing prompts, a peer review, and final comments.

Choice is not taken away when teachers focus the writer's workshop. Students continue to select their own specific topic while they learn how to write in particular forms for a variety of purposes. What is accomplished is an effective use of school time, increased support to students as they explore and refine their knowledge of writing, and greater opportunities for teachers to demonstrate how writers think with written language.

In chapters 11 and 12 you will see other examples of how you can focus writer's workshop to help students become competent writers. Basal reading series are now integrating writer's workshops into reading activities for an integrated language approach (Chapter 11). Writer's workshop also helps students think in greater depth about themes or units of study in different content areas (Chapter 12).

As you try new approaches, such as a writer's workshop, you will need models, just as students do for learning. It will help you to observe other teachers' workshops and read about the experiences of others who share through their published writing. You, too, can learn from "more knowledgeable others." In the end, however, writer's workshop in your classroom is what you make of it.

Figure 9.5 Sample writer's workshop products, eighth grade

All Men Created Equal

"Going once, going twice, sold to the man in the back row for 40 dollars."

The man stood up. He was tall and lanky, with dark hair and a mustache. He was wearing a black overcoat and black slacks. A big hat sat upon his head. He had a stern look on his face, but as I walked over to him he smiled a little.

"What's your name?" he asked.

"Clarence Tomkins," I replied.

"Mine's Bob Barley. Jump in the truck."

I got in the back of the truck quickly, and we drove off with a strong jerk. The ride lasted an hour. It was nice to get a break from work. My last owner had me working sixteen hours a day, even at night when it was dark. He finally had to sell me when my back became injured. It was apparently from the work I was doing. I was praying that this man would be different.

We got to his house and plantation. Immediately I saw three other slaves working out in the field, and as we drove up another little black girl came out of the house. She had ragged clothes on, but an apron so I guessed she worked in the house.

"Sarah," the man yelled, "I'm home with another one!"

A ~~women~~ woman came out of the house. She was petite, with blond hair. She ~~had on~~ wore a dress and apron. She looked me over for what seemed like a long time.

"Well, I guess he'll do," she said, "What's your name?"

"Clarence Tomkins."

"You had better get started. Lily here will tell you where your sleeping quarters are and everything else you need to know. Go along Lily."

The little girl took my arm and led me to a little shack over on the far side of the property.

"This is where we all sleep. There's me, Joseph, Phillip, and my ma Sally. They're out working. I work in the house cooking and cleaning. The old lady seems horrid, but she's not so bad. Just don't get in no trouble. We eat at 5:45 in the morning. Some mush and water. At 12:00 we get the same thing and at 8:00 at night we eat some bread, meat, and a small cup of milk. Sometimes I can sneak in a piece of extra bread or cheese, but not always. If you get into trouble they take away a meal, but there are not whips."

I said a silent prayer to God. For both of my sisters had been killed with whips by their masters. I myself had felt the pain of a whip before.

"Any questions Clarence?" Lily asked me.

"What about clothes?" I asked. All that I had on now was a pair of old pants.

She looked me over and said "they'll probably give you a long sleeved shirt for cold weather. When it's warm though, you'll just have to work without your shirt. These are the shoes you'll get . . .

Informal Writing across the Curriculum

As you engage students in thinking about a variety of subjects, it is important to help them learn how to capture their thinking for later use. We return here to informal writing, those bursts of writing that take a variety of forms and that may not be revised or published. Informal writing is an essential element in each subject area. To help students learn, writing their thoughts must become a "habit of mind," a way they capture ideas that helps them think about what they know.

Informal writing does not always happen naturally; you must demonstrate it. Through shared writing experiences, you may attempt various informal writing with

Figure 9.5 *continued*

Review Sheet Form #1

Name: Marie Period: 4

Title of Writing: All Men Created Equal

Draft #1

1. What is the strongest or most exciting part of piece?
The beginning – 1st couple pages
2. is the paper limited to 1 topic
yes
3. What is the topic?
One slave's life during the civil war
4. Does the lead get the writer right into the writing?
yes–
5. Which parts don't fit in and could be taken out? . . . "and as a matter of fact I think I was their favorite . . ."
6. Where could I use more description or explanation
–none–
7. Is there any part that could use dialogue?
I have it everywhere it needs to be
8. Is there anypart that could confuse the reader?
Yes, when I put in about the 2 sides, I will change those few paragraphs.
9. Have I repeated myself saying anything more than once? No–
10. Am I using particular words to often?
none–
11. Do I have paragraph breaks?
Paragraphing is fine
12. Is there information that could go in another place?
Yes, I will change it
13. How do I want my reader to feel?
Like they have a pretty good understanding of the civil war ⟶

your students. Through demonstration, on a chart or overhead projector, students can see you organize ideas and should hear you think aloud. Thinking aloud helps students understand how you decide about your writing. (This is also true for formal writing.) In writer's workshop, Kim thinks aloud so that her students can begin to understand how competent writers think.

We turn now to examples of informal writing from various subject areas. Consider how each form enables students to retain, re-collect, re-create, and re-construct their experience as a tool for learning. Try to demonstrate each of these forms with students on numerous occasions so they begin to understand the purposes and possibilities for each.

Figure 9.5 *continued*

Writers Workshop Form #2

Writers Name : Marie

Title of Writing : All Men Created Equal

Reader Editor's name : Bailey

Question : Is there enough information?

1. What is the main point the paper is making?
2. What are the strong points of this writing?
3. What would help the piece? What is unclear? Give any specific examples, details, or pieces of info. that need work.
4. Write some questions about the piece that will help the writer revise.

Yes, there is plenty of information, the end could have been drawn out alittle more?

1. That Slaves were free, and equall
2. Voice, setting is great, She reveals the info extemely well, very real
3. End needs work
5. How did he feel at the end?

Writers Workshop Form #3

Writers Name : Marie Cannon

Title of Writing : All Men Created Equal

1. What do you like about this piece of writing?
   I like that it tells a story but still has a lot of information in it.
2. What was your plan for revision?
   I took out words and phrases.
3. What would change further if you had more time, energy or desire?
   I would make the conclusion better.

Lists

Students use lists to retain information for later use or to re-collect ideas (e.g., homework assignments, types of ocean animals, steps in a problem-solving procedure, checklists for self-evaluating a class project, etc.). Lists can be descriptive (Figure 9.6) or ordered (Figure 9.7), depending on the type of information. Information in descriptive lists may not be organized. Ordered lists have an organization, such as by sequence or time. The information in lists can also be arranged into new forms, such as paragraphs, to serve the writer's specific purposes.

Clusters or Brainstorms

Students may also arrange lists visually to show how ideas relate. Such a display can be a helpful tool for retaining and re-collecting specific ideas. Initially, a brainstormed cluster may not be organized to show relationships (Figure 9.8). Re-collecting the ideas to show relationships can make the ideas more useable. Organized clusters help students see how important details can add to or replace existing schema for a topic.

Annotated Drawings

Writing can elaborate on ideas that are drawn, and vice versa. Annotations may be labels, descriptions, or explanations that comment on or clarify the illustration (Figure 9.9). Annotations may help visual learners reflect on their thinking. Some students are better able to organize their writing by first making pictorial representations.

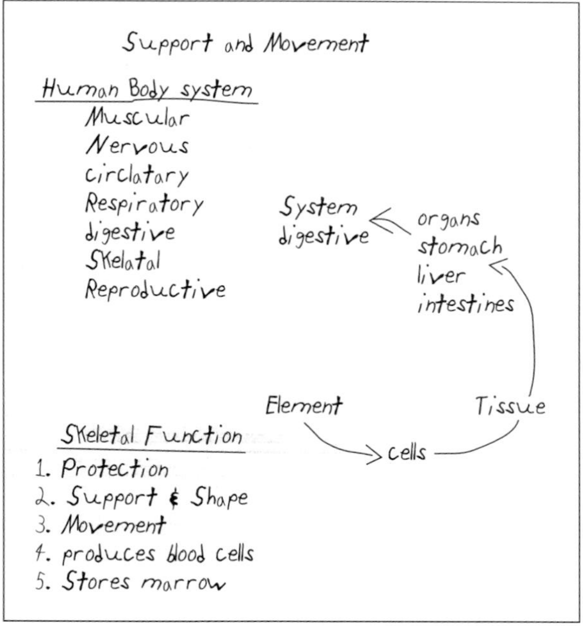

Figure 9.6 Descriptive list for science, eighth grade

Important Events in Modern Europe 1914–1961

1914	WW I begins
1917	U.S. enters the war
1919	Treaty of Versailles ends WWI
1920s	Depression in Germany
1933	Hitler becomes Nazi dictator
1935	Holocaust begins
1939	WW II begins
1941	Japan attacks Pearl Harbor
	U.S. enters war
1944	D-Day
1945	WWII ends
1956	Revolts against communism in Eastern Europe
1961	Berlin Wall built

Figure 9.7 Sample ordered list

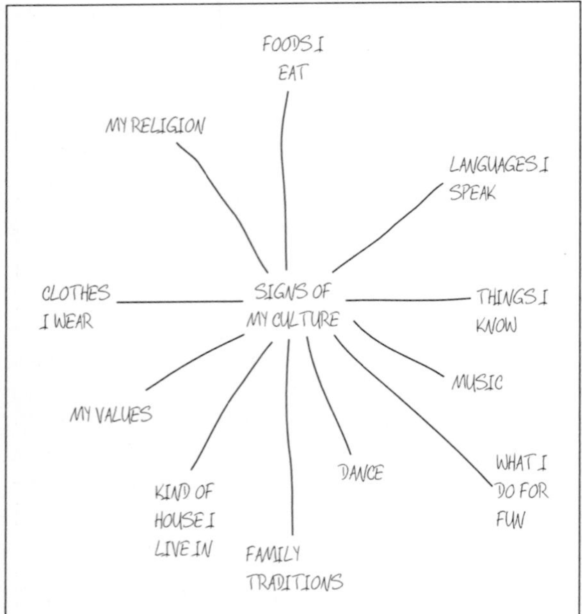

Figure 9.8 Cluster for social studies

Figure 9.9 Annotated drawing for mathematics

Venn Diagrams

The interlocking circles of a Venn diagram enable students to visually show similarities and differences between two or more categories of characteristics (Figure 9.10). They may re-construct their understanding of the relationship between groups of ideas or objects as they decide how to place each item in the Venn diagram. This exercise is an excellent rehearsal for comparative thinking and writing.

Story Maps

Another type of visual representation of thinking is a story map that shows the important literary elements and the general progression of the plot. Story maps can be as simple as a beginning-middle-end progression, or may identify more complicated relationships, such as problem-events-resolution. Maps may also include a brief description of the setting and main characters. Story maps are a planning device to re-collect or retell a story or re-create a new story drawn from a variety of our literary experiences. For example, Marie, in eighth grade, uses a map (Figure 9.11) to plan her piece of historical fiction that centers around the Civil War period and slavery. Notice how she plans to include historical facts to support her fictional characters and setting.

Graphic Organizers

A graphic organizer shows the overall structure of ideas that cluster around a topic. It may also be used as a "map" for information texts. Authors of information texts often

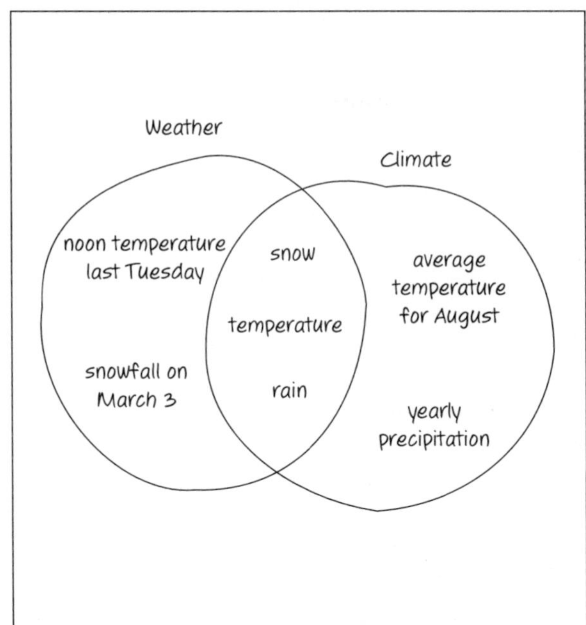

Figure 9.10 Venn diagram for science

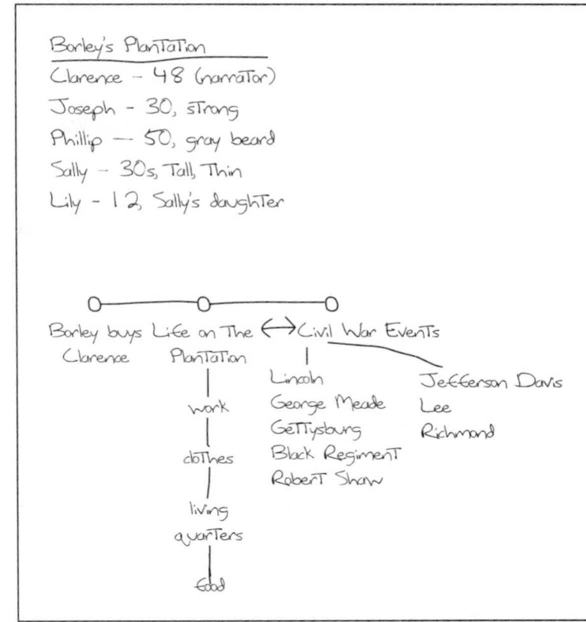

Figure 9.11 Story map for historical fiction

help readers prepare for the ideas in a chapter or section by visually showing how the ideas are organized. Students can use this same form of informal writing to re-collect ideas from an existing text or re-construct ideas in a new way, drawn from a variety of resources.

Charts

Charts can help students re-collect ideas about a topic and re-construct those ideas into related groups. The categories needed to organize ideas are dictated by the ideas' relationships. Simple charts may use only a few categories, while others may use a large number of categories and subcategories (Figures 9.12 and 9.13). Determining categories is an important part of chartmaking. You may predetermine categories, or they may emerge out of unorganized ideas when examining their relationships. For students who have little experience with setting up a chart, you must decide together about what makes appropriate categories. Another type of chart, which is actually a listing, is a K-W-L (Ogle, 1986), in which students list what they already *Know,* what they *Want* to know, and what they *Learned* about a particular topic. A K-W-L chart is an excellent tool for re-collecting ideas.

Graphs

Students also can represent ideas in symbolic form. Graphs use lines, bars, portions of circles and symbols to represent relationships. Words are used to define categories and types of relationship.

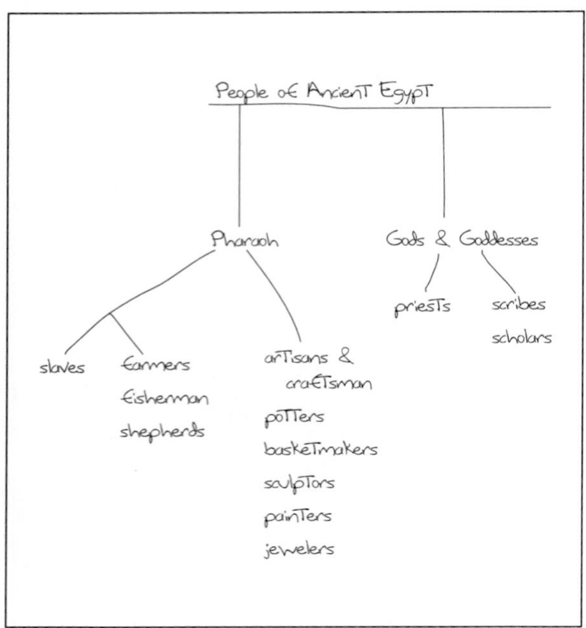

Figure 9.12 Sample chart for organizing information

Comparing world governments	Free & open elections	People control own lives	Safe guard individual freedom	Government controls economy
Communism	—	—	—	+
Constitutional monarchy	+	+	+	—
Democracy	+	+	+	—
Dictatorship	—	—	—	+
Monarchy	—	—	—	+
Republic	+	+	+	—

\+ attribute — not an attribute

Figure 9.13 Sample attribute chart

Hawaiian Islands	
1. volcanoes very old 2. islands are volcano Tops 3. melted rock, ash, gas 4. starts deep inside earth 5. cools down, hardens 6. forms mountain 7. built up from ocean floor (Pacific)	The Hawaiian Islands were made long ago by volcanoes. A volcano is an opening in the earth. Melted rock, ash and gas are forced out from deep inside. As hot rock and ash cools, they form a mountain. The islands of Hawaii are actually the tops of volcanoes that have built up from the floor of the Pacific Ocean.

Figure 9.14 Description—From list to paragraph

Kid Pay Graph

1. I brainstormed jobs that kids really do.
2. I picked 5 jobs for my graph
   raking leaves babysit
   wash the car feed pets
   mow the lawn
3. I made a survey of my parents and 5 neighbors.
4. I had to average the answers my neighbors gave so I could have 1 number for my graph.
5. I put the bars on my graph.
6. I discovered that other people pay kids more for jobs than their own parents pay.

Figure 9.15 Sample events record

Figure 9.16 Sample explanation

What do you Think This section is about?

(2-3 Scientific Notation)

This maybe about how To write numbers - (large numbers) in a way you can understand

After: I didn't Think about scientists needing a way To talk about billions and Trillions of miles. Scientific numbers would have way Too many O's To be able To read. I would have To stop To count The O's everyTime. Now I have To remember That The exponent (10^2) Tells how many O's There are in The number.

$10^2 = 100$

$10^3 = 1000$

$10^4 = 10{,}000$

$10^5 = 100{,}000$

Descriptions

Relationships among ideas can also be shown with words. Descriptions use words to build images of objects, people, places, and events; as do illustrations. In descriptions, students re-collect ideas they have already retained, or re-create a portion of an experience. Sometimes students will begin descriptions as a list and then place the ideas in paragraph form (Figure 9.14).

Note Taking

In the midst of an experience, students can use words, phrases, and sentences to capture and retain their thoughts. Notes made during experiences or immediately following retain the experience for future use. Notes should primarily be for the writer's own use. You can demonstrate note taking during activities in which retaining ideas is important.

Recording Events

Notes can be expanded to become a record of events (Figure 9.15). When it is important to recall an event in an orderly fashion, making a record of events is a useful form of informal writing (such as for a class field trip, documenting a science experiment, life events in preparation for writing an autobiography, or re-collecting the events of a group math project).

Explanations

An explanation is often useful when events require elaboration. In an explanation, the writer tells more than merely the ideas or events that occurred by providing a rationale or support for his thinking (e.g., steps in solving a math problem, response to a book or character, hypothesizing in a science experiment, or reasons for selecting a particular form for a piece of process writing). In Figure 9.16, one student explains her thinking after reading in her science text about scientific notation.

Before moving on to the next section of this chapter, take a moment and reflect on the possibilities of informal writing. What positive outcomes might you observe if students in your classroom engaged in daily informal writing experiences such as the examples in this section?

Students who frequently make lists of important information, arrange ideas into a coherent description, label diagrams to explain an idea, or organize their thinking into a multilevel chart are less likely to be intimidated by formal writing experiences and more likely to feel successful about expressing their thinking in print. ■

LEARNING LOGS: LINKING INFORMAL WRITINGS

Single-Subject Learning Logs

Learning logs are an excellent vehicle for focusing students' learning in one subject area through informal writing. For example, while working in a chapter on interpreting data in their mathematics textbook, Mary's sixth- and seventh-grade students do the following:

- Make a K-W-L *chart* that details what they already know about the topic, what they want to learn, and (at selected points throughout the chapter) what they did learn.
- Make a *list* of how they spend the money they receive from jobs, doing chores, or allowances.
- Select a project in which they will collect and analyze data, and set up a project notebook that includes *records* of all work related to the project.
- Write an *explanation* of which methods of collecting, reporting, and interpreting data they find easiest to use.
- *Record* various text exercises in their learning logs.
- Construct a variety of *graphs* and explain how the structure of various graphs reflects their purpose.
- Use mean, median, and mode to write a *description* of an average school day.
- Make *Venn diagrams* that show correlations between objects or events around them.
- *Explain* various ways to misread a stem-and-leaf plot and why a key is necessary.
- Write *notes* about the difficulties encountered in writing and conducting a survey.
- *Describe* the task enjoyed most during the unit.

A number of these writing activities appear as suggestions in Mary's mathematics textbook teacher's edition. She adds other writing experiences as needed to encourage and support students' thinking about interpreting data.

Theme or Unit Learning Logs

You also may use learning logs as vehicles for collecting a variety of writings during a theme or unit of study. When Mark, teaching in a multigrade fourth- through sixth-grade classroom, teaches a social studies unit about "Quilts," his students' learning logs contain a variety of informal writings:

- Several pages for collecting *lists* of interesting words related to quilts and quilt-making that include correct spellings, *key words* for meanings, and/or *drawings* to illustrate
- *Annotated drawings* to illustrate different types of quilt designs that the class has studied or that the student has researched independently
- *Charts* that compare and contrast quilt designs
- *Brainstormed lists* or *clusters* that indicate what the student knows about different types of quilts, with new ideas added in a different color as they occur
- *Descriptions* of particular patterns
- *Explanations* of the origins of particular quilt patterns
- A page set aside for personal *questions* about quilts
- Pages set aside for a *list* of quilt books that students have read with *annotations* or *responses* about the book
- *Notes* made while watching videos about quiltmaking
- A *record* of a field trip to a local quilter's house
- An *interview* with a relative who has made a quilt
- Sample patterns made from cloth and/or colored paper with *sequenced instructions*

Students complete these informal writings during whole-class discussions, small-group work, and independent research. If a particular form is new, Mark engages the class in a shared writing lesson to demonstrate his thinking when using that particular form of writing.

What positive outcomes do you think the students in Mary's and Mark's classes might realize from their informal learning log writing?

■

Issues in Writing Instruction

In a fully implemented writer's workshop, grammar, usage, and mechanics become meaningful as students revise and edit their work. Kim, for example, uses minilessons, small-group "workshops," individual conferences, and response or editing partners to teach specific aspects of using language for effective written communication. Some students, however, will need more explicit instruction in these areas.

Student's oral language and reading of literature form the base of their knowledge about the structure of English. The more widely students use language and the more they pay attention to the language of others when they read, the greater opportunity they have to notice language patterns. In most cases, you should provide explicit instruction, helping students recognize what they already know about language, as well as what they still need to learn in order to communicate effectively. You should draw the issues you select for explicit instruction from students' needs as writers, so they will see how the information is relevant. Figures 9.17 and 9.18 identify basic issues in grammar, usage, and mechanics and conventions that will need attention during writer's workshop.

Monitering Students' Growth as Writers

Understanding students as writers requires you to carefully observe students as they are immersed in their writing, to confer with them about their work, and to collect a variety of samples of their writing over time. Developing a set of portfolios will provide you with the most comprehensive collection of data for evaluation.

Figure 9.17 Issues in grammar and usage

Sentence types

- declarative—statement (.)
- interrogative—question (?)
- imperative—command (.)
- exclamatory—shows strong feeling (!)
- simple sentence—contains one subject and one predicate
- compound sentence—sentence made from two simple sentences, separated by a comma and joined by a conjunction (*and, but, or*)

Subject

- complete subject—who or what sentence is about
- compound subject (joined by conjunction *and, but, or*)
- subject pronouns (*I, you, he, she, it, we, you, they*)

Predicate

- complete predicate—what the subject is or does
- compound predicates (joined by conjunction *and, but, or*)
- object pronouns (*me, you, him, her, it, us, you, them*)

Subject–verb agreement

- if subject is singular, verb must be singular

Negatives

- one per sentence

Nouns

- singular
- plural
- common
- proper
- possessive

Pronouns

- stand in place of a noun
- can refer to a noun

Possessive pronouns

- before noun (*my, your, his, her, its, our, their*)
- stand alone (*mine, yours, his, hers, ours, theirs*)

Verbs

- action verbs—tell what the subject of a sentence does
- helping verbs—work with the main verb, usually changes the tense
- irregular verbs—do not add the typical inflected suffixes to show past tense

Figure 9.17 *continued*

- linking verbs—connect a subject with a word that names or describes the subject
- verb tense—tells the time in which action takes place (present, past, past participle, future)

Adjectives

- describe or tell more about a noun
- tell which one, how many, or what kind
- comparison (*-er, -est, more, most*)
- predicate adjectives—follow a linking verb, describe the subject
- demonstrative adjectives—point out a specific person or thing (which one, which kind, how many?)

Adverbs

- describe or tell more about a verb
- tell when, where, how
- comparison (*-er, -est, more, most*)

Articles

- *a*—before consonant
- *an*—before vowel
- *the*

Prepositions

- connect a noun or pronoun to another word in the sentence
- common prepositions—(*after, around, at, before, between, during, for, in, inside, of, over, through, to, until, with*)
- prepositional phrases—begin with a preposition and end with a noun or pronoun
- adjective prepositional phrases—function as adjectives
- adverb prepositional phrases—function as adverbs

Observing Writing

There is a great deal of activity in a writing process classroom. You must make a conscious effort to watch students systematically. During each workshop, when students are involved in individual writing, make careful notes about the writing behavior of one or two students, observing every student over the course of a month. Make additional informal observation notes as needed.

What behaviors might you look for? Begin with the following:

- How students respond to minilessons and shared writing activities.
- How they settle into their writing each day.
- How they give and receive help during response and editing activities.
- The attitudes they display toward their own and others' writing.

Figure 9.18 Issues in mechanics and conventions

Capitalization

- first word of a sentence
- titles of people, books, poems, stories, songs
- proper names
- initials
- proper nouns and pronouns
- greetings and closings of a letter
- first word of a direct quote
- abbreviations

Punctuation

- period
  declarative sentence
  imperative sentences
  abbreviation
- question mark
  interrogative sentences
- exclamation mark
  exclamatory sentence
- comma
  in a series (three or more items)
  with names (when spoken to)
  after introductory words
  between date, year
  between city, state/country
  inside quotation marks
  in greeting/closing of a letter
  before conjunction in a compound sentence
- apostrophe
  in possessives
  in contractions
- colon
  greeting of business letter
  between hour and minute (1:20 A.M.)
  listing

- How they sustain themselves during independent writing.
- What writing strategies they use.

Routinely review your observation notes, reflecting on each student's progress. A scarcity of information for a student should tell you that you need to make more frequent and focused observations.

Conferring About Writing

Teachers who use the writing process extensively in their classrooms confer with students in a number of different ways. From conferences during writer's workshop, make notes about each student. Keep your conference notes in a separate folder or notebook or combine them with your anecdotal records. These records will help you to evaluate those pieces of writing that you choose for your teachers' assessment portfolio.

Your conference notes should help you understand how your students think as writers. You will not be able to adequately evaluate samples of writing unless you go beyond the surface of the writing and into the processes they use. Your note format should fit the information you need about each student.

Selecting and Evaluating Samples of Writing

You should create a set of writing portfolios so you may have a comprehensive picture of each student as a writer. The portfolios should contain (1) a work folder containing most of a student's work completed during a particular grading period, (2) the student's own learning portfolio for selected pieces, and (3) your portfolio for assessment and evaluation of each student's growth.

Work Folder. During a grading period, keep all of the writing that students have begun and/or completed. From this work folder, you and the student select writing to place in that student's learning portfolio and/or your assessment portfolio. Some teachers choose to divide this writing into two folders for ease of handling—work in progress and past work.

The "work in progress" folder often holds 3-hole paper and has pockets for loose papers. Keep only the most recent pieces in this folder so that it is not cluttered. A running list of ideas and self-assessment checklists are also in this folder.

The "past work" folder holds all writing not needed daily. This folder must be accessible to the child as needed. You might divide the writing in this folder between "completed pieces" and "drafts and ideas." Even if a piece is initially abandoned, keep the first attempts in case the student decides to return to the piece.

Student Learning Portfolio. During each marking period, give students the opportunity to select pieces of writing to go into their portfolio. Graves (1994) suggests that along with selecting what students think is their "best" work, they should also select work that they feel represents growth in specific writing strategies or behaviors. For example, if developing detail or description has been a focus of that marking period, ask students to select the piece they think is their best example of using detail or description. In addition, students should also have the option of selecting a piece they want in their portfolio for their own reasons, together with a brief explanation of why they chose it.

To help students make selections, Graves (1994) suggests frequently spending time during writer's workshop reviewing past writing and reflecting on its merits. You may wish to focus minilessons on how to reflect on one's own writing by modeling reflecting on personal writing samples. Minilessons may also encourage students to share their thinking as they reflect on their past writings.

For each piece selected, students should provide an explanation for their selection. You will need to teach students how to evaluate themselves; it is not a natural process. Plan to devote minilesson time to self-evaluation, hold self-evaluation conferences with students to encourage particular strategies, and provide self-evaluation checklists for students.

Students should attach their self-evaluation to the finished piece of writing when they place it in their portfolio. Provide a self-evaluation form on which students may record their explanation. Self-evaluations may be open ended or may ask students to rate themselves on specific criteria (Figure 9.19).

The self-evaluation you encourage in students should be linked to your observations of their writing behavior and the writing strategies you have encouraged during that grading period. Students will learn more about themselves as writers if you help them focus on evaluating particular aspects of their writing, instead of giving them the impression that "whatever they want to say about their writing is fine." Writing is a complex process and involves the use of many skills and strategies. Help students evaluate by focusing their attention on particular strategies for some pieces, yet leave the evaluation of at least one piece open for them to decide the focus.

Teacher's Assessment Portfolio. During the marking period, select samples of each student's work that document areas of growth as a writer, as well as areas of need. Selecting a piece of writing for your teacher's portfolio constitutes an assessment. How you judge the piece becomes your evaluation.

Photocopy your selections so that originals can remain in the work folder or the student's portfolio. Your evaluation of each piece should clearly relate to your instructional goals during that marking period.

Evaluating Writing Traits. Many school writing programs, even district and state assessment programs, include evaluation of writing by looking for traits considered to be characteristics of good writing:

- How ideas and content are expressed in the writing
- How the author organized ideas to get the point across
- How well the voice of the author is heard
- The author's use of language, including word choice and sentence structure
- Use of conventions to communicate clearly with the reader

Figure 9.19 Evaluating specific elements

Checking my descriptive writing

Rating scale: 1 (low) to 5 (high)

_____ I created vivid pictures with words.
_____ My descriptions appeal to the sense of sight, smell, touch, hearing, or taste.
_____ I used comparisons, such as similes and metaphors to build strong images.
_____ I organized my description to lead readers from one point to the next.

Comments:

Signed ______________________________

Figure 9.20 Rubric for evaluating writing traits

Evaluating the Traits of My Writing

Ideas and Content:

5 = I know a lot about my topic, my ideas are interesting, the main point of my paper is clear, and my topic is not too broad.

3 = The reader usually knows what I mean. Some parts will be better when I tell just a little more about what is important.

1 = When someone else reads my paper, it will be hard for them to understand what I mean or what it is all about.

Organization:

5 = My beginning gets the reader's attention and makes the reader want to find out what's coming next. Every detail adds a little more to the main idea. I ended at a good place and at just the right time.

3 = The details and order of my story/paper makes sense most of the time. I have a beginning but it may not really grab the reader. I have a conclusion but it seems to sum up my paper in a ho-hum way.

1 = The ideas and details in my paper are sort of jumbled and confused. I don't really have a beginning or an end.

Voice:

5 = My paper has lots of personality. It really sounds like me. People who know me will know it is my paper.

3 = Although readers will understand what I mean, they may not "feel" what I mean. My personality comes through sometimes. I probably need to know a little more about my topic to show, rather than tell, the reader about it.

1 = I can't really hear my voice in this paper. It was hard for me to write this paper. I really need to know much more about my topic or be more willing to take a risk about what I say.

Use of Language:

5 = The sentences in my paper are clear and sound good when read aloud. Words fit just right.

3 = Some of my sentences are choppy or awkward, but most are clear. Some words are very general, but most readers will figure out what I mean.

1 = Even when I read this paper, I have to go back, stop, and read over, just to figure out the sentences. A lot of my sentences seem to be the same. The words I chose don't seem to be very interesting.

Use of Conventions:

5 = There are very few errors in my paper; it wouldn't take long to get this ready to publish.

3 = My spelling is correct on simple words, most of my sentences begin with capital letters and end with the right punctuation.

1 = There are a lot of spelling and grammar errors in my paper. Punctuation and capital letters seem to be missing. My paragraphs are not indented.

Figure 9.21 Writing traits evaluation form

For this piece, I think my writing shows:

• Ideas and content	1	2	3	4	5
• Organization	1	2	3	4	5
• Voice	1	2	3	4	5
• Use of language	1	2	3	4	5
• Use of conventions	1	2	3	4	5

What I like the best about this piece is ______________________________

____

____

One thing I think I could have done better is ____________________________

____

____

The use of traits for evaluation provides a *rubric,* a standard of expectation, that is known to both student and teacher. The qualities of writing expressed in a rubric should reflect your classroom writing program. Rubrics help students and teachers look for similar qualities of writing in one piece or across several pieces. Consider the rubric shown in Figure 9.20, adapted from Spandel and Culham (1993). It is intended for use by middle grade writers. Notice that the evaluation scale is 1, 3, 5, with 5 being high. Students learn that, in a given category, if their piece is better than a 3 but clearly not a 5, they select 4 as most representative of their work. Once the attributes and scale are familiar, you can attach a form similar to that shown in Figure 9.21 to each evaluated piece.

You must be careful to evaluate student's writing according to your instructional goals, those goals reflected in minilesson topics, shared writing topics, writing strategies suggested in conferences, and behaviors you have noted in anecdotal records of observations and conferences. You can convert these goals into a recording form that will let you quickly and clearly indicate student's overall progress in areas such as using the writing process, types of writing, organization of content, or use of conventions. The best forms are those you make yourself, because they accurately reflect your program goals, such as the sample shown in Figure 9.22.

Monitoring students' growth in writing is a continuous process, and requires your focused attention. You cannot develop an appropriate writing program for students if you do not know them as writers. You cannot know students as writers without carefully observing and talking with them. Careful monitoring is a commitment you must make if you are to have an effective writer's workshop.

RESPECTING DIVERSITY IN STUDENTS' WRITING

Throughout this chapter, it should be apparent that the writing process as used in writer's workshop, by its very nature, respects what students bring to the page. Teachers who teach writing as a process honor and validate the individual's experience and language.

Writing is a process of moving one's thinking out of the mind and onto paper. While students differ in the experience and language background they bring to school, all students are thinkers and all are capable of communicating. One purpose of your

Figure 9.22 Sample writing behaviors checklist

Growth in Using Writing Processes

Name	**Dates**			
Getting started • uses informal writing strategies • explores new topics • uses background experience				
Finding a focus • focuses after exploring ideas • abandons unproductive topics				
Composing • shows sustained effort • meaning more important than conventions				
Revising for meaning • rereads to check meaning • receives input from others • uses input from others • changes words/sentences • changes order • adds on				
Editing for conventions • receives input from others • checks for capital letters • checks for punctuation • checks for spelling (in word knowledge stage)				

writing program should be to provide whatever support and assistance students need to be able to use their language to express, explore, and appreciate their lived experiences. As students acquire new firsthand and vicarious learning experiences, they share them in your class, enriching their own and their peers' possibilities for writing.

Your writing program supports diversity of students' interests and background of experiences by letting them control the topic and content of their writing. Having choice enables students to write from firsthand experience, to write with confidence about the content of their lives. When you allow choice, you honor the importance that students place on the events of their own lives.

Finally, you respect diversity among students when you listen with sensitivity to the student as "writer" rather than focusing on the writing itself. Your talk with students should focus on their needs, interests and concerns as writers. By listening carefully, you will hear each student's voice.

TAKE A MOMENT AND REFLECT . . .

Writer's workshop provides:

- A predictable time and structure for writing
- Demonstrations of writing through minilessons and shared writing
- A block of time for sustained writing
- Choice of topic and/or content
- Response to writing through conferences, response groups, and sharing sessions

Minilessons:

- Are 5- to 10-minute lessons that offer helpful suggestions
- Can focus on the procedures of writer's workshop—
  1. writing in a particular genre
  2. using literary elements
  3. using conventions appropriately
- Are given when students demonstrate the need for specific knowledge

Writing conferences provide opportunities for:

- Students' ideas about writing to be heard at different points in the writing process
- Teachers to learn from students
- Students to learn to ask themselves questions about their writing
- Both formal and informal one-to-one conversations about writing

Writer's workshop can be linked with study in other areas to allow ample time for students to learn about varied forms of writing while retaining control of their topic choice.

Informal writing is a useful tool for helping students learn by writing:

- Descriptive or ordered lists
- Clusters or brainstorms
- Annotated drawings
- Venn diagrams
- Story maps
- Graphic organizers
- Charts
- Graphs
- Descriptions
- Note taking
- Recording events
- Explanations

Learning logs are valuable collections of informal writings that focus on learning in one subject area or in a theme or integrated unit.

You must take care to ensure that students are developing an adequate knowledge of the form and structure of the English language through attention to grammar and usage, and to mechanics and conventions.

You monitor students' growth as writers through:

- Careful observation of writing behaviors
- One-to-one conferences
- The collection of samples of writing in portfolios
- Evaluation of writing samples for traits—
  1. ideas and content
  2. organization
  3. voice
  4. use of language
  5. use of conventions

You must respect the diversity of experience and language knowledge among students, and must use it constructively to help students gain competence as writers.

REFERENCES

Calkins, L. M. (1986). *The art of teaching writing.* Portsmouth, NH: Heinemann.

Calkins, L. M. (1994). *The art of teaching writing* (rev ed.). Portsmouth, NH: Heinemann.

Douglas, D. J. (1988). *Factors that relate to choice of topic in a first grade process writing classroom.* Unpublished doctoral dissertation, Oklahoma State University.

Graves, D. H. (1973). *Children's writing: Research directions and hypotheses based upon an examination of the writing processes of seven year old children.* Unpublished doctoral dissertation, State University of New York at Buffalo.

Graves, D. H. (1994). *A fresh look at writing.* Portsmouth, NH: Heinemann.

Ogle, D. (1986). K-W-L: A teaching model that develops active reading of expository text. *The Reading Teacher, 39,* 364–370.

Smith, F. (1982). *Writing and the writer.* London: Heinemann.

Spandel, V., & Cullinan, R. (1993). *The student-friendly guide to writing traits.* Portland, OR: Northwest Regional Educational Laboratory.

Wells, G. (1986). *The meaning makers: Children learning language and using language to learn.* Portsmouth, NH: Heinemann.

CHILDREN'S LITERATURE

Hahn, M.D. (1994). *Time for Andrew: A ghost story.* New York: Clarion.

Spinelli, J. (1990). *Maniac Magee.* Boston: Little, Brown.

Yep, L. (1991). *The star fisher.* New York: Penguin.

10

Word Study

Patterns for Word Recognition and Spelling

In this chapter:

We explore possibilities for developmentally appropriate word study in the middle grades, including:

- word study activities, with emphasis on sorting words as a way to support word recognition and spelling knowledge,
- suggested sequences of instruction for within-word pattern stage, syllable juncture stage, and derivational constancy stage study, and
- assessing and evaluating students' word knowledge development.

To be effective communicators in our public and private lives we must be able to read, write, and think with a myriad of words. Our education, experience, and interest in communicating effectively with others determine how well we learn to use words.

What interests do middle grade students have in communication? At this stage of their lives, they are striving to be understood and appreciated as individuals who are making the transition from childhood to adulthood. They often struggle with communicating both inside and outside of their peer group.

With careful planning, the reading and writing program that you set up in your classroom can provide support and encouragement during this period of transition. Your word study program should be *developmentally appropriate* to your students' stage(s) of word knowledge (Bear & Barone, 1989; Henderson & Beers, 1980). Remember, the range of academic performance in a classroom can be as much as two-thirds the age of the students (e.g., an eight-year range among 12-year-olds), which means that, for example, students in a sixth-grade class could range from second to tenth grade in reading and writing performance. As you plan, you must consider how to meet the developmental needs of this range of students.

Word Study and Reading

We focus first on word study through reading. As you know, reading development typically leads writing development. As you engage students in reading activities, how will you encourage the study of words? Think back to the classrooms that we visited in previous chapters as we explored ways to organize literature-based reading. Lou, Melodia, Kim, and Kristen encourage word study during reading through teacher-mediated MLTAs and MRTAs, whole-class minilessons, individual reading conferences, and small-group discussions.

For example, as Lou plans for the reading of chapters 1 and 2 in *Hatchet* (Paulsen, 1987), he identifies language that warrants attention within the context of each chapter (see Figure 6.5), meaningful words and phrases that may need clarification depending on students' background knowledge. Focusing on language during reading activities is a valuable form of word study. It is important to draw words from those books students are currently reading. Students in Lou's sixth-grade classroom become more interested in learning new words as they realize how it adds to their understanding, and consequently to their enjoyment of reading.

Lou selects words for study by considering the background of his students, the context in which the words are used, and the level of word knowledge required to be able to decode each word.

Word study in reading focuses first on recognition and understanding, then leads to expanding vocabulary through studying related words. For example, of the words Lou identified for *Hatchet* (see Figure 6.5), most are related to airplanes and flying:

Chapter 1	*Chapter 2*
banked	turbulence
rudder	horizon
bushplane	altimeter
	transmitter
	throttle
	altitude

Also, two words, *altitude* and *altimeter,* have related word parts.

Word study is most effective as part of the study of a text, rather than in isolation. Students must have support to recognize words in their reading, then to analyze patterns and make links to words related by pattern or meaning. The progression for word study in reading follows a sequence similar to the stages of word knowledge development discussed in Chapter 4.

At any given time, the words studied in reading should be slightly more complex than those studied for writing and spelling. Students who can read words that typically come late in syllable juncture will write words (conventionally) in early to middle syllable juncture. The new words that students study in reading activities will eventually become the words for study in their weekly spelling lists. Again, we see that reading development leads writing development.

Word Study and Writing

The words your students come in contact with when reading will model the patterns in the words they write. Studying words during literature-based reading enhances your opportunities to notice patterns essential in writing, especially with multisyllable words. Once again, reading development leads writing development.

How do you use writing activities to encourage the study of words? During their literature-based reading Lou, Melodia, Kim, and Kristen ask students to make written records in journals or logs. These records require their students to think about the patterns they notice in words while reading and to use those patterns when they write. During writer's workshop (Chapter 9), Kim encourages students to give careful attention to their word choices as they structure sentences and revise and edit their work. In mathematics and social studies, her fellow teachers ask students to list, explain, chart, describe, record, label, and annotate drawings, brainstorm or cluster, and make notes in learning logs. Each of these teachers asks students to use words in writing that first appear in the students' reading material. These teachers believe that attending to the words they write enables students to become competent thinkers and communicators.

The most fundamental writing activity for word study is the weekly spelling list. As teachers, we teach spelling each week in the hope that students will notice patterns and begin to use them more consistently in their independent writing. Commercial spelling programs for each grade level are available; however, such programs typically offer only one list of words per week. With the range of students you will likely have in your classroom, it is best to use multiple lists of words for word study and spelling each week. Multiple lists enable you to engage students at a developmentally appropriate level of spelling.

Organizing a Word Study Program for Spelling

Research in spelling as a form of word knowledge indicates that instruction is most effective when word study is planned over a number of days (Templeton, 1991). A weekly routine can provide formal word study at the appropriate level for each student.

The following elements are essential to a weekly word study/spelling program:

- A list of 15 to 20 words:

  10 to 15 developmentally appropriate words that follow one or more phonic or structural patterns

  2 or 3 personal "bugaboo" words, selected by students, that they often misspell in their writing (Graves, 1994)

  2 or 3 words that each student wants to use in their writing (Graves, 1994)
- Sheets of blank word cards on which students write words that they can then cut up, sort, and categorize

- A word study notebook, usually an inexpensive spiral-bound or three-hole paper folder, in which students record their thinking about words
- A partner to talk with about sorting and patterns
- Group meetings to confirm or redirect students' thinking about patterns in words

Daily Word Study Activities

You combine these essential elements into a weeklong study of patterns, replacing the traditional spelling instruction using a single textbook, dedicating approximately 15 to 20 minutes per day to study activities. Organize the time so that all groups study at the same time. During this time your tasks are to observe students' sorting strategies, discuss patterns, and "nudge" students to explore their thinking about words.

Your weekly word study schedule will include the following types of activities for students:

Monday

- Begin with a new list of appropriate words.
- Check to be sure students can read each word.
- Write the list of words in a word study notebook.
- Make a card for each word, using blank index cards.
- Take a spelling pretest with a partner (optional).

Tuesday

- Individually review word cards.
- Do an open word sort to explore sound or meaning patterns that students already recognize.
- Write the results of the sort in the word study notebook, explaining reasons for the groupings.
- Discuss patterns observed with partner and teacher.

Wednesday

- Individually review word cards.
- Do a closed word sort according to teacher-identified categories.
- Write the results of the sort and any explanations in the word study notebook.
- Compare with open word sort from Tuesday.
- Discuss results with partner and teacher.

Thursday

- Individually review word cards.
- Do activity that focuses on using patterns, such as a word hunt in familiar reading materials or in personal writing.
- Write new words that follow the pattern in the word study notebook.
- Compare new words and word list, noting similarities and differences in the notebook.
- Discuss results with partner and teacher.

Friday

- Posttest/check patterns, including student-chosen words.
- Discuss comfort/confidence with patterns.
- Plan for next week of word study.

Teacher's Role in Word Study

Jaime teaches in a multiage classroom, with grades four, five, and six. For his word study program, Jaime has learned that he must thoroughly know word recognition theory and the stages of word knowledge development. Using this knowledge, he then develops word lists that fit patterns in each word knowledge stage appropriate for his class. He collects words from various grade levels of spelling textbooks and children's literature for these lists. (Appendix C contains lists of words sorted by stage and pattern that you may wish to use as your initial word lists.)

After determining each students' stage of word knowledge, he creates manageable word study groups of students with similar word knowledge and instructional need. These groups allow students to study sight words that are within their reach for learning to write conventionally. He prepares weekly word charts for each group and provides blank paper grids for the students to prepare as word cards for sorting activities. He circulates while students are working on sorting activities, discussing what they have noticed and mediating between what students already know and what they might need to clarify to make sense of the patterns they are studying (Vygotsky, 1962).

As Jaime implements a word study program, he helps students understand the purpose for each part of the weekly study. He teaches them to be good partners, assisting and supporting each other's efforts to learn words. To help students remember what they have learned, he has them record the results of their word sorts, as well as their thinking about the sorts, in a word study notebook.

Forming Word Study Groups

You can effectively group students for word study and reading instruction by their stage of word knowledge development (Bear & Barone, 1989). For word study to be most beneficial, students should focus on patterns that they are beginning to notice but may not yet understand, what Donald Bear calls "using but confusing" (Bear, Invernezzi, Templeton & Johnston, 1996). If you ask students to attend to patterns in words that are too far ahead of what they know, they will not be able to make full use of your instruction.

To learn what his students are noticing about language, Jaime looks at their developmental, or inventive, spellings. As students are learning about phonics and structural patterns, they often "invent" temporary spellings to stand for patterns not yet internalized (Temple, Nathan, Temple, & Burris, 1993), representing words as best they can with what they know at their independent level of performance.

Jaime uses students' writing to see what they know about written language, to see levels of word knowledge:

- Some knowledge is independent, and is used conventionally.
- Some knowledge is just becoming familiar, and is used inconsistently or unconventionally.
- Some knowledge has not yet been noticed or understood, and is absent.

Jaime analyzes the way students write a focused sample of words, representing varying stages of development, asking them to write a list of words arranged in a developmental sequence. He dictates each word, uses the word in a sentence, then repeats the word. While students write, Jaime observes students' levels of confidence. We discuss assessing and evaluating students' stage of word knowledge in greater depth in "Monitoring Students' Growth in Word Knowledge," later in this chapter.

Students will benefit most from a word study group that focuses on what they are just beginning to figure out or are using inconsistently. For example, Jaime notices that one of his fourth-grade students is aware of changes in words that end with the letter *y* in one-syllable words, but does not apply that knowledge to multisyllable words, writing *tries* and *babies*, but *apologys.* Jaime thinks this student needs to be in a study group focusing on inflected suffixes in the early syllable juncture stage. In contrast, another student writes *nation, tention,* and *creation.* Jaime places this student in a group that focuses on the suffixes *-ion, -tion,* and *-sion,* which come later in syllable juncture.

Word study is most effective with a manageable number of groups. Jaime has four groups in his multiage classroom, for students in late within-word pattern, early syllable juncture, mid–late syllable juncture, and early derivational constancy stages. Three groups will be a workable number for most single-grade classrooms.

When it is time, Jaime asks students who are in a particular word study group to move to one section of the room. Jaime's word study groups have the same words, enabling them to share their thinking with a word study partner. As Jaime circulates among the groups, he interacts with both individuals and groups of students, discussing what they have noticed about the patterns they are studying.

Developing Word Lists

To develop lists of appropriate words for study, you must know the phonics and structural knowledge focus of each stage of development. You can gather words from students' reading materials and from various levels of available spelling books, then group them into categories that coincide with each stage. Jaime finds that building word lists has made him notice word patterns and compare and contrast the difficulty level of words. (See Apendix C for sample lists.)

You must carefully select words that are appropriate to a particular part of a stage. For example, when students first study base + inflected suffix words in the syllable juncture stage, the list should contain only words in which the base does not change (*jumping, monkeys, spoiled*). After students master these words, they will be ready to consider base words that change (*baking, running, pennies*).

Sorting Activities

One excellent way for students to clearly see patterns in words is to sort them, such as by placing word cards in a column. Word sorts serve different purposes in studying patterns. Jaime uses an *open sort* when he wants students to determine categories for the word cards, showing the patterns they notice independently. In contrast, he uses *closed sorts* to direct students' attention to specific characteristics. In closed word sorts students can show their understanding about particular letter-sound patterns or word structures.

As Jaime begins a week of word study, he needs to see what students already know. As preassessment, he asks students to do an open sort (Figure 10.1). The students decide how to group the words, typically by sound, visual, or meaning patterns. In Figure 10.1, the student sorted by the visual pattern in the inflected suffix (*-er, -est, -ing, -ed*).

When Jaime wants to determine students' understanding of a particular pattern or patterns, he chooses the categories and has them complete a closed sort (Figure 10.2).

A two-level sort is easiest for students, with one set of cards that fits a particular pattern and a *crazy pile* for all cards that do not fit. Without a discard (crazy) pile, students may feel forced to place words in a category even if they are not certain about the pattern of the word. The number of levels is determined by the number of patterns being observed or compared. For example, when Jaime's students compare V/CV and VC/V words, he also includes a crazy pile for words that fit in neither category (distractors). This is a three-level sort because there will be three groupings of word cards. In Figure 10.1, the student made a four-level sort, while Figure 10.2 shows a two-level sort.

When a pattern is new, students first complete a two-level sort, asking themselves whether a word fits into the focus category or the crazy pile. As students learn patterns, they begin to compare one with another, solidifying their understanding. For example, after sorting words as in Figure 10.2, students might think of other ways that inflected suffixes can change base words. This comparing could lead to such four-level sorts as consonant doubling before adding the suffix, dropping the *e* to add the suffix, changing *y* to *i* before adding the suffix, and a crazy pile.

Figure 10.1 Open sort

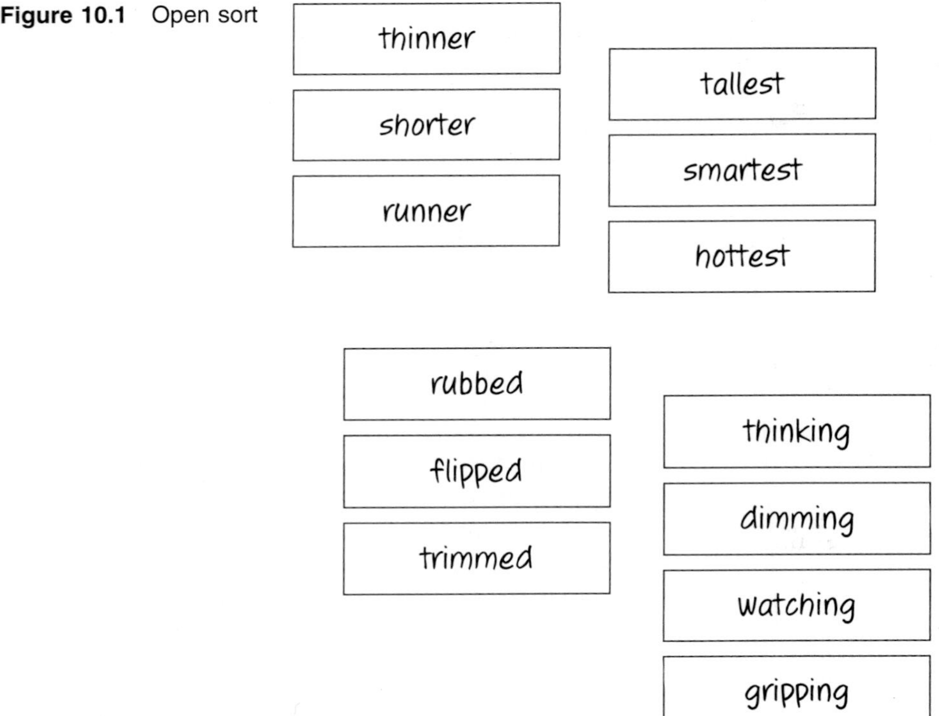

Figure 10.2 Closed sort

extra letter added to base word	Crazy Pile
trimmed	tallest
rubbed	thinking
gripping	shorter
dimming	watching
flipped	smartest
hottest	
runner	
thinner	

Try a word sort. This is a closed sort, because the categories are determined for you. Read the words below, listening carefully for silent consonants. Sort the words according to whether they include silent letters, and if so, whether the letter occurs at the beginning or end of a syllable.

ghostly	studio	wreck	solemn	fasten
castle	doubtful	listen	scribe	tombstone
knuckle	condemn	nestle	numb	stomach

What similarities do you find among the words in your two silent-consonant piles?

Let's see how our thinking compares. In the first column I placed *ghostly, knuckle, wreck, castle, nestle, listen,* and *fasten.* I see several letter combinations that typically are silent at the beginning of a syllable (*gh, wr, kn*). I also notice that four of the words (*cas-tle, nes-tle, lis-ten, fas-ten*) have a silent *t* in the middle.

I have *doubtful, condemn, numb, solemn,* and *tombstone* in the second column. I notice that the syllables that include the silent consonant end with *bt, mn,* and *mb.* These consonant combinations are not easy to pronounce and, over the years, one of the consonants in each pair has been assimilated.

Studio, scribe, and *stomach* are in my crazy pile, because they do not contain silent consonants.

■

Word Study Notebooks

Jaime provides each student with a word study notebook, a three-ring folder with inside pockets. Students record their words each week, keeping several months of study words together in the folder. Jaime often suggests that students refer to past lists and sorts to re-collect what they have learned, to encourage them to continue to make connections among patterns, and to monitor the growth in their thinking.

Jaime's students make entries in their word study notebooks each day:

- *Monday,* students record the list of words for the week.
- *Tuesday,* they record their open sort and the patterns they observed.
- *Wednesday,* they record their closed sort and explain the patterns they see. They compare this sort with Tuesday's open sort.
- *Thursday,* students record words they find as they go on a word hunt or other related activity. Again they record what they find, thinking about the weekly pattern.
- *Friday,* partners give each other their spelling test and help check for conventional spellings, discussing any ongoing confusion.

Figure 10.3 Word study notebook—Syllable juncture

Word Study Notebook

Monday (word list)

flipped	hottest	gripping
thinking	trimmed	watching
shorter	smartest	dimming
rubbed	tallest	
thinner	runner	

Tuesday (open sort)

flipped	thinking	thinner
trimmed	dimming	shorter
rubbed	gripping	runner
	watching	

smartest
tallest
hottest

I put words with the same ending together.

Wednesday (closed sort)

base word changed	no change to base word
flipped	thinking
trimmed	watching
rubbed	shorter
dimming	tallest
gripping	smartest
thinner	
runner	
hottest	

Base words that changed ended with 1 consonant. Other base words ended with 2 or 3 consonants.

Thursday (word hunt- SSR book)

base changes

slam – slammed
strap – strapped
plan – planning
grab – grabbed

base doesn't change

stack – stacking
prompt – prompted
scratch – scratched

The consonant will probably be doubled for a word that ends with a single consonant.

Friday (test)

Figure 10.4 Word study notebook—Derivational constancy

Word Study Notebook

Monday (word list)

century	autograph
biography	centipede
centigrade	telegraph
photograph	centimeter
percentage	telephone
television	graphics
geography	telescope

Tuesday (open sort)

century	autograph
centipede	biography
centimeter	photograph
percentage	telegraph
centigrade	graphics
	geography

television
telescope
telephone
telegraph

One part is the same in each word, but doesn't always have to be in the same place in the word.

Wednesday (closed sort)
What is the root of each word?
What does the root mean?

century — cent = 100
centipede
percentage
centigrade
centimeter

autograph — graph = to write or record
biography
photograph
telegraph
graphics
geography

television — tele = far
telescope
telephone
telegraph

Thursday (word hunt)
centennial — 100th anniversary
holograph — all handwritten by the author

Friday (test)

The writing in the notebook is informal, primarily for students' personal use. Jaime does not ask students to edit their responses, except for conventional spellings of study words. Jaime does evaluate students' daily effort, their completion of each day's activity, the thinking shown in the open sort, level of accuracy of the closed sort, and the spelling test.

Jaime asks students to use their word study notebooks daily. His students treat the recording they do as a valued exercise, and use their notebooks during word study group meetings to support their discussions. Figures 10.3 and 10.4. show sample notebook entries from syllable juncture and derivational constancy stage word study.

In the following sections we discuss word study at the three stages of development you are most likely to find in your students, and present developmentally appropriate content for each stage. The instructional sequences presented are suggestions only; you must base your final choices on your students' needs and your language arts curriculum. We begin with the within-word pattern stage, which includes reading levels from late first to early third grade. You may have students reading at this level in your middle grade classroom.

Word Study in the Within-Word Pattern Stage

During the within-word pattern stage students become proficient in reading most one- and two-syllable words, and are able to write most one-syllable words conventionally. Developing readers in this stage are typically reading materials from mid first-grade to early third-grade levels of difficulty. See Figure 4.7 for an overview of this stage.

Refining Phonics Knowledge

The focus of instruction in this stage is on refining consonant knowledge and continuing to develop vowel knowledge. A new concept is that consonants and vowels can represent both sound and silence. Vowel patterns are challenging because they include variants that are neither long nor short.

Appendix C contains sample words for sorting activities. Some lists are longer than others due to frequency of usage in reading and writing. For your crazy pile, select words from previous weeks to help students review and maintain patterns.

Single Long Vowels—CVCe. Suggested sequence for word sorts:

- long *a__e,* short *a,* crazy pile
- long *i__e,* short *i,* crazy pile
- long *a__e,* long *i__e,* crazy pile
- long *o__e,* short *o,* crazy pile
- long *o__e,* long *a__e,* long *i__e,* crazy pile
- long *u__e,* short *u,* crazy pile
- long *e,* short *e,* crazy pile
- long *u__e,* long *e,* crazy pile

1. Sorts begin with single long vowels—CVCe and CCVCe. Begin with long *a* (*gate*) versus not long *a* (crazy pile). The basic sorting sequence for one vowel:

   long, not long (*gate,* not *gate*)

   long, short, neither (*gate, hat,* neither)

2. Single long vowel *u* can represent two sounds, /u/ (*cute*) and /oo/ (*rude*). Encourage students to try an "either-or" strategy (try /u/, then try /oo/) and select the appropriate sound, checked by context.

Double Vowels—Common Vowel Digraphs. Suggested sequence:

- *ai/ay, a__e* short *a,* crazy pile
- *ee,* short *e,* crazy pile
- *oa, o__e,* short *o,* crazy pile
- *igh/ight, i__e,* short *i,* crazy pile
- *ea* (long *e*), *ea* (short *e*), *ea* (long *a*), short *e,* crazy pile

1. After single long vowel patterns are under students' control, begin the study of the most consistent vowel digraphs. Don't spend time studying a pattern unless students are reading or writing it. Whenever possible, emphasize frequently used rimes (*aid, ail, ain*). Identify a specific phoneme, then sort against other known patterns that have similar vowel letters.

2. Note that the common "rule," "When two vowels go walking, the first one does the talking (long sound)," is largely untrue. The first letter of a vowel digraph has a long vowel sound only about 45 percent of the time, more frequently with certain patterns than with others.

Double and Variant Consonants. Suggested sequence:

- final double consonant, crazy pile
- single and double consonants (same sound), crazy pile
- hard *c,* soft *c,* crazy pile
- hard *g,* soft *g,* crazy pile
- final *s* /z/, *s* /s/, crazy pile
- final consonant blends (*d, l, n, t*), crazy pile

1. Sort single and double consonants that represent the same phoneme in one-syllable words (*doll, dress*). Do not introduce double consonants in two-syllable words, such as *rabbit.* This pattern introduces the concept of silent letters and more than one syllable. Sorting activities should confirm that only one consonant is sounded.
2. Knowledge of single short and long vowels is needed to study single variant consonants (*c, g*). When *c* or g is followed by *a, o,* or *u,* the vowel sound is usually "hard," as in ***can*** or ***gate*;** when followed by an *e, i,* or *y,* the vowel is usually "soft," as in ***cent*** and ***gem*.**
3. The variation in sound for *s* and *x* is determined by placement in a syllable:

   initial /s/ (*sun*), or /sh/ (*sugar*)
   final /s/ (*bus*) or /z/ (*his*)
   initial /ks/ (*x-ray*) and /z/ (*xylophone*)
   final /ks/ (*fox*)

4. When the letters that are difficult to hear in final blends are beginning to show up in students' writing, study of final blends is appropriate (*ld, lt, lk, mp, nd, nk, nt*). Sorting activities should help students contrast the blend to the dominant single consonant, such as for the blend *ld*:

   ld, not *ld* (crazy pile)
   ld, -d, neither (discriminate *l*)
   ld, lt, lk, none (discriminate family)

Single R-Controlled Vowels (from Short Vowel Patterns). Suggested sequence:

- *ar,* short *a,* crazy pile
- *or/ore,* short *o,* crazy pile
- *er/ir/ur,* short *e,* short *i,* short *u,* crazy pile

1. When single short and long vowels are well understood, students are usually able to begin work with the single-vowel *r*-controlled patterns (*ar, or, ie, er, ur*).
2. Begin with *ar.* Sort /ar/, not /ar/ to distinguish its unique sound, then compare to the other known patterns with the letter *a,* such as long and short *a.* Follow a similar pattern with *or.*

3. The sounds of *er, ir,* and *ur* are the same and should be studied together. Compare to short *e, i,* and *o* to help students distinguish the influence of the letter *r.*

Variant Double Vowels—Long and Short. Suggested sequence:

- *a_e, ai, ay, ea, ei, ey* (long *a*), short *a,* crazy pile
- *e, ee, ea, ie, ey* (long *e*), short *e,* crazy pile
- *i_e, y, ie, igh* (long *i*), short *i,* crazy pile

1. Study other less consistent vowel digraphs (*ea, ie, ei, ey*). Work with vowel digraphs that are related by either sound or visual pattern.
2. Study the visual pattern (look the same—sound different). The visual pattern of these words will not help children with decoding. Use the "either-or" strategy with the possible sounds, checked by context.

   ea = long *e* (*meat*), short *e* (*bread*), long *a* (*great*)
   ei = long *e* (*receive*), long *a* (*vein*)
   ey = long *e* (*key*), long *a* (prey)
   ie = long *e* (*believe*), long *i* (*tie*)
   ou = long *o* (*soul*), short *u* (*rough*), *ow* (*out*), *oo* (*soup*)

3. Study the sound pattern (look different—sound the same). With this type of pattern, it is important for children to know that a single sound can be spelled in different ways. Sort for one sound (long *a* sound vs. not long *a*) then examine the words in the long *a* column to identify visual patterns. Re-sort by visual patterns.

Consonant Digraphs with Silent Letters.

1. Once students are familiar with silent letters, introduce consonant digraphs in which one letter is silent (*wr, kn, ck*). Sort one-syllable words with silent consonant digraphs in the initial, then final, positions in words.
2. If students have difficulty with the silent letter, sort words that begin with the single consonants. For example, for *wr* sort *wr* and *w* words to help them segment the /r/ sound.
3. Continue to examine other silent digraph patterns (*-ck, kn-, -gn, pn-, -ng, -dge, -tch*) as appropriate words are identified.

Variant Double Vowels—(Neither Long Nor Short). Suggested sequence:

- *oo* (long), *oo* (short), long *o*, short *o*, crazy pile
- *ow* (*ow*), *ow* (long *o*), short *o,* crazy pile
- *au/aw,* long *a,* short *a,* crazy pile
- *oi/oy,* long *o,* short *o,* crazy pile
- *ou* (*ow*), (long *oo*), (short *oo*), (long *o*), (short *u*), crazy pile
- *ui/ue/ew/u_e,* short *u,* crazy pile

1. While working with the vowel digraphs, you will have opportunities to study diphthongs that are appearing in students' reading and writing.
2. Look for visual patterns (look the same—sound different). With two sounds possible, encourage students to use the "either-or" strategy, checking for meaning.

3. Sorting activities should compare the different sounds for one letter pattern, then compare other vowel patterns with similar letters:

   boot, foot, crazy pile
   boot, foot, long *o*, short *o,* crazy pile

4. Listen for sound patterns (look different—sound the same):

   au (*haul*), *aw* (*saw*)
   oi (*oil*), *oy* (*boy*)
   ui (*fruit*), *ue* (*blue*), *ew* (*flew*)

   Sorting activities should compare letter patterns to show they produce the same sound, then compare the diphthong to other patterns to show the differences:

   au/aw, not *au/aw* (crazy pile)
   au/aw, long *a,* short *a,* crazy pile

R-Controlled Vowels (from Long and Double Vowels). Suggested sequence:

- *are/air, ar,* crazy pile
- *ear/eer/ere* (*eer*), *ear* (*er*), *ear* (*air*), *ear* (*ar*), crazy pile
- *ire, ir,* crazy pile
- *ure, ur,* crazy pile

1. When students are working confidently with double vowels, study those same patterns when they are influenced by the letter *r.* Sort the long *r*-controlled pattern (*are, air*) versus not long, to segment the sound.
2. Then compare the long *r*-controlled pattern to the short *ar* pattern, as well as other long and short vowel patterns.

Self-Monitoring Strategies Become Covert

Students in the within-word pattern stage have acquired much knowledge as readers. They are proficient at decoding single-syllable words, even words with variant vowels. If they have been taught and encouraged to self-monitor throughout the previous stages, monitoring for individual words and overall meaning should be on its way to becoming a natural reading behavior.

During this stage, students have begun to add knowledge of structural patterns to their repertoire of word knowledge strategies they use while reading. However, this knowledge will probably not yet be part of their "context +" strategy, which should consistently be:

   context + initial sounds,
   checked by sense and remaining letters

Success with initial and medial vowels should add consistency to their decoding.

Don't overnurture during this stage (Spiegel, 1985). Students in the within-word pattern stage know much about written language. Here they need responsive support and ample opportunity to self-monitor so they can see what they know and what they need to know.

Moving to Silent Reading

Up to now, students' reading has been dominated by the need to read orally to gain control over print to the point that ideas in written language flow together and make sense. Carefully choose texts for both instruction and independent reading to support their acquisition of phonics and structural analysis skills and to promote their use of self-monitoring strategies. Easy, low-challenge text should dominate independent reading to allow newly acquired word knowledge to move to a more automatic level, needing less conscious control. Text for instruction should be at an instructional level, offering some challenge with your assistance as needed.

In easy texts, students should be moving from oral to silent reading as their preferred mode. However, oral reading will reappear when students are in difficult texts, because these texts require too much attention to word patterns they have not yet internalized. In this stage, such difficult text should be kept to a minimum to help students build fluency and confidence.

Word Study in the Syllable Juncture Stage

Students in the syllable juncture stage are ready to apply what they know about single syllables to longer words. In this stage spelling instruction begins to include multisyllable words, which can be made from structural syllables, phonetic syllables, or a combination. See Figure 4.8 for an overview of this stage.

Refining Phonics Knowledge

Compound Words.

1. Students use compound words in oral language, and encounter them early in written language. For study, compound words should be composed of two known sight words; only the thinking strategy for compound words is then actually new.
2. Focus first on concrete compound words, then on those with implied meanings. Cluster words for study around topics such as people, places, things, animal life, and time (Rinsky, 1993).

Contractions.

1. *Contractions* are base + base combinations. Typically one base word is shortened to make the contraction. Begin with more predictable contractions, in which the first base word is pronounced and does not change.

   more predictable: *we are = we're*
   less predictable: *will not = won't*

2. Study contraction families—*not* (*can't*), *are* (*we're*), *will* (*I'll*), and *is* (*he's* & *I'm*), to encourage generalizations across a family.

Base + Inflected Suffixes (Base Does Not Change).

1. During the within-word pattern stage, students learn to write one-syllable base words. In the syllable juncture stage, help students learn to listen for and write both the base word and the suffix.
2. Word building, using cards to see each word part (base, suffix), can be beneficial for students who have difficulty hearing the two parts of these words.

Independent Prefix + Base Words.

1. Independent prefixes are studied before dependent prefixes because independent prefixes typically are attached to base words that students know. Dependent prefixes are attached to roots that usually do not stand alone as words.

2. First study words in which the prefix and base are unchanged when brought together (*un* + *tie*). The base word should be meaningful to students, so they may understand the meaning of the new prefix + base word.
3. Appropriate prefixes for study early in this stage include *un, pre,* and *re.* Focus on joining and separating prefixes and bases, with discussion of meaning changes. To best build and sort words, make separate word cards that students can join to make new words.
4. Later in this stage return to independent prefixes + base words and explore the following prefixes: *dis, en, for, fore, im, in, inter, mis,* and *non.*

Base + Inflected Suffixes (Base Changes).

1. In previous stages students have studied inflections in which the base word remains the same. In this stage you will introduce the conditions under which the base will alter as two syllables are joined. Study the following generalizations:
   - When adding *es, ed,* or *ing* to a base word that ends with *e,* the *e* in the base word is usually dropped to avoid changing the vowel sound in the suffix.

     horse + *es* = *horses,* not *horsees*
     rake + *ed* = *raked,* not *rakeed*
     hide + *ing* = *hiding,* not *hideing*

   - When adding *ed* or *ing* to a base word that ends with a single consonant, the consonant is usually doubled to preserve the short vowel sound in the base.

     grab + *ed* = *grabbed,* not *grabed*
     hop + *ing* = *hopping,* not *hoping*

   - When adding *es* or *ed* to a one-syllable base word that ends with *y,* the *y* is typically changed to *i* to form the vowel digraph *ie* (long *i* or long *e*). Note that *ye* is not a common vowel combination within a syllable.

     cry + *es* = *cries*   *baby* + *es* = *babies*
     cry + *ed* = *cried*   *hurry* + *ed* = *hurried*

Base Words + Derivational Suffixes. In the syllable juncture stage, students begin to think about words in which the suffix changes the meaning of the base word. Begin with words in which the base word remains identifiable. Focus students' attention on adding to base words to examine change in meaning and part of the speech. Encourage students to think of the original base word as a spelling aid.

Syllabication Generalizations. Suggested sequence:

- structural word, not a structural word
- base + base, not base + base
- prefix + base, base + suffix, neither
- use structure first, use phonics
- VCV, VCCV, neither
- V/CV, VC/V, neither
- V/CV, VC/V, VC/CV, none

1. Encourage students to talk about the generalizations they use for familiar multisyllable words. Then introduce unfamiliar words that use these generalizations.
   a. Structural generalizations:
      - base + base (compound, contraction)
      - prefix + base or base + suffix; this pattern could also include words with more than one affix, such as *un* + *break* + *able*
   b. Phonic generalizations:
      - V/CV—single consonant between vowels; first vowel can be open syllable (long vowel) (*fa* + *vor, mu* + *sic*)
      - VC/V—closed syllable (short vowel) (*riv* + *er, hab* + *it*)
      - VC/CV—two consonants between vowels, not a blend or digraph (*dol* + *lar, mar* + *ket*)
      - *C* + *le*—preceding consonant stays with *le,* except for *ck* (*ta* + *ble, pick* + *le*)
2. Ask students to discriminate words according to their makeup and the syllabication generalizations that would be most helpful in decoding them.
3. Schwa—Dividing words into syllables creates a vowel phenomenon called a *schwa.* In English all syllables do not receive equal emphasis when we pronounce words. When we do not stress all syllables equally, we change the vowel sound in unaccented, or unstressed, syllables, often to short *u.*

   Pronounce the following words and listen for the schwa:

   about = *a* + *bout*   *pencil* = *pen* + *cil*
   second = *sec* + *ond*   *signal* = *sig* + *nal*

In *about,* the unstressed syllable is the first—the *a* sounds like short *u.* In the other words the unstressed syllable is the second and also sounds like short *u.*

A schwa seldom occurs in base + affixed words, because each morpheme unit is stressed. Consider the following words. Is there a schwa? Is there an unstressed syllable?

foolish = *fool* + *ish*   *repaid* = *re* + *paid*
enrage = *en* + *rage*   *raincoat* = *rain* + *coat*

Notice how each structural part, or meaning unit, is stressed. Stressed syllables are not likely to have a schwa. A schwa is most likely to occur in words that are made of sound units rather than meaning units.

Sorting activities should require students to discriminate the presence or absence of a schwa:

has a schwa, does not have a schwa
schwa in first syllable, schwa in second syllable, neither

Self-Monitoring Strategies

The syllable juncture stage focuses on patterns that occur when syllables are joined. With this focus on units within multisyllable words, encourage students to expand their "context +" strategy to include syllables. Help them begin to recognize whether words are composed primarily of structural or phonetic patterns. The "context +" strategy becomes:

context + first syllable,
checked by sense and remaining syllables

Solidifying Silent Reading

During the syllable juncture stage students begin to solidify their ability to read silently. The skills they acquire during this stage enable students to decode most words appearing in independent and instructional texts. Your instructional material can be more challenging if you provide support in using these new skills. However, you must continue extensive practice in low-challenge materials to allow students to consolidate all of their word knowledge, assimilating it into their sight vocabulary. To break through into more mature reading, students' behaviors must become automatic so that they may attend almost exclusively to the ideas in a text, rather than to decoding.

WORD STUDY IN THE DERIVATIONAL CONSTANCY STAGE

During this stage students break into mature reading. You must focus here on helping students develop and use strategies for encountering a multitude of unfamiliar multisyllable words. Students will have enough background knowledge of written language to allow you to draw word study in reading and writing from the same bank of words.

Refining Phonics Knowledge

Emphasis in this stage is two-fold:

- Efficiently using what is already known to read and write new words
- Adding to existing knowledge of word parts, especially Greek and Latin roots

See Figure 4.9 (p. 90) for an overview of this stage.

Dependent Prefix + Root. Determining the meaning of words with dependent prefixes requires a different thinking strategy than that used with independent prefixes. Help students realize that the word *design* is not merely *de* + *sign*. Determining the meaning of each part of a dependent prefix word does not necessarily help determine the meaning of the whole. Knowing that the prefix *de* carries the meaning "in reverse, away, or down," along with the word's context, will not necessarily help determine overall meaning. Consider the meaning of the dependent prefixes below in relation to the example words.

com, con—together, with	compress, continue
ex—out, away	example, expensive
pro—forward, for	program, profound

Pronunciation Changes.

1. Adding an affix to a base word can change the spelling of the base, sometimes causing a change in pronunciation. Adding an affix can change the syllable that is accented or stressed, also causing a change in pronunciation. Help students explore the pronunciation changes in words that present decoding and spelling challenges. Compare base words to affixed words to help students generalize the effect of adding affixes.
2. Explore patterns of pronunciation change:
   - Change in the syllable that is stressed

     stressed to unstressed (*com **pose**′, com′ **po** si tion*)

     unstressed to stressed (*met′ **al**, me **tal**′lic*)

- Changes in letter sound due to where syllable divides for pronunciation
  vowel (*di/vide, di/vis/ion*)
  consonant (*sign, sig/nal*)

Greek Combining Forms. English has borrowed prefixes and roots from Greek that frequently occur in words related to number and scientific concepts. Help students notice how they use these word parts to determine the meaning of words:

number prefixes (*uni-, bi-, tri-, quadr-, penta-, hexa-,* etc.)
scientific forms (*bio-, tele-, therm-, aster-, auto-, micro-, phot-, hydr-, -scop, -graph, -phon*)

Study words in prefix-related groupings. Discuss how to deduce meaning from the combination of word parts. For example, discuss related *micro* words:

microscope	*microbiology*	*microorganism*
microscopic	*microbe*	*microphone*
microwave	*microfilm*	

Can students tell what *micro* means by studying these words?

Latin Roots and Related Words. English also contains many borrowed Latin word parts. While Latin roots are less obviously recognized as "words," knowing them certainly helps readers have a sense of a derived word's meaning. Provide opportunity for students in this stage to explore words that share the same root. For example, the root *dic,* meaning to speak or point, can be found in the following words:

dictate	*dictionary*	*prediction*
verdict	*dictator*	*contradict*

See Appendix C for sample words for study. An excellent resource for other word parts for study is *English Vocabulary Elements* by Keith Denning and William R. Leben (New York: Oxford University Press, 1995).

Draw study words for this stage from students' current reading, both fiction and information texts. Students will be most interested in learning words related to what they are studying. As you plan your word study program, remember that early adolescents need a meaningful learning environment if you expect them to be interested in learning words.

MONITORING STUDENT'S GROWTH IN WORD KNOWLEDGE

To assess and evaluate your students, you must collect data concerning their stages of word knowledge and spelling development. Daily reading and writing, along with focused spelling samples, will be your most accurate way to determine (1) what students know and use independently, (2) what they are beginning to notice but often confuse, and (3) what they have not yet noticed about patterns in written language.

Identifying Word Knowledge Stages

To identify and monitor students' growth in word knowledge, collect and analyze writing samples at the beginning of the school year and two or three other times during the year. Ask students to write a sample of words that represents a variety of phonic and structural patterns. Bear and Barone (1989) offer a sample list of words drawn from the range of developmental stages of word knowledge (see also Chapter 4):

bed	*train*	*preparing*	*puncture*	*confident*
ship	*closet*	*popping*	*cellar*	*civilize*
drive	*chase*	*cattle*	*pleasure*	*flexible*
bump	*float*	*caught*	*squirrel*	*opposition*
when	*beaches*	*inspection*	*fortunate*	*emphasize*

Figure 10.5 shows spelling samples from students in fourth, sixth, and eighth grade. The words are grouped by developmental stage:

Letter-name—*bed, ship*

Within-word patterns—*drive, bump, when, train, chase, float*

Syllable juncture—*closet, beaches, preparing, popping, cattle, caught, puncture, cellar, squirrel*

Derivational constancy—*inspection, pleasure, fortunate, confident, civilize, flexible, opposition, emphasize*

As students gain experience with patterns of written language, you can expect to see changes in the way they represent phonic and structural elements in words. What do you note about each student's word knowledge?

Figure 10.5 Developmental spelling samples

Word	4th Grade	6th Grade	8th Grade
bed	bed	bed	bed
ship	ship	ship	ship
drive	drive	drive	drive
bump	bump	bump	bump
when	when	when	when
train	train	train	train
chase	chase	chase	chase
float	float	float	float
caught	cot	cought	caught
closet	closit	closet	closet
beaches	beachis	beaches	beaches
preparing	prepering	prepairing	preparing
popping	poping	popping	popping
cattle	catle	cattle	cattle
puncture	punksher	puncter	puncture
cellar	seller	cellar	cellar
squirrel	skwerel	squirel	squirrul
inspection		inspecsion	inspection
pleasure		plesure	pleasure
fortunate		forchenut	fortunet
confident			confident
civilize			civulize
flexible			flexable
opposition			oposition
emphasize			emphusize

The fourth-grade student spells conventionally in the first two sections, except for *caught*. One-syllable words show confidence. Two-syllable words are not yet conventional, but do have all phonemes represented. This student would benefit from studying variant phonic patterns in late within-word (*caught*), then focusing on applying knowledge of one-syllable patterns to two-syllable words (early syllable juncture).

The sixth-grade student is somewhat successful with two-syllable words, showing the greatest confusion with phonetic elements (*c**au**ght, punc'**ture,** squir'**rel***). I would place this student in a mid–late syllable juncture group that will review base + inflected suffix words, such as *preparing*, in which the base word changes. The student's next step might be to focus on syllabication generalizations with words such as *puncture* and *squirrel*.

I would place the eighth-grade student in the derivational constancy stage. Spellings are conventional up to *squirrel*. In the last grouping it is apparent that this student is thinking more about each word's sound rather than using information from its structural (meaning) elements, as with ***civil**ize* and ***oppos(e)**ition*. This student would benefit from study that relates meaning and sound to spelling patterns.

You can design focused word knowledge assessments by having students write several words representing knowledge from one particular stage or part. For example, to assess late syllable juncture knowledge, select two- and three-syllable words that review the various syllabication patterns, such as the following:

- base + base—*overdrawn, shouldn't*
- base + affixes—*rabies, reviewing, incomplete*
- VCV, VCCV, Cle—*climate, level, splendid, knuckle*

These few words review late syllable juncture patterns. If students write the selected words a number of times over several months, you would be able to compare the samples and evaluate their growth in word knowledge. Students who have moved into the derivational constancy stage should write these words conventionally.

Focused assessments are most useful when administered individually. As you watch each word being written, decide what the writing is showing and how much farther you might go with the student in gathering useful information. For example, your assessment of the fourth-grade student in Figure 10.5 could have stopped after the word *cattle*. At that point, you knew enough about the student's beginning syllable juncture knowledge to evaluate him fairly.

In a focused assessment of word knowledge, you do not need to go more than one stage above where the student is working. This fourth-grade student already had one unconventional spelling in the second group of words (within-word pattern). The syllable juncture list shows the student's "using but confusing" knowledge and confirms that the student is just entering the syllable juncture stage.

In the work samples you keep to document students' growth, such samples of word knowledge will be a primary source of information about what phonics and structural knowledge your students know how to use independently, as well as what emerging knowledge you can make the focus of reading and writing instruction.

Keeping Records of Word Knowledge Development

You should record your observations each time that you evaluate students' reading or a piece of focused or unfocused writing for evidence of word knowledge. You can create recordkeeping forms, such as those shown in Figures 10.6, 10.7, and 10.8, that

Figure 10.6 Word knowledge development—within-word pattern

Sight Vocabulary	**Usually**	**Sometimes**	**Rarely**
1. Frequently reads low-challenge text	_____	_____	_____
2. Increasing amount of reading time	_____	_____	_____
3. Reads widely	_____	_____	_____
4. Returns to familiar texts	_____	_____	_____
Structural Patterns (no change to base)			
1. Recognizes/uses compound words	_____	_____	_____
2. Recognizes/uses contractions			
are family ('re)	_____	_____	_____
not family (n't)	_____	_____	_____
will family ('ll)	_____	_____	_____
is/am family ('s, 'm)	_____	_____	_____
3. Recognizes base + inflectional suffix	_____	_____	_____
4. Recognizes base + derivational suffix	_____	_____	_____
5. Recognizes independent prefix + base	_____	_____	_____
Self-Monitoring Strategies			
1. Uses context + beginning letters, checked by sense and remaining letters to decode 2 syllable word, no change to base	_____	_____	_____
2. Moving toward silent reading in easy material	_____	_____	_____
3. Oral reading reappears in difficult text	_____	_____	_____

Phonics Patterns: Consonants

1. Single variant consonants

reads c__, g__, s__, x__ writes c__, g__, s__, x__

2. Double consonants (1 sound, silent letter)

reads __bb, __dd, __ff, __gg, __ll, __nn, __ss, __tt, __zz

writes __bb, __dd, __ff, __gg, __ll, __nn, __ss, __tt, __zz

3. Final consonant clusters

reads __lb, __ld, __lk, __lt, __nd, __nk, __nt

writes __lb, __ld, __lk, __lt, __nd, __nk, __nt

4. Initial consonant digraphs (silent letter)

reads gh__, gn__, kn__, wh__, wr__

writes gh__, gn__, kn__, wh__, wr__

5. Final consonant digraphs (silent letter)

reads __ck, __gn, __ng, __dge, __tch

writes __ck, __gn, __ng, __dge, __tch

Figure 10.6 ***continued***

Phonics Patterns: Vowels

1. Single long vowels (CVCe, CV)
reads a__, e__, i__, o__, u__
writes a__, e__, i__, o__, u__

2. Vowel digraphs (consistent, long)
reads ai__, ay__, ee__, igh__, oa__
writes ai__, ay__, ee__, igh__, oa__

3. Vowel digraphs (long/short)
reads ea__, ei__, ey__, ie__, ou__
writes ea__, ei__, ey__, ie__, ou__

4. Diphthongs (look same-sound different)
reads oo__, ou__, ow__
writes oo__, ou__, ow__

5. Diphthongs (look different–sound same)
reads au__/aw__, oi__/oy__, eu__/ew__/ui__
writes au__/aw__, oi__/oy__, eu__/ew__/ui__

6. R-controlled (single vowel)
reads ar__, or__, er__, ir__, ur__
writes ar__, or__, er__, it__, ur__

7. R-controlled (long vowel marker)
reads are__, ere__, ire__, ore__, ure__
writes are__, ere__, ire__, ore__, ure__

8. R-controlled (double vowel)
reads air__, ear__, eer__, oar__
writes air__, ear__, eer__, oar__

reflect the knowledge and strategies that should develop at each stage. Such forms, combined with your anecdotal notes, will provide a more complete picture of student development.

Respecting Diversity in Word Study

Learning words is a very important part of the processes of reading and writing. Confidence in one's own ability to comprehend words greatly influences daily reading and writing performance. If your students are to be successful in learning words, you must consider their experiences with print, their knowledge of how to monitor their own reading and writing, and their knowledge of the language of instruction. In addition, you must provide a variety of opportunities for students to read, write, and study words.

Experience Affects Knowledge

In learning, it is often *experience* that sets students apart from one another (Allington, 1994). As you plan a word study program, expect students' differences in experience to

Figure 10.7 Word knowledge development—Syllable juncture

Structural Patterns	**Usually**	**Sometimes**	**Rarely**
1. Base + inflectional suffix			
reading			
• no change to base	____	____	____
• base changes	____	____	____
writing			
• no change to base	____	____	____
• base changes	____	____	____
2. Independent prefix + base			
reading	____	____	____
writing	____	____	____
3. Base + derivational suffix			
reading	____	____	____
writing	____	____	____
Syllabication Generalizations			
1. Recognizes word as primarily structural or phonetic	____	____	____
2. Applies base + base, base + affix			
reading	____	____	____
writing	____	____	____
3. Applies V/CV, VC/V, VC/CV, c + le			
reading	____	____	____
writing	____	____	____
4. Integrates structural and phonics knowledge as needed	____	____	____
5. Is aware of the possibility of a schwa, tries to apply to words	____	____	____
Self-Monitoring Strategies			
1. Uses context + beginning syllable, checked by sense and other syllables	____	____	____
2. Oral reading is fluent in low-challenge materials	____	____	____
3. Silent reading is rapid in low-challenge materials	____	____	____
4. Decoding is becoming fairly automatic	____	____	____

Figure 10.8 Word knowledge development—Dreivational constancy

Structural & Phonics Patterns	**Usually**	**Sometimes**	**Rarely**
1. Is refining syllabication knowledge from syllable juncture stage			
reading	____	____	____
writing	____	____	____
2. Integrates structural patterns and phonics automatically to decode new words	____	____	____
3. Explores relationship between pronunciation, spelling, and meaning	____	____	____
4. When unsure of pronunciation and/or spelling, refers to related words for help	____	____	____
5. Recognizes/uses knowledge of dependent prefixes + root	____	____	____
Greek & Latin roots	____	____	____
Vocabulary			
1. Uses knowledge of roots to determine word meaning	____	____	____
2. Continues to add to sight vocabulary	____	____	____
3. Continues to add to meaning vocabulary	____	____	____
Self-Monitoring Strategies			
1. Uses "context +" strategy efficiently and effectively	____	____	____
2. Moving toward mature reading	____	____	____

enrich the daily "talk" about words. Expect that students will make sense of their word study experiences in different ways and will, if given the opportunity, teach each other what they understand about reading and writing words.

Teaching according to developmental levels also acknowledges this difference in experience with words. Adopting one level of a spelling or phonics program for all students in a classroom does not acknowledge or respect the diversity of experience they bring.

Encourage Self-Monitoring

As you encourage students to use the "context +" strategy in their work with words, expect them also to adapt the strategy to their thinking as readers and writers. Support the diverse ways that students learn by encouraging them to think aloud about the knowledge and strategies they use as they work. Model thinking aloud through mini-lessons about using the "context +" strategy.

Consider the Language of Instruction

For students whose first language is not English, the language of instruction can be a mystery. Who else will they hear talk about variant vowels, prefixes, or Latin roots? As teachers, we have a specialized language we use in school. How well do your students know that special language? You must make it your responsibility to teach the meaning of the language of instruction to all students, so all will have an equal opportunity to benefit from word study instruction.

Provide a Variety of Opportunities

In this text, I encourage sorting as a major instructional approach for word study. However, while completed word sorts may look similar, the thought processes students use will vary. You can encourage this variety by providing opportunity for students to share their thinking with others during word study, and by accepting students' different styles of recording in their word study notebooks. Try to be open in your thinking about how students learn words.

Some students will learn words easily by reading many books or by writing for long periods of time. Some students will learn by saying words and spelling them aloud. Still others will find that repeatedly seeing word cards helps them to remember. Some students will have to think they are "playing" to learn words, such as with word games. Some students will be motivated to learn most when working on a computer. The instructional strategies suggested in this chapter are only a start, a foundation for your word study program. You will need to add to these ideas, especially as students teach you what works best for them. Be open!

TAKE A MOMENT AND REFLECT . . .

Word study is:

- Daily instruction in word knowledge that serves both word identification and spelling development
- Focused on students' developmental stages in word knowledge
- A planned program of weekly study of words by patterns
- Integrated into daily reading and writing instruction

Weekly word study programs use:

- Lists of 10 to 15 words in patterns
- Developmentally appropriate words from stages of word knowledge
- Sorting to focus children's attention of distinctive features
- Writing to retain thinking

Word sorts can be:

- open or closed
- pictures or words
- multilevel

Word study in the within-word pattern stage:

- Broadens sight vocabulary through repetition and wide reading
- Refines phonics knowledge (silent letters)
  1. consonants
     single variants
     double consonants (*ll*)
     final blends
     digraphs with silent letters

2. vowels
   single—long
   double—digraphs, diphthongs
   variant—*r*-controlled

- Self-monitoring becomes covert
  1. context + initial sounds, checked by sense and remaining letters
  2. read one- and two-syllable words
- Moves to silent reading
  oral reading reappears in difficult text

Word study in the syllable juncture stage:

- Emphasizes changes to words with the joining of syllables
  1. inflectional suffixes, adding and dropping consonants to preserve vowel sounds
  2. more independent prefixes
- Syllabication
  1. noticing differences in multisyllable words
  2. integrating the use of phonics and structural patterns
  3. generalizations
     base + base
     base + affix
     V/CV, VC/V, or VC/CV
     C + *le*
  4. schwa—vowels in unaccented syllables
- Self-monitoring, using context + first syllable, checked by context and remaining syllables
- Solidify silent reading

Word study in the derivational constancy stage:

- Emphasizes the difference between words with independent and dependent prefixes
- Notes that addition of affixes can cause pronunciation changes in multisyllable words, but does not always cause spelling changes
  1. change in which syllable is stressed
  2. change in where a word divides into syllables
- Introduces the influence on English of Greek and Latin
- Word knowledge development can be monitored through assessment of developmental spelling and by careful observation of students' writing.
- Students are diverse in (1) their experiences as readers and writers, (2) their knowledge of the language of instruction, and (3) their ability to monitor their writing.

REFERENCES

Allington, R. L. (1994). The schools we have. The schools we need. *The Reading Teacher, 48*(1), 14–29.

Bear, D. B., Invernezzi, M., Templeton, S., & Johnston, F. (1996). *Words their way.* Upper Saddle River, NJ: Merrill/Prentice Hall.

Bear, D. R., & Barone, D. (1989). Using children's spellings to group for word study and directed reading in the primary classroom. *Reading Psychology, 10,* 275–292.

Henderson, E. H., & Beers, J. W. (1980). *Developmental and cognitive aspects of learning to spell: A reflection of word knowledge.* Newark, DE: International Reading Association.

Rinsky, L. A. (1993). *Teaching word recognition skills* (5th ed.). Scottsdale, AZ: Gorsuch Scarisbrick.

Spiegel, D. L. (1985). Developing independence in decoding. *Reading World, 25,* 75–80.

Temple, C., Nathan, R., Temple, F., & Burris, N. (1993). *The beginnings of writing* (2nd ed.). Boston: Allyn and Bacon.

Templeton, S. (1991). Teaching and learning the English spelling system: Reconceptualizing method and purpose. *Elementary School Journal,* 92(2), 185–201.

Vygotsky, L. S. (1962) *Thought and language.* (E. Hanfmann & G. Vakar, Eds. & Trans.). Cambridge, MA: MIT Press.

11

Using a Basal Reading Series Effectively

Teaching from a Literature-Based Perspective

In this chapter . . .

We explore the organization and use of a basal reading series integrating reading and language arts, including:

- a brief history of basal reading series,
- the components of a basal series,
- how a basal series is organized,
- overview of a basal theme or unit,
- overview of a basal lesson, and
- planning a basal theme or unit using a combination of whole-class, small groups, and reader's workshop.

Before you begin . . .

The literature selection entitled "Kinship" in the basal lesson is actually Chapter 3 of *Woodsong* by Gary Paulsen (1990).

Imagine that you have accepted a position as a sixth-grade teacher in a school district that has recently adopted a basal reading series for the language arts program. In your new classrooms you find copies of student books, teacher's editions, and other support materials for a reading series published by Silver Burdett & Ginn (DeLain et al., 1996). As you leaf through the books, you reflect on your own reading experiences in elementary school and remember sitting at a table with other students while your teacher guided you through selections in a reading book. Those books were probably from a basal reading series!

WHAT IS A BASAL READING SERIES?

A *basal reading series* is a sequential set of instructional materials organized around a hierarchy of reading and language arts skills (Goodman, Shannon, Freeman, & Murphy, 1988). The stories in basal readers are often excerpts from children's literature. Traditionally, series editors rewrote those selections, substituting decodable words for the original language in order to teach specific vocabulary and skills (McCarthey & Hoffman, 1995). While teachers have historically used some type of printed materials to teach students to read, sets of basal readers have been part of the American educational scene only since the early 1900s (Goodman et al., 1988).

A Brief History

Teachers early in our nation's history taught reading with a Hornbook, a three- by five-inch hand-held paddle holding one page of text. Students would recite the alphabet, phonetic syllables, and the Lord's Prayer from their Hornbook each day. The only book typically available for reading by adults or children was the Bible. Books for children, as we know them today, did not exist.

By the 1840s educators became concerned with carefully controlling the rate at which new words were introduced to young readers. *McGuffey Eclectic Readers* provide an example of early attempts to control vocabulary, a characteristic of most basal readers (Bohning, 1986). A page in a beginning McGuffey *Reader* might have included words, letter patterns, and controlled text:

Tab Ann hat catch see

e ch s

See Tab! See Ann!
See! Tab has the hat.
Can Ann catch Tab?

Students pronounced words and sounds, then applied them to a simple text. The text itself bore great similarity to the basal readers used in the 1950s and 1960s. Texts for the middle grades were didactic, intending to teach values, citizenship, and patriotism through realistic stories and biographies of important people that were written by the textbook authors.

Around the beginning of the twentieth century, with dramatic increases in the schoolage population, grammar schools were organized into a graded system by age for more efficient instruction. During this period industrialization had great influence on our thinking and schools became concerned with efficiency and standardization of the "product" of schools, the students. Teachers did not always have a high level of training and there was concern that all students would not receive similar instruction (Shannon, 1989). Such concerns lead to the creation of sets of graded reading materials known as basal reading series (Betts, 1946).

Basal readers have dominated reading instruction in the United States since their inception (McCallum, 1988). As early as 1935, basal readers were seen as the foundation for classroom reading programs and the source of "expert" knowledge for instruction. Arthur Gates (1935), a well-known reading educator, suggested that basal readers freed the teacher to give more attention to the proper selection of other reading materials and the proper guidance of students in their total reading program.

From the 1940s to the 1960s, classroom instruction was dominated by basal reading series, such as the *Dick and Jane New Basic Readers,* that conveyed stereotypic images of family life (Reutzel & Cooter, 1992). With rapidly expanding global competition in the 1960s and 1970s, basal readers began to reflect a growing national concern for students' ability to demonstrate their knowledge of basic skills. During this same period, the struggle for equality by various groups in the United States led to challenges of the stereotyped portrayal of characters in basal texts (Aukerman, 1981). More recently, as a result of the whole language movement, the content of basal readers is once again changing to include high-quality literature, less isolated skills instruction, more integration of reading with other language arts and content, and greater flexibility in decision making for teachers (McCarthey & Hoffman, 1995).

Basal series continue to dominate reading instruction in the United States. Textbook adoption policies and funds for purchasing instructional materials contribute greatly to the extensive use of basal readers (Goodman et al., 1988). Textbook adoption committees at state and local levels set acceptable standards for textbooks to be used in public schools. Publishers submit materials for review by the committee, and materials that are selected can be purchased with public school funds for use in schools (Farr, Tulley, & Powell, 1987).

The demands placed on publishing companies by such heavily populated states as Texas, California, and Florida, that use state adoption processes and spend large amounts of money on basal adoptions, dramatically influence the content and organization of basal materials. For example, the state of Texas proclaimed that only texts including authentic, unedited, and unabridged children's literature would be considered for reading/language arts adoptions (Texas Education Agency, 1990). Imagine how publishers respond to such a demand by a state that buys millions of dollars of their product.

School districts often adopt a basal series as the main source of instructional materials for teaching the district curriculum. Funds are provided to purchase such materials. While school districts may allow teachers to use authentic literature rather than an adopted reading series, textbook funds for purchasing the literature may be limited. In such cases, literature-based teachers do not have equal access to funds for instructional materials.

A Call for Change

During the 1980s and 1990s basal reading series have been the target of criticism by groups that advocate holistic philosophies (Goodman et al., 1988; Shannon, 1989, 1990; Reutzel, 1991; McCarthey & Hoffman, 1995). The main areas of concern have been the quality of literature, teaching of isolated skills, and the perceived control of teaching behavior.

Authors of basal reading series select the literature that students read, provide direction to teachers, and furnish prepared practice materials for students to use. In the past the literature selected has not been authentic, but instead was often written by the editors of the series to control the level of readability and to avoid controversial issues. The readability controls led to selections in which the language was stilted, uninteresting, and difficult to understand.

Basal reading series have been criticized for teaching skills in isolation from meaningful contexts. In the past, workbooks that accompanied basal series provided practice that required students to "fill in" someone else's ideas. The number of different skills introduced or practiced in one lesson forced "reading" time to become a "skill and drill" time. In addition, the placement of skills instruction within the basal series seemed arbitrary and unrelated to the selections being read.

Authors of basal readers provided preplanned lessons for teachers to use in reading instruction. Theoretically, teachers should have been free to prepare other learning experiences for children, but often the basal reading program became the only source of students' reading materials.

Basal teacher's editions originally consisted of a few pages in the back of a student's book, the highlighting of new words in a selection, and a few suggestions for teaching a selection. During the 1970s, teacher's editions became scripts for the teacher to read during instruction. Scripting was seen as an attempt to provide teachers with information about new instructional strategies and to make their actions during reading instruction more standardized across the country.

The organization and language of basal teacher's editions led teachers to believe that educators who developed the series had "expert" knowledge about reading. Consequently, teachers followed the teacher's edition concerning decisions that they should have made at the classroom level. Apple (1982) refers to this as *deskilling*, when teachers do not trust their own knowledge and, instead, defer to an outside "expert." Over time, teachers become reskilled in basal approaches and techniques, becoming technicians who turn pages and follow directions.

What do these concerns suggest for reading instruction today? Publishers of current series have been responding to past criticisms (McCarthey & Hoffman, 1995):

- Current basal series are incorporating higher-quality literature selections.
- Formats and organizations of new texts are more diverse.
- Series are incorporating a greater variety of genres.
- The adaptations of authentic children's literature texts are minimal, preserving the richness of language.
- The selections contain more complex plots and more well-developed characters, and require readers to make interpretations.
- Many series now attempt to present skill and strategy instruction in meaningful contexts.
- Vocabulary evidence indicates that readability controls have been significantly reduced, if not abandoned.
- Series editors encourage teachers to be decision makers and to select activities appropriate for their children.
- Editors now include process writing, thematic units, and numerous extension activities that reflect current trends in integrated instruction.

The change in basal series over the decade from 1986 to 1996 is dramatic, showing the influence of the movements in literature-based reading, whole language, and integrated thematic instruction.

Decision Making with a Basal Reading Series

The authors of a basal reading series offer suggestions for planning learning experiences for students, but do not make the decisions for you. You make the decisions in your own classroom. The format of the teacher's edition offers prepared lessons and activities, but the series' authors clearly expect that you will select what is best for your students.

If you view a basal reading/language arts series as multiple copies of literature selections and a series of skill and strategy lesson plans with support materials, you will find that you may use your knowledge of literature-based reading and writing more effectively. Before you teach with basal materials, you must decide the types of experiences your students need, just as you would if you were teaching with authentic literature. Keeping your objectives in mind, you can select the portions of the basal materials that will help you meet those objectives.

In the sections that follow, you will become familiar with one basal series and think about the decisions you might make if you use basal materials with middle grade students. Basal reading series can be very effective for reading/language arts instruction if you make informed decisions regarding their use.

Overview of an Integrated Reading/Language Arts Basal Series

Let's return to your new sixth-grade classroom. Imagine that you are looking over all of the materials that come with the reading series. You see that there are two large, spiral-bound teacher's editions entitled *Literature Works* (DeLain et al., 1996). Turning to the front pages of one of the volumes, you find references to the components of the program, listed in Figure 11.1.

Current basal series are quite comprehensive. Publishers typically provide anthologies of literature selections for students, consumable materials to practice skills and strategies, supplemental materials to extend beyond the literature selections, an assessment program for monitoring students' progress, and a comprehensive teacher's manual that includes illustrations of student and supplemental materials. The impact of technology can be seen in the inclusion of CD-ROMs, laser discs, and other supporting media. While the program is comprehensive, many materials must be purchased separately. *Note:* Be aware that some school districts may not provide textbook funds for the purchase of materials considered a supplemental part of the program.

While surveying the basal materials, you become keenly aware that over the years instructional materials for reading have grown into well-developed management systems for integrated classroom reading/language arts programs. A number of basal reading series, including *Literature Works,* also integrate content area materials for a more comprehensive program. For example, one of the themed units in the sixth-grade program focuses on ancient Egypt, which is typically a topic of study in social studies during that year.

How Components Are Organized

Most current basal reading/language arts series are organized around units of instruction that contain literature selections, skill and strategy instruction, extension activities, and assessment materials. In *Literature Works,* for example, the two volumes of the sixth-grade collection are each divided into three units, for a total of six units:

Volume 1

- Perspectives
- Uncovering the Past: Ancient Egypt
- Finding Common Ground

Figure 11.1 Basal program components

Literature Resources
Collection (student anthology)
Theme Magazine
Theme Trade Books

Practice and Support Materials
Practice Book & Language Arts Handbook
Spelling Source: An Integrated Approach to Spelling
English Language Support Program

Teacher Resources
Teacher's Guide
SourceBank
Home Connections
Teaching Transparencies

Technology Resources
CD-ROM & Videodiscs
Story Tapes
Videotapes

Assessment Components
Guide to Student Portfolios & Classroom Assessment
Reading Process Assessment
Reading and Language Arts Skills Assessment
Writing Assessment Guide
Placement Assessment
Informal Reading Inventory
Phonics Inventory

Volume 2

- Strange Encounters
- Survival
- Journeys of Change

The publishers suggest that you spend approximately five to six weeks on each theme unit.

First Steps in Planning

Before we study this basal unit and consider the decisions you might make, let's think about your planning processes. If you are planning to teach a themed unit of your own, you would probably do the following:

- Determine what you want students to learn.
- Gather available resources.
- Select activities to help students reach the unit goals and objectives.
- Consider how to assess student learning.

All of these aspects of unit or theme planning are included in the themes developed by the authors of the basal series. Your task is to decide how well their suggestions meet your goals, as well as the needs and interests of your students. As you make decisions about a basal reading/language arts program, you find that some suggested activities are appropriate and should be kept just as they are; some activities meet your goals but must be modified to meet students' needs, and some are inappropriate for your goals and/or students' needs and interests and either should be discarded or revisited at a more appropriate time. *Remember:* Your decision making is the key to effective use of any commercially produced teaching materials.

How a Basal Theme Is Organized

We now turn our attention to one of the themes in the basal series, "Survival," and see how it is organized. Understanding the organization of a unit or theme in a basal series can be a key element to understanding the organization of the entire grade level. To aid your understanding, this chapter contains pages from the teacher's edition for the "Survival" theme from *Literature Works* (Figure 11.2). Although the pages of the actual student text are reproduced in the teacher's edition, our discussion focuses on the instructional suggestions made by the authors of the basal series, rather than on the actual pieces of literature taught. From your study of this text, you are familiar with teaching literature selections from a literature-based perspective.

Theme Planner. (*See TE 884–885.*) To facilitate unit planning, the teacher's edition provides a two-page chart that highlights important unit resources and activities found in the lesson plans for each selection. On the left side of the Theme Planner is an overview of the four selections contained in the student anthology, *Collection.* On the right are suggestions for resources and activities to take you "Beyond the Collection."

Many basals now use authentic literature. For example, the following selections are included in the "Survival" unit:

- "Kinship," from *Woodsong* by Gary Paulsen (1990)
- "Leader of the Pack," from *Champions: Stories of Ten Remarkable Athletes* by Bill Littlefield (1993)
- "The Grandfather Tree," from *Morning Girl* by Michael Dorris (1992)
- "Four Against the Sea," from *A Boat to Nowhere* by Maurene Crane Wartski (1980)

The resources identified in Beyond the Collection may or may not be included in the materials purchased by the school district. The "Writing Process" and "Theme Project" pages appear in the teacher's edition. Other materials shown are considered supplemental and are typically purchased separately.

Management Options. (*See TE 886–887.*) The teacher's edition offers three possible management options. You may choose to use the selections in *Collection* as a major focus, or you may focus on either the Theme Magazine that is available or the suggested Theme Trade Books. Each option includes theme projects, writing process,

Figure 11.2

Survival

Theme Planner

Integrated Language Arts

WITHIN THE COLLECTION	READING	WRITING	LISTENING/SPEAKING/VIEWING
Kinship from *Woodsong* **pages T894–925** **Key Concept:** The resourcefulness and loyalty of sled dogs	**Building Background** Activating Prior Knowledge Developing Vocabulary **Comprehension** Compare/Contrast **Literature** Theme **Vocabulary** Compound Words; Forms/Applications	**Writing Workshop** Descriptive Writing: Using Sensory Words **Grammar Workshop** Adverbs: Definition, Use; Adverbs of Time, Place, Manner **Spelling Workshop** Endings *-ion, -tion, -sion*	**Responding** Reader Response Groups **Speaking Workshop** Using Visual Aids to Explain or Illustrate
Leader of the Pack from *Champions* **pages T926–963** **Key Concept:** What it takes to win the grueling Iditarod	**Building Background** Activating Prior Knowledge Developing Vocabulary **Comprehension** Main Idea **Vocabulary** Multiple-meaning Words **Study Skills** Graphic Aids; Reference Sources	**Writing Workshop** Topic Sentences and Supporting Details **Grammar Workshop** Contractions: *not, have* Adverbs of Comparison **Spelling Workshop** Endings *-ence, -ance, -able, -ible*	**Responding** Reader Response Groups **Listening/Speaking Workshop** Conducting an Interview
The Grandfather Tree from *Morning Girl* **pages T976–1015** **Key Concept:** Finding strength to survive a storm	**Building Background** Activating Prior Knowledge Developing Vocabulary **Comprehension** Conclusions **Literature** Setting; Figurative Language **Vocabulary** Synonyms and Antonyms	**Writing Workshop** Organizing Comparisons **Grammar Workshop** Commas, Capitalization in Greeting, Closing in Letters **Spelling Workshop** Spellings of Consonant Sounds	**Responding** Reader Response Groups **Viewing Workshop** Using and Interpreting Nonverbal Communication
Four Against the Sea from *A Boat to Nowhere* **pages T1024–1065** **Key Concept:** Surviving a shipwreck	**Building Background** Activating Prior Knowledge Developing Vocabulary **Comprehension** Make Inferences; Authors Purpose **Vocabulary** Analysis **Study Skills** Dictionary/Glossary; Library Skills	**Writing Workshop** Expository Writing: Using Order Words **Grammar Workshop** Negatives Grammar Review **Spelling Workshop** Prefixes *com-* and *con-*	**Responding** Reader Response Groups **Listening Workshop** Determining Problem/Solution With Role-playing

Estimated Time for Theme Completion: 5–6 Weeks

BEYOND THE COLLECTION

Theme Trade Books *Drylongso* (easy) and *The Crystal Drop* (challenging) provide opportunities to explore characterization and drawing conclusions. **For instructional support, see pages T1074–1085.**

Theme Magazine *Danger Zone* employs a variety of writing and visual styles. Specific articles can be used to access the Collection, to build context, and to apply reading and writing skills. **For instructional support, see pages T1070–1073.**

Writing Process: Comparison and Contrast Writing This lesson provides a structure in which students can develop a piece of expository writing using comparison and contrast. Begin the Writing Process lesson during the second week of the theme so that students will have time to revise their writing. **For instructional support, see pages T1086–1091.**

Writing Process
Exposition: Comparison and Contrast

Theme Project: Making Survival Handbooks This feature suggests steps to assist students in developing booklets with tips for staying safe in dangerous circumstances. **For instructional support, see pages T1092–1095**

CROSS-CURRICULAR

Science
Explore the Tundra;
Report on Primitive Knowledge

Mathematics
Calculate Average Speed

Social Studies
Explore the Last Frontier

Science Research Dog Breeds

Health and Safety
Cold-Weather Safety Tips

Mathematics
Determine Workload

Social Studies
Compare Living Environment;
Map an Iditarod

Science Learn About Clouds;
Learn About Islands

Social Studies
Report on Caribbean Peoples

Music
Use Percussion Instruments

Mathematics
Locate Islands on a Map

Science Investigate South China Sea Storms

Health and Safety Understand the Body's Need for Fluids

Music Listen to Southeast Asian Music

Social Studies Learn About Vietnamese Culture

Mathematics Chart a Course

Theme Resources

Story Tape

Spelling Source

Practice Book

Word Power CD-ROM

SourceBank
English Language Support
Home Connections

Figure 11.2 *continued*

Management Options

Think about your students' interests and abilities as you decide which reading materials you will emphasize during the theme. Select the focus best suited to your class: Focus on the Collection, Focus on the Theme Magazine, or Focus on Theme Trade Books. The choice is yours!

Rationale To teach reading, writing, and oral language through a variety of award-winning classics and contemporary pieces

OPTION 1 Focus on the Collection

Theme Project "Kinship," page 400, and "Four Against the Sea," page 464, provide students with details about life-threatening situations to which they can refer when writing a survival handbook.

Writing Process The lesson provided with "Leader of the Pack" on main idea and supporting details in paragraphs can help students prepare for comparison-and-contrast writing.

Theme Trade Books Use Drylongso and The Crystal Drop for more survival-related readings and experience with novel-length fiction.

Theme Magazine "Into the Storm," page 18, provides background information on the disaster faced by the characters of "The Grandfather Tree" in the Collection.

Collection

Rationale To support second-language learners and students reading below grade level by providing high-interest, accessible reading materials; to emphasize real-world literacy and cross-curricular learning for all students

OPTION 2 Focus on the Theme Magazine

Theme Project The background information in "Into the Storm," page 18, can lead students to research other natural disasters as they plan their survival handbooks.

Writing Process In "I Will Survive!" page 7, ask students to compare the effects of adding different action verbs, adjectives, and emotions to the story.

Theme Trade Books "Around the World: Emergency Shelters" has tips on surviving varied weather. Students may apply this information to understand how Lindy's family survived the dust storm in Drylongso.

Collection Discuss the experiences of a musher in "Win by a Nose" to build interest in the selection "Leader of the Pack."

Theme Magazine
Danger Zone

OPTION 3 Focus on the Theme Trade Books

Theme Project In The Crystal Drop and in Drylongso, characters make careful preparations to cope with drought conditions. Suggest that students mention their techniques in the survival handbooks.

Writing Process Use the contrast between Megan and her brother and between their home and their uncle's in The Crystal Drop to help students understand how authors use comparison and contrast.

Theme Magazine Have students consider how the refugees who brave the sea in "Risk Taking, Hope Making" are like Lindy and her family in Drylongso, who struggle bravely with drought.

Collection Compare Obeah, the dog who rescues the narrator of the selection "Kinship," with the dog Charlie, who hunts for Megan and Ian as they cross a drought-stricken landscape in The Crystal Drop.

Rationale To promote learning through experience with novels and other complete, self-contained pieces of literature

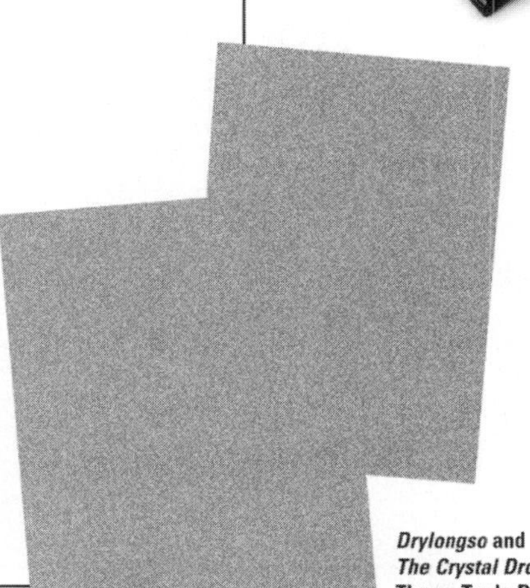

Drylongso and
The Crystal Drop
Theme Trade Books

Figure 11.2 *continued*

T888 Theme 5 Survival

Ongoing Assessment

The following Learning Goals build on skills and strategies learned in this theme. As you observe students' reading, writing, speaking, listening, and viewing, look for these specific indicators to determine whether the Learning Goals are being reached.

A

Formal end-of-theme assessment is addressed on pages T1096–1097.

	LEARNING GOALS	PERFORMANCE INDICATORS
Constructing Meaning	• Students monitor and evaluate the meaning they construct.	• Students can compare ideas between selections. • Students can make judgments about what they have read.
	• Students can use their knowledge of text structure to construct meaning.	• Students can identify main ideas and supporting details. • Students can discuss the theme and setting of a selection.
	• Students use strategies to improve understanding as they read.	• Students can choose among reference sources to locate necessary information. • Students draw conclusions about ideas in selections.
Learning About Language	• Students use knowledge of word meanings to construct meaning.	• Students can use knowledge of compound words, prefixes, and suffixes to determine meaning for new words. • Students can use a dictionary to select the appropriate meaning of a word with multiple meanings. • Students discuss the purpose of figurative language.
	• Students can recognize and appreciate an author's craft in literature.	• Students can determine the theme of a story. • Students can discuss how tone and mood affect the construction of meaning.
Appreciating Language and Literature	• Students are interested and excited by what they read and write.	• Students ask for more books about the same topics or by the same author. • Students are eager to share with others something they have read.
	• Students appreciate narrative and expository texts as an adventure and an escape to new worlds and lives.	• Students discuss the suspense of a survival story. • Students voluntarily select texts dealing with adventures and challenges.

Portfolios

Classroom observations, students' written work, reading logs, and skills and process tests all reflect students' growth, progress, and attitudes about reading, writing, and oral communication. While tests document the hard facts of reading and writing, ongoing personal observations and checklists, such as the Learning Goals Checklist, help you collect information on the intangibles, such as interests, commitment, and motivation.

Getting stranded in the wilderness can be a life-or-death situation, whether you're in the desert or the Arctic tundra. In either place, you must find shelter to survive the harsh weather. The glaring desert sun can cause your body to dehydrate if you're out in the middle of the day. In contrast, nighttime presents the greatest danger in the tundra because of the bitterly cold temperatures. If you're planning a trip to either climate, learning how to build a shelter could save your life.

Select material that demonstrates students' progress.

A Learning Goals, Theme 5

Learning About Language

Name: Grade: Theme:

Theme Selections	Kinship			Leader of the Pack			The Grandfather Tree			Four Against the Sea		
Learning Goals	Emerging	Developing	Accomplished	Emerging	Developing	Accomplished	Emerging	Developing	Accomplished	Emerging	Developing	Accomplished
Students use knowledge of word meanings to construct meaning.												
• Students can use knowledge of compound words, prefixes, and suffixes to determine the meaning of new words.												
• Students can use a dictionary to select the appropriate meaning of a word ...												

Observation Checklists for this theme, such as the one shown here, can be found in the Grade 6 Guide to Student Portfolios and Classroom Assessment.

Gathering Materials for a Student's Portfolio

Periodically adding selected pieces of students' work to their theme portfolios will create a running record of their progress. Include your own written observations of indications that students are becoming independent readers and writers with improving comprehension and critical thinking skills. The Portfolio Checklist for this theme suggests one way to track students' progress as they participate in reading, writing, and oral language activities throughout the theme. Opportunities are indicated throughout the theme by the symbol above.

Survival

Portfolio Checklist

- ☐ Survival Reading and Writing checklists in the Grade 6 Guide to Student Portfolios and Classroom Assessment
- ☐ Anecdotal records
- ☐ Practice Book worksheets
- ☐ SourceBank: Writer's Notebook pages
- ☐ Writing Process
- ☐ Spelling Source extension and review pages
- ☐ Teacher evaluations of student's growing knowledge of theme content
- ☐ Family Involvement Form
- ☐ Student's self-selected work
- ☐ Tape recordings of student's reading
- ☐ Theme Project
- ☐ Skills Assessment
- ☐ Reading Process Assessment
- ☐ ____________
- ☐ ____________
- ☐ ____________

The Portfolio Checklist can be found in the Grade 6 Guide to Student Portfolios and Classroom Assessment. Teachers should choose from among the listed items according to their teaching styles and curriculum requirements.

trade books, and collection ideas, and provides a variety of materials you may use to meet student needs and interests. You also may choose to combine parts of the different management options.

Ongoing Assessment. (*See TE 888–889.*) You begin planning a theme by deciding what students should learn and what behaviors will indicate such learning. These pages provide information about the learning goals that the basal's authors suggest and have planned for learning experiences. You can see the focus of this theme is on constructing meaning, learning about language, and appreciating language and literature. Each focus appears with appropriate learning goals and performance indicators.

You must decide which learning goals and performance indicators are appropriate for your students, and at what particular time. Basal series authors carefully plan and sequence their goals throughout the series. The activities suggested typically build on previously introduced skills and strategies, and generally allow sufficient learning time.

As a part of your ongoing assessment, series authors encourage you to have students keep a portfolio that demonstrates their growth as readers and writers. They have developed a "Guide to Student Portfolios and Classroom Assessment." A sample "Portfolio Checklist" for the "Survival" theme appears on TE 889. Your knowledge of portfolio assessment will help you decide about using materials in the basal series.

Theme Launch. The next section in the teacher's edition is entitled "Theme Launch," and contains suggestions for capturing students' attention, suggested literature to read aloud, ideas for a theme bulletin board, and an introductory selection available on videodisc. As in all unit teaching, you need to "hook" your students right from the start. You may choose to begin with the teacher's edition suggestions and then add ideas of your own.

Literature Selections. The "Survival" theme is presented through four literature selections, each with a fully developed lesson plan. Each plan begins with a "Selection Planner" that gives an overview of the integrated lesson plan. We discuss here one of these plans, that for "Kinship" (Chapter 3 of *Woodsong*, by Gary Paulsen [1990]). The literature selection from the student text is not included. Our emphasis here is on using the components of the teacher's edition.

Other Theme Components. The final pages of the theme plan contain other suggestions for this theme study as a whole, including the following:

- Theme Wrap-Up
- More Books and Technology
- Theme Magazine
- Trade Book Support
- Writing Process
- Theme Project
- Assessing Growth
- Home Connections

Theme Wrap-Up. Bringing closure to learning is an important issue in effective instruction. For the "Theme Wrap-Up," the series authors suggest ways to help students reflect on the selections and make connections to the overall theme. Rather than wait until the end of a theme, you should continually help students make connections among theme learning experiences.

More Books and Technology. The series authors have researched books related to the theme, and suggest books on a variety of levels to better meet students' needs and interests. You may display these books, and others you are familiar with, throughout the theme. Encourage students to make selections for independent reading at home and school. The authors also identify supplemental technology that supports the unit theme.

Theme Magazine. If you have access to the "Theme Magazine," supplemental selections in magazine format, the series authors provide suggestions for integrating it with other theme materials. One or more articles or activities in the Theme Magazine support or extend each major selection in the student anthology, *Collection.* The formats of the articles vary, and are accessible to most students.

Trade Book Support. In this basal series, the authors suggest two pieces of authentic literature for study in each theme. Since the selections in the student anthology are excerpts from literature, it is important that your students also engage in extended reading. Chapter books, in particular, build a stamina for reading that excerpts cannot. The trade books suggested for the "Survival" theme are *Drylongso* (Hamilton, 1992) and *The Crystal Drop* (Hughes, 1993). For each trade book, the series authors have developed plans for engaging students with each book. You are free to include other trade books for study or substitute other texts. In earlier chapters we studied *Hatchet* (Paulsen, 1987). You could choose to include it in the survival theme. I would be inclined to use this piece as a whole-class study to accompany other survival selections, including the sequel to *Hatchet*, *Brian's Winter* (Paulsen, 1996).

Writing Process. This basal series is a complete integrated reading/language arts program. In each theme, the authors suggest at least one extended piece of writing that is taken through the writing process to publication. In the "Survival" theme, students are provided opportunity and instruction in writing with "Exposition: Comparison and Contrast," including suggestions to you for helping students with each phase of the writing process. If you have a writer's workshop each day, you may use these suggestions in your minilessons, shared writing, small-group instruction, and conferences.

Theme Project. Units of study typically engage students in demonstrating what they learn by letting them choose to complete open-ended projects. One project students might enjoy that appears in this unit is making a "Survival Handbook." Quality projects require time and preparation to develop, and to succeed must be part of your initial planning.

Assessing Growth. (*See TE 1096–1097,* shown later in this chapter.) To follow up the beginning section, Ongoing Assessment, the series authors make suggestions for informal assessment, such as conferences and student self-assessment, as well as more formal assessment of specific skills and strategies developed in the unit. Once again, the Portfolio Checklist reminds you of options for assessing students' learning.

Home Connections. Finally, the series authors make suggestions for strengthening the connections among student, family, and school. Encouraging students to read at home should always be a mainstay of your literacy program. If you want students to read at home, you must have a varied collection of appropriate texts to support and stimulate their interests. You must also work with parents to provide an environment in the home that will encourage reading.

Keeping parents informed about theme studies can also promote home connections. The series authors suggest that you consider (1) using a theme newsletter to involve families in theme-related activities and (2) encouraging family assessment of the work in a student's portfolio. These suggestions can be catalysts for other successful ways to build connections between home and school.

The basal series authors have tried to put together suggested lessons and materials that you can weave into a theme or unit. The ideas presented can be a springboard into an integrated unit of study with more emphasis in content area learning, or you may treat the material as an integrated reading/language arts unit. The direction that a unit goes is your decision.

What is your impression thus far of current basal reading/language arts programs? How do you feel about what a program of this type offers you as a teacher? Can you see yourself as a decision maker, selecting materials that meet your instructional goals and are appropriate for your students?

Planning a Basal Selection

Before we go further in planning the unit, I want to be sure that you understand your options for each selected piece of literature. The "Survival" unit contains lesson plans for engaging students with four literature selections, as well as ideas for introducing and extending skills and strategies that are important in the language arts. I include in this chapter the complete lesson plan for "Kinship" by Gary Paulsen (1990) to focus and enhance our discussion. (I will be using the teacher's edition page numbers for reference throughout.)

Format of Basal Lesson Plans

Each selection begins with a "Selection Planner" (TE 895) that provides an overview of the reading, writing, speaking, listening, and viewing lessons developed for each selection, as well as possible cross-curricular connections. The series authors intend that you spend as much as one week on a single selection and related theme activities.

Looking at the Selection Planner for "Kinship," note that the teaching of a selection is broken into three parts:

- Part 1: Reading and Responding
- Part 2: Literature-based Instruction
- Part 3: Integrated Curriculum

Part 1, "Reading and Responding" (TE 896–911), focuses on activities that typically occur before and during the reading of a selection. Note in the reading column on page T895 such prereading activities as building background knowledge, activating prior knowledge by making a concept web, developing vocabulary, and phonics. The

Kinship

"Kinship," taken from the book *Woodsong,* describes several episodes from dog musher and writer Gary Paulsen's life that taught him never to underestimate the intelligence and compassion of animals.

Learning Opportunities

"Kinship" provides the following learning opportunities.

Theme Link Students can learn how Paulsen's team of sled dogs helped him survive a treacherous accident in the frozen Minnesota wilderness.

Writing Model The selection provides a model of autobiographical narrative that students will find engaging and thought-provoking.

Reading/Writing Link Students will gain an appreciation for the author's techniques of characterization and theme development, which they can apply to their own writing.

Cross-curricular Link Students will have the opportunity to study ecosystems and animal characteristics, use math skills to compare data related to dog sledding, find information about exploring frontiers, and study nutrition.

Selection Planner

Integrated Language Arts

READING	WRITING	LISTENING/SPEAKING/ VIEWING	CROSS-CURRICULAR
Part 1: Reading and Responding, pages T894–911			
Building Background **Activating Prior Knowledge** Concept Web **Developing Vocabulary** steeped, whirlpool, mystified, alleviate, exaltation, awakening, dwelling, chagrin **Phonics** Long *i* **Strategic Reading** Preview and Predict Set Purposes Visualize Check Predictions Fix-up: Reread KWL	**Spelling Preview** Endings *-ion, -tion, -sion* **Author's Craft** Autobiographical Narrative Characterization Theme **In Response** Learning from Dogs **Responding** Write in journal Write a short story	**In Response** Looking for Insight **Responding** Discuss responses to selection Role-play a scene Discuss author's argument	**Building Background** Social Studies: History of trapping in Minnesota Science: Canine family of animals
Part 2: Literature-based Instruction, pages T912–917			
Comprehension Compare/Contrast **(T)** Forms and Applications **Literature: Story Structure** Theme **Word Study: Vocabulary** Compound Words	**Theme** Write theme statements **Compare/Contrast** Write descriptions that compare and contrast **Compound Words** Write compound words with common roots **Forms/Applications** Write information for applications	**Theme** Discuss selection themes **Compare/Contrast** Discuss entries for a Venn diagram **Compound Words** Discuss compound words organized in a word web **Forms/Applications** Talk about guidelines for filling out forms	
Part 3: Integrated Curriculum, pages T918–925			
	Writing Workshop Using Sensory Words **(T)** **Grammar Workshop** Adverbs Adverbs of Time, Place, Manner **(T)** **Spelling Workshop** Endings *-ion, -tion, -sion*	**Viewing** Using Visual Aids to Explain	**Science** Creating a "Recipe" for Balance Reporting on Primitive Knowledge **Mathematics** Calculating a Winning Speed **Social Studies** Exploring the Last Frontier **Health and Safety** Developing a Diet

(T) = Tested Skill

Materials

Collection
pages 400–409

Theme Magazine
Danger Zone

Theme Trade Books
Drylongso
See support on pages T1074–1079.

The Crystal Drop
See support on pages T1080–1085.

Additional Resources

- **Story Tape**
- **Practice Book**
  pages 172–180
- **Spelling Source**
  pages 55, 56
- **Teaching Transparencies**
  pages 80–84
- **Word Power: CD-ROM**
- **SourceBank**
- **English Language Support**

Building Background

SELECTION SUMMARY

In this selection from his book *Woodsong,* Gary Paulsen recalls two experiences with his team of sled dogs that changed his life. In one instance, he observed one dog planning and executing a complicated joke on another dog. In another, Paulsen was rescued from a life-threatening situation by the ingenuity of his team. These experiences taught Paulsen that animals are much smarter and more complex than human beings normally give them credit for.

Activating Prior Knowledge

Concept Web Tell students that the selection they will read next is written by a man who runs dog sleds. Elicit information about dogs and people's relationship with dogs using questions like the following. You may wish to record students' responses in a concept web.

- **What kinds of relationships do dogs have with people? What work can dogs do?**
- **Do dogs have feelings? Can they think? What makes you believe this?**
- **What other characteristics of dogs can you name?**

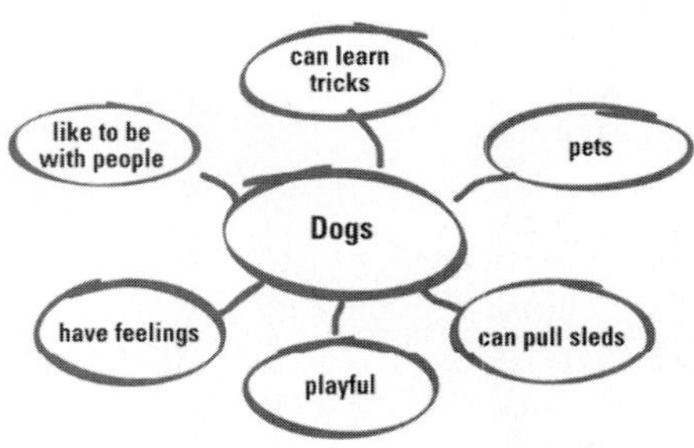

To help students build further background for reading the selection, share with them the information on the opposite page.

Theme Magazine
Danger Zone

How Cold Can You Go?

Brrrr! Does cold weather give you the shivers? Find out how to survive when the temperature falls.

Not Too Hot, Not Too Cold

Whether it's 1° F or 101° F outside, your body temperature usually hovers at a comfortable 98.6° F. How does your temperature stay so steady?

Like a car engine, the cells in your body "burn" fuel. The fuel is the food you eat. Food supplies energy that your body uses to keep all its cells working. When the food is "burned," it gives off heat. It is this heat that keeps your body at 98.6° F.

When the outside temperature drops way down, your body may not be able to stay warm just by burning fuel. Then two automatic processes kick in to warm you up. Goose bumps pop out and you begin to shiver.

Goose bumps slow down heat loss. They push up the hair on your arms and allow air to become trapped between the hairs. Actually, goose bumps work much better in furry animals or in birds whose feathers trap air.

Shivering warms you by cranking up your body's heat production. Most of your body's heat is produced in the muscles. That's why jogging or exercising can make you warm. When you shiver, your twitching muscles also warm you up.

DANGER ZONE 29

To build background about the human body's reaction to extremely cold temperatures such as those described in "Kinship," students can read the article "How Cold Can You Go?" on pages 29–31 of the theme magazine.

Jackals, dogs, foxes, and wolves (shown here, top to bottom) all evolved from a common ancestor and are members of the canine family, which makes their feet and toes especially suited for running. Dogs used for sled running also have thick coats to protect them from cold.

The state of Minnesota, where Gary Paulsen and his dogs live, has a long history of commercial fur trapping and trading. Beavers and muskrats (inset) were heavily trapped for their warm fur, and beaver skins were considered a unit of money in the region until 1820.

AUTHOR PROFILE

Award Winner

As a child, Gary Paulsen was a voracious reader. Years later, when he was working as an aerospace engineer, he realized that he wanted to write professionally. He talked his way into a job as a magazine editor, where he began learning to write. In the next twelve years, he published 40 books of all kinds, over 200 articles and short stories, and two plays. In 1977, purely by chance, he was given a sled dog team. Working with the team and eventually running the Iditarod was a transforming experience for Paulsen and motivated him to write books such as *Canyons*, *The Haymeadow*, and *Mr. Tuckett*. His awards include the Newbery Honor Book (1986, 1988), the ALA's Best Young Adult Books (1983, 1984), and the New York Public Library's Books of the Teen Age (1980, 1981, 1982).

Building Background continued

Key Words

steeped: *completely filled with; absorbed in*

whirlpool: *water spinning swiftly around and around*

mystified: *puzzled or bewildered*

alleviate: *to make easier to bear; to relieve*

exaltation: *a feeling of great joy or pride*

awakening: *reviving*

dwelling: *a house or home*

chagrin: *a feeling of being embarrassed or annoyed*

Developing Vocabulary

Developing Definitions Work with students as they read the context sentences on Transparency 80 and create a definition for each underlined word.

Building Associations Use these questions to help students further develop vocabulary by associating key words with prior knowledge.

- **If you were steeped in knowledge about plants, would you know a lot about plants or nothing about plants?** *(a lot)*
- **What are some words that describe a whirlpool? (Sample:** *circular, powerful, wet)*
- **If you were mystified by a magic trick, would you understand how it was done?** *(no)*
- **What could you do to alleviate thirst while hiking in the desert? (Sample:** *take a drink of water)*
- **Would you feel greater exaltation from winning a race or from losing a race?** *(from winning a race)*
- **How do you feel after awakening from a sound sleep? (Sample:** *refreshed)*
- **Which kind of dwelling is constructed of bricks made of sun-dried clay—a pueblo or a wigwam?** *(a pueblo)*
- **If you accidentally dropped your friend's birthday cake, would your face show chagrin or happiness?** *(chagrin)*

Transparency 80

Developing Vocabulary

1. In order to write convincing historical fiction, an author must be steeped in information about the time period in which the story is set.
2. The oar was caught in a massive whirlpool and was sucked to the bottom of the lake.
3. Most people are mystified by professional magicians who seem to pull birds right out of the air.
4. Many people are attracted to the health care professions because of a strong desire to alleviate the suffering of others.
5. The director had a sense of exaltation and satisfaction when her play received a standing ovation.
6. The time he spent on the island turned out to be an awakening experience for Lester, causing him to look at his life in a new way.
7. As I looked out over the valley, I could see no home or dwelling of any kind.
8. A feeling of chagrin came over me when I realized I had left my notebook on the bus.

Practice Book 172

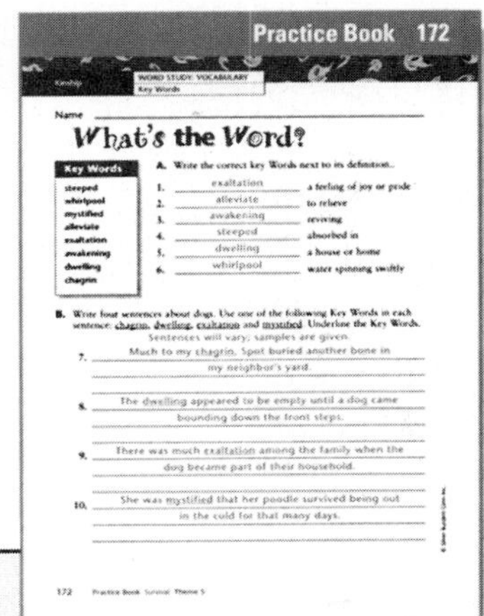

WORD STUDY: VOCABULARY
Key Words

Name

What's the Word?

Key Words: steeped, whirlpool, mystified, alleviate, exaltation, awakening, dwelling, chagrin

A. Write the correct key Words next to its definition.

1. exaltation — a feeling of joy or pride
2. alleviate — to relieve
3. awakening — reviving
4. steeped — absorbed in
5. dwelling — a house or home
6. whirlpool — water spinning swiftly

B. Write four sentences about dogs. Use one of the following Key Words in each sentence: chagrin, dwelling, exaltation and mystified. Underline the Key Words.

Sentences will vary; samples are given.

7. Much to my chagrin, Spot buried another bone in my neighbor's yard.
8. The dwelling appeared to be empty until a dog came bounding down the front steps.
9. There was much exaltation among the family when the dog became part of their household.
10. She was mystified that her poodle survived being out in the cold for that many days.

172 Practice Book Survival Theme 5

Meeting Individual Needs

English Language Support

Building Fluency You may wish to pair students acquiring English with more fluent partners. Have pairs work together to understand each vocabulary word, using pictures, gestures, context sentences, and cognates in other languages to work out definitions. Pairs who are having difficulty with a word may ask for help from another pair.

Optional Independent Practice
Practice Book page 172 gives students extra practice in learning key words from the selection.

English Language Support This component provides additional help in building vocabulary and concepts for "Kinship."

Spelling Preview

Endings *(-ion, -tion,* and *-sion)* The selection includes several words with the endings *-ion, -tion,* and *-sion.* Invite students to keep track of these and other interesting words as they read the story. See the Spelling Workshop on page T923 for a minilesson on these word endings.

The pretest and posttest for these words can be found on page R24 of the Teacher's Resource Section.

* *Word or form of the word appears in the selection.*

Spelling Support

Spelling Strategy As students read "Kinship" and do related writing, they will encounter words they find difficult to spell. Explain that one good strategy for learning new words is to think of related words. For example, knowing that *infect* and *infection* are related will help students realize that the */sh/* sound in *infection* is spelled by the letter *t* (rather than *s,* for example).

Kinship

from *Woodsong* by Gary Paulsen

Prereading Strategies

Preview and Predict: Nonfiction
Invite students to preview the first two pages of "Kinship." Then have them predict what they will learn from the selection. Prompt them with questions like *Why is the selection called "Kinship"? Why is cold weather important to the story? Can you guess why the narrator is telling the story?*

Set Purposes
Prompt students to fill in the "W" section of their KWL charts. They should note what they want to learn from the selection about dogs, sledding, survival, or other topics suggested by their preview.

Meeting Individual Needs

Reading Options

- Independent Reading
- **Supported Reading**
- Teacher Read Aloud
- Cooperative Reading

Most students will be able to read "Kinship" without major difficulties, but you should be ready to give support. Have students begin reading on their own, and suggest strategies provided in the notes as needed.

SLED DOGS	
K	• Dogs pull sled over snow. • Dog sledding takes place in Alaska.
W	• How did Columbia's behavior show a sense of humor? • How did Columbia's sense of humor convince the author to stop trapping?
L	

Author's Craft 

Genre By using the pronoun *I*, the author gives readers a clue that this selection is autobiography. Help students recall that autobiography is a form of nonfiction—the events in the story really happened. An autobiographical narrative does not recount every detail of the author's life, however. For "Kinship," Gary Paulsen selected certain significant events from his life and put them together to create a meaningful story.

Comprehension

Author's Purpose Point out the phrase *as with many changes*. Tell students that dashes allow a writer to insert a comment on the rest of the sentence. Here, it provides a clue to the author's purpose for writing the selection. Ask students what the phrase reveals. (Sample: *The author wants to tell readers about the many changes his dogs have caused.*)

Challenge

Researching a Controversial Issue Hunting and trapping are frequently criticized by environmentalists and animal-rights activists. Interested students can use the *Readers' Guide to Periodical Literature* to find articles (both pro and con) about hunting and trapping. They might also investigate controversies in their community through local newspapers or by interviewing local officials.

Comprehension Support

Story Tape Students who need additional support can listen to the selection on the Survival Story Tape.

Reading Strategy

Visualize
Prompt students to visualize the arrangement of the kennel area. Point out that each dog is chained so that it can move in a circle. You might model the strategy for students.

Think Aloud
Each dog has a house; it must be located inside his circle. The kennel probably covers a large area, with the dogs' circles next to and across from each other. As I read about Columbia's prank, I realize that the dogs' circles nearly touch but do not overlap.

Vocabulary

Compound Words Remind students that a compound word is two words put together. Ask them to find four compound words on pages 402–403. (Sample: *notebook, something, outside, anything, everything*)

Further Instruction:
Compound Words on page T916

Meeting Individual Needs

Comprehension Support

Building Meaning Invite students to use a chart to describe the dogs' lives in the summer. They might list boredom, Bone Wars, chewing on bones, and running with wheeled carts. See if they can find clues to other aspects of their life. Encourage the students to add an additional column to their charts for words that describe the dogs' winter activities later in the selection.

A Dog's Life	
Summer	**Winter**
runs wheeled carts	runs sleds
boredom	
Bone Wars	
chews bones	

Comprehension

Compare/Contrast The author gives many details about Olaf and Columbia so that readers will understand their actions. The dogs have some characteristics in common, but they are also different in many ways. Students may use a Venn diagram to keep track of Olaf's and Columbia's traits. Their diagrams should list ways in which the two dogs are similar as well as ways in which they differ.

Further Instruction:
Compare/Contrast on pages T914–915

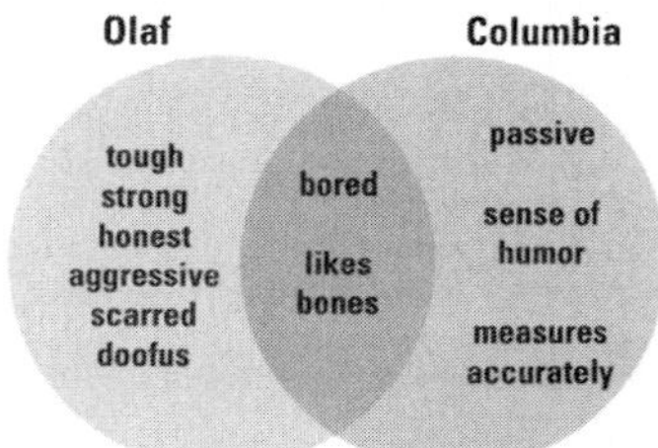

English Language Support

Building Fluency Draw students' attention to these adjectives on pages 402–403: *aggressive, good, strong, honest, tough, dumb, smart, big.* Discuss their meanings in the story. Model sentences using the words: *Would it be fair to call Olaf strong? Yes, he was certainly strong.* Then write each word on an index card and have students pick words, formulate questions using them, and let partners answer.

Reading Strategy

Check Predictions

Prompt students to check their predictions about why the author is telling this story. You might direct them to the sentence *I wanted to run them and learn from them* on page 404.

Author's Craft

Characterization Have students find words Paulsen uses to describe his dogs' unique personalities and actions. (Sample: *posturing and bragging, honest, argue, laughed*)

Theme Also point out that many of these words are usually associated with humans rather than animals. Ask students how this might be related to Paulsen's message, or theme. (Sample: *It suggests that there is a kinship between dogs and humans.*)

Further Instruction:
Theme on pages T912–913

Meeting Individual Needs

INFORMAL ASSESSMENT
COMPREHENSION

Comprehension Check

1. *Which of Olaf's characteristics did Columbia observe and use to trick him?* (Sample: *aggressiveness, determination, stupidity*)
2. *What trait shown by Columbia caused the author to make a change in his life?* (*Columbia's sense of humor made Paulsen decide to stop trapping and killing animals.*)

Critical Thinking

3. *Why might the author want to share this story with other people?* (Sample: *He might hope that others will stop killing animals, too.*)

Appreciating Multilingualism 

Share Knowledge Point out that *gully* and *canyon* name similar landforms (channels cut into the earth by running water) that differ in size. Ask students to identify words in other languages that have a similar relationship. Translations of *hill/mountain*, *grotto/cave*, and *stream/river* are other examples.

English	Spanish	Pronunciation
gully	la hondonada	lah ohn-doh-NAH-dah
canyon	el cañón	ehl kah-NYOHN

Appreciating Cultural Diversity 

Appreciation and Acceptance Point out that different cultures have differing ideas about killing and eating animals. Students might share their own ideas on this topic.

Challenge

Diagraming a Dogsled Students who have an interest in how things work might investigate the construction of a dogsled. They could draw a diagram of the brake mechanism and explain its operation. Mushers usually run beside the sled but sometimes ride on its runners. The students might explain what factors determine the musher's choice of action.

Students with mechanical aptitudes will enjoy investigating how brakes work as a way to enrich their experience with this selection.

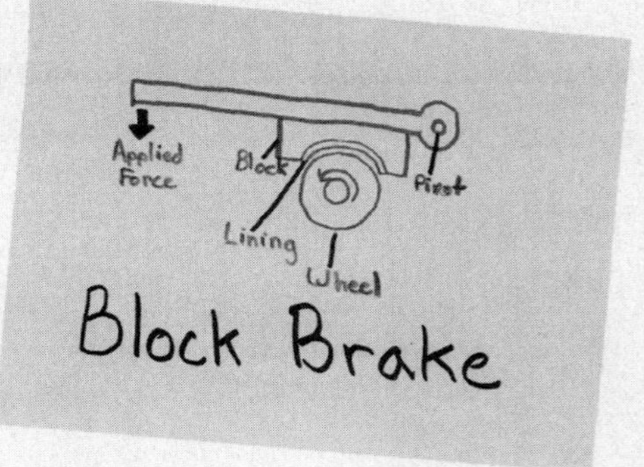

Reading Strategies

Fix-up Strategy: Reread
Have students stop reading after Paulsen describes landing on his injured knee and ask themselves if they have understood how he came to be lying on the frozen pond. If the sequence of events is unclear, they might go back and reread the section that begins on page 405 with the words *There was a point where an old logging trail.*

Visualize
As students read or reread the section describing Paulsen's fall, suggest that they visualize each event as it happens. They should try to create a vivid mental picture of the landscape: the gully, the stream, the waterfall, and the frozen pond below.

Meeting Individual Needs

Comprehension Support

Connecting to Personal Experience Many students will be able to connect with Gary Paulsen's response to his injury. Some of them may have bumped their heads and "seen stars." Others may have fallen while playing a game and required a few minutes to shake off the fall's effects. Invite students to chart Paulsen's reaction to his injury and check off the responses that are familiar.

Paulsen's Reactions	Personal Experiences
"brain exploded"	
screamed	✓
eyes closed	✓
squirmed	
shock, pain in waves	✓
minutes seem like hours	✓

Comprehension

Making Inferences Have students review the author's assessment of his situation as he lies on the ice: the dogs have left (he assumes); he cannot walk; he is miles from the nearest dwelling. Remind them of the description of cold weather's effects on page 400. Ask students to infer, from these details, what fears may be in Gary Paulsen's mind at this point. (Sample: *that he might freeze to death before anyone rescues him*)

Phonics Support

Long *i* Point out the words *whined* and *whining* in the eighth paragraph. Both are forms of *whine* and have the same long *i* sound even though they do not end in a silent *e.* Remind students that a word with a long vowel and silent *e* simply adds *d* to form the past tense; it drops the *e* and adds *ing* to form the participle. The vowel remains long. Students may list other long-*i* words in their notebooks.

INFORMAL ASSESSMENT
CHECKLIST

Learning Goal
Students can use their knowledge of text structure to construct meaning.

Performance Indicators

- ☑ Students can identify main ideas and supporting details.
- ☑ Students can discuss the theme and setting of a selection.
- ☑ Students can use their understanding of genre to discuss aspects of the selection.

Reading Strategy

KWL
After reading, students can fill in the "L" sections of their KWL charts. Have them review the "K" and "W" sections for accuracy and to see if their questions were answered.

Meeting Individual Needs

INFORMAL ASSESSMENT
COMPREHENSION

Comprehension Check

1. *What events showed Paulsen that the dogs could teach him?* (Sample: *Columbia's sense of humor; Obeah's rescue effort*)
2. *How did these events lead him to this conclusion?* (Sample: *They showed the dogs were smarter and wiser than he expected.*)

Critical Thinking

3. *How can we learn from animals?* (Sample: *Observe their actions and thought processes; trust them to help make decisions.*)

SLED DOGS	
K	• Dogs pull sled over snow. • Dog sledding takes place in Alaska.
W	• How did Columbia's behavior show a sense of humor? • How did Columbia's sense of humor convince the author to stop trapping?
L	• Columbia planned a joke on Olaf and then laughed about it. • Paulsen realized that if Columbia could plan a joke, other animals could be very smart, too.

IN RESPONSE

Learning From Dogs

Gary Paulsen says, "The dogs could teach me." Write a brief newspaper article describing what Mr. Paulsen might learn from or about his dogs. Include examples from the story.

Looking for Insight

In a group, discuss what happened to Mr. Paulsen as he watched Columbia push the bone toward Olaf. What did Mr. Paulsen see in the dogs' actions? How did he react to what he saw? How do you think you would react if you had seen the dogs' actions?

AUTHOR AT WORK

Gary Paulsen recalls changing schools often and receiving average or below-average grades. Then a librarian gave him a library card. "When she handed me the card, she handed me the world. . . . It was as though I had been dying of thirst and the librarian had handed me a five-gallon bucket of water. I drank and drank."

Of writing Mr. Paulsen says, "I write because that's all I can do. Every time I've tried to do something else I cannot, and have to come back to writing, though often I hate it—hate it and love it." He has managed to write over two hundred articles and nearly forty books.

★ Award-winning Author

Another Book by . . .

Gary Paulsen

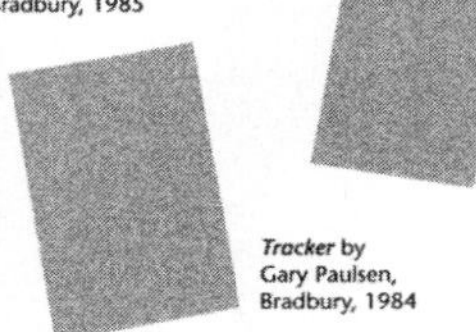

Dogsong by Gary Paulsen, Bradbury, 1985

Tracker by Gary Paulsen, Bradbury, 1984

Library Link This story was taken from *Woodsong* by Gary Paulsen. You might enjoy reading the entire book to learn more about Paulsen's experiences with his dogs.

409

In Response

Learning from Dogs You may wish to review the structure of newspaper articles with students before they begin writing.

Looking for Insight Encourage students to draw on their own experiences with animals as they discuss.

Other Books

by Gary Paulsen

Dogsong A Village elder helps 14-year-old Russel to understand the traditional ways of his people. Russel also learns how to rely on himself in the Alaskan wilderness.

Tracker Thirteen-year-old John has an experience while hunting in the Minnesota woods that helps him cope with the imminent death of his grandfather.

ESL Spanish-speaking Students

Help students to appreciate the diversity of Gary Paulsen's career "detours" by explaining something about each career he has tried. Encourage students to provide this information cooperatively for the jobs that are familiar to them.

English	Spanish	Pronunciation
teacher	maestro / a	mah-EHS-troh
field engineer	ingeniero de campo	een-heh-nee-EH-roh deh KAHN-poh
soldier	soldado	sohl-DAH-doh
farmer	hacendado	ah-sehn-DAH-doh
truck driver	camionero	kah-mee-oh-NEH-roh
trapper	cazador con trampas	kah-sah-DOHR kohn trahm-PAHS
archer	flechero	fleh-CHEH-roh

Responding

Personal Response

Suggest that students record their responses to "Kinship" in their personal journals. To stimulate writing ideas, you might ask such questions as:

- **How did reading "Kinship" make you feel about Gary Paulsen's dogs and about other animals?**
- **What questions would you like to ask Gary Paulsen?**
- **Did Paulsen's experiences remind you of any experiences you have had with animals?**

Students may speculate about why Gary Paulsen wrote the selection the way he did. How did the story of Columbia's joke and the story of Obeah's rescue effort support the author's theme? Students may also wish to draw a sketch of their favorite part of the selection.

Drawing a favorite scene reinforces students' comprehension while allowing them to respond creatively to the selection.

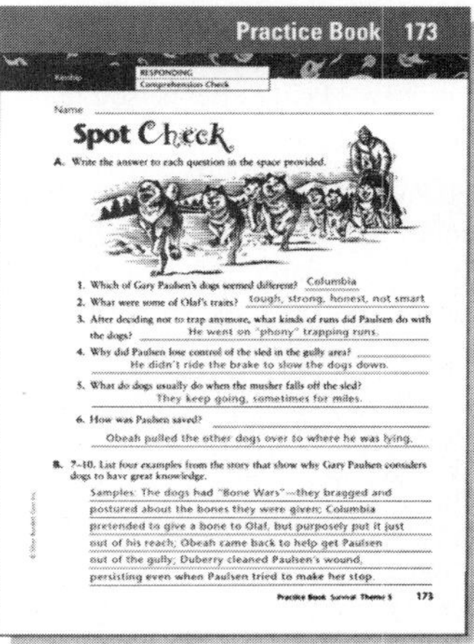

Practice Book 173

RESPONDING
Comprehension Check

Name ________

Spot Check

A. Write the answer to each question in the space provided.

1. Which of Gary Paulsen's dogs seemed different? Columbia
2. What were some of Olaf's traits? tough, strong, honest, not smart
3. After deciding not to trap anymore, what kinds of runs did Paulsen do with the dogs? He went on "phony" trapping runs.
4. Why did Paulsen lose control of the sled in the gully area? He didn't ride the brake to slow the dogs down.
5. What do dogs usually do when the musher falls off the sled? They keep going, sometimes for miles.
6. How was Paulsen saved? Obeah pulled the other dogs over to where he was lying.

B. 7–10. List four examples from the story that show why Gary Paulsen considers dogs to have great knowledge.
Samples: The dogs had "Bone Wars"—they bragged and postured about the bones they were given; Columbia pretended to give a bone to Olaf, but purposely put it just out of his reach; Obeah came back to help get Paulsen out of the gully; Duberry cleaned Paulsen's wound, persisting even when Paulsen tried to make her stop.

Practice Book Survival Theme 5 173

▲ **Optional Independent Practice Practice Book page 173 provides a comprehension check for the selection.**

Reader Response Groups

Have students form small discussion groups to discuss their responses to the selection. The notes and questions they recorded in their journals should provide ideas. Students from each group may then share any particularly interesting issues or unresolved questions with the class.

Creative Response

The following suggestions give students the opportunity to respond creatively to "Kinship."

Write Write a short story or an autobiographical account about a sixth grader who learns something from an experience with an animal. The animal might be a pet or a wild animal, and the writing may be from the point of view of either the person or the animal.

Role-play Pretend you are one of the dogs mentioned in "Kinship." Working with a group of your classmates, role-play one of the scenes from the selection, such as Columbia's joke on Olaf or Obeah's rescue of Gary Paulsen. Say aloud what thoughts and feelings you think are going through the dog's mind.

Design Create a board game based on Gary Paulsen's life. Include the experiences described in "Kinship" as well as other adventures he might have while running his sled dogs.

Critical Response

Ask students whether, after reading "Kinship," they are convinced that dogs have senses of humor, can use reasoning to solve problems, and have emotions such as compassion, anger, love, and concern. If they accept Paulsen's argument about dogs, do they agree that it applies to other animals as well? Students may work independently or in small groups to develop arguments for their positions and then share these arguments with the class.

Creating a board game requires students to use logical reasoning skills as well as imagination.

MAKING CONNECTIONS

Reflecting on the Theme

Invite students to discuss what "Kinship" says about survival. For example, is survival a matter of instinct, careful planning, or sheer luck? Is it easier to survive alone or in cooperation with others? Students may begin by discussing these questions in small groups and then share the results of these discussions with the entire class.

Connecting Across Literature

Students might compare Gary Paulsen's experiences with his sled dogs to Jack's experiences with Peanut in the story "Rabies." Although Jack's relationship with Peanut is an antagonistic one, he must figure out how the dog's mind works in order to track him down. Once he finds Peanut, he feels compassion for the dog, who is frightened and confused.

English Language Support This component provides additional help for reading and responding to "Kinship."

Literature: Story Structure

Theme

Skills Trace	Theme
Introduce	T912–913
Reteach	T913

1 Teach

Teaching from the Literature Explain that the theme of a piece of writing is the central message or idea that the author wants readers to understand. The theme is usually not stated directly; instead, readers must analyze the setting, characters, and plot in order to identify the theme.

To begin a discussion of the theme of "Kinship," you might prompt students to talk about what Gary Paulsen learned from each of the following incidents.

- the dogs' nervousness at the edge of the frozen whirlpool
- Columbia's conscious prank on Olaf
- the dogs' rescue of Paulsen

Write any preliminary theme statements that students suggest on the board. Then call on a volunteer to read aloud the closing passage on page 408.

Literature Connection

> ...later I thought of the dogs.
>
> How they came back to help me, perhaps to save me. I knew that somewhere in the dogs, in their humor and the way they thought, they had great, old knowledge; they had something we had lost.
>
> And the dogs could teach me.
>
> —Gary Paulsen, "Kinship"

Ask students whether they think this passage contains a direct statement of Paulsen's theme and, if so, what it is. (Sample: *"I knew that somewhere in the dogs...they had great, old knowledge...And the dogs could teach me."*) Suggest that a better theme statement might be slightly broader or more general, taking into account everything Paulsen learned in the experiences described in the selection.

2 Practice

Developing Independence Have students work in pairs to further discuss the theme of "Kinship." You might display Transparency 81 while students are working.

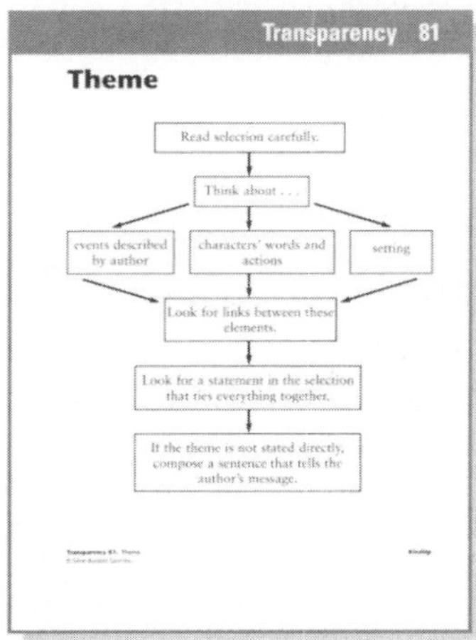

Students might follow these steps as they work with their partners.

- First, write in their own words the theme of "Kinship"; that is, what they think the author wanted readers to understand.
- Then, reread the selection together to find support for their theme idea. They may decide to modify their theme statement based on evidence from the selection.
- Next, finalize their theme statements based on their rereading and discussion.
- Finally, present the theme and supporting passages to another pair of students for discussion.

You might ask volunteers to present final versions of their theme statements to the class. (Sample: *Dogs, and perhaps all animals, have much to teach people if we seek their knowledge rather than just use them for our own narrow purposes.*)

3 Apply

Going Beyond the Literature Ask students to return to the story "Aunt Millicent" in Theme 4 of the Collection. Have pairs of students work together to develop theme statements for the story, following the same steps they used for "Kinship." Encourage a lively debate among the pairs of students when they meet as a class to discuss their theme statements. Remind them that a story may have more than one theme woven together. The important issue is whether they can support their ideas with evidence from the story. The following themes may emerge from students' discussions.

- A good fantasy can change reality.
- Stories and rumors often take on a life of their own.
- Tell one lie and you'll probably have to tell another.

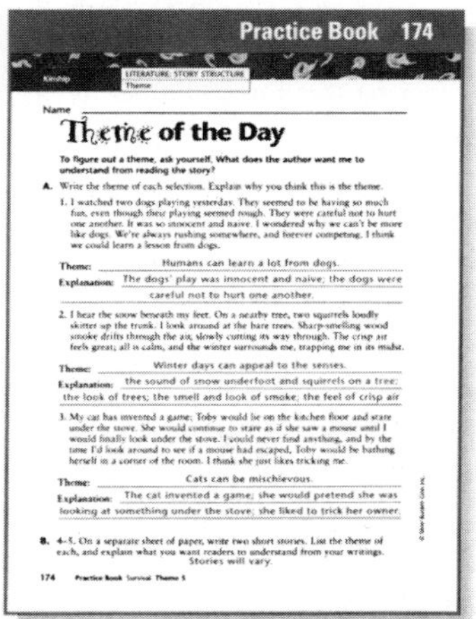
Practice Book 174

LITERATURE: STORY STRUCTURE
Theme

Name ______

Theme of the Day

To figure out a theme, ask yourself, What does the author want me to understand from reading the story?

A. Write the theme of each selection. Explain why you think this is the theme.

1. I watched two dogs playing yesterday. They seemed to be having so much fun, even though their playing seemed rough. They were careful not to hurt one another. It was so innocent and naive. I wondered why we can't be more like dogs. We're always rushing somewhere, and forever competing. I think we could learn a lesson from dogs.

Theme: Humans can learn a lot from dogs.

Explanation: The dogs' play was innocent and naive; the dogs were careful not to hurt one another.

2. I hear the snow beneath my feet. On a nearby tree, two squirrels loudly skitter up the trunk. I look around at the bare trees. Sharp-smelling wood smoke drifts through the air, slowly cutting its way through. The crisp air feels great; all is calm, and the winter surrounds me, trapping me in its midst.

Theme: Winter days can appeal to the senses.

Explanation: the sound of snow underfoot and squirrels on a tree; the look of trees; the smell and look of smoke; the feel of crisp air

3. My cat has invented a game; Toby would lie on the kitchen floor and stare under the stove. She would continue to stare as if she saw a mouse until I would finally look under the stove. I would never find anything, and by the time I'd look around to see if a mouse had escaped, Toby would be bathing herself in a corner of the room. I think she just likes tricking me.

Theme: Cats can be mischievous.

Explanation: The cat invented a game; she would pretend she was looking at something under the stove; she liked to trick her owner.

B. 4–5. On a separate sheet of paper, write two short stories. List the theme of each, and explain what you want readers to understand from your writings. Stories will vary.

174 Practice Book Survival Theme 5

◀ Optional Independent Practice

Students can work in pairs to complete Practice Book page 174.

Meeting Individual Needs

Reteach

Auditory Activity Have students work in small groups. Suggest a theme for each group and have students relate incidents from their experiences that illustrate the theme. Possible themes are "A friend can really help in a bad situation," "Persistence pays off," and "We can learn from our parents."

Further Support

See SourceBank, Reteaching page 17.

Comprehension

Compare/Contrast

Skills Trace	Compare/ Contrast
Introduce	T394–395
Review	T914–915
Assess	T439, T1097
Reteach	T395, T915

1 Review

Teaching from the Literature Remind students that authors often use comparisons and contrasts to highlight certain aspects of their topics. One way to describe something vividly is to say how it is similar to or different from some other thing. Sometimes, especially in short texts, the author will make explicit comparisons with signal words such as *all, always, both, every, also, same,* and *similar.* Explicit contrasts might be signaled with words such as *on the other hand, however, now/then,* and *before/after.*

One way students can understand Gary Paulsen's "Kinship" is to compare his attitudes and activities before and after he watched his dog Columbia trick Olaf. Read aloud the following paragraph that discusses the turning point in Paulsen's life.

Literature Connection

After a time I stopped trapping. That change—as with many changes—occurred because of the dogs. As mentioned, I had hunted when I was young, trapping and killing many animals. I never thought it was wrong until the dogs came. And then it was a simple thing, almost a silly thing, that caused the changes.

Columbia had a sense of humor and I saw it.

—Gary Paulsen, "Kinship"

Then work with students to create a Venn diagram comparing and contrasting Paulsen's life before and after Columbia's prank. Following is an example of some of the responses you might elicit from students.

2 Practice

Developing Independence Remind students that one way to compare and contrast two or more things is to create a diagram to summarize the characteristics of each. A Venn diagram like the one used in this lesson is perhaps the most common type of diagram used for this purpose. Transparency 82 shows another example.

Transparency 82

Compare/Contrast

"Kinship"	"Rabies"	
	Similar	Different
nonfiction		
dogs as major characters		
speaker is male		
speaker writes for a living		
speaker is injured		
tone is not humorous		

Sentences to describe comparison/contrast: ___________

To give students practice in comparing and contrasting, display Transparency 82 and have them work in pairs to list characteristics of "Kinship." They should then decide whether each characteristic is similar to or different from the Collection story "Rabies." When they have completed this, they might write sentences—using signal words when appropriate—that express the information in their charts. (Sample: *Both "Kinship" and "Rabies" have dogs as major characters. "Kinship," however, is nonfiction, whereas "Rabies" is fiction.*)

3 Apply

Going Beyond the Literature Have students write two short descriptions using their compare/contrast skills. The first description should include signal words to make comparisons or contrasts; the second should make them without using signal words. Encourage students to use Venn diagrams to plan their writing. Following are some suggested topics.

Compare/contrast the interests, habits, and appearances of two friends or relatives.

Compare/contrast the goals, strategies, and players of three sports.

Describe two stories read recently, including the similarities and differences between their genres, plots, characters, or themes.

Compare and contrast the strategies, action, and graphics of several computer or video games.

Meeting Individual Needs

Reteach

Visual/Auditory Activity Display photographs of two related and familiar events—e.g., a baseball game and a wrestling match, a rock band and a solo saxophone player—or play brief excerpts of two different types of music. Ask students to talk about ways in which the things are different and similar.

Further Support
See SourceBank, Reteaching page 27.

Challenge

Extending Meaning Have students conduct research to compare what Paulsen calls the "knowledge" of animals such as wolves, dolphins, and dogs to the knowledge that humans have. What traits do humans and animals share? What differences do we have? Students may want to limit the scope of their research, for example, to forms of communication or kinship structures.

Word Study: Vocabulary

Compound Words

Skills Trace	Compound Words
Introduce	T40–41
Review	T126, T916
Reteach	T41, T126, T916

1 Review

Teaching from the Literature Remind students that a compound word is formed from two words put together. A compound word may appear as a single word (*notebook*), as two separate words (*sled runner*), or as a hyphenated word (*short-sighted*). Write these sentences from "Kinship" on the board. Have volunteers identify the compound words and discuss how knowing the words that compose them helps reveal their meanings.

Forty, fifty, even sixty below zero—actual temperature, not windchill*—seems to change everything. (p. 400)*

There was a point where an old logging trail went through a small, sharp-sided *gully—a tiny canyon. (p. 405)*

When things settled down to something I could control, I opened my eyes and saw that my snow pants *and the jeans beneath were ripped in a jagged line for about a foot. (p. 407)*

2 Practice/Apply

Going Beyond the Literature To give students practice in recognizing and defining compounds, write *wind* at the center of a word web and compounds formed with *wind* around it. Discuss the meanings of these compounds and how they relate to the meaning of *wind*.

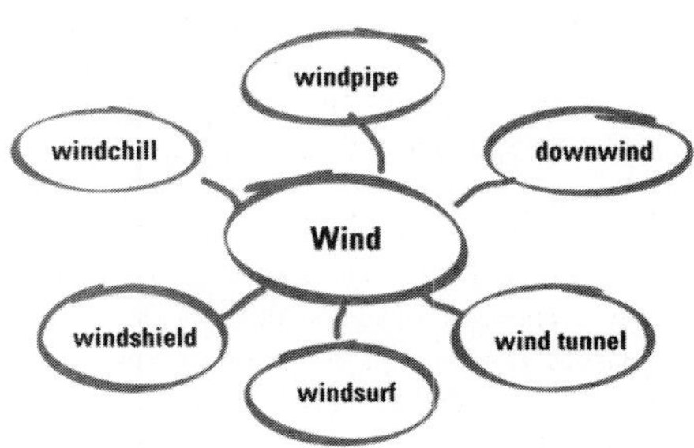

Meeting Individual Needs

Reteach

Hands-on Activity Work with students to make a collection of word cards with a single word that can be used to form compound words written on each. Then have students match up words to create compounds and then define them. They can verify the spellings by checking a dictionary.

Optional Independent Practice Practice Book page 176 gives students additional practice with compound words.

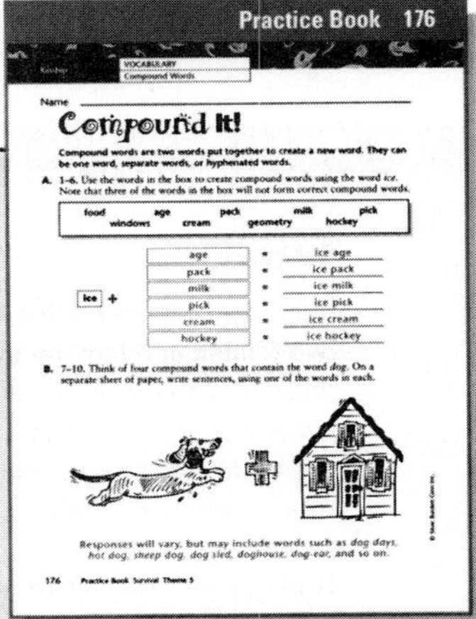

Practice Book 176

Kinship | VOCABULARY Compound Words

Name ______

Compound It!

Compound words are two words put together to create a new word. They can be one word, separate words, or hyphenated words.

A. 1–6. Use the words in the box to create compound words using the word *ice*. Note that three of the words in the box will not form correct compound words.

food age pack milk pick windows cream geometry hockey

ice + age = ice age
ice + pack = ice pack
ice + milk = ice milk
ice + pick = ice pick
ice + cream = ice cream
ice + hockey = ice hockey

B. 7–10. Think of four compound words that contain the word *dog*. On a separate sheet of paper, write sentences, using one of the words in each.

Responses will vary, but may include words such as *dog days, hot dog, sheep dog, dog sled, doghouse, dog-ear,* and so on.

176 Practice Book Survival Theme 5

Study Skills

Forms/Applications

Skills Trace	Forms/ Applications
Introduce	T917
Reteach	T917

1 Teach

Teaching from the Literature Recall with students that Gary Paulsen trains his dogs for the Iditarod race. To enter the race, mushers must submit an application and pay an entry fee. Many events and organizations require applications for entry or membership. You may wish to display Transparency 83, which gives some general guidelines for filling out forms and applications. Discuss some instances in which students might need to complete forms, and have them explain why following the guidelines is important.

Transparency 83

Forms/Applications

How to Complete an Application

1. Skim the entire form to see what is required. You may need to locate information at home before you can complete it.
2. Note directions, such as "Please Print," that apply throughout.
3. Provide all information requested.
4. Fit each answer into the space provided.
5. Write neatly; spell all words correctly.
6. Reread your answers before signing the form to make sure they are readable and accurate.

2 Practice/Apply

Going Beyond the Literature Ask students to bring to class blank copies of forms and applications they have completed in the past few months. Make photocopies or use an overhead projector to display a sampling of the forms. Ask the student who brought each one to teach others to fill it out.

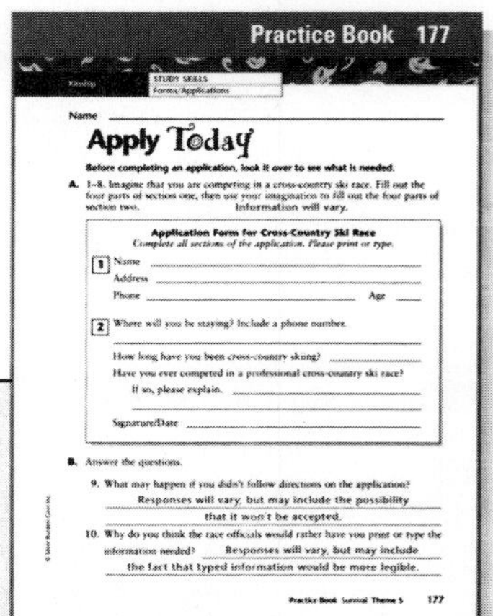
Practice Book 177

Kinship | STUDY SKILLS Forms/Applications

Name ____

Apply Today

Before completing an application, look it over to see what is needed.

A. 1–8. Imagine that you are competing in a cross-country ski race. Fill out the four parts of section one, then use your imagination to fill out the four parts of section two. Information will vary.

Application Form for Cross-Country Ski Race
Complete all sections of the application. Please print or type.

1 Name ____
Address ____
Phone ____ Age ____

2 Where will you be staying? Include a phone number.
____
How long have you been cross-country skiing? ____
Have you ever competed in a professional cross-country ski race?
If so, please explain. ____
____
Signature/Date ____

B. Answer the questions.

9. What may happen if you didn't follow directions on the application?
Responses will vary, but may include the possibility that it won't be accepted.

10. Why do you think the race officials would rather have you print or type the information needed? Responses will vary, but may include the fact that typed information would be more legible.

Practice Book Survival Theme 5 177

▲
Optional Independent Practice
Students can work individually to complete Practice Book page 177.

Meeting Individual Needs

Reteach

Hands-on Activity Work with students to fill out forms obtained in your local area, such as the application for a library card, a local youth organization, or a business that employs young people. Model the process taught above and review the vocabulary and abbreviations that may appear on these forms.

Further Support
See SourceBank, Reteaching page 57.

Writing Workshop

Using Sensory Words

1 Teach

Ask a volunteer to read aloud the first three paragraphs of "Kinship." Remind students that the five senses are sight, sound, touch (or feeling), smell, and taste, and ask them which senses the writer appealed to in these paragraphs. (*sight, sound, feeling*) Then ask which sense dominates the description. (*feeling*) Tell students that writers can appeal to all five senses in a description but that often one sense dominates.

Ask students to reach into their memory and draw out a sight, sound, smell, taste, or feeling that left a strong impression on them. Have them share their experience with the class by using sensory words and phrases to describe it.

Spark a discussion on the importance of using sensory images in descriptive writing by asking students how Gary Paulsen was able to communicate the sense of extreme cold so effectively. Guide them to understand that sensory words help readers enter a scene in their imagination and experience what the writer is describing.

Call attention to Transparency 84 and invite students to study the list. Ask them to consider the words on the list and to name specific people, animals, objects, or settings that the words might describe. Then have students read the first sentence and identify the sensory words. Ask them where the terms *ring* and *filled with diamonds* would appear on the list. Continue with the rest of the sentences. Encourage students to skim through "Kinship" to find other sensory words and phrases to add to the list.

Transparency 84

Using Sensory Words

Sight	Sound	Smell	Taste	Touch
narrow	screech	musty	sweet	greasy
bright	soothing	spoiled	bitter	pointed
round	splash	sharp	spicy	smooth
scarlet	loud	mildewy	salty	fuzzy

Sound seems to ring and the very air seems to be filled with diamonds when ice crystals form.

Sometimes dogs . . . will hold their bones up in the air, look at each other, raise their hair, and start growling at each other.

Columbia leaned back and laughed. "Heh, heh, heh . . ."

. . . the jeans beneath were ripped in a jagged line for about a foot.

Shock and pain came in waves and I had to close my eyes.

I heard some more whining and growling, then a scrabbling sound.

Optional Independent Practice
Practice Book page 178 gives students extra practice in using sensory words.

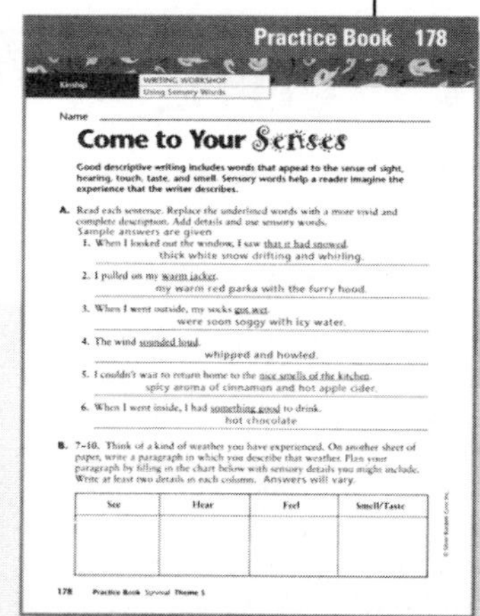

Practice Book 178

Kinship | WRITING WORKSHOP Using Sensory Words

Name ______

Come to Your Senses

Good descriptive writing includes words that appeal to the sense of sight, hearing, touch, taste, and smell. Sensory words help a reader imagine the experience that the writer describes.

A. Read each sentence. Replace the underlined words with a more vivid and complete description. Add details and use sensory words.
Sample answers are given

1. When I looked out the window, I saw that it had snowed.
   thick white snow drifting and whirling.
2. I pulled on my warm jacket.
   my warm red parka with the furry hood.
3. When I went outside, my socks got wet.
   were soon soggy with icy water.
4. The wind sounded loud.
   whipped and howled.
5. I couldn't wait to return home to the nice smells of the kitchen.
   spicy aroma of cinnamon and hot apple cider.
6. When I went inside, I had something good to drink.
   hot chocolate

B. 7–10. Think of a kind of weather you have experienced. On another sheet of paper, write a paragraph in which you describe that weather. Plan your paragraph by filling in the chart below with sensory details you might include. Write at least two details in each column. Answers will vary.

See	Hear	Feel	Smell/Taste

178 Practice Book Survival Theme 5

2 Practice

In different areas of the board, write *dog*, *eating pizza*, and *concert*. Using each word or phrase as the center of a word web, have students brainstorm for sensory words and phrases that could be used in a description of the subject, such as the following.

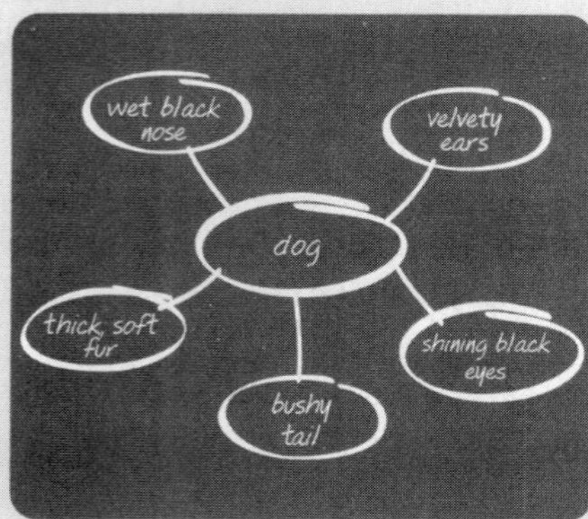

Remind students to consider all five senses as they imagine and suggest images for each subject. As students develop each cluster, ask them to notice which sense most of their words and phrases appeal to, and whether any of the senses are being left out. For example, the description of *eating pizza* should focus on taste, smell, and touch. The description of *concert* should focus on sound and sight.

3 Apply

Challenge students to write a paragraph in which they describe something without mentioning what they are describing. Remind them to use sensory words and phrases that appeal to as many of the five senses as possible. When they have written a draft, have them read it aloud to a partner to see if their partner can identify the subject. Encourage students to point out parts that were especially vivid and parts that need to be made clearer. Students can revise their work according to their classmate's suggestions and make a final copy.

REVISING TIPS

Sensory Words

Have students revise the word choices in their paragraphs.

- Did I include enough details to help the reader imagine what I am describing?
- Did I include details that appeal to a variety of senses?

Grammar Workshop

Adverbs

Oral Language Options

Ask students to find sentences with adverbs in the selection. Have volunteers read their sentences, identify the adverbs, and give the verbs, adjectives, or adverbs they describe.

1 Teach

On the board, write the following sentences from "Kinship."

> He was sitting quietly on the outside edge of his circle, at the maximum length of his chain.
> While Columbia was relatively passive, Olaf was very aggressive.

Have students identify the verb in the first sentence. (*was sitting*) Tell students that a word that describes a verb is an adverb and that many adverbs end in *-ly*. Ask them to point out the adverb in the first sentence. (*quietly*) Then tell students that an adverb can also describe an adjective or another adverb. Ask a volunteer to read the second sentence and to name the adjectives. (*passive, aggressive*) Have a volunteer identify the adverb that describes each adjective. (*relatively, very*) Point out that *very* is an adverb that does not end in *-ly*.

Daily Language Activities

The sentences on page R13 of the Teacher's Resource Section feature the grammar concepts taught in this lesson.

2 Practice/Apply

Write the following sentences on the board. Have students identify each adverb, the word it describes, and the part of speech of that word.

I was terribly afraid. (*terribly*, describes the adjective *afraid*)

We were going too fast. (*fast*, describes the verb *were going*; *too*, describes the adverb *fast*)

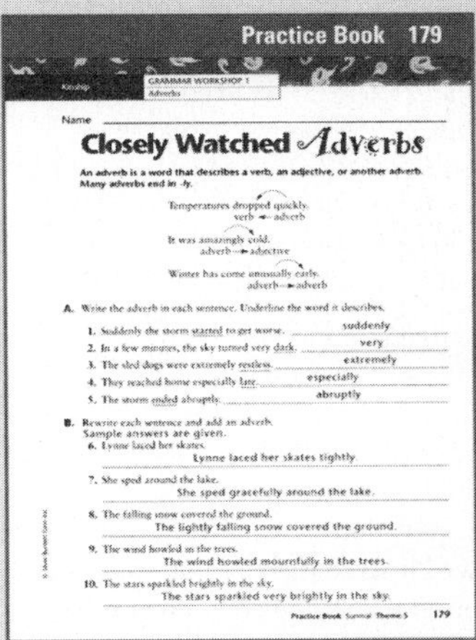
Practice Book 179

Kinship | GRAMMAR WORKSHOP 1 Adverbs

Name ______

Closely Watched Adverbs

An adverb is a word that describes a verb, an adjective, or another adverb. Many adverbs end in -ly.

Temperatures dropped quickly.
verb ← adverb

It was amazingly cold.
adverb → adjective

Winter has come unusually early.
adverb → adverb

A. Write the adverb in each sentence. Underline the word it describes.

1. Suddenly the storm started to get worse. suddenly
2. In a few minutes, the sky turned very dark. very
3. The sled dogs were extremely restless. extremely
4. They reached home especially late. especially
5. The storm ended abruptly. abruptly

B. Rewrite each sentence and add an adverb.
Sample answers are given.

6. Lynne laced her skates.
Lynne laced her skates tightly.
7. She sped around the lake.
She sped gracefully around the lake.
8. The falling snow covered the ground.
The lightly falling snow covered the ground.
9. The wind howled in the trees.
The wind howled mournfully in the trees.
10. The stars sparkled brightly in the sky.
The stars sparkled very brightly in the sky.

Practice Book Survival Theme 5 179

▲ **Optional Independent Practice**
Practice Book page 179 provides practice in using adverbs.

Reteach See SourceBank page 92.

Adverbs of Time, Place, and Manner

1 Teach

On the board, write the following sentences.

Later I thought about the dogs.
They were sleeping nearby.
They had behaved lovingly.
I was extremely grateful.

Tell students that adverbs can answer the questions *When? Where?* and *How?* or *To what extent?* Write these questions on the board as headings for a chart. Have volunteers identify the adverb in each sentence and the question it answers, and write the adverb under the appropriate heading. Then read students the following sentences and have them add the adverbs to the chart:

We were completely surprised.

There he found a bone.

They will leave soon.

The moon shone brightly.

When	*Where*	*How/To what extent*
later	*nearby*	*lovingly*
soon	*there*	*extremely*
		completely
		brightly

Tell them to skip a line between each sentence, allowing room to draw an arrow from the adverb to the word it describes. Ask them to write *When? Where?* or *How?* above the adverbs. Then have students exchange papers and check each other's work.

2 Practice/Apply

Have students write sentences using two adverbs from each column on the board.

Oral Language Options

Have a student give a sentence with an adverb. Ask a volunteer to identify the adverb and identify whether it tells when, where, or how/to what extent.

Daily Language Activities

The sentences on page R13 of the Teacher's Resource Section feature the grammar concepts taught in this lesson.

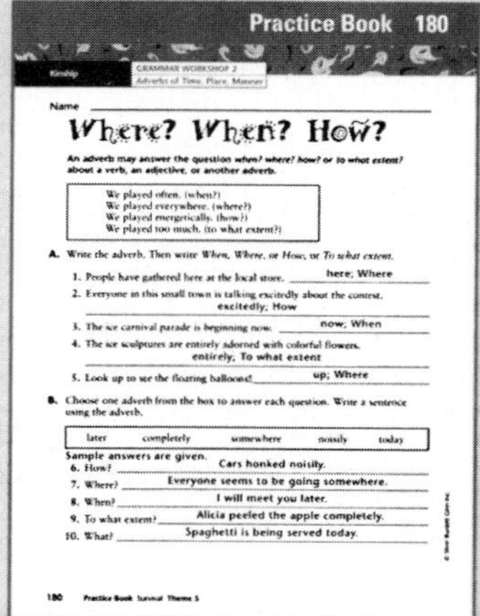
Practice Book 180

Kinship | GRAMMAR WORKSHOP 2 | Adverbs of Time, Place, Manner

Name ______

Where? When? How?

An adverb may answer the question *when? where? how?* or *to what extent?* about a verb, an adjective, or another adverb.

We played often. (when?)
We played everywhere. (where?)
We played energetically. (how?)
We played too much. (to what extent?)

A. Write the adverb. Then write *When, Where,* or *How,* or *To what extent.*

1. People have gathered here at the local store. here; Where
2. Everyone in this small town is talking excitedly about the contest. excitedly; How
3. The ice carnival parade is beginning now. now; When
4. The ice sculptures are entirely adorned with colorful flowers. entirely; To what extent
5. Look up to see the floating balloons! up; Where

B. Choose one adverb from the box to answer each question. Write a sentence using the adverb.

later completely somewhere noisily today

Sample answers are given.

6. How? Cars honked noisily.
7. Where? Everyone seems to be going somewhere.
8. When? I will meet you later.
9. To what extent? Alicia peeled the apple completely.
10. What? Spaghetti is being served today.

180 Practice Book Survival Theme 5

▲ **Optional Independent Practice**
Practice Book page 180 provides practice in using adverbs.

Reteach See SourceBank page 93.

Viewing Workshop

Using Visual Aids to Explain

1 Teach

Ask students, "If Gary Paulsen wanted to tell someone how to follow the old trail he had discovered, what could he do to make his explanation clearer?" (*draw a map*) Then ask what other kinds of visual aids speakers can use to explain different types of information. (*pictures, diagrams, charts, demonstrations*) Invite students to suggest specific learning situations in which each visual aid might be useful. Mention some of the visual aids that have been used in class recently and ask students to explain how each one helped them learn.

Share the following guidelines for using visual aids to explain.

Using Visual Aids Effectively

- *Outline your presentation first. Then prepare the visual aid.*
- *Be sure the visual aid is neat, clear, and big enough to see.*
- *Practice using your visual aid with your presentation.*

2 Practice/Apply

Ask students to think of something they know about or know how to do that could best be explained with the help of a map, chart, diagram, picture, or demonstration. Allow time for them to plan their explanation, prepare their visual aid, and practice their presentation with a partner. Then have volunteers present their explanations to the class. Encourage students to discuss how the visual aids were helpful and how they could have been improved.

English Language Support This component provides activities that develop language skills related to "Kinship."

Spelling Workshop

Endings *-ion, -tion,* and *-sion*

1 Teach

Write the Spelling Words on the board, and have students pronounce them. Point out that each word ends with the letters *-tion* or *-sion* pronounced /shən/ or /zhən/. Also point out that many of the words are formed by adding the ending *-ion* to a base word. For example, *tension* and *infection* are formed by adding *-ion* to *tense* and *infect*. Have students identify other base words among the Spelling Words. *(discuss, populate, define, elevate, explode, educate, persuade, create, satisfy)*

2 Practice/Apply

Ask students to create two columns on a sheet of paper and label them *-tion* and *-sion*. Students should work in pairs, one student reading the Spelling Words aloud as the other student writes each word in the appropriate column. When both students have written the words, have them exchange papers and check each other's spelling.

Challenge Words: *compassion,* exaltation,* precision, proportion*

See page 63 of Spelling Source for optional independent practice.

Home Connections: See the Take-home Letter for this lesson in the Spelling Source Teacher's Edition.

Spelling Words

- mention*
- reaction*
- position*
- infection*
- discussion
- population
- tension
- definition
- mission
- elevation
- explosion
- education
- persuasion
- recreation
- satisfaction

*Word or form of the word appears in the selection.

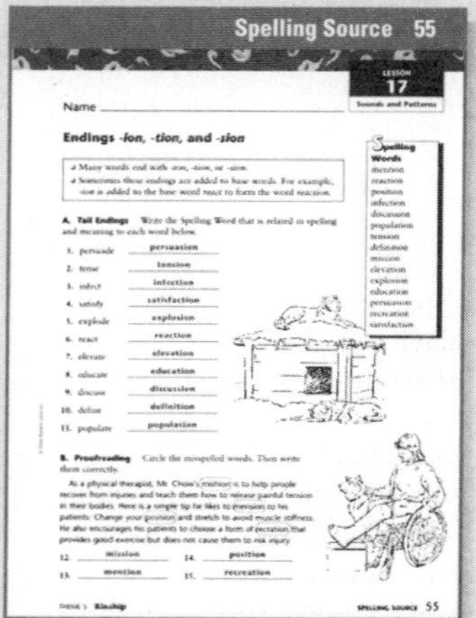

Spelling Source 55

Lesson 17 — Sounds and Patterns

Name ______

Endings *-ion, -tion,* and *-sion*

- Many words end with -ion, -tion, or -sion.
- Sometimes these endings are added to base words. For example, -ion is added to the base word *react* to form the word *reaction*.

A. Tail Endings Write the Spelling Word that is related in spelling and meaning to each word below.

1. persuade — persuasion
2. tense — tension
3. infect — infection
4. satisfy — satisfaction
5. explode — explosion
6. react — reaction
7. elevate — elevation
8. educate — education
9. discuss — discussion
10. define — definition
11. populate — population

B. Proofreading Circle the misspelled words. Then write them correctly.

12. mission
13. mention
14. position
15. recreation

Theme 5 Kinship — Spelling Source 55

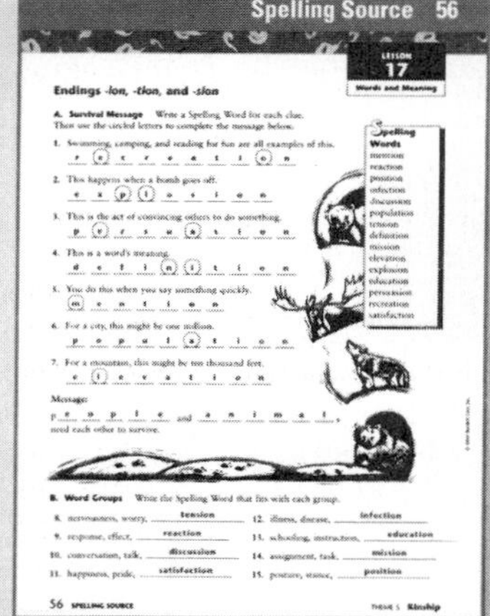

Spelling Source 56

Lesson 17 — Words and Meaning

Endings *-ion, -tion,* and *-sion*

A. Survival Message Write a Spelling Word for each clue. Then use the circled letters to complete the message below.

1. Swimming, camping, and reading for fun are all examples of this. r e c r e a t i o n
2. This happens when a bomb goes off. e x p l o s i o n
3. This is the act of convincing others to do something. p e r s u a s i o n
4. This is a word's meaning. d e f i n i t i o n
5. You do this when you say something quickly. m e n t i o n
6. For a city, this might be one million. p o p u l a t i o n
7. For a mountain, this might be ten thousand feet. e l e v a t i o n

Message: p e o p l e and a n i m a l s need each other to survive.

B. Word Groups Write the Spelling Word that fits with each group.

8. nervousness, worry, tension
9. response, effect, reaction
10. conversation, talk, discussion
11. happiness, pride, satisfaction
12. illness, disease, infection
13. schooling, instruction, education
14. assignment, task, mission
15. posture, stance, position

56 Spelling Source — Theme 5 Kinship

Daily Language Activities

The sentences on page R24 of the Teacher's Resource Section feature the Spelling Words taught in this lesson.

Optional Independent Practice

Pages 55 and 56 of Spelling and Vocabulary Book provide additional practice with the Spelling Words.

Cross-curricular Connections

SCIENCE

Supporting Science Goals:
Studying Ecosystems

Explore the Tundra The tundra is an elaborate ecosystem with many interdependent species. Provide encyclopedias and almanacs for students to investigate the plants, wildlife, and insects that have adapted to this harsh environment. After researching, students may present posters with captions that help to illustrate the various components of the tundra ecosystem. Challenge students to explain the changes that humans have made in the tundra and the effect of these changes on the environment.

Students can present their findings about the tundra ecosystem to the class.

MATHEMATICS

Supporting Math Goals:
Comparing Data

Calculate Average Speed
Explain to students that the Iditarod Trail crosses two mountain ranges and frozen waterways to cover 1,790 kilometers. To help students understand the physical difficulty of the race, have them calculate the trail's total number of miles. (The metric conversion is 0.6214.) If the winning musher completes the course in 11 days, how many miles are completed in a day? In a 12-hour day, what is the average miles traveled per hour? If another musher finishes the course in 15 days, how many miles are completed a day? In a 12-hour day, what is the average miles traveled per hour? How much faster would the slower racer need to be traveling in order to beat the winner? *(1,112 miles; 101.1 miles/day; 8.4 mph; 74.1 miles/day; 6.2 mph; 2.3 mph faster)*

SCIENCE

Supporting Science Goals:
Researching Animal Characteristics

Report on Primitive Knowledge Gary Paulsen's theme implies that dogs retain a primitive knowledge humans have lost. Encourage students to find out about the instincts and adaptations of animals.

- What do animals "know" that humans do not? For example, deer can sense approaching danger, and they possess a keen sense of direction.
- How are animals physically equipped to survive in their environment? For example, the wolf has a thick coat for protection and special circulation to keep paws warm, and it can survive for two weeks without food.

Help groups of students investigate various animals and report their findings to the class.

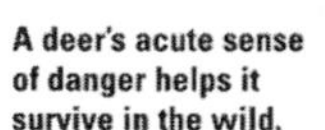

A deer's acute sense of danger helps it survive in the wild.

SOCIAL STUDIES

Supporting Social Studies Goals:
Researching Arctic Environment

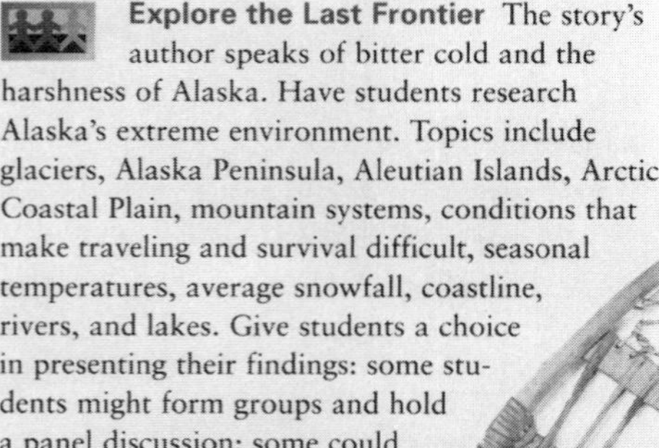

Explore the Last Frontier The story's author speaks of bitter cold and the harshness of Alaska. Have students research Alaska's extreme environment. Topics include glaciers, Alaska Peninsula, Aleutian Islands, Arctic Coastal Plain, mountain systems, conditions that make traveling and survival difficult, seasonal temperatures, average snowfall, coastline, rivers, and lakes. Give students a choice in presenting their findings: some students might form groups and hold a panel discussion; some could prepare a class chart listing their findings; others might like to create a map and label features.

remaining activities in this section typically occur during the guided reading of a selection—preview and predict, setting purposes, checking predictions, and so on.

Activities in Part 1 are similar to the steps in a directed reading activity (DRA) (Betts, 1946), which has dominated the format of basal reading instruction for decades. A DRA emphasizes preparing students for a selection by preteaching concepts and vocabulary, guided silent reading and discussion, rereading for a closer look at key concepts, and instruction in reading skills that are often isolated from the context of the story. You also can see the influence of literature-based and holistic approaches with the inclusion of fixup strategies, attention to literary elements and the author's craft, and written response to literature.

Part 2, "Literature-based Reading Instruction" (TE 912–917), focuses on activities that typically occur after the first reading. The activities in this section are enhanced by knowledge of the selection, which is often used as illustration of the skill or strategy being developed or reinforced.

Part 3, "Integrated Curriculum" (TE 918–925), is a new addition to most basal reading lessons. Only recently have publishing companies attempted to integrate the language arts, and other curricular areas as appropriate. Spelling and grammar, typically taught through other commercially developed programs, are now a part of one lesson plan. You must decide whether the words identified, for spelling especially, are appropriate for your students' level of word knowledge development.

As we discuss the planning of the first selection in the "Survival" theme, "Kinship," by Gary Paulsen (1990), you will see how each part of the lesson plan is developed. You can compare suggestions made by the series authors with your own ideas about effective reading/language arts instruction.

Part 1: Reading and Responding

Building Background. (*See TE 896–897.*) On page T896 we find a summary of the selection and activities for building background for the reading of the selection. We know there is a strong relationship between students' background knowledge and their ability to make meaning with text. We can see why the series authors suggest that we help students activate their prior knowledge before reading the selection. The selection that students are about to read focuses on the ingenuity of dogs. Making a concept web about dogs, as suggested, is one option for helping students re-collect their knowledge. The authors also suggest reading a selection in the Theme Magazine, titled "How Cold Can You Go?" (see inset at bottom of page T896).

After reading the selection summary on T896, what type of background knowledge will help students prepare for the content of the selection?

While the weather certainly may be cold, Paulsen focuses on his understanding of his sled dogs. Students would benefit most by considering what they already know about the types of dogs that will appear in the story.

Developing Vocabulary. (*See TE 898.*) Basal reading series traditionally suggest preteaching any vocabulary in the selection that you may not yet have introduced to students. Middle grade students, especially those who read widely, are likely to encounter a variety of words in other texts. The issue you must consider is whether or not the author presents each "new word" in a context that allows students to apply their word knowledge to sense the author's intended meaning. If so, let students first try to use what they know. To preteach the words, Transparency 80 (see inset on page T898) provides sentences for discussion of the words; however, the sentences are not drawn from the context of the story. Let's examine the identified words:

- *Steeped* (steep), *mystified* (mystery), *awakening* (awake), *dwelling* (dwell), and *exaltation* (exalt) are affixed words that students are likely to have encountered in other forms, which combined with the context should help them figure out the gist of each word.
- *Whirlpool* is a compound word that is quite literal, and students are likely to know the component parts.
- *Alleviate* and *chagrin* may be new. Consider the context in which *alleviate* and *chagrin* appear in "Kinship":

> To *alleviate* the boredom we give the dogs large bones to chew and play with. (p. 22)
>
> There was some self-pity creeping in, and not a little *chagrin* at being stupid enough to just let them run when I did not know the country. (p. 28)

Your Turn

Would you preteach the suggested words, practicing the words before students read "Kinship"? Would you use Transparency 80 with its sentences that are not drawn from the text?

My Turn

Using the context of the selection, I think students can get a sense of word meaning. I want to see which word knowledge strategies they use effectively. After reading the text, I can check their understanding of word meanings in context. If I have been teaching using base words and affixes plus context to determine word meanings, I should give students opportunities to apply that knowledge.

Spelling Preview and Support. (*See TE 899.*) In this basal series, one list of spelling words is identified for each selection. The words for this particular selection are a mixture of *-ion, -tion,* and *-sion* words, with spelling clues from the base word (*infect, infection; tense, tension*). These words are studied typically late in the syllable juncture stage. If your students are all in late syllable juncture, this list will be appropriate. If not, you may want to create additional lists that provide words that are developmentally appropriate for students' spelling stages, as discussed in Chapter 10.

Reading Options. (*See TE 900.*) The suggested reading option is "Supported Reading," providing support to students as needed during the reading. To begin the reading, we are urged to have students preview the text and predict what they will learn from the selection and complete the "W" section of their KWL chart. (This suggestion leads me to assume that the brainstorming about dogs, in the earlier section, was intended to be entered on the "K" section of the KWL chart, although this is not specified.)

Strategic Reading. (*See TE 900–908.*) As the reading begins, other suggestions for teacher–student interaction about the text appear in the margins. Comprehension,

Author's Craft, Visualizing, Vocabulary, Appreciating Multilingualism and Cultural Diversity, and Fix-up Strategies are suggested for calling students' attention to particular aspects of this text. You may discuss these suggestions as students progress through the text, as well as after the initial reading.

Your Turn

Examine each of the suggestions in the side margins of the teacher's edition. Which suggestions seem essential to understanding the text during the first reading? Which suggestions might be more useful to the reader if discussed after the reading of the text? Are there any suggestions that you probably would not incorporate? Give your reasons.

- W in the KWL
- Author's Craft—Genre
- Comprehension—Author's Purpose
- Reading Strategy
  Visualize
  Think Aloud
- Comprehension—Compare/Contrast
- Reading Strategy—Check Predictions
- Author's Craft
  Characterization
  Theme
- Appreciating Multiculturalism—Share Knowledge
- Appreciating Cultural Diversity—Appreciation and Acceptance

My Turn

Since the reading of this nonfiction piece is suggested as supported reading, I would use an MRTA technique for mediating between the students and the text. I would preview the text with students, encourage them to predict what they might learn, complete the "W" section of the KWL, and clarify the point of view (I) of this autobiography (Author's Craft, page T901). I would plan stopping points in the MRTA to incorporate most of the suggestions made in the teacher's edition. After the reading I would discuss characterization, theme, multilingualism, and diversity issues. I probably would not include the suggestions made for compound words, except for the meaning of *whirlpool* made earlier, because the suggested words seem inappropriate for this level.

■

Informal Assessment. (*See TE 908.*) The performance indicators provided assist you to consider how students respond to the reading. Questions to check comprehension are also suggested. The KWL chart can be completed at this point.

Meeting Individual Differences. Suggestions appear on each page below the story for ways to challenge students and to provide additional comprehension or language support. You know that the range of students in your classroom will require you to adapt instruction to meet students' needs. The series authors offer ideas for such adaptations that you may incorporate after the initial reading of the text, when students' background knowledge can be used to make stronger connections.

Responding. (*See TE 910 & 911.*) Students should have the opportunity after the reading to respond to the selection. The series authors suggest a variety of response opportunities:

- Personal response in a journal
- Reader response groups, using journal entries
- Creative response through writing, role playing, and designing a board game
- Critical response through problem solving

Response suggestions also appear in the student text (see page T909). In addition, suggestions at the bottom of page T911 make connections to the unit theme, survival, and to other pieces of literature.

Your Turn

What choices might you make for encouraging students' responses to the selection?

My Turn

As we discovered with book clubs, making a personal written response helps prepare students for sharing their responses with others. I would certainly encourage personal journal responses. Other types of response depend on your students and their interaction with the selection. Supported reading was suggested for the reading of "Kinship," so I assume that students have already had some opportunity for discussion with their peers. In this situation, then, I might consider creative or critical responses.

Part 2: Literature-Based Reading

This section of the basal lesson plan contains teaching ideas for skills and strategies that, for the most part, support the reading of the selection. For each selection you are provided lessons for specific aspects of literature, comprehension, word study, and study skills.

Literature: Story Structure—Theme. (*See TE 912–913.*) This literature lesson focuses on learning to identify the theme of the selection "Kinship," then applies that knowledge to a selection read previously. Being able to identify the theme of a selection makes it possible for students to learn life lessons for themselves. For other selections, this section of the lesson might focus on other literary elements such as characters or point of view or setting.

Comprehension: Compare/Contrast. (*See TE 914–915.*) In "Kinship," Paulsen describes the impact of his relationship with his dogs on his attitude and behavior. This lesson asks students to compare and contrast Paulsen's attitude and behavior before and after he observes his dog, Columbia, trick another dog, Olaf. A Venn diagram is suggested and a practice work sheet for comparison to another piece of literature is provided (see inset on page T914).

Word Study: Vocabulary—Compound Words. (*See TE 916.*) Word study can be most effective when words are related by common meaning units. This lesson suggests the study of compound words that share a common base word, *wind.* The compound word, *whirlpool,* was identified in the vocabulary list at the beginning of this selection. By this stage of word knowledge development, because students are well aware of how compound words are formed, studying related compounds can be effective for word study.

Study Skills: Forms/Applications. (*See TE 917.*) One reason for learning to read and write is to perform basic literate tasks such as completing forms and applications. Paulsen must complete applications when he wants to enter an Iditarod race. This lesson provides practice with forms that are either familiar to the students or that appear in the Practice Book.

Your Turn

Which of the four lessons above might you include when you teach the selection, "Kinship"? Explain your reasoning.

My Turn

Before addressing theme I would lead students back into the selection to compare and contrast Paulsen's attitude about dogs before and after observing Columbia and Olaf. The Venn diagram is an excellent informal writing technique to use to re-collect story events for comparison. After we had a good sense of Paulsen's attitude, we would be ready to consider theme. Studying compound words can be a valuable way to expand vocabulary, but they are not an important part of this selection. While reading "Kinship," I would prefer to focus on descriptive words, which are an important part of this selection and will be needed in the expository writing for this unit. Attention to completing forms and applications would be more appropriate in a life skills unit. How did our thinking compare?

Part 3: Integrated Curriculum

In this section, the series authors have provided lessons that make connections among the language arts and other curricular areas. While these lessons are labeled "Part 3" and appear at the end of the selection lesson plan, they are not necessarily intended to come at the end. If the suggested lesson is appropriate, you must decide where to include it in your study of the selection.

Writing Workshop: Using Sensory Words. (*See TE 918–919.*) Gary Paulsen uses many words that appeal to the senses and help to build strong images for the reader. This lesson begins with a minilesson that focuses students' attention on the use of sensory words in the selection, and that enables students to practice with familiar subjects, then apply their knowledge to writing a descriptive paragraph about a familiar subject.

Grammar Workshop: Adverbs. (*See TE 920–921.*) This workshop begins with a minilesson about adverbs and what they are, followed by practice in identifying, describing, and using adverbs of time, place, and manner. Like the use of sensory words, knowledge of adverbs can help writers communicate more vividly, especially in comparison writing.

Viewing Workshop: Using Visual Aids to Explain. (*See TE 922.*) This lesson provides an opportunity to help students explore representing their ideas in graphic form. Students are urged to consider how a visual presentation helps to make information easier to understand.

Spelling Workshop: Endings *-ion, -tion, -sion.* *(See TE 923.)* Targeted words having these endings were introduced at the beginning of the selection. During the week students are able to practice this pattern through Daily Language Activities (editing sample sentences) and pages from the Practice Book. The asterisk next to a word in the list indicates that it appears in some form in the selection.

Cross-Curricular Connections. (*See TE 924–925.*) To connect with the content of the "Kinship" selection, two lessons are suggested: exploring the tundra and calculating the average speed that Iditarod dog teams travel. These suggestions would probably be interesting to students. Questions you must ask are, "How much time must be committed to explore these issues adequately?" and "Do I want to devote such time at this point in the theme study?"

Your Turn

Which suggested lessons would you decide to use from Part 3? Would any of these suggested lessons be better accomplished through other activities already occurring in your classroom?

The Writing Process section, near the end of the theme, suggested that students should be engaged in writing an expository piece involving comparing and contrasting. In my classroom I would have a daily writer's workshop, in which I would incorporate the types of writing suggested by the series authors. I would use the suggested lessons for Writing Workshop and Grammar Workshops in my minilessons for our daily writer's workshop, because these lessons help students with word choices that improve their ability to make written comparisons and contrasts. The Viewing Workshop would be saved until a point in a theme study when students are beginning to prepare visual aids for class sharing. In my classroom, I would have daily word study for spelling. The suggested words for the Spelling Workshop would be added to existing lists for the syllable juncture stage, the stage in which these words are appropriate for spelling instruction. I would pull together the Cross-curricular Connections for each selection as theme choices that capture student interest and enhance our theme study, especially suggestions that require extended time.

Now that we have examined most parts of the theme plan for "Survival," you must extend your planning beyond the separate selections, to the theme as a whole. How will you tie lessons, materials, and activities together to achieve your goals? You might try a flexible unit plan that will cover the suggested five to six weeks and incorporates whole-class literature study, literature circles or book clubs, and the individual reading of reader's workshop.

Teaching the Basal Unit

A flexible unit plan integrates language arts instruction for middle grade readers by using whole-class literature study, literature circles/book clubs, and reader's workshop over a period of several weeks. You will need a wide array of literature related to your theme.

Developing a Flexible Unit Plan

A flexible unit will include the following:

- Whole-class literature study to introduce the unit and provide teacher-led instruction that focuses students' attention on accomplishing the unit goals and objectives.

- Literature circles or book clubs to enable students to further explore the concepts introduced in the whole-class study and deepen their understanding, with moderate teacher guidance.
- Reader's workshop to culminate the unit, allowing students to focus on that portion that especially interests them and to apply what has been developed in the previous whole and small groups.

You might also choose to begin with a whole-class study, then spend the remaining time in reader's workshop, especially if you do not have sets of multiple copies of appropriate literature.

Figure 11.3 presents examples of how you can divide the flexible time period among the three types of study groupings. Time frames are adjusted according to the length of the text chosen for whole-class study and the number of different texts to be read by the small groups. The figure shows four-, six-, and nine-week periods to illustrate flexibility.

Sample Six-Week Basal Unit Plan—"Survival"

Imagine, again, that you are teaching sixth grade and are planning to teach the "Survival" unit provided in your reading/language arts basal series. Your class is already familiar with whole-class literature study through other chapter book studies. Students also have participated in literature circles and book clubs earlier in the school year. While you have not used reader's workshop as a consistent part of your reading program, students do have a predictable time for independent reading each day. The pieces are all in place for you to teach your basal theme through a flexible unit format.

To begin planning this flexible unit, look back at the basal unit reproduced in this chapter. What literature is available in the unit for a whole-class study, for literature circles or book clubs, and for reader's workshop? Would you need to collect other literature for this unit? What other types of literature will you need?

I would begin my search for materials by going back to the beginning of the unit and reviewing each page, searching for suggested literature. Here are the possibilities:

Figure 11.3 Flexible literature units

Type of Grouping	4 Weeks	6 Weeks	9 Weeks
Whole-class study	1 week	1–2 weeks	2–3 weeks
Literature circles or book clubs	2 weeks	2–4 weeks	3–4 weeks
Reader's workshop	1 week	1–2 weeks	2–3 weeks

- Whole-class—*The Crystal Drop* (Hughes, 1993), a chapter book, and *Drylongso* (Hamilton, 1992), a picture book. The series authors share ideas for teaching with these books.
- Literature Circles/Book Clubs—the four selections included in *Collection* are available in multiple copies with developed lesson plans and support activities—"Kinship," "Leader of the Pack," "The Grandfather Tree," and "Four Against the Sea."
- Reader's workshop—Seventeen books are listed for More Books and Technology and articles in the Theme Magazine.
- Additional—Suggested read-alouds are *Abel's Island* and *The Big Wave*.

Using many of the materials provided by the basal program, you might organize the six-week unit as shown in Figure 11.4. Note how the materials provided by the basal program fulfill your needs for whole-class and small-group literature study. You will need additional books for reader's workshop beyond those suggested in the More Books and Technology section of the unit plan.

Figure 11.4 Survival unit—Six Weeks

Whole-Class Study (2 weeks):	**Read** ***The Crystal Drop*** (class set in basal program)	**Reading/Writing Strategies** • introduce theme and solving problems • small-group discussion skills • point of view • descriptive language
Small Groups, select 3 of 4 (3 weeks):	"Kinship" "The Leader of the Pack" "The Grandfather Tree" "Four Against the Sea"	• reinforce theme and problem solving • theme/main ideas • draw conclusions, make inferences • using descriptive language (sensory, setting, etc.)
Independent (1 week):	offer wide assortment of books, magazines, and newspaper articles	• apply strategies independently • focus on sustained reading/writing • confer once with each student

Whole-Class Literature Study

To get the unit started with a clear focus on survival, engage students in a whole-class literature workshop (see Chapter 6) using a class set of *The Crystal Drop* (Hughes, 1993). The series authors have developed a lesson plan for literature study that links this text to the theme, as well as to other curriculum areas. The lesson plan includes a chart that provides chapter summaries, key vocabulary, strategic reading suggestions, and response options.

Response options are divided between personal response, reader response groups, and critical/creative responses. These divisions provide ideas for possible journal/log entries and small-group discussions as a followup to the whole-class reading. You can develop discussion guides from the response options to support small-group discussions, just as we did for *Hatchet* (Chapter 6) and for *A Taste of Blackberries* (Appendix A).

Literature Circles/Book Clubs

After completing the whole-class study, several weeks of small-group study provide opportunity for more focused interaction with students. In this survival unit, three weeks out of six will be allotted for small-group work. Literature circles allow students to select the literature they prefer to read, or you may form book clubs, with everyone reading the same selections. (See Chapter 7 for more small-group possibilities.) The lesson plans developed by the series authors are full of ideas that you may use for small-group discussions, learning logs, and extension activities. Refer to the "Kinship" selection as an example.

Reader's Workshop

The culmination of the "Survival" unit is a week of reader's workshop in books related to the theme, providing opportunity for students to select their own "survival" reading. During the other five weeks of the unit, students should have time for daily independent reading, but that reading need not be connected to a unit of study.

The More Books and Technology section of the theme plan includes suggestions for 17 additional books on a variety of levels. You will, however, need more than 17 books for reader's workshop. You might choose from the following titles:

Between a Rock and a Hard Place (Alden Carter, 1995)
Brian's Winter (Gary Paulsen, 1996)
The Camp Survival Handbook (Lisa Eisenberg, 1995)
The Cay (Theodore Taylor, 1987)
Frantic Lightning Strike (Larry Strauss, 1996)
Low Tide (William Mayne, 1993)
The River (Gary Paulsen, 1991)
The Shark Callers (Eric Campbell, 1994)
Signs of Survival (Nancy McKinley, 1991)
Survival Camp (Eve Bunting, 1992)
Survival on Cougar Mountain (J. Cunnyham, 1995)
Sweet Friday Island (Theodore Taylor, 1994)
The Tested Man (John Fine, 1994)

Thunder Cave (Roland Smith, 1995)
Timothy of the Cay (Theodore Taylor, 1993)
To Touch the Deer (Gus Cazzola, 1981)
Toughboy and Sister (Kirkpatrick Hill, 1992)
Trial by Wilderness (David Mathieson, 1990)
The Voyage of the FROG (Gary Paulsen, 1993)
When the Road Ends (Jean Thesman, 1992)
Wish Me Luck (James Henegan, 1997)

The week of independent reading can include the following:

- Whole-class meetings and minilessons to support continued development of independent reading strategies
- Students self-selecting books and reading silently for a sustained period
- Opportunity for students to have personal conferences with you about their reading

Writer's Workshop

Students should continue to participate in writer's workshop throughout the six-week unit. The series authors have provided suggestions for one extended piece of writing as well as for informal pieces that build background for that writing experience. These suggestions, along with grammar and spelling lessons and activities, are most useful to students if you integrate them into the writer's workshop. You also may include minilessons for grammar, mechanics, and word choice. Revising and editing groups can help students apply their knowledge from the minilessons.

Word Study

If you want your students to grow as both readers and writers, you must continue daily word study throughout the unit. Remember, you have a dual focus in word study of both reading and writing. For reading, consider the vocabulary and word study activities already developed by the series authors. In addition, you may add to your study words from the basal selections or other literature of interest to your students.

With the range of readers and writers that are likely to be in your classroom, you should continue to use a multilevel approach to spelling by developing your own lists for sorting each week. The list suggested by the basal authors may be appropriate for one or more of your word study groups. If so, you should certainly consider the suggested activities.

Monitoring Students' Progress in Basal Reading Programs

In previous chapters we have explored observation, conferences, and collecting samples of students' work as key sources of information you need to monitor their progress in reading and writing. In a basal reading series, we add a fourth dimension, the series' own assessment materials.

In *Literature Works,* assessment is ongoing and includes both informal and formal assessment, as well as portfolio assessment (see Figure 11.5). Informal assessment includes conferences and student self-assessment, both of which are familiar to you. Formal assessments, typically paper-and-pencil assessments, are available for reading, language arts, spelling, and writing. You are encouraged to maintain student portfolios.

Figure 11.5

T1096 Theme 5 Survival

Assessing Growth

Informal Assessment

You may choose to observe and record students' progress using the following methods.

Conferences With Students Review students' portfolios, asking them questions such as the following.

- **Why did you choose to share this writing?**
- **What new things have you learned as a reader? as a writer?**
- **Which parts of the theme were difficult or challenging?**

Talk about progress you have noticed, commenting on portfolio pieces that indicate understanding of skills and concepts taught in the theme. Together set some personal learning goals, and decide how to work toward them in the next few weeks.

Student Self-assessment To support students' self-assessment, you might encourage them to

- listen to a recording of themselves reading so that they can determine whether their oral reading has improved
- assess their project work by asking themselves how they solved their hardest problems and what part they enjoyed the most
- select work to add to their portfolios
- complete the self-assessment page in the Practice Book

Getting stranded in the wilderness can be a life-or-death situation, whether you're in the desert or the Arctic tundra. In either place, you must find shelter to survive the harsh weather. The glaring desert sun can cause your body to dehydrate if you're out in the middle of the day. In contrast, nighttime presents the greatest danger in the tundra because of the bitterly cold temperatures. If you're planning a trip to either climate, learning how to build a shelter could save your life.

Jackie's main idea is supported by relevant details.

Jackie used both comparison and contrast to make her point.

Jackie drew a logical conclusion from the facts she presented.

Figure 11.5 *continued*

Assessing Growth T1097

Formal Assessment

You may want to use the following components to assess students' growth.

Reading Process Assessment	Skills Assessment	Writing Assessment Guide
Using holistic measures, students will • demonstrate their ability to use details in pictures and text to build meaning • demonstrate their ability to make connections across texts and their experiences	Assessed skills include • Main Idea and Details • Author's Purpose • Compare and Contrast • Draw Conclusions • Multiple-meaning Words • Study Skills • Grammar Skills	The prompts, exemplars, and scoring rubrics for expository writing in the Writing Assessment Guide will enable you to formally assess your students' proficiency in that mode. Use either the Writing Process Test or the Timed Writing Test.

Test booklets support formal testing of skills.

Spelling Source

Use the following to assess formally or informally your students' spelling progress:

- unit spelling tests
- lesson and unit dictation sentences
- practice and review pages for Spelling Words
- personal word lists

Portfolio Assessment

Portfolios offer insights into students' thought and work processes and document reading and writing growth in a dynamic form. When evaluating portfolios, you might wish to consider the following areas:

- evidence of improvement in comparing and contrasting characteristics or ideas, drawing conclusions, and using graphic aids to improve comprehension
- evidence of effort
- attempts at unfamiliar kinds of reading
- attempts at expository writing
- range of projects completed, such as a survival handbook
- students' goals and self-evaluation

Survival

Portfolio Checklist

- ☑ Survival Reading and Writing checklists in the Grade 6 Guide to Student Portfolios and Classroom Assessment
- ☑ Anecdotal records
- ☑ Practice Book worksheets
- ☐ SourceBank: Writer's Notebook pages
- ☐ Writing Process
- ☐ Spelling Source extension and review pages
- ☑ Teacher evaluations of student's growing knowledge of theme content
- ☐ Family Involvement Form
- ☑ Student's self-selected work
- ☑ Tape recordings of student's reading
- ☐ Theme Project
- ☐ Skills Assessment
- ☐ Reading Process Assessment
- ☑ *Folk-hero Tale*
- ☑ *Drought Diary*
- ☐ __________

A theme checklist helps organize each student's achievements.

Note the "Portfolio Checklist" (TE 1097) and the variety of assessments available for you to use.

If your school district has adopted a basal series, you may be required to use all or part of the assessment program. Before you begin teaching a unit, be aware of what skills/strategies you will teach, and be sure to include your objectives for students' learning in the assessment instruments.

Respecting Diversity in Basal Instruction

Like most facets of our society, basal reading series are showing greater sensitivity to the diverse needs and interests of middle grade learners. For example, the following activities to meet individual needs are suggesteed throughout the "Kinship" lesson plan:

- ESL language support for building fluency
- Varied reading options depending on the type of text
- Appreciating multilingualism
- Challenging students
- Providing additional support
- Appreciating cultural diversity

The main characters in the literature selections across the unit represent a range of differences in gender orientations, ethnicity, cultural groups, and time periods. Basal materials provide opportunity to address issues of diversity and urge teachers to be the decision makers.

TAKE A MOMENT AND REFLECT . . .

A basal reading series is a set of sequential instructional materials organized around a hierarchy of reading and language arts skills and strategies.

Since their inception, basal readers have dominated reading instruction in the United States.

The content and organization of basal reading series are being influenced by the movement in literature-based reading:

- More authentic literature is being included.
- Fewer adaptations of literature occur.
- Fewer controls on vocabulary exist.
- Suggestions to teachers are less prescriptive.
- Skill/strategy instruction is less isolated, more meaningful.
- More integration of the language arts.

Basal series are comprehensive and include a range of materials to meet varied needs and interests of students.

Planning for basal themes or units should include:

- Determining what students need to learn
- Gathering resources for learning
- Selecting activities that are appropriate for students
- Considering how to assess student learning

Basal themes/units frequently have most of the components of teacher-developed themes:

- Introductory engagements
- Extension activities
- Varied reading and writing activities
- Open-ended activities

Writing process, including attention to grammar and spelling, is encouraged as a part of the basal lesson.

The teacher's edition does not make decisions! Teachers must make decisions about which activities best meet instructional goals and student needs and interests.

A basal lesson plan includes several components:

- Reading and responding
- Development of skills and strategies in literature, comprehension, work study, and study skills
- Cross-curricular connections

A basal theme or unit can include a variety of instructional formats:

- Whole-class literature study (large group)
- Literature circles/book clubs (small group)
- Readers' workshop (individual)

To monitor students progress, basal reading programs include suggestions for:

- informal assessment
- formal assessment
- portfolio assessment

Basal programs show sensitivity to diversity through suggested activities for meeting individual needs.

REFERENCES

Apple, M. (1982). *Education and power*. Boston: Routledge & Kegan Paul.

Aukerman, R. (1981). *The basal reader approach to reading*. New York: Wiley.

Betts, E. A. (1946). *Foundations of reading instruction*. New York: American Book Company.

Bohning, G. (1986). The McGuffey Eclectic Readers: 1836–1986. *The Reading Teacher, 40,* 263–269.

DeLain, M. T., Englebretson, R., Florio-Ruane, S., Galda, L., Grant, C., Hiebert, E. H., Juel, C., Moll, L. C., Paratore, J., Parson, P. D., Raphael, T. E., & Rueda, R. (1996). *Literature works: Grade 6, volume 2.* Needham, MA: Silver Burdett & Ginn.

Farr, R., Tulley, M. A., & Powell, D. (1987). The evaluation and selection of basal readers. *The Elementary School Journal*, 87(3), 276–279.

Gates, A. I. (1935). *The improvement of reading*. Upper Saddle River, NJ: Merrill/Prentice Hall.

Goodman, K. S., Shannon, P., Freeman, Y. S., & Murphy, S. (1988). *Report card on basal readers*. New York: Richard C. Owens.

McCallum, R. D. (1988). Don't throw the basals out with the bath water. *The Reading Teacher, 42,* 204–209.

McCarthey, S. J., & Hoffman, J. V. (1995). The new basals: How are they different? *The Reading Teacher*, *49,* 72–75.

Reutzel, D. R. (1991). Understanding and using basal readers effectively. In B. Hayes (Ed.), *Effective strategies for teaching reading* (pp. 254–280). New York: Allyn & Bacon.

Reutzel, D. R., and Cooter, R. B. (1992). *Teaching children to read*. Upper Saddle River, NJ: Merrill/Prentice Hall.

Shannon, P. (1989). *Broken promises*. Granby, MA: Bergin & Garvey.

Shannon, P. (1990). *The struggle to continue*. Portsmouth, NH: Heinemann.

Texas Education Agency. (1990). Proclamation of the State Board of Education advertising for bids on textbooks: Proclamation 68. Austin, TX: Author.

CHILDREN'S LITERATURE

Paulsen, G. (1990). *Woodsong.* New York: Viking Penguin.

12

Teaching with Integrated Units

Balancing Information and Narrative Texts

In this chapter . . .

We explore combining time and subject matter to create cohesive units of instruction that provide integrated learning experiences for middle grade students, including:

- answering the question, "What is integration?"
- types and levels of integration,
- the role of language arts in integration,
- issues related to reading information text,
- developing content-mediated reading thinking activities (C-MRTA), and
- planning, organizing, and implementing an integrated unit.

What Is Integration?

We cannot discuss integrated units and what they offer for teaching and learning, without first considering what we mean by *integration*. I first learned of "integration" when I read about teaching practices in British primary schools and "open classrooms" during the 1960s. I first tried to implement it in the learning centers that I began using in the 1970s. During the past decade there has been a renewed and intensified interest in integration and I find that educators hold differing definitions and practice it in a variety of ways.

Integration Is Whole Learning

Tarry Lindquist, a fifth-grade teacher and author of *Seeing the Whole through Social Studies* (1995), states that integration is whole learning. She describes *whole learning* as "a way of balancing content and instructional strategies to nurture and nudge the whole child away from self-centeredness toward self-realization and self-actualization" (p. 5). Isn't this the place where we find our middle-grade students—pulled back to childhood by self-centeredness, while desperately seeking the self-realization of adulthood? Perhaps more than any other age group, middle grade students should be engaged in whole learning that nurtures and nudges them as learners.

Integration Is the Fabric, Not the Threads

Integration is the key to whole learning. Imagine that integration is represented by a loom:

> Think of language arts skills and processes as the warp of learning, with each specific skill or understanding symbolized by a thread running vertically through the loom. Then picture another discipline, such as social studies, as the horizontal threads providing the pattern and individuality of the fabric eventually woven by the learner (Lindquist, 1995, p. 5).

This is integration—the fabric of learning in which we see and appreciate the pattern in the fabric, rather than the individual threads. We weave our knowledge of language, communication, and thinking around and through other subject areas.

Integrated curriculum should help students relate learning experiences across disciplines.

Integration Is a Process

Integration is the process of *how* we go about planning, developing, implementing, and evaluating learning experiences, rather than being only the product of the experience.

Integration is the process of making connections. "Integration calls upon the teacher, initially, and later the students to identify the connections or overlaps between content areas, between similar processes of applications of skills, and then build on those connections" (Lindquist, 1995, p. 7). In an integrated curriculum, units of study focus on "how concepts and ideas in one curriculum area are related to those in another area" (Morrison, 1993, p. 87).

Two Types of Integration

The most obvious type of integration is an *integrated curriculum.* Shoemaker (1991) identifies a number of ways that teachers integrate the curriculum:

- Teachers select an organizing theme or topic, such as "Working Together" or "Ancient Egypt," and then select subject matter appropriate to the organizing topic.
- Teachers look for ways to infuse skills from one curriculum area into another, such as using critical thinking skills in social studies.
- Teachers organize the entire school year around a concept or theme, such as change or habitats.
- Teachers take advantage of natural links between subject areas, such as integrating the language arts together, using mathematical calculations to solve problems in science, or using writing to explore thinking in mathematics.

A second type of integration is *integrated learning*, which "occurs when we specifically consider and plan for the continued development of the cognitive, physical, affective, and moral dimensions of each child" (Shoemaker, 1991, p. 793). Integrated learning occurs when we use what we know about our students to consciously select learning experiences that enhance and extend their individual growth and ability to learn.

Levels of Integration

Selecting a topic, usually from science or social studies, and using the language arts to support learning in that topic was my first conscious step into integrating the curriculum. From there I moved on to making links across several subject areas, committing larger and larger blocks of time to integration each day. As a teacher, I did not integrate all subjects or learning experiences in the same way.

There are several levels at which we can provide integrated learning experiences for our students. Lindquist (1995) identifies four levels in her own development as a teacher:

- Level 1—Few connections, carefully planned, rather formal.
- Level 2—Blending skills and content, connecting subject areas.
- Level 3—Highly integrative, natural connections, no longer focus on consciously connecting subjects because learning is not seen as subjects, but rather concepts, behaviors, ways of thinking.
- Level 4—The whole student, not the subject or topic, is the focus of the planning.

The level of integration at which we function has a lot to do with our knowledge of (and comfort with) the curriculum at the particular grade level we teach, the depth of our understanding about human development and learning, and our knowledge of our students as individual people and learners. As we examine our school year (or any other increment of time), we can find ourselves working at various levels of integration. As elementary or middle school teachers, we know a little about a lot of topics, but those topics we know intimately enable us to function at a higher level of integration than those we merely "know about."

Integration and Language Arts

Reading, writing, listening, and speaking are integral to all learning. In units of study, the language arts are integrated, drawing on listening, speaking, reading, and writing to explore and inquire. Without the language arts, the construction of meaning would be virtually impossible. The language arts are vehicles for exploring ones' own thinking and inquiring into the thinking of others. Oral and written language become tools for exploration and inquiry in integrated units.

Listening and speaking are the easiest links for us to make. These modes of communication enable us to receive the thinking of others and to share our own. We often do not think of using these modes as part of integration. However, the possibilities for integrated learning would be truly limited without verbal communication.

Reading is a link we make with other subject areas when firsthand experience is either not practical or possible. We read to inquire into new areas of knowledge, to expand our background knowledge, to solve problems, and the like. Abundant literature for children and young adults, both narrative and informational, now makes the reading link even stronger than in the past.

Writing is the link we use when we need to re-collect, re-create, and re-construct our thinking in subject areas. Getting our ideas outside of ourselves enables us to "see" what we know, to step back and reflect, to understand our own thinking, and to see our thinking in a new way (revision).

The Role of Literature

Literature, narrative and informational, is a mainstay for most integrated units. Allen and Piersma (1995) suggest that the literature be used in units either as the central focus, as a supplement to content study, or infused into content area study:

- A *literature-centered model* focuses primarily on the literary value of narrative literature. While some students may explore content that is embedded (such as by exploring survival while reading *Hatchet* [Paulsen, 1987]), such content is not the main focus of the unit.
- A *literature-supplemented model* uses literature to supplement content area instruction. Literature is used to create interest and motivate students to engage in content study. The literary value of text, however, is not the focus of the unit.
- A *literature-infused model* places equal importance on narrative and information texts in the development of concepts in the unit. Information texts are integral to developing content background. Narrative texts play a vital role by helping students understand and appreciate content through interactions with characters and themes that relate to unit concepts.

Throughout this text, we have discussed narrative texts and their use in middle grade classrooms. Integrated units will include both narrative and information texts. Before we launch into how to plan units, the following discussion will strengthen your knowledge of helping students make meaning with information texts.

Reading Information Texts

Rosenblatt (1989) states that readers have different expectations for narrative and information texts and, consequently, approach them in different ways, for different purposes. In narrative, a reader has a great deal of latitude for interpreting an author's ideas in light of the reader's experiences. A reader's purpose for reading narrative may be purely aesthetic, for the pleasure of the experience. In contrast, readers often approach information texts with different expectations. Because readers expect to need to retain, use, or act on the information in such texts, they must inspect the author's ideas and intentions much more closely.

Your Turn

Through your experiences as a reader, what differences do you note in the way that you read narrative and information texts? How do you explain them?

My Turn

Part of the difference I feel between texts lies in my purposes for reading. Depending on my purposes, I determine how much effort I give to making meaning, especially if I find the text challenging. There are also fundamental differences in the way that texts are written, the way that ideas are organized on the page.

While authors of narrative use their own unique way (style) of telling a story (plot), I know (from my experience as a reader) that the story will focus on a particular person or group of people (characters) at a particular place in time (setting). I also know that either the author or a character will tell the story (point of view), and that through the telling of the story the author urges me to think about the lessons I learn about life (theme). Regardless of the genre in which a narrative is written (historical fiction, fantasy, etc.), narratives seem to have in common the telling of life stories. My own experiences with life help to connect me to the lives of others, even those who live in other places and times. The use of the literary elements feels "predictable." I know what to expect much of the time.

In contrast, information texts can address an infinite range of topics. I may possess little firsthand knowledge of the topics I read about, making building or revising my schema more difficult. The less I know about a topic, the harder it is to build a schema through reading. Unlike the use of literary elements in narrative text, the arrangement of ideas in information text does not seem "predictable." I sometimes do sense patterns in the way that authors organize and share their ideas, which makes me feel that I must constantly adjust my thinking to stay up with the author.

Thinking in Information Texts. Part of the difference between narrative and information texts can be explained by the ways we must think when we read. Moore, Moore, Cunningham, and Cunningham (1994) suggest that nine thinking processes account for a large portion of the cognitive activity involved in reading, writing, and learning information:

- *Call up* what we already know.
- *Connect* new ideas to what we already know.
- *Predict or anticipate* what is to come.
- *Organize* information into a useful framework.
- *Generalize* information into similar groupings after noting patterns or commonalities.

- *Form an image* using sensory information.
- *Monitor* internally to determine how well learning or thinking is progressing and repairing breakdowns in understanding.
- *Evaluate or judge* the contents of passages and author's writing style.
- *Apply* knowledge or select the most appropriate response from all those acquired.

A reader may simultaneously use several of these thinking processes in a learning experience.

Mediated Reading of Information Text. As you prepare to engage students in the study of an information text, you must think about how you will mediate between students and the text. Remember that mediated instruction includes the following (Dixon-Krauss, 1996):

- Your *purpose* for engaging students in thinking about the text
- The *strategy(s)* you will use to assist students as they make meaning before, during, and after reading the text
- *Reflection* on how you will adjust support to students as indicated by their feedback during discussion

Students should think about how they link the author's ideas with what they already know. The more students know about the topic of the text, the easier it will be for them to follow the author's ideas. In information writing, however, it is often difficult to anticipate where the author is leading the reader.

The MRTA (mediated reading thinking activity) presented in Chapter 6 for narrative texts focused on using background knowledge, combined with the ideas in the text, to anticipate and respond to the story. In information texts the emphasis is not on prediction and personal response, but rather on questioning whether the author's ideas are being understood and how to use personal knowledge to support understanding.

Given the differences in texts, it would stand to reason then that you will need to revise the MRTA techniques you use with narrative texts when you mediate students' reading of information. Figure 12.1 shows a comparison of thinking between MRTA and content-MRTA (C-MRTA).

In information texts, you must help students realize how their reading (or listening, if you are reading aloud to students) may be different than with narrative texts. They must pay careful attention to the author's ideas. Readers (listeners) are not as free to make personal interpretations in information texts as in narrative texts. Retaining, using, or acting on the information in the text is a purpose of the reading, therefore, readers must be actively involved in linking new information to their existing schema. Students must come to realize that they are responsible for monitoring what is or is not making sense.

Content-Mediated Reading Thinking Activity (C-MRTA)

To promote thinking and meaning making before, during, and after the reading of a text, stop at key points and discuss the text by asking open-ended questions. Because of the structure of ideas in information texts, guide students to explain the information in a text and make connections among ideas and between the text and their own knowledge. Let the particular structure of ideas in a text guide how you support students' thinking and connecting.

Figure 12.1 Comparing MRTA and C-MRTA

MRTA	C-MRTA
Before the reading, you think: • What is this possibly going to be about? • What do I already know?	**Before the reading, you think:** • What is this going to be about? • What information do I already know about this topic? • Can I tell by looking at the text what I might need to think about to understand the author's ideas?
During the reading, you think: • How does this fit with what came before? • How does this fit with what I already know? • What will happen next? • Do I need to change what I am thinking?	**During the reading, you think:** • Am I finding the important details? • Which ideas are the main or most important ideas? • How do these ideas fit with what I already know? • Do I need to rethink my own ideas?
After the reading, you think: • How do I feel about this? • What do I want to remember about this?	**After the reading, you think:** • Now, what was that all about? • What do I really need to remember? • How will I use these ideas?

In an MRTA with narrative text, we used a predict-read-respond-connect cycle to mediate between students and text. In a C-MRTA, because of differences between narrative and information text (readers' purposes for reading, the way the text is written, and the ways readers must think while reading), readers do not *respond* to text. Instead, readers first *explain* the ideas they found in the text, then make connections to their schema for the topic. We thus revise the C-MRTA cycle to be: predict, read, explain, connect.

For example, imagine your sixth grade classroom is beginning a study of ancient Egypt. Chapter 3 in your social studies textbook focuses on ancient Egypt, as one of several chapters about the beginnings of civilization. The unit you are planning begins with a look at the Nile River as the base of Egyptian civilization. After brainstorming and clustering what students already know about the Nile (rather than ancient Egypt as a whole), you engage students in reading pages 65–69 in the textbook using a C-MRTA. You begin by asking students to preview the text and predict what the text might contain. The following sample dramatizes how your C-MRTA might proceed.

Sample C-MRTA—The Geography of Ancient Egypt

Predict: "The heading of this section of the text is 'The Geography of Ancient Egypt.' Think about this heading as you look at the subheadings on pages 65–69. What do you think we might learn about in this part of the textbook? How do these predictions compare to our Nile cluster?" (students make comparisons and contrasts)

Read: "Let's look at the first subheading, 'The Nile River Valley.'" (read the first three paragraphs out loud to set the tone for the reading, referring students to the map on page 66 as suggested in the second paragraph) "What do we know so far? The authors of this textbook remind us how much the geography of a place influences people's lives. Please read the reminder of this subsection silently."

Explain: "What did we find out about the Nile?" (take responses)

Connect: "Should we add to or revise our cluster?" (add "flows from south to north," and "Egypt divided into Upper and Lower")

Predict: "Look at the map on page 66. What differences might there have been between Upper and Lower Egypt?" (pause for responses) "What does the next subheading make you think about?"

Read: "Let's read 'The Overflow of the Nile' silently to check our ideas."

Explain: "What did we find out about the overflow?" (take responses) "What do you know about silt? Does the text explain why the overflow happened every summer? How can we explain it?" (guide students to look at Africa on the classroom world relief map)

Connect: "Do we need to add to or revise our cluster?" (pause for responses) "The next section is titled, 'The Nile Delta.' What do we already know about that?" (students refer back to cluster and the map on page 66)

Predict: "What else might we find out about the Nile Delta in this section?" (take responses)

Read: "Please read this section on page 67 silently."

Explain: "What do we know about the delta?" (pause) "What do you think about the comparison of the delta to the lotus flower?"

Connect: "How do these ideas compare to the ideas on our cluster?" (take responses)

Predict: "The remaining sections have something to do with farming. Why do you think the textbook authors put these section next?" (pause for responses) "As you read silently, make note of the details about farming and the Nile that you think are important for us to discuss."

Read: Students read pages 68 & 69 silently.

Explain: "What details did you notice as you read?" (take responses) "Did anyone use the drawing on page 69 to better understand the way ancient Egyptians used irrigation? How did the drawing help?" (pause for responses)

Connect: "In the last paragraph on page 69, the textbook authors stated that the Nile helped to unite Egypt. What do we know that could support that statement?" (pause for responses). "Do we need to make any other revisions to our cluster for today?" (take responses) "What are the most important ideas we want to remember from this reading?" (take responses) "Let's highlight the most important ideas on our cluster."

What students are able to take from a text depends on what they bring to it. Remember that students with more extensive background knowledge and more book experience may be more successful initially than less experienced students. As you observe students' responses during C-MRTAs, you must watch the responses of the less experienced as a gauge of effectiveness.

We turn our attention now to using information and narrative texts in units of study, as we explore using the language arts as tools for supporting and enhancing content area integration.

Planning an Integrated Unit

In integration, *process* is a key word. Planning an integrated unit is actually the process of selecting and organizing materials and activities that will have the greatest impact on student attitude and learning. The process different teachers follow to plan and develop integrated units may vary in their order, but will usually include the following actions:

- Considering the required curriculum areas, topics, and objectives.
- Brainstorming possibilities for units throughout a school year, including purposes for the use of the language arts in a unit.
- Identifying available and appropriate resources, especially literature.
- Matching curriculum objectives and resources.
- Selecting appropriate organizing ideas and activities that meet learning objectives.
- Deciding on a time frame for the unit.
- Organizing and implementing unit activities.
- Monitoring students' progress during the unit.
- Evaluating the unit's effectiveness.

From your reading in other chapters, you know many things that can become a part of developing successful integrated units:

- A variety of ways to teach through literature and writing
- How to integrate your use of the language arts to enhance learning experiences
- How to consider curriculum requirements
- How to select appropriate objectives and experiences for instruction
- Options for monitoring student progress

Now, your task is to apply what you already know to linking learning experiences between the language arts and one or more content areas.

Imagine yourself once again in a sixth-grade classroom, preparing a unit about ancient Egypt. Your planning begins with considering the curricular experiences you are expected to offer students.

Consider the Curriculum

Topics of content area study are usually clearly identified by school district curriculum guides. It is quite possible in your school district that you are expected to help your sixth-grade students develop the following skills and strategies:

Social Studies

1. Tell how laws are needed in world civilizations.
2. Examine the causes and effects of major historical events.
3. Place historical events in chronological sequence.
4. Recognize how people's needs are met in different cultures.
5. Recognize the importance of cultural and religious differences.
6. Explore the relationship of economics to natural resources and civilization.
7. Interpret the role of geography in the lifestyles of inhabitants.
8. Define and locate examples of different geographical formations.
9. Recognize the hemisphere in which countries are located.
10. Use legends accurately.

Reading/Language Arts

1. Distinguish types and purposes of a variety of works of literature.
2. Explore the role of literary elements in the development of fiction, including plot, character, setting, voice (point of view), style (language, mood, tone), and theme.
3. Compare/contrast characteristics of fiction and information texts, including that authors write in different ways for different purposes.
4. Generalize, infer, and draw conclusions.
5. Read and effectively use resource references.
6. Interpret charts, tables, and diagrams.
7. Practice productive reading strategies.
8. Write multiparagraph narrative, expository, and descriptive pieces, letters, and poems.
9. Organize information by strategies such as note taking, outlining, and summarizing.
10. Write a report using at least three sources, and include a bibliography and note cards.
11. Improve effectiveness at revising and editing.
12. Improve oral expression through oral reports, recitations, and drama.

As a starting point, which of these skills and strategies might you develop in a unit about ancient Egypt?

My Turn

I believe all of the items listed under social studies and language arts could potentially appear in an ancient Egypt unit, although I would emphasize some more than others. As I gather information and develop a clearer sense of the unit's focus, I would return to these objectives and identify a few to receive greater emphasis.

Consider Adopted Textbooks

While an adopted textbook is not "the curriculum," it certainly can be a valuable resource as you learn to integrate the curriculum. Imagine that the adopted social studies textbook in your school district focuses on the eastern hemisphere, with unit topics such as the beginnings of civilization, and ancient and modern times in the continents of Europe, Africa, and Asia. If you are new to integration, the textbook may be a starting point for your planning.

The social studies textbook authors (Beyer et al., 1990, teacher's edition, p. 63-A) identify the following chapter theme and content objectives:

> *Theme:*
>
> The ancient Egyptians developed the world's first civilization by organizing themselves and their use of their geographical environment
>
> *Content Objectives:*
>
> In the civilization of ancient Egypt, identify, explain, or describe:
>
> - the geography of the Nile River
> - the importance of irrigation to farming along the Nile
> - important events that lead to Egypt's rise to power
> - the absolute power of the pharaohs
> - features of the Egyptian system of writing
> - the importance of religion in Egyptian society
> - the impact of the social system on Egyptian life

Your Turn

What do you think of these content objectives? Do you think your students would benefit by studying them? How do they compare with the school district's social studies objectives?

The textbook provides some background about the geography of Egypt, with limited information about the culture and daily life. The school district's objectives go beyond what the textbook offers. I would need to supplement the information in the textbook to meet the school district's goals and objectives for sixth grade.

■

Review and Select Literature Resources

For most units, there will be more literature available than you can possibly use. Some resources, but not all, will be useful for your students and/or the topic. It is important to carefully review the available narrative and information texts and select appropriate ones that meet the scope of the unit and the diverse reading levels and interests of your students.

Norton (1994) suggests the following guidelines to help you select quality information texts:

- All facts are accurate.
- Stereotypes have been eliminated.
- Illustrations enhance and clarify the text.

Figure 12.2 Literature possibilities—Information

Whole-Class Read-Aloud

Koenig, V., & Ageorges, V. (1992). *The Ancient Egyptians.* Brookfield, Ct: Millbrook.

Reeves, N. (1992). *Into the Mummy's Tomb: The Real-Life Discovery of Tutankhamen's Treasures.* New York: Scholastic/Madison.

Literature Circles

McCaulay, D. (1982). *Pyramid.* Boston: Houghton Mifflin.

Wilcox, C. (1993). *Mummies and Their Mysteries.* New York: Scholastic.

Independent Reading and Research

Aldred, C. (1980). *Egyptian Art.* New York: Oxford University Press.

Brandenberg, A. (1985). *Mummies Made in Egypt.* New York: First Harper Trophy.

Berrill, M. (1990). *Mummies, Masks, and Mourners.* New York: E. P. Dutton.

Brander, B. (1993). *The River Nile.* Washington, DC: National Geographic Society.

Caselli, G. (1986). *An Egyptian Craftsman.* London: Macdonald.

Claiborne, R. (1974). *The Birth of Writing.* New York: Time-Life Books.

Clayton, P. (1996). *The Valley of the Kings.* New York: Thomson Learning.

David, A. R. (1988). *The Egyptian Kingdoms.* New York: Peter Bedrick.

Giblin, J. (1990). *The Riddle of the Rosetta Stone.* New York: Thomas Crowell.

Harris, N. (1990). *Everyday Life in Ancient Egypt.* New York: Franklin Watts.

Hart, G. (1990). *Eyewitness Books: Ancient Egypt.* New York: Alfred A. Knopf.

Katan, N. (1981). *Hieroglyphs: The Writing of Ancient Egypt.* New York: McElderly.

Lauber, P. (1983). *Tales Mummies Tell.* New York: Scholastic.

Marston, E. (1996). *The Ancient Egyptians.* New York: Benchmark Books.

Millard, A. (1995). *Mysteries of the Pyramids.* Brookfield, CT: Copper Beech Books.

National Geographic. (1984). *Great Rivers of the World.* Washington, DC: National Geographic.

Nicholson, R., & Watts, C. (1994). *Ancient Egypt.* New York: Chelsea Juniors.

Odijk, P. (1989). *The Ancient World of the Egyptians.* Hong Kong: Silver Burdett.

Oliphant, M. (1989). *The Egyptian World.* New York: Warwick.

Osborne, M. P. (1993). *Mummies in the Morning.* New York: Scholastic.

Price, C. (1990). *Made in Ancient Egypt.* Toronto: Clarke, Irwin.

Roehrig, C. (1990). *Fun With Hieroglyphics.* New York: Metropolitan Museum of Art.

Scott, J., & Scott, L. (1974). *Hieroglyphics for Fun.* New York: Van Nostrand Reinhold.

Stanley, D., & Vennema, R. (1994). *Cleopatra.* New York: Morrow Junior Books.

Strouhal, E. (1992). *Life of the Ancient Egyptians.* Norman, OK: University of Oklahoma Press.

Terzi, M. (1992). *The Land of the Pharaohs.* Chicago: Childrens Press.

Watts, F. (1992). *Craft Topics.* New York: Franklin Watts.

Woods, G. (1988). *Science in Ancient Egypt.* New York: Franklin Watts.

- Analytical thinking is encouraged.
- The organization of the text aids understanding.
- The style of writing stimulates interest.

For your unit on ancient Egypt, it is particularly important that you have texts with excellent photographs of artifacts from that period to help students develop a sense of the culture.

As you select appropriate literature, you want to ensure variety of use: texts you can read aloud to the whole class, texts that might be studied by a small group, and texts that will support individual study and research. Such variety will enrich the way you use literature to engage students in the unit topic and enable you to meet reading/language arts and social studies objectives at the same time. Literature possibilities for ancient Egypt are listed in Figures 12.2 (information books) and 12.3 (narratives).

Figure 12.3 Literature possibilities—Narrative

Whole-Class Read-Aloud

dePaola, T. (1987). *Bill and Pete Go Down the Nile.* New York: Putnam.

Lattimore, D. N. (1992). *The Winged Cat: A Tale of Ancient Egypt.* New York: HarperCollins.

Stolz, M. (1988). *Zekmet, The Stone Carver.* San Diego: Harcourt Brace Jovanovich.

Literature Circles

Climo, S. (1989). *The Egyptian Cinderella.* New York: Thomas Crowell.

Dexter, C. (1992). *The Gilded Cat.* New York: Morrow Junior Books.

Roden, K. (1996). *In the Footsteps of the Mummy.* Brookfield, CT: Copper Beech Books.

Snyder, Z. K. (1976). *The Egypt Game.* New York: Atheneum.

Independent Reading

Bradshaw, G. (1991). *The Dragon and the Thief.* New York: Greenwillow.

Carter, D. S. (1987). *His Majesty, Queen Hatshepsut.* New York: Lippincott.

Ellerby, L. (1980). *King Tut's Game Board.* New York: Lerner.

Harris, R. (1972). *The Bright and Morning Star.* New York: Macmillan.

Lepon, S. (1988). *The Ten Plagues of Egypt.* New York: Judaica.

McGraw, E. J. (1986). *The Golden Goblet.* New York: Puffin.

McGraw, E. J. (1988). *Mara, Daughter of the Nile.* New York: Puffin.

Service, P. (1988). *The Reluctant God.* New York: Atheneum.

Somper, J. (1993). *Pyramid Plot.* New York: EDC.

Stine, M., & Stine, H. (1992). *The Mummy's Curse.* New York: Random House.

Stine, R. L. (1993). *Goosebumps: The Curse of the Mummy's Tomb.* New York: Scholastic.

Strouhal, E. (1991). *Indiana Jones Explores Ancient Egypt.* New York: Little, Brown.

Involve Students in Planning

As you begin the planning process, discuss the unit topic with students, exploring what they already know about Egypt. You also want the unit to reflect their needs and interests, so discuss what they want to learn about Egypt. Sixth-grade students often raise the following questions:

- What was ancient Egypt like?
- How did the Egyptians make a mummy?
- Why did the Egyptians mummify people?
- Who got to be mummified?
- Who built the pyramids?
- How did the Egyptians make the pyramids without machines?
- Why did the Egyptians build the pyramids?
- Were all pharaohs buried in pyramids? Was King Tut?
- How did people figure out hieroglyphs? Why didn't Egyptians write with letters?

Students' interests typically focus on pyramids and the mummification process. Your challenge, then, is to find ways to weave their interests with your goals and objectives.

Look back at the school district goals and objectives. How can you weave students' interest in mummies and pyramids into the objectives listed?

The discovery of Tutankhamen's Tomb was certainly a major historical event (Goal/Objective 2), the pyramids were inspired by religious beliefs (5), the mummification process resulted from religious and cultural beliefs (5), materials to build the pyramids and treasures in the tomb were related to natural resources and economics (6), and who was buried in pyramids and tombs related to the laws of the civilization (1). Students' needs and interests easily link to what we are expected to teach.

■

Develop Organizing Ideas and Activities

Now, you have some basic ideas around which you can organize this unit. As you find out more about students' knowledge and interests, you can add to or revise your plans. You should, however, begin to make the following decisions:

- The basic organization and scope of the unit
- Initiating activities for the unit
- Activities that will be important for all students
- Activities that could be choices for students

Overall Organization. Considering the goals and objectives for social studies identified in an earlier section, what the adopted textbook offers, the literature that is available, and the organization of the school in which you teach, you could organize your unit around three central issues:

- Life along the Nile River
- Pyramids and the Valley of the Kings
- The social pyramid

You can develop the concept of civilization through the study of the Nile, including the influence of the geography on life and culture, the forming of a government, economic issues, and communication. Both the pyramids and the social pyramid will return you to students' interest in mummies and the mummification process. Exploring the social pyramid will allow you to look at Egyptian culture, religion, and writing.

Initiating Activities. Believing that the language arts undergird learning, you would probably choose to begin with a whole-class literature selection to capture interest and set the tone for the unit. Figures 12.2 and 12.3 identify several whole-class books. To get a feel for life in another time, it would be best to begin with narrative selections. Probing students' background knowledge is also important. Focusing on the K- (What do I *know?*) and W- (What do I *want* to know?) in a K-W-L chart could be a start.

Activities for All Students. From a language arts perspective, it is important for all students to participate in whole-class discussions that process the information being found in small groups and independently. In addition, all students should participate in some form of reading experience that provides opportunity for discussion and reflection through writing. New vocabulary will be abundant. All students need opportunity to collect and consider new words, especially words that are related to contemporary language.

Activities for Choice. Middle grade students need the sense of becoming independent and making successful decisions. Choice must be an integral part of any unit. With the wealth of information available on this topic, it is difficult to defend the idea that all students must learn the same content. Middle grade students will benefit from pursuing areas of interest as they apply reading, writing, and thinking strategies. They can then share what they learn in a variety of forums.

Plan for Adequate Time

As you select a theme/topic and begin to collect resources to plan for possible activities, you should have a general sense of the time that you can devote to the theme study. Think about both the duration of the unit and the daily time devoted to unit activities. At the beginning of each school year it is a good idea to survey your curriculum and anticipate the units you might teach during the year. This survey gives you a better sense of the number of weeks you may devote to any single unit. For example, after conducting your survey, you might decide to devote three to four weeks to this unit about ancient Egypt.

How you organize your daily time for the unit depends, in part, on the organization of your school:

- If you have one class of students for the entire day, you have the choice of integrating within time blocks or across time blocks in your daily schedule.
- If you have a class for a block of time, such as when departmentalizing by subject areas, you can plan jointly with other teachers to accomplish the unit goals.

In a self-contained classroom, you typically will have blocks of time for reading/ language arts, mathematics, and science/social studies experiences. In an integrated

Integrated units require blocks of time for study that allow students to become deeply engaged in their learning.

unit, you must decide how much time to devote each day to unit activities. Will you use only your science/social studies time or will you also think of language arts and/or mathematics instruction time as possibilities for inclusion? You will make these decisions as the unit takes shape.

Organizing and Implementing the Unit

Starting with your organizing ideas and activities, plan the basic structure of the unit. If integrated teaching is new, you might consider keeping the daily schedule you have already established (e.g., reading/language arts time, math, read-aloud, SSR/DEAR, science/social studies time) and using the time in one or more blocks to explore unit concepts and objectives in the unit.

A workshop framework, similar to reader's and writer's workshop, is a useful way to arrange work time. Whole-class activities can set a focus, lead to small-group and independent activities, then bring closure. Depending on your daily schedule, you can have one or more workshop periods during a day (reading/language arts, unit study).

During integrated units, you might allocate typical subject time blocks in the following ways:

- Reading/language arts block—Whole group, small-group, and/or independent study of information and narrative texts about Egypt, write in response to reading, and make records of learning about Egyptians.
- Mathematics—Whole-group instruction in math concepts that have some relationship to the unit study, such as the mathematics of the pyramids, with exploration and application in work centers.

- Science/social studies—Whole-group hands-on activities, time for independent exploration and research related to ancient Egypt.
- SSR/DEAR—Self-selected reading in books related to the unit, continuation of reading for literature groups, or independent research.
- Read-aloud—Reading and rereading of texts that contribute to unit theme.

The more that you experiment with integration and the more familiar you are with the unit topic, the more you are able to think flexibly about daily instructional time and "blur" the lines dividing subject matter. In the beginning, however, "integrated" thinking will be very challenging.

Grouping for Instruction

In your ancient Egypt unit, you decide to arrange learning experiences as combinations of whole-group, small-group, and independent activities.

- Whole group—Introductory experiences are whole-class activities to help students become aware of concepts in the theme and possibilities for activities within the theme.
- Small group—Processing experiences are small-group activities where you can interact more closely with students to support and extend their thinking.
- Independent—Exploration and personal interest experiences are partner/independent activities, giving individual students the time they need to learn.

You have a number of ideas now for organizing a unit on ancient Egypt. Let's put these ideas to work. The following section presents a sketch for a sample four-week unit. Following the sample, we discuss how to monitor and evaluate students' progress when working with integrated units.

Sample Unit: Ancient Egypt—Uncovering the Past

Week 1—Social Studies Workshop.

Monday

- Independent drawing—"When you think of ancient Egypt, what do you think life was like? Draw a picture of your thinking." (Assess students' conceptions/misconceptions.)
- Opening reading—Whole-class read-aloud of *Bill and Pete Go Down the Nile* (just for fun!).
- "What do you already know (K-) about the Nile River?"

  Small-group discussions, begin K- part of K-W-L chart, record in learning log.

  Return to whole class, share, compile class K- chart.
- Video—*What Was Ancient Egypt Like?* (Pyramid School Kit, PBS).
- Small-group discussions with discussion guide:

  Why is Egypt called "the gift of the Nile"?

  What was Upper Egypt and Lower Egypt?

  Why did ancient Egyptians live close to the Nile?

  Place discussion guide in learning log

- Closure

  Share discussion guides with class.

  Add to or revise class/personal K- chart.

  Plan for Tuesday.

Tuesday

- Opening—Recall video highlights of the Nile and early Egypt.
- C-MRTA—Social studies textbook (geography of the Nile, farming, irrigation).
- Revisit K- chart, re-construct what students know, cluster around broad topics (geography, farming, government, economics, communication). Be sure topics are researchable.
- Small groups work on one topic.

  Discuss what is already known, what information is needed.

  Collect additional data on topic (log).

  Use materials collected in unit resource area.
- Closure

  Process how small groups worked.

  Suggestions for Wednesday groups.

Wednesday and Thursday

- Opening

  C-MLTA, read selected portions of *The River Nile,* discussion.

  Review small group tasks. Introduce data disk (Figure 12.4) for recording small group research.
- Small-group work.

  Continue research.

  Make notes, sketches, charts, etc. in log.

  Make a group data disk for sharing research.
- Closure on Thursday

  Present results of research and group data disks.

  Create bulletin board, with Nile River backdrop and data disks.

Friday

- Opening

  Minilesson—Finding information in stories.

  Read-aloud, *Zekmet, The Stone Carver.*

  Role-play Khafre (pharaoh), Ho-tep (vizier), Zekmet (stone carver), and Senmut (Zekmet's son).
- Small-group discussions with discussion guide

  What did you learn about Egyptian social class?

  What would you like to learn about Egyptian people?
- Closure

  Divide class by lottery into social groups (farmer, slave, pharaoh, scribe, artisan, priest, embalmer, etc.). Students prepare to research social roles and "be" that person.

Figure 12.4 Data disk

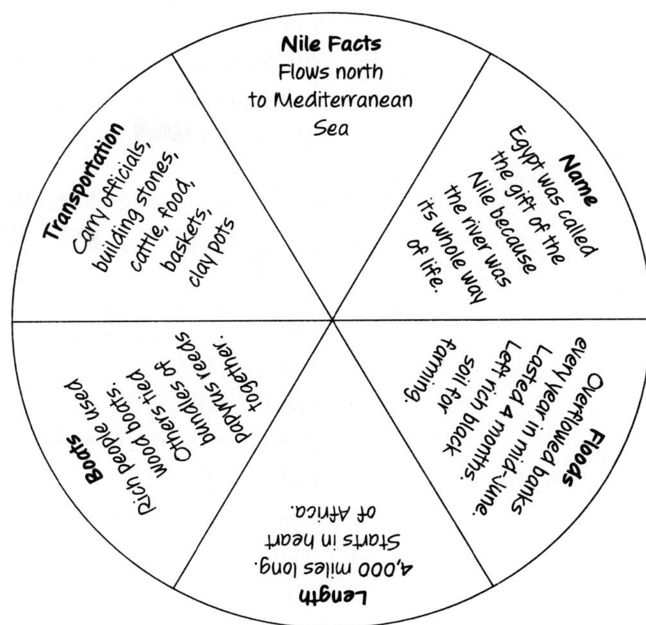

Give book talks for next week's literature circles, students select books by first and second choice on ballot.

Week 2—Social Studies Workshop.

- Group and individual research for roles in social pyramid.
- Students make icons that represent their roles' social class for the Social Pyramid bulletin board.
- Students prepare a skit, advertisement, videotaped commercial, song, etc. to share research on social roles during Week 3.

Reader's Workshop.

- Literature circles for the week:

  Pyramid

  Cleopatra

  Mummies and Their Mysteries

  The Egyptian Cinderella

  In the Footsteps of the Mummy
- Groups meet, agree on a reading plan, discuss first impressions, make predictions, share background knowledge.
- Learning logs, open response to reading, collect three to five new words or interesting phrases, information about Egyptian life.

Writer's Workshop.

- Writing from a point of view:

  Students take perspective of assigned social role.

  Form is student's choice (diary, personal narrative, poem, letter, etc.).

Students plan to share writing orally during Week 3.

- Minilessons during the week:

  Example of Two-Voice Poem (Figure 12.5) as a writing option.

  Examples of writing in first person.

Weeks 3 and 4—Social Studies Workshop.

- C-MLTA, "The Day of Days" from *Into the Mummy's Tomb,* describes the discovery of King Tut's tomb in the Valley of the Kings.
- MLTA, *The Winged Cat: A Tale of Ancient Egypt,* a myth about Egyptian gods.
- Form interest groups

  1. Pyramid Group

  Research question, How were the pyramids built?

  View video (Pyramid School Kit, PBS).

  Simulate building procedures, build a replica pyramid.

  Make records in "Architect's Manual" (log).

  Become an "expert" on a tool used for building.

  2. Burial Customs

  Research questions, Why were pyramids built? What was the significance of items placed in the tomb?

Figure 12.5 Sample two-voice poem

The Social Pyramid—A Poem for Two Voices

Pharoah's Voice	Both Voices	Slave's Voice
	1. What makes us different? We are so much the same.	
2. I am pharoah.		3. I am slave.
4. Our worlds must be separate.		
	5. We both marvel at the beauty of the Nile.	
		6. Why can't we live together?
7. Because we are not equal.		
		8. But I am human just as you.
9. You are less.		
		10. I wish I was more.
11. I look forward to the life hereafter.		
		12. So do I.
	13. What makes us different? We are so much the same.	

View video (Pyramid School Kit, PBS).

Research mummification process, mummify a chicken.

Prepare a "How To" book for burial and mummification, a "Book of the Dead", or stela or mural of important life events.

3. Gods and Goddesses

   Research questions, What did Egyptians believe about life and afterlife? Why did the Egyptians have so many gods and goddesses?

   Read myths about gods and goddesses.

   Compile information on data disks or make a "Guide to Gods and Goddesses."

   Write a myth that demonstrates the power of a particular god or goddess.

Reader's Workshop.

- Independent reading in narrative and information texts related to unit topics.
- Respond in learning log each day, in a variety of format options (double-entry, Venn diagram, annotated drawing, description, etc.).
- Confer with teacher once during week:

  Share log entries.

  Share favorite or interesting selections.
- Small-group sharing of related texts (pyramids, mummies, etc.).
- Give book talks to promote books on topics of interest.

Writer's Workshop.

- Integrate workshop into projects for pyramids, burial customs, and gods and goddesses.
- Minilessons

  Effective spatial organization of information (in preparation for sharing with class).

  Selecting a form of writing that fits the author's intention.

Culminating Activity.

- Create a "Living Museum" of vignettes of Egyptian life, including student created art, poetry, plays, etc.

Monitoring Students' Progress in Integrated Units

In past chapters we have organized monitoring around observing students at work, conferring with them about their work, and collecting samples of their work over time. In integrated units, you will use similar procedures to consider students' growth in reading, writing, and content areas.

Observing Students

During the four weeks of this unit there would be opportunities to observe students in guided whole-group activities, in cooperative small-group activities, and in independent reading, writing, and research activities. You can make anecdotal records of students during the unit to see patterns of learning behavior, maintaining individual record forms. You also may make records of learning behavior that meets your instructional goals. Unit objectives become a frame of reference for observing students' progress. A simple form, with space for observations, can remind you of your overall objectives.

Conferring with Students

During independent reading, writer's workshop, and personal research time you have opportunities to confer with students about their progress in learning, focusing on the students as learners, as well as on the concepts they are acquiring. In the ancient Egypt unit, conferring is most practical during weeks 3 and 4 when students are engaged primarily in independent work. Even though your objectives address more than one subject area, one general conference record per student should suffice for the entire unit.

Samples of Student Work

As you think back over the unit, what samples of work could be saved to reflect student learning? Writing from a perspective in week 2 and research in the interest groups in weeks 3 and 4 should yield good samples. What about the learning log? It should contain a number of samples of informal writing used to capture thinking across all four weeks. Consider these two types of writing for each student.

In addition, you might ask students to select one or two other samples of work, unique to the individual, that will show the following:

- Effort during the unit
- Creative or critical thinking
- Something that was hard to do
- Something the student is most proud of

You should evaluate all work in light of student's personal goals and unit instructional goals.

Observing, conferring, and collecting samples of students' work during integrated units enable you to help students reflect on their own growth, as well as to share their progress with parents and administrators. While you may be able to "blur" the lines among subject matter in unit activities, you are still accountable for documenting growth on report cards and other evaluation systems used by your school district.

Evaluating an Integrated Unit

As you monitor students' progress in a unit, you are also gathering information that enables you to evaluate the unit's effectiveness. You plan your unit to be engaging and beneficial for learning, but how can you be sure that actually happens? You cannot know if your planning was appropriate until you implement the unit and observe students' progress.

Your evaluation should focus on asking the following questions:

- Were the unit objectives and activities appropriate for the needs and interests of my students?
- Did students have adequate learning time to meet the unit objectives?
- Did I provide appropriate support to enable all students to be successful in gaining new knowledge and connecting their past experiences to that new knowledge?

- Did the instructional materials I selected meet the varying needs and interests of my students?

Evaluation should focus heavily on the decisions that you made while planning and implementing your instructional activities. When instruction is not as successful as you hope, the cause may lie in not understanding your students as individuals and as learners. That understanding should influence your objectives for instruction, the materials you select to help you meet those objectives, and the instructional strategies you use to engage students in learning. In reality, you are not evaluating your students, but rather yourself and your decision making processes.

Respecting Diversity Through Integrated Units

Integrated units may be the most genuine way for you to respect and support diversity in your classroom. The range of curricular experiences in a well-planned integrated unit makes it possible to meet the diversity of your students' interests and needs. Every student should find success in the range of unit activities and projects. Including students in developing and planning your units enhances your opportunities for success.

Consider for a moment the chapter's sample integrated unit on ancient Egypt. This unit drew on nearly all of the instructional strategies and approaches that we have discussed in this text. Reading experiences combined whole-class, small-group, and independent opportunities, as well as reading aloud to students, in a variety of fiction and information texts. Writing experiences included both writing process and informal writing. The teacher mediated some experiences, while others were initiated and guided by students. Many activities were open-ended to allow for diversity in student thinking.

We have considered issues of diversity in each chapter of this text. I suggest that you reread the "Respecting Diversity" sections at the end of each chapter to review the range of possibilities you have for meeting the needs and interests of diverse groups of middle grade students.

As Lindquist (1995) stated at the beginning of this chapter, the more knowledgeable you are about your curriculum, your teaching materials, and your students, the more natural teaching through integration will become, and the more you will grow to respect the wonderful diversity of your students.

TAKE A MOMENT AND REFLECT . . .

Integration is:

- whole learning
- the woven fabric, not the individual threads
- a process

Two types of integration are:

- Integrated curriculum, including
  1. Selecting appropriate subject matter for a topic
  2. Infusing skills from one area to another
  3. Organizing the school year around a theme
  4. Natural links between subject areas
- Integrated learning that focuses on the child

Levels of integration include:

- Few connections, formal planning
- Blending skills and content, connecting subject areas
- Natural connections, focus is not on subjects
- Focus on whole student

The language arts are naturally integrative and support all learning.

Use of literature in units serves different purposes:

- Focus on literature and literary value
- Use literature to supplement content
- Blend literature and content experiences

Readers read information text differently than narrative text:

- Purposes for reading
- Ways of thinking in text

In information texts, readers:

- Call up what they know
- Connect new ideas
- Predict or anticipate what may come
- Organize information
- Generalize
- Form an image through the senses
- Monitor internally
- Evaluate or judge
- Apply knowledge

Use a C-MRTA (or C-MLTA) to guide students' reading (or listening) of information text as they learn to use thinking processes as they read:

- Teachers guide students by asking open-end questions
- In response to teacher's questions, students
  1. Predict/anticipate what might come next
  2. Read or listen to a portion of text read aloud
  3. Explain their thinking by referring back to text
  4. Connect new ideas to what is already known

To develop units of instruction, you must:

- Consider the required curriculum areas, topics, and objectives
- Consider content of adopted textbooks
- Brainstorm possibilities for units, including purposes for using language arts to support learning
- Identify available and appropriate resources, including literature
- Involve students in planning
- Match curriculum objectives and resources
- Select appropriate activities that meet your learning objectives
- Plan adequate time for the unit
- Organize and implement unit activities
- Monitor students' progress during the unit
- Evaluate the effectiveness of the unit

Integrated units:

- Maximize instructional time in an already crowded school day
- Balance the use of narrative and informational texts to better meet students' needs and interests
- Use reading and writing as tools for learning rather than focusing on the processes of learning to read and write

REFERENCES

Allen, D. D., & Piersma, M. L. (1995). *Developing thematic units*. Albany, NY: Delmar.

Beyer, B. K., Craven, J., McFarland, M. A., & Parker, W. C. (1990). *The world around us: Eastern hemisphere.* Upper Saddle River, NJ: Merrill/Prentice Hall.

Dixon-Krauss, L. (1996). *Vygotsky in the classroom: Mediate literacy instruction and assessment.* New York: Longman.

Lindquist, T. (1995). *Seeing the whole through social studies.* Portsmouth, NH: Heinemann.

Moore, D. W., Moore, S. A., Cunningham, P. M., and Cunningham, J. W. (1994). *Developing readers & writers in the content areas K–12.* New York: Longman.

Morrison, G. S. (1993). *Contemporary curriculum K–8.* Boston: Allyn & Bacon.

Norton, D. E. (1994). *Through the eyes of a child: An introduction to children's literature* (4th ed.). Upper Saddle River, NJ: Merrill/Prentice Hall.

Rosenblatt, L. M. (1989). Writing and reading: The transactional theory. In J. Mason (Ed.), *Reading and writing connections* (pp. 153–176). Boston: Allyn & Bacon.

Shoemaker, B. J. E. (1991). Education 2000 integrated curriculum. *Phi Delta Kappan, 73*, 793–797.

CHILDREN'S LITERATURE

Paulsen, G. (1987). *Hatchet.* New York: Viking Penguin.

Appendix A

Whole-Class Literature Study: A Taste of Blackberries,

by Doris Buchanan Smith
(New York: Thomas Y. Crowell, 1973)

This study includes:

- Chapter lesson plans
- Discussion guides
- Sample forms for literature log entries

Recommended for 4th or 5th grade.

Chapter 1 Lesson Plan

Summary

We meet Jamie and the unnamed narrator ("I") and learn of their friendship, woven around picking blackberries, stealing apples, and rock-hopping a creek. Narrator agrees to get children to pick Japanese beetles off of Mrs. Houser's grapevines.

Discussion Points and Key Words

Before Reading

- Read the title and information about the book available on the dust jacket. From the title and jacket copy, what do we know so far about this story? What do you think might happen?

During Reading

- Read first two paragraphs. Clarify point of view. Who is "I"?
- Note how Jamie and "I" overhear other children talking about them while in the blackberry thicket.
- Pause at the beginning of the apple stealing incident (after Jamie "up-an-overed" the fence) for children to anticipate what is going to happen, and why "I" didn't join in.
- After the stealing incident, encourage brief responses. Note the statement, "My heart was beating *paradiddles,*" to emphasize how "I" felt.
- Pause after Mrs. Houser calls to "I", anticipate what might happen (we already know that "I" is afraid of her).

After Reading

- Engage in brief retelling of key ideas before children go to small groups.
- Children respond to the chapter in small groups using the discussion guide.

Developed by: Ginny Beck, Vickie Cannon, Martha Combs, Janet DeLano, Stacy Drum, Liz Lean, Paula McLaughlin, Kae Moreno, Lisa Reger, and Judy Smith.

- Return to whole class for in-depth discussion using discussion guides.
- Additional suggestions for discussion:
  1. What do we know so far about Jamie? About "I"?
  2. Hyphen-words from Chapter 1:

     every which-a-way
     rock-hopped the creek
     up-and-overed the fence
     playground merry-go-round
     sour-sweetness spilled into my mouth
     sat down cross-legged
     across-the-street neighbor
     far-away feeling
- Anticipate what might happen in the next chapter. Say, "What do you think might happen in the next chapter? What makes you think that?" Think back to "I"'s conversation with Mrs. Houser.

Discussion Guide Questions

See Chapter 1 Discussion Guide.

Literature Log Possibilities

- Start a character chart to show what you are learning about Jamie and "I" as people and as friends (see sample log form, Figure A.1). What have you learned about them in Chapter 1? (Suggestion: Begin this as a whole class, then move to independent recording.)
- Start lists of words on separate pages (see sample log forms, Figures A.2 and A.3):

  Interesting words and phrases

  Words I want to know more about

Chapter 2 Lesson Plan

Summary

Jamie and "I" take Martha, Jamie's four-year-old sister, for a walk as they get children to pick beetles off Mrs. Houser's grapevines. Heather, the boys' best friend, is the first one they ask. Trying to show Martha their school, the children get stuck in a storm and "hitch" a ride from a stranger who is actually the father of a schoolmate.

Discussion Points and Key Words

Before Reading

- Read the first two sentences of the chapter, then recall the end of Chapter 1, where "I" volunteers to get other children to help remove the Japanese beetles from Mrs. Houser's grapevines.

During Reading

- Pause before Jamie and "I" start toward their school with Martha, and discuss how the boys feel about helping Mrs. Houser. Note the description, "She guarded her property as if every inch was a diamond mine."
- Pause when the stranger stops and offers a ride. Anticipate what might happen.

- Note narrator's reaction to his mother standing at the door and his feeling that "She had the *uncanniest* ability to suspect things. . . ."

After Reading

- Brief retelling to confirm important events in chapter.
- Children meet in small groups with discussion guide.
- Return to large group for in-depth discussion.
- Additional suggestions for discussion:

  1. Did anything the author said make you anticipate that something bad might happen.
  2. How words can make images in our minds ("streaks of angel wings").
  3. More hyphen-words:

     four-year-old sister Jamie big-mouth
     I was tongue-tied

- Anticipate what might happen in the next chapter.

Discussion Guide Questions

See Chapter 2 Discussion Guide.

Literature Log Possibilities

- Begin a double-entry log, which allows readers to select specific quotes from the text or an event to which they wish to respond (see sample log form, Figure A.4).

Example:

In the text	*My response (student)*
Mrs. Houser "guarded her property as if every inch was a diamond mine."	The lady on my corner was like that. Once my ball got in her yard. She wouldn't give it back to me. My dad went to see her. He got it back!

- Add to character chart and word lists in the log.

Chapter 3 Lesson Plan

Summary

While the children are scraping Japanese beetles off of Mrs. Houser's grapevines, Jamie pokes a stick in a hole where bees live and is stung. He has an acute reaction. "I" thinks Jamie is acting, so he goes home and eats a popsicle. An ambulance comes and takes Jamie way. "I" returns to scraping beetles.

Discussion Points and Key Words

Before Reading

- Recall how the chapter ended yesterday (collecting children to pick off the beetles).
- The chapter opens with a foreshadowing of Jamie's death. Read first paragraph aloud, then pause and ask children what this paragraph might mean, why the author might have started the chapter this way.

During Reading

- Pause after, "It's just a bunch of Heather-bees" to anticipate what might happen. Why did the author use the word *Heather-bees*?
- Note the language used to describe the bees: "The bees came swarming up out of the hole in *a ball of fury* . . . . Those bees went after the kids in *arrow formation;* just like in the cartoons."
- Discuss narrator's reaction to Jamie's falling down. What does "I" know about Jamie that would make him think Jamie is acting?
- Pause after "I" finds out the ambulance is for Jamie and discuss his reaction.

After Reading

- Brief retelling to confirm important events in the chapter.
- Children meet in small groups with discussion guide.
- Return to large group for in-depth discussion.
- Additional suggestions for discussion:
  1. Return to the foreshadowing and discuss how authors use this literary device.
  2. Why did the author spend time describing the popsicle scene? What purpose did it serve?
  3. More hyphen-words:

     Heather-bees whoop-whoop-whoop
- Anticipate what might happen in the next chapter.

Discussion Guide Questions

See Chapter 3 Discussion Guide.

Literature Log Possibilities

- Start collecting phrases and sentences that make pictures in your head (see sample log form, Figure A.5). You might begin with the description of the sun from Chapter 2:

  At the same time the sun burst through the clouds in streaks of angle wings.

  Possibilities from Chapter 3:

  arrow formation

  the neighborhood flowing down the hill like water behind a moving dam
- Add to character chart and word lists.
- Make a double-entry log entry.

Chapter 4 Lesson Plan

Summary

"I" finds out that Jamie is dead. He thinks back on the event and considers what being dead really means.

Discussion Points and Key Words

Before Reading

- Read aloud first paragraph, pause and help children connect back to Chapter 3. Realize that it is still the same day. Recall predictions from yesterday.

During Reading

- Pause just after narrator's mother tells him Jamie is dead and question whether "I" knew. What in the text makes you think that?
- Discuss the meaning of *allergic:* "It wasn't the number of stings, it was that Jamie was *allergic* to them."
- Discuss meaning of *freak:* "It was a *freak* accident. It hardly ever happens." Contrast with previous use, "Jamie was a *freak.*"
- Help children realize that narrator's thoughts about making a string telephone and learning Morse code to communicate across the street is really his thinking back to something that happened in the past (flashback).

After Reading

- Brief retelling to confirm important events in the chapter.
- Children meet in small groups with discussion guide.
- Return to large group for in-depth discussion.
- Additional suggestions for discussion:
  1. Revisit portions of chapter that describe narrator's actions and feelings.
  2. Why "I" would think back over the event and other past experiences with Jamie.
  3. More hyphen-words:

     show-off   blue-sky and white-cloud day   floppy-eared dogs
- Anticipate what might happen in the next chapter.

Discussion Guide Questions

See Chapter 4 Discussion Guide.

Literature Log Possibilities

- Personal response to Jamie's death.
- Add to character chart and word lists.
- Make a double-entry log entry.

Chapter 5 Lesson Plan

Summary

"I" begins to realize that Jamie is dead and starts to deal with his grief and with his view of death, which is based on his experience with his uncle's funeral.

Discussion Points and Key Words

Before Reading

- Reread the last paragraph of Chapter 4, ask for predictions about Chapter 5.

During Reading

- Why do you think "I" decided to go to the funeral parlor? Why would he have felt panicky? What does *panicky* mean?
- How did Jamie in his casket look to the narrator? Discuss meaning of *casket*.
- Before the setting shifts from the funeral parlor to home, pause to make clear that this is a viewing and not the funeral.

After Reading

- Brief retelling to confirm important events in the chapter.
- Children meet in small groups with discussion guide.
- Return to large group for in-depth discussion.
- Additional suggestions for discussion:
  1. Notice word pictures the author uses to help us "see" and "feel":

     Soapy whiskers covered my chin.

     Jamie slept all bunched up.

     I imagined the crack of light slicing across the room.

     The sight of her turned my tear faucets on so suddenly that I was surprised.

     My face was tight where the tears had dried.

     He sat me on his lap and cradled my head to his chest.
  2. Did you think "I" would go to the funeral?
  3. What does "I" discover about his dad's lap?
  4. Why do you think "I" tears up the yellow flower?
- Anticipate what might happen in the next chapter.

Discussion Guide Questions

See Chapter 5 Discussion Guide.

Literature Log Possibilities

- When you feel sad, what do you do to make yourself feel better?
- If you sent a sympathy card to Jamie's family, what would you say?
- Add to character chart and word lists.
- Make a double-entry log entry.

Chapter 6 Lesson Plan

Summary

"I" is having trouble with the fact that everything is remaining the same after Jamie's death. People and things are continuing as if Jamie had never died. "I" sneaks into Mrs. Mullins's garden to sit and think and ends up having a conversation with her about Jamie and death.

Discussion Points and Key Words

Before Reading

- Share literature log entries from previous day.

- When you feel sad, what do you do to make yourself feel better?
- Based on what we know about ourselves and "I", what do you think "I" might do to help himself feel better about Jamie's death?

During Reading

- Pause after "I" talks about going into the garden (end of p. 39).
- What do we already know about Mrs. Mullins's garden? Reread description of the garden from Chapter 3. Have children close eyes to visualize. Ask, Do you think "I" will go into the garden.
- Note the words used to describe objects in the garden.

  [The granite] was *speckledy black and white.*

  I could almost *hear the colors in my ears.*

  And there was a hummingbird, *hovering like a helicopter.*

After Reading

- Brief retelling to confirm important events in the chapter.
- Children meet in small groups with discussion guide.
- Return to large group for in-depth discussion beginning with discussion guide.
- Additional suggestion for discussion:

  Are there times when you needed to talk with someone else, and doing it helped you feel better?

- Anticipation what might happen in the next chapter.

Discussion Guide Questions

See Chapter 6 Discussion Guide.

Literature Log Possibilities

- The author uses a lot of words and phrases in this chapter that help to make pictures in your head. Look back through the chapter. Add to your list of words and phrases that help you make pictures in your head.
- In this chapter, and also in Chapter 3, the author vividly describes Mrs. Mullins's garden. It is bright compared to narrator's dark mood. The book's illustrations are in black, white, and gray. Draw a picture of Mrs. Mullins's garden. Go back through the chapter and look for the descriptions of the flowers and creatures in the garden: colors, shapes, animals, and insects that are there.
- Add to character chart and word lists.
- Make a double-entry log entry.

Chapter 7 Lesson Plan

Summary

"I" is coming to terms with Jamie's death by talking to Martha, attending Jamie's funeral, and going to the cemetery.

Discussion Points and Key Words

Before Reading

- Ask students to share any experience they have had with someone dying, such as attending a viewing or a funeral, or going to a cemetery. Think back to Chapter 5 and the viewing.

During Reading

- Pause after Martha says "Heaben." What is the word supposed to be? Why did the author spell it like that?
- In the scene during the funeral, after reading the paragraph that begins, "I began . . ." (p. 49), pause to discuss the meaning of two phrases:

  brace myself against time

  reverse gravity

- Discuss other interesting words:

  procession—What is a procession?

  strictly taboo—What does that mean?

  foxholes—What is a foxhole? What might have they been playing if they dug foxholes?

After Reading

- Brief retelling to confirm important events in the chapter.
- Children meet in small groups with discussion guide.
- Return to large group for in-depth discussion.
- Additional suggestions for discussion:
  1. While narrator's mind was wandering during the funeral and at the cemetery, what was really happening?
  2. "I" talked about wanting to be near his family during the funeral and in the car. Why do you think he wanted to be with his family instead of his friends?
- Anticipate what might happen in the next chapter.

Discussion Guide Questions

See Chapter 7 Discussion Guide.

Literature Log Possibilities

- Follow up the small-group discussion of the things "I" noticed during the funeral. Ask students to sit quietly and write for 10 minutes (Graves, 1994) about things they notice and/or think about. Encourage them to think of a recent event that they have strong memories about.
- Write about a time when you were happy to be with your family. What were you doing? Why did you want to be with your family?
- Add to character chart and word lists.
- Make a double-entry log entry.

Chapter 8 Lesson Plan

Summary

This is a turning point for the narrator's acceptance of Jamie's death. "I" gives into his hunger. He picks blackberries and takes them to Jamie's mother. After talking briefly to her, "I" runs off to play.

Discussion Points and Key Words

Before Reading

- Briefly review what happened in Chapter 7.
- Encourage predictions. This is the last chapter of the book. Remember, I haven't eaten, played, or talked to Jamie's mother. What things do you think "I" still needs to deal with? How do you think the author will tie everything together in this last chapter?

During Reading

- Pause and discuss the meaning of the following:

  Suddenly I thought about blackberries. They'd be ripe now. It seemed important to pick blackberries.

  I wished I was invisible. I didn't want anyone to see me, even Heather. I wanted to go blackberry picking with Jamie.

  And you be sure to come slam the door for me now and then.

- Discuss the following key words as they appear in the chapter:

  I *rummaged* under the sink and brought out two *peck* baskets.

  It seemed a long time since Jamie and I had *snickered* while the kids talked about us from the outside edge of the *thicket*.

After Reading

- Brief retelling to confirm important events in the chapter.
- Children meet in small groups with discussion guide.
- Return to large group for in-depth discussion.
- Additional suggestions for discussion:
  1. What do you think about the way the story ended?
  2. Solicit open responses to the story as a whole, and to favorite parts.

Discussion Guide Questions

See Chapter 8 Discussion Guide.

Literature Log Possibilities

- Do you think "I" will still think of Jamie? What kind of things do you think he will remember and feel?
- Imagine you are the narrator. Write a letter to Jamie's mother explaining why it took you so long to go over to her house and talk to her.
- Make the following double-entry log entry:

In the text	*My response*
At supper I no longer felt it	______________________
was disloyal to eat. If a miracle	______________________
could have brought Jamie back,	______________________
it would have been done already.	______________________

Discussion Guide Questions

Chapter 1 Discussion Guide

After reading this chapter, I wonder . . .

1. Do Jamie and "I" seem like good friends? What parts of Chapter 1 make you think that?

2. Would you have gone over the fence to get the apples? Why/why not?

3. When Doris Smith (author) writes, she likes to use hyphens (-) to make up words that fit her purpose, such as,

> We *rock-hopped* the creek and sat down on the other side where there was a fence to lean on. (p. 3)

The word *rock-hopped* lets you know exactly what the boys did and it is more interesting than just saying the boys hopped on rocks. Find other hyphen-words in Chapter 1 and talk about their meaning. Make up a hyphen-word and be ready to tell what it means to you.

Our group also talked about. . . (group members can add to teacher prompts)

Chapter 2 Discussion Guide

After reading this chapter, I wonder . . .

1. How does Jamie feel about his sister, Martha? What happens in Chapter 2 that helps you know that?

2. Would you have hitchhiked in the thunderstorm? Why/why not?

3. While the children are riding with the stranger, you read:

> "Here's the turn," Jamie said. His voice squeaked. I didn't breathe until the man slowed the car and began to turn. Then Jamie and I looked at each other and grinned. *At the same time the sun burst through the clouds in streaks of angel wings.* (p. 14)

What kind of pictures do you get in your mind when the author talks about the sun? On the back of this paper, make a sketch of the picture you have in your mind. Be ready to share your sketch.

Our group also talked about. . .

CHAPTER 3 DISCUSSION GUIDE

After reading this chapter, I wonder . . .

1. How did "I" react to Jamie's falling down act and being taken away in the ambulance? Were you surprised by the way that "I" reacted? Why/why not?

2. Did the author help you make a picture in your head when she wrote the following?

   The whole neighborhood flowed down the hill like water behind a moving dam. (p. 23)

   How did you picture the neighborhood?

3. What did the author mean by the italicized phrase in this quote?

   In the distance I heard a siren wail and *cocked my ear* to decide if it was the police, a fire engine or an ambulance (p. 21)

   What clues did you use to help you figure out this phrase? Were the clues in the book? Were some of the clues in you from things you already know?

Our group also talked about. . .

CHAPTER 4 DISCUSSION GUIDE

After reading this chapter, I wonder . . .

1. How did "I" act when he heard that Jamie was dead? Why do you think he acted that way?

2. Have you ever known someone who is *allergic* to something? What were they allergic to? How did their allergy affect them?

3. What do you think you might have done if you were the narrator?

Our group also talked about . . .

CHAPTER 5 DISCUSSION GUIDE

After reading this chapter, I wonder . . .

1. How did "I" see Jamie in a different way than other people?

2. Why do you think "I" doesn't want his parents to know that he is awake?

3. Explain what you think "I" meant when he said, "I wasn't glad the bees were dead." (p. 34).

Our group also talked about . . .

CHAPTER 6 DISCUSSION GUIDE

After reading this chapter, I wonder . . .

1. In this chapter "I" talks about not wanting things to be the same since Jamie died. Why do you think he feels this way? Would you feel the same? Why or why not?

2. On page 40, what do you think the word *speckledy* means? At first glance it looked gray, but if you looked closely it was *speckledy* black and white.

   Use the word in a sentence of your own.

3. Discuss what you think the author means when she writes the following:

   the air felt empty (p. 42)

   This time the air didn't need to be filled. (p. 43)

Our group also talked about . . .

Chapter 7 Discussion Guide

After reading this chapter, I wonder . . .

1. Reread the three paragraphs (pp. 46–47) that begin, "Where is Martha?"
   - Do you think Martha understood what had happened to Jamie? What makes you think that?
   - Do you think Martha should have gone to the funeral? Why or why not?
   - Does it help someone to go to the funeral of someone they cared for? Why do you think that?

2. Make a list of things that "I" was noticing and thinking about during the funeral and at the cemetery.

Our group also talked about . . .

Chapter 8 Discussion Guide

After reading this chapter, I wonder . . .

1. Look back at your character chart of Jamie and "I". Talk about how you think "I" has changed since the beginning. Find examples in the story to support your ideas.

2. Why was it important for "I" to pick blackberries in the last chapter?

3. How did it help "I" end the "main sadness" when Jamie's mother said, "And be sure to come slam the door for me now and then" (p. 56)?

Our group also talked about . . .

Sample Literature Log Forms

Figure A.1 Character chart

Character Chart

Jamie	I

Figure A.2 Interesting words and phrases

Interesting words and phrases

Page ______

Word/phrase ______________________________

To me, it means ______________________________

Page ______

Word/phrase ______________________________

To me, it means ______________________________

Page ______

Word/phrase ______________________________

To me, it means ______________________________

Figure A.3 Words I want to know more about

Words I want to know more about

Page ______ Word/phrase ____

In the dictionary it means ____

Page ______ Word/phrase ____

In the dictionary it means ____

Page ______ Word/phrase ____

In the dictionary it means ____

Page ______ Word/phrase ____

In the dictionary it means ____

Page ______ Word/phrase ____

In the dictionary it means ____

Figure A.4 Double-entry log

Double–entry Log

In the text	My response

Figure A.5 Phrases that make pictures in my head

Phrases that make pictures in my head

Page ______ ____

Page ______ ____

Page ______ ____

Page ______ ____

Page ______ ____

Appendix B

Sample Study Topics with Suggested Literature

RECENT FAVORITES AND RECOMMENDED TITLES

Alice in April (Phyllis Naylor, 1993, Gr. 3–5)

Aliens For Dinner (Stephanie Spinner, 1994, Gr. 3–5)

Almost a Hero (John Neufeld, 1995, Gr. 5–8)

The Arkadians (Lloyd Alexander, 1995, Gr. 6–9)

The Barn (Avi, 1994, Gr. 6–8)

The Booford Summer (Susan Mathias Smith, 1995, Gr. 4–6)

Cat Running (Zilpha Keatley Snyder, 1994, Gr. 3–6)

Catherine, Called Birdy (Karen Cushman, 1994, Gr. 6–8)

Climb or Die (Edward Myers, 1994, Gr. 3–6)

Crosstown (Kathryn Makris, 1993, Gr. 5–8)

Deep Dream of the Rain Forest (Malcolm Bosse, 1994, Gr. 6–8)

Dogteam (Gary Paulsen, 1993, Gr. 3–5)

Dragon's Gate (Lawrence Yep, 1994, Gr. 6–8)

Fig Pudding (Ralph Fletcher, 1995, Gr. 3–5)

Flip-Flop Girl (Katherine Paterson, 1994, Gr. 5–8)

Frankenlouse (Mary James, 1994, Gr. 6–8)

The Ghost of Popcorn Hill (Betty Ren Wright, 1993, Gr. 3–5)

The Giver (Lois Lowry, 1993, Gr. 5–8)

Goodbye, Vietnam (Gloria Whelan, 1994, Gr. 3–5)

Grab Hands and Run (Frances Temple, 1994, Gr. 6–8)

Harris and Me: A Summer Remembered (Gary Paulsen, 1994, Gr. 6–8)

Heart of a Champion (Carl Deuker, 1994, Gr. 6–8)

Help, I'm Trapped in My Teacher's Body (Todd Strasses, 1994, Gr. 5–8)

The Hostage (Survive!) (Larry Weinberg, 1994, Gr. 3–5)

In the Middle of the Might (Robert Cormier, 1995, Gr. 6–8)

Just One Tear (K. L. Mahon, 1994, Gr. 5–8)

The King's Shadow (Elizabeth Alder, 1995, Gr. 6–8)

Loch (Paul Zindel, 1994, Gr. 6+)

The Man in the Ceiling (Jules Feiffer, 1994, Gr. 6–8)

The Midwife's Apprentice (Karen Cushman, 1995, Gr. 6–8)

Moonshiner's Son (Carolyn Reeder, 1993, Gr. 5–8)

My Brother, My Sister and I (Yoko Kawashima Watkins, 1994, Gr. 6–8)

Nightjohn (Gary Paulsen, 1993, Gr. 5–8)

Out of the Storm (Patricia Willis, 1995, Gr. 5–7)

Phoenix Rising (Karen Hesse, 1994, Gr. 6–8)

Somewhere Around the Corner (Jackie French, 1994, Gr. 6+)

Songs in the Silence (Catherine Murphy, 1994, Gr. 4–6)

The Tent: A Parable in One Sitting (Gary Paulsen, 1995, Gr. 6–8)

Tiger, Tiger, Burning Bright (Ron Koertge, 1994, Gr. 6–8)

Time for Andrew: A Ghost Story (Mary Downing Hahn, 1994, Gr. 4–7)

Timothy of the Cay (Theodore Taylor, 1994, Gr. 5–8)

Toning the Sweep (Angela Johnson, 1994, Gr. 6–8)

Under the Blood-Red Sun (Graham Salisbury, 1994, Gr. 6–8)

Venus Among the Fishes (Elizabeth Hall & Scott O'Dell, 1994, Gr. 5+)

Walk Two Moons (Sharon Creech, 1994, Gr. 6–8)

The Well (Mildred Taylor, 1995, Gr. 6–8)

White Lilacs (Carolyn Meyer, 1994, Gr. 6–8)

AFRICAN AMERICANS

African Migrations (Hakim Adi, 1994, Gr. 5+)

The Ballad of Belle Dorcas (William Hooks, 1990, Gr. 4–6)

Black Eagles: African Americans in Aviation (Jim Haskins, 1994, Gr. 6–8)

Black Stars in Orbit: NASA's African American Astronauts (Khephra Burns & William Miles, 1994, Gr. 4+)

Circle of Fire (William Hooks, 1982, Gr. 5–8)

Come a Stranger (Cynthia Voight, 1986, Gr. 5+)

Cousins (Virginia Hamilton, 1990, Gr. 6–9)

The Day That Elvis Came to Town (Jan Marino, 1991, Gr. 6–9)

Down in the Piney Woods (Ethel Smothers, 1992, Gr. 6–8)

Finding Buck McHenry (Alfred Slote, 1991, Gr. 4–6)

Fish & Bones (Ray Prather, 1992, Gr. 6–9)

The Friendship (Mildred Taylor, 1987, Gr. 4–6)

From AFAR to ZULU: A Dictionary of African American Cultures (Jim Haskins & Joann Biondi, 1994, Gr. 5+)

The Gift-Giver (Joyce Hansen, 1980, Gr. 4–6)

A Girl Called Bob and a Horse Called Yoki (Barbara Campbell, 1982, Gr. 4–6)

The Glory Field (Walter Dean Myers, 1994, Gr. 5+)

The Green Lion of Zion Street (Julia Fields, 1988, Gr. 3–5)

Have a Happy . . . A Novel (Mildred Pitts Walter, 1989, Gr. 6–8)

Hold Fast to Dreams (Andrea Pinkney, 1995, Gr. 5–7)

Julian, Dream Doctor (Ann Cameron, 1990, Gr. 3–5)

Just an Overnight Guest (Eleanora Tate, 1980, Gr. 4–6)

Just Like Martin (Ossie Davis, 1992, Gr. 6–9)

Just My Luck (Emily Moore, 1983, Gr. 4–6)

Justin and the Best Biscuits in the World (Mildred Pitts Walter, 1986, Gr. 3–6)

Mariah Loves Rock (Mildred Pitts Walter, 1988, Gr. 3–6)

Mississippi Bridge (Mildred Taylor, 1990, Gr. 4–6)

The Mouse Rap (Walter Dean Myers, 1990, Gr. 6–10)

Paris, Pee Wee, and Big Dog (Rosa Guy, 1985, Gr. 3–5)

The Righteous Revenge of Artemis Bonner (Walter Dean Myers, 1992, Gr. 7–10)

The Road to Memphis (Mildred Taylor, 1990, Gr. 6–8)

Roll of Thunder, Hear My Cry (Mildred Taylor, 1976, Gr. 5–8)

Scorpions (Walter Dean Myers, 1988, Gr. 6–8)

The Secret of Gumbo Grove (Eleanora Tate, 1987, Gr. 5–8)

The Shimmershine Queens (Camille Yarborough, 1990, Gr. 6–8)

Skeeter (K. Smith, 1989, Gr. 7–10)

Somewhere in the Darkness (Walter Dean Myers, 1992, Gr. 6–8)

Sort of Sisters (Stacie Johnson, 1992, Gr. 6–8)

Sweet Whispers, Brother Rush (Virginia Hamilton, 1982, Gr. 5–8)

Talking Turkey (Lila Hopkins, 1989, Gr. 6–8)

Thank you, Dr. Martin Luther King, Jr. (Eleanora Tate, 1990, Gr. 3–5)

Tough Tiffany (Belinda Hurmence, 1980, Gr. 5–7)

The Underground Railroad (Raymond Bill, 1994, Gr. 3–6)

The Ups and Downs of Carl Davis III (Rosa Guy, 1989, Gr. 6–9)

When the Nightingale Sings (Joyce Thomas, 1992, Gr. 6–8)

Willy's Summer Dream (Kay Brown, 1990, Gr. 6–8)

ASIAN AMERICANS

April and the Dragon Lady (Lensey Namioka, 1994, Gr. 6+)

Baseball Saved Us (Mochizuki, 1993, Gr. 6+)

The Best Bad Thing (Yoshiko Uchida, 1983, Gr. 4–6)

The Chi-Lin Purse (Linda Fang, 1994, Gr. 4–7)

Children of the River (Linda Crew, 1989, Gr. 5+)

Cranes at Dusk (Hisako Matsubara, 1985, Gr. 6+)

Dara's Cambodian New Year (Sothea Chiemroum, 1992, Gr. 3–5)

Dragonwings (Lawrence Yep, 1975, Gr. 6+)

El Chino (Allen Say, 1990, Gr. 3–5)

Hello, My Name is Scrambled Eggs (Jamie Gilson, 1985, Gr. 6–8)

Her Own Song (Ellen Howard, 1988, Gr. 3–6)

I am an American: A True Story of Japanese Internment (Jerry Stanley, 1994, Gr. 4+)

In The Eye of the War (Margaret Chang, 1990, Gr. 4–6)

In the Year of the Boar and Jackie Robinson (Bette Bao Lord, 1984, Gr. 4–6)

The Invisible Thread (Yoshiko Uchida, 1991, Gr. 4–6)

A Jar of Dreams (Yoshiko Uchida, 1981, Gr. 4–6)

Journey to Topaz (Yoshiko Uchida, 1971, Gr. 4–6)

Kim/Kimi (Hadley Irwin, 1987, Gr. 6+)

Molly by Any Other Name (Jean Davies Okimoto, 1990, Gr. 7–10)

My Name is San Ho (Jayne Pettit, 1992, Gr. 6–8)

The Rainbow People (Lawrence Yep, 1989, Gr. 6–8)

Sadako and the Thousand Paper Cranes (Eleanor Coerr, 1977, Gr. 3–5)

Shortstop from Tokyo (Matt Christopher, 1988, Gr. 6–8)

So Far From the Bamboo Grove (Yoko Kawashima Watkins, 1986, Gr. 4–6)

The Star Fisher (Lawrence Yep, 1991, Gr. 6–8)

Tales From Gold Mountain: Stories of the Chinese in the New World (Paul Yee, 1990, Gr. 6–8)

A Time Too Swift (Margaret Poynter, 1990, Gr. 7–10)

When Justice Failed: The Fred Korematsu Story (Steven Chin, 1993, Gr. 6–8)

Yang the Youngest and His Terrible Ear (Lensey Namioka, 1992, Gr. 6–8)

Year of Impossible Goodbyes (Sook Nyui Choi, 1991, Gr. 6–10)

Youn Hee & Me (C. S. Adler, 1995, Gr. 3–6)

COMING OF AGE

Across the Grain (Jean Ferris, 1990, Gr. 8+)

Against the Storm (Gaye Hicyilmaz, 1990, Gr. 7–9)

Are You Alone on Purpose? (Nancy Werlin, 1994, Gr. 5+)

Athletic Shorts: Six Short Stories (Chris Crutcher, 1991, Gr. 8–12)

Becoming Gershona (Nava Semel, 1990, Gr. 6–8)

Blue Skin of the Sea (Graham Salisbury, 1992, Gr. 8+)

Canyons (Gary Paulsen, 1990, Gr. 7–10)

Celine (Brock Cole, 1989, Gr. 8+)

The Crystal Garden (Vicki Grove, 1994, Gr. 5–8)

Dawn River (Jan Hudson, 1990, Gr. 5–8)

The Dying Sun (Gary Blackwood, 1989, Gr. 7–10)

Fools' Hill (Barbara Hall, 1992, Gr. 7–10)

Funnybone (William Coles & Stephen Schwandt, 1992, Gr. 7–10)

A Hand Full of Stars (Rafik Schami, 1990, Gr. 7–10)

Haunted Journey (Ruth Riddell, 1988, Gr. 7–12)

In Your Dreams (Colin Neeman, 1994, Gr. 6+)

Looking at the Moon (Kit Pearson, 1992, Gr. 7–10)

Me and the End of the World (William Corbin, 1991, Gr. 6–8)

Newfound (Jim Miller, 1989, Gr. 8+)

The Original Freddie Ackerman (Hadley Irwin, 1992, Gr. 6–8)

Shabanu: Daughter of the Wind (Suzanne Staples, 1989, Gr. 7–10)

The Shadow Brothers (A. E. Cannon, 1990, Gr. 7–10)

FAMILY RELATIONSHIPS AND PROBLEMS

The Absolutely True Story (Willo Roberts, 1994, Gr. 3–6)

Amazing Gracie (A. E. Cannon, 1991, Gr. 6–9)

Ask Me Something Easy (Natalie Honeycutt, 1991, Gr. 7–10)

The Baby Grand, the Moon in July, & Me (Joyce Barnes, 1994, Gr. 4–6)

Babyface (Norma Fox Mazer, 1990, Gr. 7–10)

The Best School Year Ever (Barbara Robinson, 1994, Gr. 3–6)

Blue Heron (Avi, 1992, Gr. 6–9)

The Brightest Light (Colleen O'Shaughnessy McKenna, 1992, Gr. 7–10)

C, My Name is Cal (Norma Fox Mazer, 1990, Gr. 7–9)

Cages (Peg Kehret, 1991, Gr. 6–9)

Come The Morning (Mark Harris, 1989, Gr. 5–8)

Cruise Control (Lisa Fosburgh, 1988, Gr. 7–10)

Danny Ain't (Joe Cottonwood, 1992, Gr. 7–10)

Del-Del (Victor Kelleher, 1992, Gr. 7–10)

Dixie Storms (Barbara Hall, 1990, Gr. 7–10)

Earthshine (Theresa Nelson, 1994, Gr. 5–8)

Eclipse (Kristine Franklin, 1994, Gr. 6–9)

Fig Pudding (Ralph Fletcher, 1994, Gr. 3–6)

Free Fall (Elizabeth Barrett, 1994, Gr. 6+)

From the Notebooks of Melanin Sun (Jacqueline Woodson, 1995, Gr. 6+)

The Glass House People (Kathryn Reiss, 1992, Gr. 7–10)

Going the Distance (Mary Jane Miller, 1994, Gr. 4–6)

Gruel and Unusual Punishment (Jim Arter, 1991, Gr. 7–9)

Homecoming (Cynthia Voigt, 1981, Gr. 5–8)

How Could You Do It, Diane? (Stella Pevsner, 1989, Gr. 7–10)

I Am the Universe (Barbara Corcoran, 1986, Gr. 5–8)

If You Need Me (C. S. Adler, 1988, Gr. 6–8)

Jason and the Losers (Gina Willner-Pardo, 1995, Gr. 4–6)

Junglerama (Vicki Grove, 1989, Gr. 6–9)

Just an Overnight Guest (Eleanora Tate, 1980, Gr. 4–6)

Just as Long as We're Together (Judy Blume, 1987, Gr. 6+)

The Kite Song (Margery Evernden, 1984, Gr. 6–7)

The Last Safe Place on Earth (Richard Peck, 1995, Gr. 6+)

The Latchkey Kids (Susan Terris, 1986, Gr. 4–7)

The Leaves in October (Karen Ackerman, 1991, Gr. 5+)

Like Seabirds Flying Home (Marguerite Murray, 1988, Gr. 7–10)

Linc (Mary Christian, 1991, Gr. 7–10)

Love, David (Dianne Case, 1991, Gr. 6–8)

Mama's Going to Buy You a Mockingbird (Jean Little, 1984, Gr. 5–8)

Maizie (Linda High, 1994, Gr. 4–6)

Missing Pieces (Norma Fox Mazer, 1995, Gr. 6+)

The Mona Lisa of Salem Street (Jan Marino, 1994, Gr. 5+)

More Than a Name (Candice Ransom, 1995, Gr. 3–6)

Past Forgiving (Gloria Miklowitz, 1995, Gr. 6+)

Several Kinds of Silence (Marilyn Singer, 1988, Gr. 7–10)

Shadows (Dennis Haseley, 1991, Gr. 3–5)

The Solitary (Lynn Hall, 1986, Gr. 6+)

Something Terrible Happened (Barbara Porte, 1994, Gr. 6+)

Tallahassee Higgins (Mary Downing Hahn, 1987, Gr. 5–7)
Tree by Leaf (Cynthia Voight, 1988, Gr. 7–9)
Under Seige (Elisabeth Mace, 1988, Gr. 7–10)
Vikki Vanishes (Peni Griffin, 1994, Gr. 5–8)
With a Wave of the Wand (Mark Harris, 1980, Gr. 4–6)
You'll Miss Me When I'm Gone (Stephen Roos, 1988, Gr. 7–10)
You're Dead David Borelli (Susan Brown, 1994, Gr. 4–7)

FANTASY/SCIENCE FICTION

An Acceptable Time (Madeleine L'Engle, 1989, Gr. 8+)
Ambrosia and the Coral Sun (Sherri Board, 1994, Gr. 6+)
The Ancient One (Thomas Barron, 1992, Gr. 7–10)
Antar and the Eagles (William Mayne, 1990, Gr. 6–9)
Bailey's Window (Ann Lindbergh, 1984, Gr. 3–6)
Below the Root (Zilpha Keatley Snyder, 1975, Gr. 5–7)
Castle in the Air (Diana Jones, 1991, Gr. 7–12)
The Castle in the Attic (Elizabeth Winthrop, 1985, Gr. 4–6)
The Chronicles of Narnia (7 vols.) (C. S. Lewis, 1950–1956, Gr. 3–6)
The Crystal Stair (Grace Chetwin, 1988, Gr. 6–8)
Dark Heart (Betsy James, 1992, Gr. 7–10)
The Dark Is Rising (Susan Cooper, 1973, Gr. 5–7)
Diggers (Terry Pratchett, 1991, Gr. 6–9)
Dr. Gravity (Dennis Haseley, 1992, Gr. 7–10)
The Dragon and the Thief (Gillian Bradshaw, 1991, Gr. 7–10)
Follow a Shadow (Robert Swindells, 1990, Gr. 7–10)
Gameplayers (Stephen Bowkett, 1986, Gr. 7–10)
Gemini Game (Michael Scott, 1994, Gr. 6+)
The Gold Dust Letters (Janet Lisle, 1994, Gr. 4–6)
Hero's Song (Edith Pattou, 1991, Gr. 7–10)
Hexwood (Diana Jones, 1994, Gr. 6+)
Hob and the Goblins (William Mayne, 1994, Gr. 5+)
Into the Land of the Unicorns (Bruce Corville, 1994, Gr. 3–6)
Lizard Music (Daniel Pinkwater, 1976, Gr. 4–8)
Long Night Dance (Betsy James, 1989, Gr. 8–12)
Mazemaker (Catherine Dexter, 1989, Gr. 6–8)
Minnie (Annie Schmidt, 1994, Gr. 3+)
My Name is Amelia (Donald Sobol, 1994, Gr. 4–7)
One Good Tern Deserves Another (Eric Kimmel, 1994, Gr. 5–7)
The Phantom Tollbooth (Norton Juster, 1961, Gr. 4–8)
The Promise (Monica Hughes, 1992, Gr. 6–8)
The Same But Different (Perry Nodelman, 1994, Gr. 3–6)
Sandwriter (Monica Hughes, 1988, Gr. 7–10)
The Sleep of Stone (Louise Cooper, 1991, Gr. 7–12)
Touch the Moon (Marion Dane Bauer, 1987, Gr. 3–5)
Tuck Everlasting (Natalie Babbit, 1975, Gr. 5–7)
The Van Gogh Cafe (Cynthia Rylant, 1994, Gr. 3–6)
Wings (Bill Brittain, 1991, Gr. 5–7)
A Wizard of Earthsea (Ursula Le Guin, 1968, Gr. 5+)

FRIENDSHIP

Across the Creek (Myra Smith, 1987, Gr. 5–7)
Afternoon of the Elves (Janet Lisle, 1989, Gr. 5–8)
All But Alice (Phyllis Naylor, 1992, Gr. 6–8)
Always and Forever Friends (Carol Adler, 1988, Gr. 5–8)
And One For All (Theresa Nelson, 1989, Gr. 6–10)
Anne of Green Gables (L. M. Montgomery, 1908, Gr. 5–9)
Backfield Package (Thomas Dygard, 1992, Gr. 7–10)
The Berkley Street Six Pack (Mary Francis Shura, 1979, Gr. 3–5)
Best Friend Insurance (Beatrice Gormley, 1983, Gr. 5–7)
Best Friends Tell the Best Lies (Carol Dines, 1989, Gr. 7–10)
The Best of Friends (Margaret Rostkowski, 1989, Gr. 6–12)
Better Than a Brother (Edith McCall, 1988, Gr. 6–9)
Between the Cracks (Joyce Wolf, 1992, Gr. 6–8)
Bones on Black Spruce Mountain (David Budbill, 1978, Gr. 5+)
The Broken Boy (Karen Ackerman, 1991, Gr. 6–8)
Bridge to Terabithia (Katherine Paterson, 1977, Gr. 5–7)
Buddies (Barbara Park, 1985, Gr. 5–8)
Came Back to Show You I Could Fly (Robin Klein, 1990, Gr. 6–10)
Changeling (Zilpha Keatley Snyder, 1970, Gr. 5–8)
Charlotte's Web (E. B. White, 1952, Gr. 3–6)
The China Year (Emily Neville, 1991, Gr. 7–9)
Class Pictures (Marilyn Sachs, 1980, Gr. 5–6)
The Cold and Hot Winter (Joanna Hurwitz, 1988, Gr. 4–6)
Commander Coatrack Returns (Joseph McNair, 1989, Gr. 6–9)
Cricket and the Crackerbox (Alane Ferguson, 1990, Gr. 5–6)
Crutches (Peter Hartling, 1988, Gr. 6+)
Cute Is a Four Letter Word (Stella Pevsner, 1980, Gr. 5–6)
The Cybil War (Betsy Byars, 1981, Gr. 4–6)

Daphne's Book (Mary Downing Hahn, 1983, Gr. 5+)

Diving For the Moon (Lee Bantle, 1994, Gr. 5+)

The Divorce Express (Paula Danziger, 1982, Gr. 5–6)

Dog Days (Colby Rodowsky, 1990, Gr. 4–6)

The Double Life of Angela Jones (Hila Colman, 1988, Gr. 7–10)

Dump Days (Jerry Spinelli, 1988, Gr. 4–7)

Dynamite Dinah (Claudia Mills, 1990, Gr. 5–6)

Eben Tyne: Powdermonkey (Patricia Beatty, 1990, Gr. 5+)

The Empty Window (Anne Evelyn Bunting, 1980, Gr. 3–5)

An End to Perfect (Suzanne Newton, 1984, Gr. 6–8)

Enemies (Robin Klein, 1989, Gr. 3–5)

Eunice (the Egg Salad) Gottlieb (Tricia Springstubb, 1988, Gr. 4–6)

A Fine White Dust (Cynthia Rylant, 1986, Gr. 5–7)

The Flying Fingers Club (Jean Andrews, 1988, Gr. 3–5)

Fourteen (Marilyn Sachs, 1983, Gr. 5–8)

Fourth Grade Celebrity (Patricia Reilly Giff, 1979, Gr. 4–5)

Friends First (Christine McDonnel, 1990, Gr. 6–8)

Golden Girl (Nancy Tilly, 1985, Gr. 5–8)

Good-bye, Billy Radish (Gloria Skurzynski, 1992, Gr. 6–8)

The Great Gilly Hopkins (Katherine Paterson, 1978, Gr. 5–6)

Hear the Wind Blow (Patricia Pendergraft, 1988, Gr. 5–7)

The Hermit of Fog Hollow Station (David Roth, 1980, Gr. 4–6)

Hunt for the Last Cat (Justin Denzel, 1991, Gr. 6–8)

I Hate Being Gifted (Patricia Hermes, 1990, Gr. 4–6)

The Iceberg and Its Shadow (Jan Greenberg, 1980, Gr. 5–6)

Instant Soup (Brenda Guiberson, 1991, Gr. 5–7)

Jennifer, Hecate, Macbeth, William McKinley and Me, Elizabeth (E. L. Konigsburg, 1967, Gr. 3–5)

The Josey Gambit (Mary Francis Shura, 1986, Gr. 5–7)

Just as Long as We're Together (Judy Blume, 1978, Gr. 6+)

Just Between Us (Susan Pfeffer, 1980, Gr. 5–6)

Just Good Friends (Dean Marney, 1982, Gr. 5–8)

Just Like a Friend (Marilyn Sachs, 1989, Gr. 7–9)

Just Like Always (Elizabeth-Ann Sachs, 1981, Gr. 5+)

The Kid in the Red Jacket (Barbara Park, 1987, Gr. 4–6)

Kiss Me, Janie Tannenbaum (Elizabeth-Ann Sachs, 1992, Gr. 6–8)

Libby on Wednesday (Zilpha Keatley Snyder, 1990, Gr. 5–6)

Like Everyone Else (Barbara Girion, 1980, Gr. 5–6)

Losing Joe's Place (Gordon Korman, 1990, Gr. 6–9)

Ludie's Song (Shirlie Herlihy, 1988, Gr. 6–8)

Mariposa Blues (Ron Koertge, 1991, Gr. 7–9)

Maybe I'll Move to the Lost and Found (Susan Haven, 1988, Gr. 7–9)

My Life in the Seventh Grade (Mark Geller, 1986, Gr. 5–7)

My Summer Brother (Ilse-Margaret Vogel, 1981, Gr. 3–5)

Next Thing to Strangers (Sheri Sinykin, 1991, Gr. 6–9)

Nothing's Fair in Fifth Grade (Barthe DeClements, 1981, Gr. 4–6)

Number the Stars (Lois Lowry, 1989, Gr. 4–6)

One of Us (Nikki Amdur, 1981, Gr. 4–6)

The Other Side of the Fence (Jean Ure, 1988, Gr. 8–10)

Part-Time Boy (Elizabeth Billington, 1981, Gr. 3–4)

Philip Hall Likes Me, I Reckon Maybe (Bette Greene, 1974, Gr. 5–6)

The Pinballs (Betsy Byars, 1977, Gr. 5–6)

Pink Slippers, Bat Mitzvah Blues (Ferida Wolff, 1989, Gr. 6–8)

The Planet of Junior Brown (Virginia Hamilton, 1971, Gr. 5+)

Rabble Starkey (Lois Lowry, 1987, Gr. 5–6)

Remember Me to Harold Square (Paula Danziger, 1987, Gr. 4–6)

Rhonda, Straight and True (Roni Schotter, 1986, Gr. 5–7)

Rish 'n Roses (Jan Slepian, 1990, Gr. 5–7)

Sam and the Moon Queen (Alizon Herzig & Jane Mali, 1990, Gr. 6–8)

Sarah and Me and the Lady From the Sea (Patricia Beatty, 1989, Gr. 6–8)

Shoeshine Girl (Clyde Bulla, 1975, Gr. 3–5)

The Silent Treatment (David Carkeet, 1988, Gr. 7–10)

Soup (Robert Newton Peck, 1974, Gr. 3–6)

The Strange Case of the Reluctant Partners (Mark Geller, 1990, Gr. 6–8)

Stuart Little (E. B. White, 1945, Gr. 3–6)

Such Nice Kids (Eve Bunting, 1990, Gr. 7–10)

Thatcher Pain-in-the-Neck (Betty Bates, 1985, Gr. 4–6)

The Trouble With Lemons (Daniel Hayes, 1991, Gr. 7–9)

What If They Knew? (Patricia Hermes, 1980, Gr. 4–5)

The Young Landlords (Walter Dean Myers, 1979, Gr. 5–7)

Zucchini (Barbara Dana, 1982, Gr. 3–5)

HISPANIC AMERICANS

All For the Better: A Story of El Barrio (Nicholasa Mohr, 1993, Gr. 3–5)

Baseball in April and Other Stories (Gary Soto, 1990, Gr. 6–10)

Best Friends Tell the Best Lies (Carol Dines, 1989, Gr. 7–10)

Centerfield Ballhawk (Matt Christopher, 1992, Gr. 6–8)

Champions of Change: Biographies of Famous Hispanic Americans (Thomas Powers & José Galvan, 1989, Gr. 3–5)

Class President (Joanna Hurwitz, 1990, Gr. 3–5)

Crews: Gang Members Talk to Maria Hinojosam (Maria Hinojosam, 1994, Gr. 6+)

Don't Look at Me That Way (Caroline Crane, 1970)

El Bronx Remembered: A Novela and Stories (Nicholosa Mohr, 1975)

Everett Alvarez, Jr: A Hero of Our Time (Susan Clinton, 1990, Gr. 3–5)

Extraordinary Hispanic Americans (Susan Sinnott, 1991, Gr. 6–8)

Felita (Nicholosa Mohr, 1989, Gr. 4–6)

A Fire in My Hands: A Book of Poems (Gary Soto, 1990, Gr. 6–8)

Gaucho (Gloria Gonzalez, 1977, Gr. 4–6)

Going Home (Nicholasa Mohr, 1986, Gr. 6–8)

Gonzalo: Coronado's Shepherd Boy (Mary Clendenen, 1990, Gr. 6–8)

Hispanic, Female and Young (Phyllis Tashlik, 1994, Gr. 7+)

I Speak English For My Mom (Muriel Stanek, 1989, Gr. 3–5)

Jesse (Gary Soto, 1994, Gr. 6+)

Juanita Fights the School Board (Gloria Velasquez, 1994, Gr. 6+)

Leona (Elizabeth de Trevino, 1994, Gr. 5+)

Local News (Gary Soto, 1994, Gr. 6–8)

Lupita Manana (Patricia Beatty, 1981, Gr. 6–8)

The Maldonado Miracle (Theodore Taylor, 1973, Gr. 5–8)

Maria Luisa (Winifred Madison, 1971, Gr. 5–6)

The Me Inside of Me: A Novel (T. Ernesto Bethancourt, 1985, Gr. 6–8)

New York City, Too Far From Tampa Blues (T. Ernesto Bethancourt, 1975, Gr. 5–8)

The One Who Came Back (Joann Mazzio, 1992, Gr. 7–10)

Our Tejano Heros: Outstanding Mexican-Americans in Texas (Sammye Munson, 1989, Gr. 6–8)

Pacific Crossing (Gary Soto, 1992, Gr. 6–9)

Stories From El Barrio (Piri Thomas, 1978)

Taking Sides (Gary Soto, 1991, Gr. 6–8)

Vilma Martinez (Corinne Cody, 1991, Gr. 3–5)

Where Angles Glide at Dawn: New Stories From Latin America (Lori Carlson & Cynthia Ventura, 1990, Gr. 6–8)

Who Needs Espei Sanchez (Terry Dunnahoo, 1977)

HUMOR

Agnes the Sheep (William Taylor, 1991, Gr. 6–8)

Alan Mendelsohn, The Boy From Mars (Daniel Pinkwater, 1979, Gr. 5–8)

Alias Madame Doubtfire (Anne Fine, 1988, Gr. 6–9)

Almost Starring Skinnybones (Barbara Park, 1988, Gr. 4–6)

The Amazing and Death-Defying Diary of Eugene Dingman (Paul Zindel, 1987, Gr. 7–10)

Andie and the Boys (Janice Harrell, 1990, Gr. 7–10)

Be a Perfect Person in Just Three Days (Stephen Manes, 1982, Gr. 3–5

Bingo Brown and the Language of Love (Betsy Byars, 1989, Gr. 6–8)

Borgel (Daniel Pinkwater, 1990, Gr. 6–8)

The Boy Who Owned the School (Gary Paulsen, 1990, Gr. 7–10)

Buffalo Brenda (Jill Pinkwater, 1989, Gr. 7–9)

Dear Mom, You're Running My Life (Jean Van Leeuwen, 1989, Gr. 4–7)

Family Reunion (Caroline Cooney, 1989, Gr. 7–10)

Fat Men From Space (Daniel Pinkwater, 1977, Gr. 3–6)

Fudge-a-Mania (Judy Blume, 1990, Gr. 3–6)

Funny You Should Ask (David Gale, 1992, Gr. 5–8)

The Ghost Belongs to Me (Richard Peck, 1975, Gr. 5–9)

The Hoboken Chicken Emergency (Daniel Pinkwater, 1977, Gr. 3–5)

How to Eat Fried Worms (Thomas Rockwell, 1973, Gr. 3–5)

If Pigs Could Fly (John Lawson, 1989, Gr. 6–8)

Just the Two of Us (Jan Greenberg, 1988, Gr. 6–8)

Like Some Kind of Hero (Jan Marino, 1992, Gr. 7–10)

Lizard Music (Daniel Pinkwater, 1976, Gr. 4–6)

Mariah Delaney's Author-of-the-Month Club (Sheila Greenwald, 1990, Gr. 4–6)

Matilda (Roald Dahl, 1988, Gr. 4–7)

Mom is Dating Weird Wayne (Mary Jane Auch, 1988, Gr. 6–8)

The Richest Kid in the World (Robert Hawks, 1992, Gr. 6–8)

Sideways Stories From Wayside School (Louis Sachar, 1989, Gr. 3–6)

Sixth Grade Secrets (Louis Sachar, 1987, Gr. 4–6)

The Snarkout Boys and the Avocado of Death (Daniel Pinkwater, 1982, Gr. 5–9)

The Snarkout Boys and the Baconburg Horror (Daniel Pinkwater, 1984, Gr. 5–9)

Something's Rotten in the State of Maryland (Laura Sonnenmark, 1990, Gr. 7–10)

Summer of the Monkeys (Wilson Rawls, 1976, Gr. 4–6)

There's a Girl in My Hammerlock (Jerry Spinelli, 1991, Gr. 6–9)

Wanted: Mud Blossom (Betsy Byars, 1991, Gr. 6–8)

You'll Never Guess the End (Barbara Wersba, 1992, Gr. 7–10)

Young Adults (Daniel Pinkwater, 1985, Gr. 6–8)

The Zucchini Warriors (Gordon Korman, 1988, Gr. 6–8)

MYSTERIES/SUSPENSE

The Accident (Todd Strasser, 1988, Gr. 7–10)

Adventure in Granada (Walter Dean Myers, 1985, Gr. 5–8)

Beyond the Magic Sphere (Gail Jarrow, 1994, Gr. 3–6)

The Blue Empress (Kathy Pelta, 1988, Gr. 4–6)

The Bones in the Cliff (James Stevenson, 1995, Gr. 5+)

Breaking the Ring (Donna Inglehart, 1991, Gr. 7–10)

Callender Papers (Cynthia Voigt, 1983, Gr. 5–8)

Cameo Rose (Robbie Branscum, 1989, Gr. 6–8)

A Candidate for Murder (Joan Lowery Nixon, 1991, Gr. 7–12)

Cold as Ice (Elizabeth Levy, 1988, Gr. 7–9)

Companions of the Night (Vivian Velde, 1995, Gr. 6+)

Deadly Games (Peter Nelson, 1992, Gr. 8–12)

Finders (Jan Dean, 1994, Gr. 6+)

Fire in the Heart (Liza Murrow, 1989, Gr. 7–10)

Following the Mystery Man (Mary Downing Hahn, 1988, Gr. 5–7)

The Ghost Children (Eve Bunting, 1989, Gr. 5–7)

Graven Images (Paul Fleischman, 1983, Gr. 5–8)

The Haunting of Holroyd Hill (Brenda Seabrooke, 1995, Gr. 4–6)

High Trail to Danger (Joan Lowery Nixon, 1991, Gr. 4–6)

Interstellar Pig (William Sleator, 1984, Gr. 6–9)

Is Anybody There? (Eve Bunting, 1988, Gr. 6–8)

Keeper of the Light (Jan Klaveness, 1990, Gr. 7–10)

Kept in the Dark (Nina Bawden, 1982, Gr. 5–8)

Knee-Knock Rise (Natalie Babbit, 1970, Gr. 3–5)

Lake Fear (Ian McMahon, 1985, Gr. 5–7)

Mystery on Ice (Barbara Corcoran, 1985, Gr. 5–8)

On the Edge (Gillian Cross, 1984, Gr. 5–6)

The Sandman's Eyes (Patricia Windsor, 1985, Gr. 6–10)

The Search for Jim McGwynn (Marcia Wood, 1989, Gr. 5–8)

Show Me the Evidence (Alane Ferguson, 1989, Gr. 7–10)

Something Suspicious (Kathryn Galbraith, 1985, Gr. 4–6)

The Spirit House (William Sleator, 1991, Gr. 7–10)

Steal Away Home (Lois Ruby, 1995, Gr. 3–6)

Terror Train (Gilbert Cross, 1987, Gr. 4–6)

Tom Tiddler's Ground (John Townsend, 1986, Gr. 4–7)

Trapped in Death Cave (Bill Wallace, 1984, Gr. 5–8)

The Turquoise Toad Mystery (Georgess McHargue, 1982, Gr. 4–6)

Up From Jerico Tel (E. L. Konigsburg, 1986, Gr. 4–6)

The Vandemark Mummy (Cynthia Voigt, 1991, Gr. 6–9)

The Watcher in the Garden (Joan Phipson, 1982, Gr. 5+)

The Way From Sattin Shore (Philippa Pearce, 1984, Gr. 5–8)

The Westing Game (Ellen Raskin, 1978, Gr. 5–6)

NATIVE AMERICANS

Apache: The Long Ride Home (Grant Gall, Gr. 7+)

Ashana (E. P. Roesch, 1990, Gr. 7+)

Barefoot a Thousand Miles (Patsey Gray, 1984, Gr. 6–8)

Bearstone (Will Hobbs, 1989, Gr. 6–9)

The Bone Wars (Kathryn Lasky, 1988, Gr. 8+)

The Brave (Robert Lipsyte, 1991, Gr. 8+)

Brother Moose (Betty Levin, 1990, Gr. 6–9)

A Brown Bird Singing (Frances Wosmek, 1986, Gr. 4–6)

Canyons (Gary Paulsen, 1990, Gr. 7–10)

Cherokee Summer (Diane Hoyt-Goldsmith, 1993, Gr. 3–5)

A Circle Unbroken (Sollace Hotze, 1988, Gr. 7–10)

Crossing the Starlight Bridge (Alice Meade, 1994, Gr. 4–6)

The Crying For a Vision (Walter Wangerin, Jr., 1994, Gr. 6–9)

Dawn Rider (Jan Hudson, 1990, Gr. 5+)

Eyes of Darkness (Jamake Highwater, 1985, Gr. 6–8)

False Face (Welwyn Katz, 1988, Gr. 7–10)

The Fledglings (Sandra Markle, 1992, Gr. 7–9)

The Ghost of Eagle Mountain (L. E. Blair, 1990, Gr. 5+)

Gone the Dreams and Dancing (Douglas C. Jones, 1985, Gr. 8+)

Guests (Michael Dorris, 1994, Gr. 3–6)

I am Regina (Sally Keehn, 1991, Gr. 7–10)

Island of the Blue Dolphins (Scott O'Dell, 1960, Gr. 5–7)

Jenny of the Tetons (Kristiana Gregory, 1989, Gr. 6–9)

Kunu: Escape on the Missouri (Kenneth Thomasma, 1989, Gr. 6+)

Legend Days (Jamake Highwater, Gr. 6–8)

The Legend of Jimmy Spoon (Kristiana Gregory, 1990, Gr. 6–8)

Maggie Among the Seneca (Robin Moore, 1990, Gr. 5+)

Mak (Belle Coates, 1981, Gr. 6+)

Mother's Blessings (Penina Keen Spinka, 1992, Gr. 6–9)

Music From a Place Called Half Moon (Jerrie Opughton, 1994, Gr. 5–8)

Navajo Code Talkers (Nathan Aaseng, 1992, Gr. 5+)

Only Brave Tomorrows (Winifred Luhrman, 1989, Gr. 6–9)

The People Shall Continue (Simon Ortiz, 1988, Gr. 3–5)

The Primrose Way (Jackie French Koller, 1992, Gr. 7–10)

Quiver River (David Carkeet, 1991, Gr. 7–10)

Racing the Sun (Paul Pitts, 1988, Gr. 5–7)

The Rattle and the Drum (Kisa Sita, 1994, Gr. 4–6)

Sarah Winnemucca (Mary Morrow, 1992, Gr. 3–5)

Saturnalia (Paul Fleischman, 1990, Gr. 7–10)

The Secret of the Seal (Deborah Davis, 1989, Gr. 6–8)

The Shadow Brothers (A. E. Cannon, 1990, Gr. 5+)

The Sign of the Beaver (Elizabeth Speare, 1983, Gr. 5–7)

Sing Down the Moon (Scott O'Dell, 1970, Gr. 5–7)

Sing For a Gentle Rain (J. Alison James, 1990, Gr. 8+)

Smoke on the Water (John Ruemmler, 1992, Gr. 8+)

So Sings the Blue Deer (Charmayne McGee, 1994, Gr. 3–6)

Speak to the Rain (Helen Passey, 1989, Gr. 7–10)

Sweetgrass (Jan Hudson, 1989, Gr. 6–10)

The Talking Earth (Jean Craighead George, 1987, Gr. 6–8)

Thunder Rolling in the Mountains (Scott O'Dell & Elizabeth Hall, 1992, Gr. 6–9)

Turtle Dream: Collected Stories from the Hopi, Navajo, Pueblo, and Havasupai People (Gerald Hausman, 1989, Gr. 6–8)

Uncle Smoke Stories: Nehaawka Tales of Coyote the Trickster (Roger Welsch, 1994, Gr. 3–6)

Vision Quest (Pamela Service, 1989, Gr. 6–9)

Wild Man of the Woods (Joan Clark, 1986, Gr. 4–7)

A Woman of Her Tribe (Margaret Robinson, 1990, Gr. 7–10)

Appendix C

Sample Lists for Word Sorts

The sample word lists in Appendix C will help you construct your own lists of words appropriate for your students. The number and type of words you select depend on your assessment of how students are progressing in weekly word study activities. Each list shows the types of words suggested for comparison. The number of words in each list decreases as the number of categories increases.

Always provide students with the option of a "crazy pile" for discarding words they believe do not fit the pattern(s) being studied. To encourage such comparisons, you may choose to provide words from patterns students have already studied. It is especially helpful for students in the within-word pattern stage to continue to think about previously learned related patterns.

Within-Word Pattern Stage

1. Single Long Vowels—CVCe

long a_e		***short a***		***crazy pile***
name	skate	am	bath	(high-frequency sight words)
tape	brave	jam	flat	
lake	plane	mat	that	
gave	shape	bag	snap	
case	grade			

long i_e		***short i***		***crazy pile***
I	crime	big	if	(short *a* long *a_e*)
time	shine	six	hid	
wife	slide	drip	chin	
five	smile			
nine	chime			

long a_e		***long i_e***		***crazy pile***
game	bathe	nine	smile	(short *a* short *i*)
skate	race	bike	five	
plane	shake	time		
lake	grave			
chase	maze			

long o_e		***short o***		***crazy pile***
so	stove	not	stop	(short *a, i* long *a, i*)
rope	pole	dot	frog	
note	broke	mom	hop	
joke	stone			
home	choke			

long o_e	***long a_e***	***long i_e***	***crazy pile***
stroke	grate	wife	(for discards)
probe	shape	ride	
stove	grade	hike	
home	name	smile	
bone			

long u_e		***short u***		***crazy pile***
cute	flute	rug	plug	(long *a, i,* or *o,* short *a, i,* or *o*)
cube	crude	cup	drum	
mule	June	bus		
rule	tube			
tune				

long e		***short e***		***crazy pile***
he	feet	them	step	(long *a, i, o, u* short *a, i, o, u*)
we	see	then	leg	
me	free	yes		
be	sweet	red		
he	tree			

long u	***long e***		***crazy pile***
cube	tree	me	(long *a, i,* or *o,* short *a, e, i, o*)
flute	sheep	she	
rule	feet		
June	green		

2. Double Vowels—Common Vowel Digraphs

ai/ay		***a_e***	***short a***	***crazy pile***
train	play	grate	path	(for discards)
rain	tray	game	sash	
stain	may	made	clap	
mail	say	shake		
wait	day			

ee		*short e*	*crazy pile*
feet	steep	then	(other long or short vowels)
street	jeep	sled	
tree	deed	fret	
free	eel	help	
feel	steel		

oa		*o_e*	*short o*	*crazy pile*
boat	toast	joke	drop	(for discards)
coat	goal	rope	spot	
float	loaf	stove	moth	
goat	roast	home		
soap	toad			

igh/ight		*i_e*	*short i*	*crazy pile*
sigh	night	five	big	(for discards)
high	flight	smile	him	
right	sight	nine	sit	
light	might	kite	grin	
fight	tight		clip	

ea (long e)		*ea (short e)*	*ea (long a)*	*short e*	*crazy pile*
clean	meat	spread	great	step	(for discards)
team	each	dead	break	red	
beat	read	head	steak	then	
sea	please	read			
teach		deaf			
		bread			

3. Double and Variant Consonants

double	*consonant*	*crazy pile*
will	add	(end in single consonant)
all	buzz	
small	egg	
well	sniff	
class	off	
mess	dress	

final l/ll		*final s/ss*	*final f/ff*	*final g/gg*	*final d/dd*
will	doll	bus	off	leg	mad
pal	pill	dress	if	egg	add
small		class	sniff	bag	slid
well		yes			odd

soft c		***hard c***	***soft g***	***hard g***	***crazy pile***
cent	mice	cat	cage	bag	(for discards)
face	face	cape	age	frog	
race	ice	coat	stage	game	
nice		cute	huge	go	

s /z/		***s /s/***		***crazy pile***
his	close	dress	said	(for discards)
as	goes	sat	bus	
was	nose	see		
has	these	glass		
use	wise	kiss		

final blend (short vowel patterns)		***no final blend***	***crazy pile***
belt	next	mat	(for discards)
milk	left	hid	
help	bank	cap	
and	think	let	
hand	fast	had	
plant	ask	hike	

final blend (long vowel patterns)			***no final blend***	***crazy pile***
old	child	odd	thin	(final blend with short vowels)
cold	wild	fin	pin	
told		kid		
find		that		
kind				

4. Single *R*-Controlled Vowels—From Short Vowel Patterns

ar		***short a***	***crazy pile***
car	mark	ran	(for discards)
star	sharp	jam	
jar	far	fan	
farm	arm	flag	
barn		bath	

or/ore		***short o***	***crazy pile***
for	fork	on	(for discards)
more	chore	pot	
store		stop	
or		frog	

er/ir/ur		***short e***	***short i***	***short u***	***crazy pile***
her	first	hen	did	fun	(for discards)
bird	dirt	bed	slip	bud	
girl	stir	step		gun	
fur					

5. Variant Double Vowel—Long and Short

long a		***crazy pile***
cape	they	(short *a*)
shake	eight	
mail	rein	
rain	great	
stay	break	
play		

long e		***crazy pile***
he	key	(short *e*)
need	field	
heap	chief	
sweet	dream	
each	treat	

long i		***crazy pile***
five	knight	(short *i*)
smile	high	
pipe	light	
drive	tie	
fly	lie	
try	pie	

6. Consonant Digraphs With Silent Letters

wr(w)	***kn(k)***	***gh(g)***	***wh(w)***	***wh(h)***	***crazy pile***
write	know	ghost	when	who	(for discards)
wrote	knife		white	whole	
	knit		whale	whose	
			which		
			wheel		

ck(k)	***mb(m)***	***gn(n)***	***lf(f)***	***tch(ch)***	***dge(j)***	***crazy pile***
duck	comb	sign	calf	match	fudge	(for discards)
trick	lamb		half	witch	bridge	
black				catch		

7. Variant Double Vowels—Neither Long Nor Short

oo (long)		***oo (short)***		***long o***	***short o***	***crazy pile***
boot	broom	foot	wood	stone	hop	(for discards)
soon	tooth	look	good	robe	not	
boom	roof	book		road		
moon	cool	took		goat		
hoop	tool	hook				

ow (ow)		***ow (long o)***		***short o***	***crazy pile***
cow	brown	row	throw	hot	(for discards)
now	crown	bow	slow	box	
bow	down	know	show	sock	
how	plow	grow	flow		

au/aw		***long a***	***short a***	***crazy pile***
haul	jaw	lake	snap	(for discards)
law	crawl	day	chat	
draw	dawn	clay	match	
paw		rain		
saw		snail		

oi/oy		***long o***	***short o***	***crazy pile***
oil	joy	bone	on	(for discards)
coin	boy	road	not	
boil	toy	rope	box	
noise		stove	job	
join		boat	stop	

ou patterns

(ow)	***(long oo)***	***(short oo)***	***(long o)***	***(short u)***	***(au)***
mouth	you	would	though	tough	ought
cloud	through	could	soul	rough	fought
round	soup	should		young	bought
bounce	group				
shout					

ue/ui/ew/u_e		***short u***	***crazy pile***
blue	flute	bug	(for discards)
true	tube	sun	
suit	use	club	
fruit	stew	crush	
juice	blew		

8. *R*-Controlled Vowels—From Long and Double Vowels

are/air		***ar***		***crazy pile***
care	stairs	car	start	(short *a*, long *a_e*)
rare	chair	mark	far	
share	pair	cart	barn	
scare	fair	dark		

ear/eer/ere(eer)		***ear(er)***	***ear(air)***	***ear(ar)***	***crazy pile***
ear	here	earth	bear	heart	(*ea*)
dear	deer	learn	pear	hearth	
fear	clear	earn	wear		
near	year				

ire	***ir***	***crazy pile***
fire	dirt	(long *i_e*, short *i*)
wire	girl	
tire	first	
hire	third	

ure	***ur***	***crazy pile***
pure	fur	(long *u_e*, *ui*)
sure	burn	
cure	turn	
	nurse	

Syllable Juncture State

1. Compound Words

compound word		***not a compound word***	
bedroom	playground	room	day
goldfish	daydream	dog	chair
houseboat	baseball	house	
doghouse	snowman	ground	
armchair			

compound—literal meaning		***compound—implied meaning***	
bedroom	textbook	starfish	hardship
doghouse	evergreen	butterfly	uproar
wheelchair	round-trip	homesick	however
daytime	twenty-four	software	fallout
weekend	son-in-law	overdrawn	everywhere
newscast	drumstick	breakfast	runaway
eyesight	vice president		

2. Contractions

contraction		***crazy pile***
can't	you'll	(not a contraction)
didn't	haven't	
you're	we've	
we'll	he's	
I'm	I've	

contractions by families

not	***are***	***will***	***is/am***	***have***	***crazy pile***
aren't	you're	I'll	he's	I've	(for discards)
can't	we're	you'll	she's	you've	
don't	they're	we'll	it's	we've	
haven't		they'll	I'm	they've	
wouldn't					
shouldn't					

3. Base + Inflected Suffix Words (no change to base)

inflected suffix		***crazy pile***
dogs	taller	(no suffix)
hits	smartest	
dishes	washed	
writes	jumped	
barking		

s added	***ed added***	***ing added***	***er added***	***est added***
dogs	washed	barking	taller	smartest
hits	jumped	matching	shorter	fastest
wants	eating			

4. Independent Prefix + Base

independent prefix		***crazy pile***
untie	forget	(no prefix)
preview	forgive	
reuse	unload	
prepay	unkind	
repay	undo	

same prefix (meaning)—with increasing complexity

un	***re***	***pre***	***dis***
untie	reuse	preview	discuss
unkind	review	prepay	dismiss
unload	repay	preschool	discover
undo	recall	presume	discovery
unhappy	repeat	prehistoric	dissolve
unknown	relief	prearrange	disrupt
unwrap	rejoice	precinct	disapprove
unsure	remark	precaution	disappear
unhealthy	refresh	prerecorded	discard
unexpected	reappear	precede	disagree
unreliable	rearrange	preparing	disappoint
unfortunate	retrieve	precipitation	discriminate

in	***inter***	***en***
invite	interview	enlist
include	interfere	enroll
inspire	interrupt	enable
incomplete	interaction	endanger
incorrect	intercept	enlarge
inevitable	intersection	engrave
inferior	intervene	enrich
inquiry	intermittent	enclose

5. Base + Inflected Suffixes (base changes)—Early to Middle Syllable Juncture

e drop		***no e drop***		***crazy pile***
raked	horses	jumped	matching	(for discards)
baking	places	washed	sleeping	
nicer	making	thinking	playing	
hoping	liking			
using	smiling			

consonant double		***no consonant double***		***crazy pile***
hitting	rubbed	thinking	smartest	(for discards)
runner	chopped	watching	tallest	
hottest	hopping	shorter		
stopping	bigger			

ends with y		***y changes to i***		***y doesn't change***
baby	ugly	babies	tried	flying
fly	puppy	candies	flies	trying
pretty	cry	cried	puppies	crying
try	candy	prettiest		

6. Base + Inflected Suffixes (base changes)—Late Syllable Juncture

s added	***es added***	***y to i***	***ed added***	***ing added***
solos	heroes	supplies	spoiled	guiding
lives	leaves	tiniest	created	gripping
patios	potatoes	copied	trimmed	gardening
alleys	wolves	chillier	attached	whispering
chimneys	dominoes	diaries	refused	dangling
sheriffs	latches	horrified	exchanged	preparing

7. Base Words + Derivational Suffixes

derivational suffix		***no derivational suffix***		***crazy pile***
careful	helpful	care	help	(for discards)
slowly	wisely	slow	wise	
sleepy	waiter	sleep	wait	
cloudy	really	cloud	real	
painless	kindness	pain	kind	
friendly		friend		

Sort by same suffix, with increasing complexity, no pronunciation change

-ful	***-ly***	***-less***	***-ness***
useful	really	spotless	brightness
beautiful	lightly	hopeless	kindness
sorrowful	finally	timeless	darkness
handful	angrily	helpless	emptiness
hopeful	hopefully	restless	quickness
harmful	apparently	penniless	stubbornness
doubtful	silently	relentless	happiness
skillful	hesitantly	careless	selfishness

-ent	*-ant*	*-able*	*-ible*
parent	servant	favorable	flexible
decent	merchant	reasonable	sensible
present	radiant	comfortable	edible
absent	observant	remarkable	legible
talent	distant	capable	horrible
efficient	pleasant	changeable	convertible
obedient	occupant	valuable	irresistible
ingredient	assistant	admirable	
continent		lovable	
permanent			

-ion		*-tion*	*-sion*
collection	elevation	determination	permission
confession	tension	mention	possession
association	protection	position	extension
reaction	connection	condition	decision
infection	action	addition	persuasion
discussion	operation		mission
pollution	creation		

8. Syllabication Generalizations

structural word		*phonetic word*		*crazy pile*
floating	repay	towel	squirrel	(for discards)
thirsty	driver	river	early	
winner	dresses	bubble	butter	
carefully	friendly	giant	buffalo	
we're	starlight	dollar	family	
untie				

base + base	*prefix + base*	*base + suffix*	*crazy pile*
starfish	untie	swimming	(for discards)
didn't	prepay	horses	
I'll	recall	washed	
daydream	forgive	careful	
you're	unkind	slowly	
houseboat		kindness	
weekend			

VC/CV (same letters)		***VC/CV (different letters)***		***crazy pile***
kitten	pretty	picnic	winter	(for discards)
summer	yellow	pencil	monkey	
rabbit	lesson	garden	person	
pillow	hammer	circus	signal	
little	dollar	doctor		

V/CV		***VC/V***	
cider	defeat	river	gravel
about	patience	second	minute
later	meter	clever	relish
water	female	sugar	public
music	vacate	ticket	finish
pilot	notice	travel	feather
open	library	rocket	rapid
secret	lagoon	linen	nephew
student	puny	lizard	popular
apart	cubic	pocket	meadow
father	weapon	radish	melon

VC/CV		***V/CV***	***VC/V***	***C + le***
after	platter	afraid	brother	purple
balloon	issue	cement	cousin	eagle
basket	villain	diner	never	fable
carrot	captain	equal	travel	fiddle
chimney	barrel	hotel	visit	pebble
dinner	kitchen	music	lizard	turtle
harvest	carton	open	pocket	candle
hungry	arrive	recess	river	cycle

Derivational Constancy Stage

1. Dependent Prefix + Root

com	***con***	***de***
compress	continue	design
compute	conference	deprived
common	contestant	depress
comma	control	desirable
comrade	confine	descent
comic	convince	departure
compound	contract	devotion
commendable	condense	devour

ex	***pro***
example	program
examination	procedure
exercise	protection
exploration	prolong
expression	proportion
exhaust	propeller
expensive	profound
excellent	pronounce

2. Pronunciation Change

change in stressed syllable, changes sound

combine	combination	disable	disability
inspire	inspiration	stable	stability
prepare	preparation	repeat	repetition
confide	confident	reform	reformation
product	production	local	locality

syllable division changes sound

crumb	crumble	mortal	mortality
magic	magical	family	familiar
crime	criminal	electric	electricity
compete	competent	divide	division
magic	magician	music	musician

3. Greek Combining Forms

uni (one)	***bi (two)***	***tri (three)***
unicorn	biannual	tricycle
unified	bicycle	triangle
uniform	biceps	triceps
unity	bicentennial	tripod
unilateral	biennium	trio
unicycle		triple

auto (self, same)	***astro (star)***	***bio (life)***
autobiography	astronomy	biography
autocratic	astronomer	biology
autograph	astronomical	biopsy
automatic	astrological	biosphere
autopsy	astrophysics	biosynthesis
automobile	astronaut	

tele (far)	***thermo (heat)***	***photo (light)***
telecast	thermal	photo finish
telegraph	thermometer	photograph
telephone	thermostat	photographer
telephoto		photogenic
telescope		photosynthesis
telescopic		

hydro (water)	***-graph (write/record)***
hydrant	autograph
hydrogen	telegraph
hydroelectric	paragraph
	geography
	photograph
	biography

-phon (speech, sound)

homophone
microphone
megaphone
saxophone
symphony
telephone
phonograph

4. Latin Roots and Related Words

aud (hear)	***aqu (water)***	***cis (cut/kill)***
audible	aquarium	scissors
audio	aquatic	precise
audition	aquamarine	incisor
auditorium		incision
audience		exercise

jec (throw, lay, lie, extend)
reject
eject
projector
object
injection

mit/mis/miss (send, do)
dismiss
mission
admit
submit
missionary
transmit

ped/pod/pus (foot)
centipede
pedal
pedestrian
pedestal
podiatrist

port (carry)
important
reporter
support
portfolio
import

spect (to look)
spectator
inspection
spectacles
suspect
expectation

scrib (write)
prescribe
manuscript
subscribe
scribble
describe

Author Index

Subject Index